Agencies of

CW01454722

# Agencies of the Frame:
# Tectonic Strategies in Cinema
# and Architecture

By

## Michael Tawa

**CAMBRIDGE**
**SCHOLARS**

P U B L I S H I N G

Agencies of the Frame: Tectonic Strategies in Cinema and Architecture, by Michael Tawa

This book first published 2010. The present binding first published 2011.

Cambridge Scholars Publishing

12 Back Chapman Street, Newcastle upon Tyne, NE6 2XX, UK

British Library Cataloguing in Publication Data
A catalogue record for this book is available from the British Library

Copyright © 2011 by Michael Tawa
All drawings and photographs © Michael Tawa
Cover Image: Barcelona, 1995. Photograph © Michael Tawa

All rights for this book reserved. No part of this book may be reproduced, stored in a retrieval system, or transmitted, in any form or by any means, electronic, mechanical, photocopying, recording or otherwise, without the prior permission of the copyright owner.

ISBN (10): 1-4438-2942-0, ISBN (13): 978-1-4438-2942-7

# TABLE OF CONTENTS

Preface ............................................................................................. ix
Pretecton, *Jean-Luc Nancy*

Introduction ...................................................................................... 1
O(u)verture—*similarities and differences; transdisciplinarity and deterritorialisation; cinema and reality; unsettling the real.*
Architecture *and—disciplinary conjunctions; conjugational and strategic function of the* and; *difference and deferral.*
Drawing parallels—*drawing* from *and drawing* for; *precedents; drawing for strategic and tactical benefit; selection of films and built projects; validity of readings; assemblages; intentional and non-intentional features of assemblages; adaptability and sustainability; reading for proliferating sense.*
Framing the look—*the image; regimes of visuality; representational and presentational capacities of the image; ethics of looking; towards a non-representational architecture of enablement.*
User's manual—*purpose and uses of the book; thematic synopsis of the five main themes.*

Chapter One ...................................................................................... 42
Place and Setting
Setting—*setting and work; framing and unsettling; symbolic settings; Asplund and Lewerentz's Woodland Crematorium; Cordoba Mosque.*
Place—*space and place; place, memory, identity; place and Simondon's "individuation"; place as "metastable" setting;* ethos *and* topos; *place, placelessness and modernity; displacement and dislocation.*
Taking place—*"at home in homelessness," the taking place of place,* Ngannyatjarra *country; kinaesthetic spatial practices; framing landscape in Burgess'* Uluṟu-Kata Tjuṯa *Cultural Centre, Herzog's Where the Green Ants Dream, Ian Dunlop's People of the Western Desert, Roeg's Bad Timing, Kurosawa's Sunshine Through the Rain and Throne of Blood.*
Framing place—*incontinent "Nature"; apparatuses of control; Heidegger's reading of Aristotle's* phusis *(nature); kinematics; potentiality; the right to concealment; Modernity and nature; landscape in Godard and Tarkovsky.*
Displacement—*presence, absence and withdrawal; oblivion of the gods; the uncanny; framing landscape in Antonioni's l'Avventura and Blow Up.*

Chapter Two ........................................................................................ 91
Spatiality
Setup—*space and place; form and rhythm;* rhuthmos; *geometric setups and regimes; frames and framing;* hors d'œuvre, *Derrida's* parergon, *out-of-frame and out-of-field; limit,* leimma *and residue; spatial framing and dynamics in Paradjanov's Sayat Nova, Kazan's Baby Doll and Dreyer's Joan of Arc; limit and surface in Miralles and Tagliabue's Torre de Gas Natural, Nouvel's Fondation Cartier and Quai Branly.*
Looking away—*frame and look; Steigler's attentiveness; care; gaze of betrayal; close-up in Pasolini's Gospel According to St Matthew; Agamben's "whatever being" and Deleuze's "whatever space"; framing space in Antonioni's The Passenger; makeshift spaces; framing enablement.*
Narrative frames—*framing for the Other; spatial narratives in Le Corbusier's Villa Savoye, Kahn's Korman House, Burgess' Hackford House, Zumthor's Sumvigt Chapel and Strasbourg Cathedral.*

Chapter Three .................................................................................. 131
Temporality
Time: *time, division and the instant; past, present and future; time and tempo; Bergman's Cries and Whispers; time and space.*
Limit, caesura—*time, limit, limbo; time of the look;* khronos, kairos *and opportunity.*
Other times—*duration; tempo and temporality; structures of temporality in Wilder's Double Indemnity, Inarritu's 21 Grams, Roeg's Bad Timing and Antonioni's The Passenger, l'Eclisse and Blow Up; time, image, duration; time pressure and affective time in Tarkovsky's Mirror; infinitely finishing; The Necks' Aether; overlaid times in Arvo Pärt's Festina Lente; time and facticity in Tarkovsky and Herzog.*
Time of the shot—*time in Godard's Éloge de l'Amour, Jarmusch's Stranger than Paradise, Paradjanov's Sayat Nova and Lynch's Lost Highway, Mulholland Drive and Inland Empire; time and virtuality in Lynch; gaze and duration in Godard's Éloge de l'Amour and Herzog's Fata Morgana.*
"It is boring for one"—*Heidegger's profound boredom; the moment of vision.*
Witholding potential—*Agamben's potentiality; Jullien's "blandness"; preservation of potential in space; symbolic and experiential registers of time in architecture; Jai Singh's Jantar Mantar observatory; the musical columns of Vijayanagar; programmatic potential in architecture; designing for the unprogrammable; adaptational potential in architecture; designing for enablement; transmuting context; light and time at Chartres Cathedral and the Baños Almirante of Valencia; architectural registers of time, place and memory.*

Chapter Four .................................................................................... 200
Materiality
Light, sound, architecture—*regimes of visuality; light and space; light and dark; knot, joint and connection; sound and space; symbolism of sound and light; Plato's Myth of Er.*
Light and sound in cinema—*grains of image and textures of sound; Jarmusch's Year of the Horse and Dead Man; Bergman's Cries and Whispers, Persona and Winter Light; materiality of the image in Tarkovsky; the desert in Antonioni; light in Lynch and Godard.*
Materialised sense—*vision and hearing; vibration and resonance; listening and attentiveness; conjugation and augmentation;* mantra *(sound) and* yantra *(space); the sound of the earth in Mahler and Godard; sound of altereity in Taverner's The Protecting Veil; sound and assemblage; soundtracks in Pasolini, Lynch, Roeg, Tarkovsky and Antonioni.*
Monstrous images—*image and monstration; resonant presence; violence of the image; evidence and appearance; architectural violations.*
Grounds of artifice—*ground, grounding, grounds; Heidegger's "The essence of Ground."*
Surfeit—*surface and excess; materiality of the image in Paradjanov's Sayat Nova; substance and materiality of space in Siza and Lewerentz.*

Chapter Five ..................................................................................... 258
Agency, Crisis, Disestablishment
Assemblage—*assemblage and agency; mobilising potential; Deleuze's "Plane of Immanence"; Simondon's "metastable field" and "transduction"; buildings, ensembles and systems.*
Agencies of the frame—*plane and plan(e) of consistency; Deleuze's* agencement; *frame as an apparatus for mobilising potential; spatial framing in Hitchcock's Rear Window; spatial dynamics in Antonioni's l'Avventura; technology and "enframing" in Heidegger; prosthetic apparatuses and technical catastrophe; Martin Arnold's Cinemnesis; time and space in Galeta.*
Crisis—*multiplicity, virtuality and actuality; memory and recollection in Tarkovsky's Mirror; geometric potentiality; virtuality in geometry, space and architecture; Simondon's "supersaturation" and the crisis of sense.*
Disestablishment—*montage, stability and instability; rhythm and destabilisation; disturbance, and crisis; subversive tactics in Antonioni, Godard and Haneke's Caché; framing and incommunicability; subversive montage in the Palace Museum Beijing, Markli's La Conjiunta, Scarpa's Brionvega and Lewerentz' St Peter*

Notes .............................................................................................. 310

Bibliography ................................................................................... 338

Index .............................................................................................. 349

# PRETECTON

Architecte: *tektôn* en chef ou en premier, c'est-à-dire charpentier principal, couvreur principiel, constructeur initial.

Peut-être même: bâtisseur du principe—et du commandement, et du commencement. L'*archi-* intégral, radical, authentique, c'est-à-dire l'*archi-* tout court, et très simplement, se précède lui-même.

Il s'encadre avant de s'être posé, placé, situé de quelque façon que ce soit. L'*archi-*, de manière très générale, est le cadre des cadres et donc le cadre d'avant les cadres, les places, les délimitations, les distributions, les rapports de forces, de volumes, de tensions.

L'architecte donc devrait se précéder lui-même. Appelons "tectonique" la qualité de la structure, de la tenue principielle, de la mise en place par conséquent de l'Idée sans laquelle nul agencement, nulle disposition ne saurait s'engager. Le tectonique, donc, est antérieur à toute position, proposition, exposition de quelque montage, construction, instruction que ce soit.

Archi et tectonique dans cette mesure se recouvrent. Tout *archi-* est tectonique et réciproquement: le premier mot indique dans la direction du principe ce que le second indique dans la direction du bâtiment. Commencer et bâtir se recouvrent là où on commence à bâtir en même temps qu'on bâtit un commencement (qui est toujours aussi commandement).

Tout commencement commence une espèce ou une autre de bâti—cadre, dispositif, structure, constantes et variables, jeu des résistances, convergences et divergences, attractions et répulsions. Inversement tout bâtir fait commencer quelque chose, un volume, un lieu, un espace, une bâtisse ou un bâtiment—qu'il soit temple, usine ou cabane.

Même la grotte, même la caverne—l'invention de la grotte ou de la caverne, le geste troglodyte—est architectonique. La caverne existe, mais il faut en saisir la forme, l'ampleur, il faut s'y disposer en tous les sens de l'expression: se disposer à y pénétrer, à en ouvrir le lieu, et se disposer en elle, s'y assied, s'y coucher, y faire le feu. Bientôt on y décore les parois. Elles deviennent des murs.

\*\*\*

Le geste architectonique encadre mais il fait plus qu'encadrer: il ouvre la possibilité du cadre et pour cela avant de plier et fermer un triangle, un carré ou un rectangle, un volume quelconque, tube ou boîte, il entame l'espace. Il entaille. Il découpe, il taille des épaisseurs, des profondeurs, des avancées, des soutiens, des assises. Il taille dans l'espace brut qui est un bloc d'étendue indifférenciée. Le *tektôn* est charpentier ou bien sculpteur, dit-on. En réalité c'est un seul métier: c'est la taille qui extirpe le bloc, la poutre, l'étançon ou la dalle.

La taille n'est pas seulement de blocs. Les formes ne sont pas seulement des tracés. Ce peuvent être des mouvements, des élans, des motions. C'est aussi un chemin vers une porte. C'est aussi un escalier ou une échelle. C'est comment on regarde au dehors ou au-dedans. C'est le corps en marche, allongé, accroupi. C'est la veille et le sommeil, la vigilance et l'oubli.

L'entaille ouvre la possibilité du cadre, de la découpe, dans un regard qui est une pensée qui est un mouvement, une tension: comment j'espace l'espace lorsque j'y prends place. Le philosophe appelle cela *Dasein*: être un *là*. Comment je suis non pas "ici" mais moi-même cet *ici*. Je ne m'y trouve que parce que je l'ouvre.

Chaque corps ouvre l'espace et l'entaille, se met à le tailler en morceaux, en pièces, en masses, en nappes, rubans, pans, panneaux et voiles. Chaque corps est une caméra qui cadre et qui monte ses cadres selon ses mouvements, avances, reculs, glissades, montées, descentes: rien d'autre qu'un corps ouvert et mobile dont la kinésie découpe les champs, les plans, les portées successives de la perception. Mais que veut dire "perception"? C'est entrée d'un corps dans le monde et poussée du monde en lui. Procession ou promenade, dérapage ou étirement, prises, déprises, saisies, dessaisissements. Toutes les espèces, les sortes, les allures d'entaille que peut faire un corps, une pensée, un tact, une approche.

Michael Tawa est une caméra, un corps à son travail d'entaille dans la masse épaisse qui se trouve à la fois dans le monde et posée sur lui: la masse signifiante des discours, théories, propositions, analyses, rhétoriques et poétiques où se jouent d'autres façons d'entaille, d'entame et de cadre. Car on veut aussi dire ce que fait le corps cadreur qui, lui, ne parle pas. On veut le cadrer à son tour dans des mots, des propositions, des énoncés, ce qu'on dit faire du sens mais qui surtout met à vif la richesse, la profusion des tectoniques indéfiniment renouvelées et qui pour finir échappent quand même aux prises du discours. Il parle de "sacré" par exemple, ou de "durée," ou de "présence," il parle de "violence" ou de "rencontre," de "territoire" ou de "flux": autant d'entailles, parfois profondes, parfois légères, brèves, de simples encoches et parfois des rayures, des stries: de l'une ou de l'autre manière ce sont des échappées vers des espaces qu'aucun mot ne contient, des espacements, des extensions, des appuis et des tremplins parmi lesquels il nous fait avancer, sentir la tectonique toujours à l'œuvre non pas devant mais derrière nous: l'architectonique qui le commande lui-même comme un pilote qui serait très loin derrière lui, très loin en lui, la première entaille qu'est son corps même d'architecte.

—Jean-Luc Nancy

# PRETECTON

Architect: chief or first *tektôn*, that is to say principal carpenter, principal roofer, initial constructor.

Maybe even: builder of the principle—and of the commandment, and of the commencement. The integral, radical, authentic *archi-*, that is to say, in one word and very simply, the *archi-* precedes itself.

He frames himself before having been posed, placed, situated in one manner or another. The *archi-*, in a very general way, is the frame of frames and thus the frame from before frames, places, delimitations, distributions, relationships of force, of volumes, of tensions.

The architect should therefore go before himself. Let us call "tectonic" the quality of the structure, of the principial disposition, of the consequent putting into place of the Idea without which no setup, no disposition could be engaged. The tectonic, then, is anterior to any position whatsoever—to any proposition, exposition of montage, construction or instruction.

In that sense, archi and tectonic overlap each other. Every *archi-* is tectonic and reciprocally: the first word indicates in the direction of the principle what the second indicates in the direction of the building. Commencement and building overlap each other right there where we commence to build at the same time as we build a commencement (which is also always commandment).

Every commencement commences one or another species of framework—cadre, apparatus, structure, constant and variable, play of resistances, convergences and divergences, attractions and repulsions. Inversely all building makes something begin, a volume, a place, a space, a construction or a building—be it a temple, factory or cabin.

Even the grotto, even the cavern—the invention of the grotto or the cavern, the troglodytic gesture—is architectonic. The cavern exists, but one must grasp its form, its amplitude, one must be disposed to it in every sense of the term: disposed to enter it, to open it as a place, and to dispose oneself within it, to sit there, to lie down, to make a fire. Soon we decorate its sides. They become walls.

\*\*\*

The architectonic gesture frames but it does more than frame: it opens the possibility of the frame and therefore, before folding and closing a triangle, a square or a rectangle, any volume whatsoever, tube or box, it initiates space. It gashes. It cuts up, it carves thicknesses, depths, projections, supports, seatings. It carves into brute space which is a block of undifferentiated extension. The *tektôn* is a carpenter, or else a sculptor as we say. In reality it is a single trade: carving is what extirpates the block, the beam, the prop or the pavement.

Carving is not only of blocks. Forms are not only tracings. They could be movements, élans, motions. It is also a path towards a door. It is also a stairway or a ladder. It is how we look to the outside or to the inside. It is the body walking, lengthened, crouched. It is waking and sleep, vigilance and oblivion.

The prop opens the possibility of the frame, of the cutting out, in a look that is thinking in motion, a tension: how I space out space when I take place there. The philosopher names this *Dasein*: being a *there*. How it is that I am not "here" but am myself this *here*. I only find myself there having founded it.

Every body opens space and carves it, sets about cutting it up in portions, in pieces, in sheets, ribbons, flaps, panels and veils. Every body is a camera which frames according to its movements, advances, retreats, slidings, ascents, descents: nothing other than an open and mobile body whose kinetics carves up fields, shots, the successive reaches of perception. But what does "perception" mean? It is entry of a body into the world and thrust of the world within it. Procession or promenade, skid or stretch, takes, releases, seizures, relinquishments. Every species, sort and aspect of carving that can make a body, a thought, a tact, an approach.

Michael Tawa is a camera, a body at work carving into the thick mass that finds itself in the world and placed upon it: the signifying mass of discourses, theories, propositions, analyses, rhetorics and poetics in which are played out other means of carving, slicing and framing. Because one also wants to say what a framing body does, which itself does not speak. One wants in turn to frame it in words, propositions and enunciations which we hold to make sense, but which above all animate the richness, the profusion of indefinitely renewed tectonics, and which when all is said and done nevertheless evade the framings of discourse. He speaks of "sacred" for example, or of "duration," or of "presence," he speaks of "violence" or of "encounter," of "territory" or of "flux": so many carvings, sometimes deep, sometimes light, brief, simple notches and sometimes stripes, streaks: in one or another way they are escapements towards spaces that no word can contain, spacings, extensions, supports and springboards with which he enables us to advance, to sense the tectonic always at work not before but behind us: the architectonic that commands him like a pilot, that would be very far behind and deep within him, and whose first carving would be his own architectural body.

—Jean-Luc Nancy

# INTRODUCTION

## O(u)verture

The main purpose of this book is to help inform and enrich the spatial and tectonic dimensions of architectural design. The intent is to discern within cinema those qualities, conditions and techniques that might be useful for design strategies, tactics and practices. Although the main focus is on drawing implications from cinema for architectural design, the same might be possible in reverse, as well as across into other disciplines. There are evident parallels between cinematic ways of constructing film and architectural ways of constructing space. The major emphasis is on drawing parallels rather than implying identity between the two art forms. They are substantially, even radically different in purpose, scope and practice. Nevertheless, there are significant overlaps and resonances that are worth mapping out and investigating for common ground.

A parallel relationship maintains difference and distance between two entities. It does not allow direct transfer across the divide that separates them. This means that something irreconcilable must be preserved between them, something that is not accidental or contingent but constitutive and revealing. What separates identities also defines them individually and conjointly in fundamental ways. For example, time is a major constitutive condition of cinema. It cannot-not be broached and worked conceptually and technically. This applies even if time is not the central thematic concern of a film. In architecture time generally does not represent a critical condition. It forms part of the general environment in which architecture is situated, but may not be explicitly conceived of, theorised or worked by architects. It is nevertheless an inescapable component of existential space whether or not it is brought into consideration, and it will condition the quality and experience of built environments.

In the past, time constituted a fundamental register for architecture, particularly in sacred buildings. Many landscapes, buildings and structures explicitly embody the numbers, ratios, proportions, cycles and rhythms of time into their physical fabric.[1] But architects, unlike cinematographers, cannot literally manipulate chronological time, slowing or speeding up it's duration by design. What they can do however, like cinematographers, is modify existential time or the sense of time that is felt in the experience of space. It is possible to convey particular temporalities—for example by certain alignments between built form, light, and environmental conditions. There are therefore parallels between cinema and architecture in terms of the manipulation of existential temporality. Such parallels do not represent equivalences between the two, since the worlds that they each operate within are fundamentally unlike. There are nevertheless resonances, and it is the potential of such resonances that this study looks to investigate.

Architecture is unlike cinema in fundamental ways. Cinema is essentially time-based, even though it clearly would not exist and could not be experienced without space—without the key spatial condition of the interval which makes *here* different from *there*. It deals with moving two dimensional images projected for an audience whose spatial position is fixed and whose engagement is largely limited to vision and sound. The particular framing and sequence of viewing are predetermined, uncontestable and irreversible. Visual regimes and points of view established by the camera and the manner, geometry and dynamics of the camera's motion fundamentally affect the nature and reception of films. This takes place according to their disposition towards the world and to worlds that they create, as well as to the relationships between characters, narratives, spaces and times that they valorise. For its part, architecture is fundamentally space-based even though it clearly couldn't be designed, produced or experienced without time. It deals with the installation of stable forms in space, experienced by individuals and collectives whose engagement is largely kinaesthetic and multi-sensory. The sequencing of experience in architecture, or the spatial sequences and narratives it makes available—although evidently limited in many ways—are open to multiple possibilities of trajectory, rhythm and infiltration. Architectural experience will generally be of a self-consistent subject whose ultimately unknowable subjectivity conditions the visual regime they deploy, the equally unknowable and unpredictable points of view they take up, the circuits they trace and the tempo of their movement. They will be engaged to a greater or lesser extent in the milieu they are moving through, and they will make particular demands on that milieu depending on their functional, recreational, commercial or other disposition towards it.

Such limits form part of what defines architecture and cinema, but they also represent opportunities for transformation through practices of place making and cinematography. It is a question of how assumptions and limits can be put to the test in order to eclipse disciplinary, material and technical constraints. It is when cinema can say something about the timeless presence that arrests its passage, and when architecture can say something about the transient moment which unsettles its permanence, that the extraordinary and the uncanny are enabled to take place and come to pass.

The construction of place remains fundamental to architecture, irrespective of the disciplinary transformations that take place from time to time by design, necessity or crisis. Architects must deploy skills of spatial organisation and manipulation, calibrated and geared to articulating enduring places for human inhabitation. Among the many dimensions that architects must engage with and manipulate to achieve these ends—space, time, materiality, structure, construction, environment—those of space, time and materials will predominate in this study. The fundamental gesture of architecture is the performance of spatial moves and the enactment of spatial and material strategies that determine enclosure, dispose and compose patterns of form, mobilise and make possible sequences and rhythms of motion and rest. Experienced architects draw on multiple typologies and vocabularies of such formal and kinaesthetic gestures, bringing to bear a vast legacy of architectural reflection to the processes of design and production of buildings and places. The richer the vocabularies, the more flexible, adaptable and effective the process becomes.

Architecture has its own formal and gestural histories; its own typologies, vocabularies, tropes and syntaxes. At the same time, architecture has always deferred to other disciplines in order to clarify and elaborate its own procedures and its own problems. In a surprising sense architecture is a discipline with intrinsic rules—geometric, spatial, configurational, and technical—but without the means to implement them other than by consorting with others. It inhabits the intersections between so many disciplines across the arts, humanities and sciences that it can only be adequately known in terms of a foundational otherness, rather than in terms of anything intrinsic to itself. In that sense, architecture is radically improprietous and delinquent. It might claim authority over space, but so do sculpture and dance; over place, but so do landscape architecture, cartography and geography; over time, but so do music and cinema; over materials, technology and environment, but so does engineering; over procurement but so do law, building and project management; over well-being but so do medicine and psychology. It might defer to philosophy for its ideas; to history for its types; to astronomy, music and arithmetic for its canons of measure; to astrophysics or cybernetics for its metaphors; to aeronautics, biomemimetics and parametrics for its forms and materials; to industrial manufacturing for its assemblage, and so forth. The question *What is* proper *to architecture? What is architecture* per se? is an uncomfortable one. What is it that

remains for a discipline so greatly dependent on others to outline its
identity, define its scope and articulate its practices?

In his *Abécédaire*, Gilles Deleuze elaborates the interiority and
exteriority of disciplines through the motif of *desire*:

> "For me, as soon as we do something, it is a question of getting out, it is a
> question of remaining and getting out at the same time. So, remaining
> within philosophy is also a question of how to get out of it. But getting
> out of philosophy doesn't mean doing something else. That's why one has
> to get out while remaining inside… I want to get out of philosophy by
> way of philosophy."[2]

He then recounts correspondence received after publication of his book
*The Fold*—numerous letters from surprising sources, among them the
French Movement of Paper Folders, and ocean surfers who saw
themselves inhabiting and riding "the mobile folds of nature." Deleuze's
evident point is that, through philosophy, philosophy gets out of itself,
deterritorialises itself by way of drawing latent implications across into
other domains. For him these instances represent the true sense of
encounter—which is not to meet other people, but to encounter other ideas
and other practices. "We encounter things before we encounter people…
we encounter the charm of people, the work of people, not people." What
we encounter is desire, and desire is not desire for the singular but for
multiplicities and ensembles of elements associated within assemblage that
have agency—that is, that have the capacity to produce:

> "You never desire someone or something. You always desire an
> ensemble… what is the nature of the relationships between elements so
> that there can be desire, so that they can become desirable?… I do not
> desire a woman, I also desire a landscape that is enveloped in that
> woman… I never desire something on its own… I don't desire an
> ensemble either… I desire within an ensemble… there is no desire that
> doesn't flow… that doesn't flow in an assemblage. So much so that desire
> for me has always been… constructivism. To desire is to construct an
> assemblage, to construct an ensemble… to construct a region… that is
> truly to assemble. For an event to take place there has to be a difference of
> potential. For there to be difference in potential there has to be two levels.
> At that moment something takes place, lightning passes or a small
> stream… Desire… constructs an assemblage, it establishes itself in an
> assemblage, it always puts into play several factors… In an assemblage
> there is always a collectivity: collective, constructivism… Never interpret.
> Experiment with assemblages. Look for assemblages that suit you. There
> are four constituents of assemblages: an assemblage comprises states of
> things and enunciations, styles of enunciation. Every assemblage applies a
> style of enunciation. Then it applies territories, every one to their

territory... Even when we are in a room, we chose our territory. I enter an unfamiliar room. I look for the territory—that is, the place in that room where I will feel most comfortable. Then there are processes that we have to call deterritorialisations. That is to say the manner in which we leave the territory. I would say that an assemblage includes these four dimensions: states of things, enunciations, territories and movements of deterritorialisation. In such ways, desire flows."[3]

It is in this sense that architecture and cinema operate as sites of deterritorialisation for each other. They are an outside in which the other's desire for encounter plays itself out and begins to produce. Cases can be made for multiple disciplinary associations for architecture—for example with music, theatre, philosophy, gastronomy, viticulture and so forth. But with cinema it can avail itself of distinctive and instructive alignments of concern with place, space, time and materiality. Cinema frames places, landscapes and environments. It organises the screen spatially in particular ways. It modulates duration and montage to construct specific temporalities. It manipulates light, sound and the technologies of film production to convey particular ambiances and atmospheres. What cinema does *not* do is remain open ended as to the sequencing of its reception. The viewer is obliged to experience a film according to an order that is both predetermined and inescapable. In fact this is one of the key conditions that cinema has sought to eclipse through various techniques of montage by unsettling chronological sequence and spatial hierarchy, so as to suggest folds and returns in the fabric of space and time. Nevertheless, the cinematic sequence must be set in order to be projected and it must be experienced as set in order to be received.

A common proposition is that architectural experience has no such imposed constraints. People can infiltrate spaces from several directions, cross and crisscross them at will, revisit some and avoid others, remain in one place for a long time and bypass another in no time at all, chose to move in a line or in returning circuits. Hence the claim as to the freedom available in architecture compared to the constraining regime of reception in cinema. But things are not that simple. Firstly, a significant proportion of the space of the world is out of bounds or otherwise inaccessible—by law, by design or by the nature of things. Dwellings, civic and commercial buildings, industrial estates, government and military installations, gated communities, the service zones of buildings such as lift shafts, machine rooms, security facilities and so on—all of these are spaces of exception. This means that spatial infiltration is always already limited by at least pragmatic and technical conditions. There are political conditions which establish power relations determining accessibility and inaccessibility; preventing access by certain people to certain spaces, but also allowing

pervasive surveillance and therefore access to all spaces by others. There
are then the designed conditions conceived by architects and others who
install particular spatial practices by determining specific geometric forms
and typologies, spatial organisations and layouts, circulation patterns,
solids and voids, structures and services, and the facilities (or lack of
facilities), furnishings, materials, signage and surveillance that support
these practices. Part of these designed conditions flow from implicit
philosophical, religious, socio-cultural, political and aesthetic registers that
often remain undeclared, but which affect the reception of architecture, the
spatial disposition and kinaesthetic comportment of those who inhabit and
use it. This deterministic capacity of architecture further masks the
apparent freedom to come and go where and as one pleases. The greatest
works are always those that test the disciplinary limits and constraints
supposed to condition their conception, production, reception and
consumption. They do not eliminate these limits but maintain them—
working with them liminally and subjecting them to significant stress so
they dilate and become open to other possibilities. Consider for example
the question of how multiple temporalities (past, future and present, slow
and fast time) could be conveyed in cinema within a framework that must
remain strictly chronological, sequential and linear, and in architecture
within a framework that must remain strictly orthogonal, immobile and
centred.

Following his assertion that the proper concern of cinema is not to
"realistically" convey the factuality of events but to capture their reality,
Andrey Tarkovsky makes a telling observation about the way imagination,
dreams and recollections can be conveyed in cinema:

"How is it possible to reproduce what a person sees within himself, all his
dreams, both sleeping and waking? ... It is possible, provided that dreams
on the screen are made up of exactly these same observed, natural forms
of life. Sometimes directors shoot at high speed, or through a misty veil...
But that mysterious blurring is not the way to achieve a true filmic
impression of dreams or memories. The cinema is not, and must not be,
concerned with borrowing effects from the theatre. What then is needed?
First of all we need to know what sort of dream our hero had. We need to
know the actual material facts of the dream; to see all the elements of
reality which were refracted in that layer of the consciousness which kept
vigil thorough the night... And we need to convey all of that on screen
precisely, not misting it over and not using elaborate devices. Again, if I
were asked, what about the vagueness, the opacity, the improbability of a
dream?—I would say that in cinema `opacity' and `ineffability' do not
mean an indistinct picture, but the particular impression created by the
logic of the dream: unusual and unexpected combinations, and conflicts

between, entirely real elements. These must be shown with the utmost precision. By its very nature, cinema must expose reality, not cloud it."[4]

The implication is that in order to convey the real character of a situation, event, object, person, place or world—that is, its *this-ness, quidditas* or *haecceity*—there must be a significant element of unreality and artificiality, of playing with and distorting the "realistic" in such a way as to amplify its "real" content. For Tarkovsky this is not to be sought in special effects or literal translation, but in the focussed and intensified working of the materials and technologies of film itself, paying close attention to the inherent logic of the moment being conveyed and being willing to suspend disbelief in order to perfect that conveyance. Tarkovsky's conceptual and tectonic modes of working have significant implications for architecture.

Much current architectural theory and practice declares an urgency for engaging with contemporary realities in which certainty and stasis no longer hold, where universals have no purchase, where fluctuation and interminable variation condition experience and where the disconnected and fragmented are commonplace. In response, architects look to formal systems and modes of working which privilege the dynamic and the ambiguous. Attracted to so-called non-Euclidean geometries and rhizomatic networks, embedding design in the diagramming of fluctuations in global markets, political deterritorialisations or other kinds of statistical analyses and parametric modelling, architects look for relevance in the conditions, needs and demands of a contemporary world in a state of crisis. As a result architecture becomes a mimetic and formal representation of the dynamic, fluctuating, unsettled, unpredictable and catastrophic lineaments of that crisis. But doing so it merely trades one form of *mimesis*—the imitation of transcendent permanent realities—for another: the imitation of immanent impermanent fluxion. It continues to adhere precisely to the literalness that Tarkovsky warned against. It is not a question of finding "elaborate devices" to represent certain conditions or to displace certain accepted modes of working. Rather, it is a question of remaining and working with the foundational and familiar existential characteristics, elements and processes of reality in order to convey its unsettling and uncanny dimensions. The implication for architecture is that the most unsettling, the most unfamiliar and extraordinary experiences happen to take place precisely in the midst of the most ordinary and mundane of circumstances.

# Architecture *and...*

Architecture *and* cinema. Why this particular conjunction? Architecture and: music, gastronomy, viticulture, philosophy, religion, geography, politics. Always architecture *and* something else—as if architecture had no intrinsic being and could exist only in relation to something else, to something outside of its bounds. It may be that architecture's primitive role has always been the implementation of commissions and directives from outside its own domain through the application of organisational and technical know-how, skills and resources to realise them. Architecture originates in the field, in the workshop and with the guilds. It comes very late into the ambit of art, the humanities and the university. Before then such alliances were without value or function. Architecture proceeded by the application of commonly accepted practices and techniques in geometry and construction. These constituted the "content" of architecture— what was proper to it, what determined its identity as an applied practice. The complexity and sophistication of this applied content and tecnics can be gauged in traditional buildings across different cultures, constructed when architecture as a discipline and profession existed only in a latent state: Medieval cathedrals and Hindu temples, Roman and Arab baths, Mesoamerican cities and so forth. The appearance of "Architecture" as a distinct discipline and profession also meant the appearance of distinct "content" that could be abstracted from its traditional practices. The complex conceptual and ritual framework of Masonry is a case in point. Once introduced into the academy and displaced from the field and the workshop, architecture needed to define its disciplinary boundaries and justify its contents. The more it did this, the more it distanced itself from its primitive conditions. This distantiation has a limit. The intensification of architecture's dalliance with theory appears to have reached a state of excess and overburdening of this limit. The corollary of excess is an impoverishment of the kind of primitive know-how that characterised architecture before "Architecture." This is evidenced as much in the quality of built architecture as it is in the nature of architectural education, curricula and practices.

Regaining what is proper to architecture does not imply returning to past circumstances, nor does it imply a-conceptual un-theoretical perspectives on practice and education. The point I would make here is that much of the theory adopted into architecture—whether it be Pythagorean cosmology in Vitruvius or Derrida's trace in Eisenman—is improprietous to the extent that it does not engage what is at the same time proper and radical to architecture. Traditional architectural know-how and techniques for articulating and constructing buildings, irrespective of how pragmatic or unconsciously held they happen to be, are, like every idea held and every gesture enacted, susceptible of being theorised. Processes of organising space through geometric patterning and repartition can be diagrammed, codified, classified and converted to repeatable patterns that require no theoretical or conceptual undertaking in their application to particular projects. However these geometries and patterns do have ideational dimensions which connect them into complex webs of symbolic registers for example. Likewise all technical figures in construction, no matter how mundane, connect to registers beyond the pragmatic in similar ways. Consider for example the terms *door furniture* and *housing* in carpentry. With the first, the notion and reality that a door is inoperative without being furnished with hinges, a latch, handle, lock and so forth, is self evident practically. Theoretically however this term gives leave to think the concept of furniture as what is necessary to operability—whether it be a door, a room, a street or a public square. Door furniture, room furniture, street furniture—these might all be designed on purely aesthetic grounds, or they might reference Derrida's trace and Eisenman's overmapped geometries. But they can also engage with a different kind of theory which derives from their pivotal necessity for the operability of the equipment and spaces that they furnish and furnish-*with*.[5] As for *housing*, the term refers to the creation of a joint in carpentry, where one member of the connection allows a place for the other by modifying itself. Normally this is done by having some material removed which the other member can then occupy. Japanese timber joinery has made of this possibility an extraordinarily sophisticated art. Connections vary in complexity from simple housings to very complex joints in which two or more members each give something away to receive the others. The most remarkable examples in Japanese carpentry are those which require no third element— such as glue, dowels, nails or bolts—to fasten the housing assembly. Here, it is the precise mutual compliance of each component with each other component that creates a locked joint with practical, structural and aesthetic value. This architectural moment—something proper to construction in other words—implies and entails its own theorisation. No other discipline can approach the concept of housing in the same way, and only this approach can yield distinctive insights and directions for theoretical investigation. Such technical instances of housings have something foundational and radical to say about the theme—for example, that housing is about reception, receptivity, hospitality, hosting, allowance, making room for, affordance, sacrifice, compliance, deferral, complementarity, interlocking, strength, inseparability, demountability, adaption, reuse and so forth. The particular constellations of words, ideas and themes opened up by architectural notions like housing and furniture are not possible in any other discipline. These constellations are fields which enable the production of sense—of *architectural* and *architectonic* sense that can be elaborated into frameworks and assemblages with substantial implications for design.[6]

The *and* in *architecture and cinema* would then be a gesture of reappropriating sense, of recovering assemblages whose components have become dispersed in music, philosophy, poetry, religion; or else appropriated by other conditions and disciplines, by cinema for example. In such cases the conjunction *and* takes on a formative or semantic role. Philosophy, music, or whatever else, supply meanings and concepts that architecture might convey or communicate, but which it does not in itself have the capacity to produce. The danger is a setting up of architecture as primarily concerned with signification, with an instrumental function of communicating or expressing ideas. It then operates as an empty container—informed, animated, ordered and organised by meanings drawn from outside to shape and articulate it. It depicts and represents those ideas, becoming *metaphorical* or *symbolic* in the process. The clearer the representation, the more efficacious the depiction, the better the communication and the more successful the architecture. This trope is Platonic and follows the motifs of *mimesis* (imitation of the archetype or *eidos*) and *methexis* (participation in the *eidos*), developed notably in the Republic, and of the *khora*, developed in the Timaeus. There, space (*khora*) is the "nurse of becoming"—formless potentiality or pure inarticulate capacity in need of an idea or archetypal pattern to shape, organise and give it purpose. In phrases like "architecture and cinema," the *and* will commonly establish a relationship of hierarchical dependence implying that the first needs the second in order to be meaningful.

Another sense of the *and* is the implication of an intrinsic, secret alliance. If we take "architecture and music" as an example, the *and* would imply that the two art forms and practices are affiliated according to some essential commonalities—such as number and geometry, proportion and rhythm, tonality and atmosphere, timbre and materiality. These identities refer both arts and practices to a more essential state of being. The *and* provides a circuit of continuity between them, across which their affiliation can be played out. Again the trope is Platonic and its lineage Pythagorean. In the Republic, Plato lists four key stages on the way to truth. Each is associated with a science. They are arithmetic (static one-dimensional number), geometry (static number in two and three dimensions), music (number in motion) and astronomy (three dimensional number in motion). These four became the *Quadrivium* of Medieval pedagogy. The four sciences are completed by the "capstone" of Dialectics, towards which all learning must be directed. Number and the logic of its operations regulate all things, from quantitative calculation to the qualitative dimensions of discernment, wisdom and truth—all things in proper order and proportion. This allows Plato to venture a quantification of ontological relationship by defining the various states of being in the form of a proportion: "as being is to becoming, so is pure intellect to opinion, and as intellect is to opinion so is science to belief and understanding to the perception of shadows."[7] In such a register, architecture *and* music would imply that there is some intrinsic kinship between the two, that they are analogues, alternate expressions or modulations of a single condition, or that there is a foundational measure of identity between them. This alliance would allow both art forms and practices to share common content and to reflect each other. The study of architecture and music would then concern itself with demonstrating essential correlations, with the subtext being that *and* means *equal to*: architecture = music.

The sources and persistence of this ideology and its mobilisation for architectural practice are well documented. It rests on a harmonic conception of existence and a hermeneutic framework for creative practice. It can only be sustained where the ambition is to correlate human production, through *mimesis*, with a cosmic production that has sacred status worthy of imitation. In this framework, the *and* represents a relationship of logocentric and hierarchical dependence implying a dual rhythm of deduction/induction. The alliance is reinforced by etymology since name (*logos*) and number are cognates and convey two states of the same entity. Every existent has a name and every name a corresponding number, so that the name (*NAM) is the being *in principle*, while the number (*BR) is the being *in vibration*—that is, in rhythmic operation. The world is constituted of such vibratory states and harmonic configurations which are available to human endeavour as a means of according human and cosmic conditions. The harmonies embedded in human works are thereby deduced from and induce cosmic harmonies embedded in the world, themselves deduced from and inducing the first harmonic utterance: the *logos*, word or verb.

With Roland Barthes, the *and* takes on a radically different function. Instead of drawing together two entities to form a unity it operates to concatenate without fusion, but also to ramify. It works in a conjugational and not merely additive or integrative manner. The conjunction is not summative but excessive. In Barthes' terminology, the resulting concatenated system produced tends to overcoding. It develops to a liminal state of crisis which is both catastrophic and transformative. The entities thus gathered remain distinct while the collectivity is marked by an increase and intensification. By virtue of the excess produced, the entities begin to resonate and imply others which are not concrete but immanent and virtual within the collectivity, and whose potential is actualised by the resonances. A personal experience from music might illustrate this. I recall a performance by the musician Keith Jarrett at the Sydney Opera House. Jarrett's overture consisted in playing a series of chords, repeated in a sustained cycle of iterations. The chord sounds produced remained clearly distinct and the pattern of repetition scrupulously maintained. At a certain moment during the sequence, an additional melodic line could be faintly heard above the repeating chords. But Jarrett was not playing a melody. This additional layer was being produced entirely through the resonances activated by the separate chords, themselves comprising distinct, though related tones. The melodic line was smooth and continuous across the chords and, as it were, *floated* some way above them. This was not a solitary experience. Several in the audience who realised what was developing were sufficiently taken aback to look for confirmation from others. Jarrett had managed to mobilise the potential of these chords, to actualise without explicit articulation their propensity to unfold entire scales or modes, and to foreground their latent melodies. In this example, the *and* which linked the chords kept them singular but also produced, because of the acoustic prolongation, overlap and resonance of sound either side of each chord, something supplementary, emergent, unexpected and surprising.

This is equally the Deleuzian function of the *and*. A concatenation of singularities which produces something new, unplanned, possibly unplannable and unprogrammable.[8] For Deleuze, the *and* belongs to the motif of the *milieu*—the midst and middle. It constructs a site in which the focus shifts away from the terms of a relation towards the mediating relation itself. That is, away from the stable *being* (*être, est*) of the terms to the *and* (*et*) which mobilises a deployment of "conjunctions, disjunctions, alternations and interlacements, of additions the total of which is never achieved, of subtractions the remainder of which is never fixed."[9] This priority of being and privileging of essence is foundational in language and philosophy:

> "All of grammar, all of syllogism, is a means of maintaining the subordination of conjunctions to the verb to be, and to make them gravitate around the verb to be. We have to go further: make it so that the encounter with relations penetrates and corrupts everything, mines being, makes it tumble. Substitute and (*et*) for being (*est*). A and B. The AND is not even a particular relation or conjunction, it is what subtends all relations, the route of all relations which makes all relations flee outside their term, outside the ensemble of the terms, and outside everything that could be determined as Being, One or All. The AND as extra-being, inter-

being. Relations could establish themselves between their terms, or between two ensembles, from one to the other, but the AND gives another direction to relations and forces terms and ensembles to flee, one and the other, on the line of flight that it actively creates. To think *with* AND, instead of thinking BEING, to think *for* BEING: empiricism has never had any other secret... The multiple is no longer an adjective subordinated to a One which divides itself, nor to the Being which encompasses it. It has become substantive, a multiplicity which never ceases to inhabit every thing. A multiplicity is never in the terms, no matter how numerous, nor in their ensemble or totality. A multiplicity is only in the AND, which does not have the same nature as the elements, the ensembles and even their relations."[10]

The *and* therefore has a creative and productive function. Its use shifts, unclenches, accelerates and mobilises language, bringing it to a state of stammering or stuttering (*begaiement*), carrying it to an encounter with the strange, unfamiliar and uncanny within itself.[11] Philosophy then becomes a practice of putting into work, of functioning, of agency, of preparing or making room for what arrives and eventuates. The components of philosophy, of thought, of community are not distinct, stable entities or eternal ideas. When people enter a room, he writes, "they are not persons, characters or subjects, but an atmospheric variation, a change of hue, an imperceptible molecule, a discrete population, a fog or a dripping storm cloud... Real entities are events, not concepts."[12] By implication, spaces are not defined formal configurations that have a separable existence. Rather, they are settings, milieux and ambiances subject to interminable modification, changes of state, reorientations, densifications and rarefactions caused by whatever assemblages happen to take place within them and affect them fundamentally.

The efficacy of the *and* is to unclench assemblages and agencies whose interminable deterritorialisations provoke a surfeit and fulguration of production. It operates as the pivot of assemblage, the trope which affords a development of agency and desire. In Barthes' terms, the *and* triggers a state of *jouissance,* accompanying the experience of overcoding to excess of signification. It is a mark of radical difference and interminable deterritorialisation between elements which the *and* simultaneously separates and concatenates, divides and conjugates. It makes possible the difference of potential necessary for there to be communication, negotiation and commutation between the elements—for it to be possible for something to spark, flow or resonate between them. In that sense, the *and* initiates an open system of dynamic interaction, of constantly unfolding conditions which, while not bringing terms into cohesion nevertheless triggers or brings them into production. Bringing elements and conditions into neighbourhood through the *and*, through juxtaposition, collage, montage and other assembly and editing strategies, is not a process destined to specific outcomes. It is not the means to an end. The process may well deliver outcomes, but the outcomes are not the point. The process and what it produces are equally not convergent or predetermined but *emergent*. The focus of this process is on creating conditions and circumstances of preparedness and readiness—limit conditions of crisis and emergency within a system that is attentive to the advent of whatever comes, of whatever presents itself in the midst.

Architecture *and* cinema means that we are faced with two fundamentally unlike and irreconcilable entities. Two singularities that do not refer to a transcendent commonality or unity, but which nevertheless produce between them an enabling site of assemblage and agency. The relationship is neither closed nor symmetrical but parallel. This means that the two do not touch and do not meet, that the discrepancy between them is sustained. The gap between them is a field of potential difference and therefore of potential resonance and vibration. They are parallel in the sense of interminably shuttling between and deferring to each other, and beyond each other to yet others through a disconnected connectivity which is vitally productive. This parallelism becomes a mechanism for reading, producing, mapping and implementing new configurations of thought, figures of speech, states of being, gestures, trajectories, geometries, strategies, tactics, techniques and technologies. At least that is the sense intended for architecture *and* cinema in this book. The framework approaches Deleuze's contention of philosophical practice as a kind of multilingualism—in the sense that architecture and music are two systems that are brought into strategic relationship through the analyses and parallels proposed:

> "We have to be bilingual even in a single language, we have to have a minor language in the interior of our language, we have to make of our proper language a minority usage. Multilingualism is not only the possession of several systems each of which would be homogenous in itself; it is first a line of flight or of variation which affects each system by preventing it from being homogenous. Not to speak like an Irish person or a Romanian in a language other than one's own, but on the contrary to speak in one's own language as a stranger. Proust says: 'Great books are written in a sort of foreign tongue'… That is the definition of style."[13]

This might mean that its dalliance with cinema enables architecture to become estranged, to create a foreign condition for itself within itself, to find trajectories which deterritorialise it from within. It would not do this by acting "cinematically" or working outside its confines, but precisely by working the limits of its own milieu through the strangeness that the other promotes within itself. This strangeness is the uncanny condition that architecture finds with its own resources, in itself and by itself, through the agencies and circuits that an encounter with cinema provokes. And it is for Deleuze entirely a question of encounter:

"When we work, we are in absolute solitude. We do not constitute a school, nor belong to any school. The only work there is is black and clandestine. Only it is an extremely populated solitude. Not populated with dreams, phantasms or projects, but with encounters. An encounter is maybe the same thing as a becoming or a party (*des noces*). It is in the depth of this solitude that we can realise such encounters. We encounter people... but also movements, ideas, events, entities. These things all have proper names, but the proper name does not designate a person or a subject at all. It designates an effect, a zigzag, something which passes or which passes between two as if by a difference of potential... We were saying the same thing about becomings: it is not a term which becomes another, but each one encounters the other, one sole becoming which is not common to both, since they have nothing to do with one another, but which is between the two of them, which has its proper direction, a block of becoming, an a-parallel evolution. It is this, the double capture, the wasp and the orchid: not even something that would be in one, or something that would be in the other, even if it were a question of exchange, mixture, but something which is between the two, outside the two, and which flows in another direction. To encounter is to find, to capture, to steal, but there is no method for finding, nothing but a long preparation. Stealing is the opposite of plagiarising, of copying, of imitating or or doing likewise. Capture is always a double-capture, theft, a double-theft, and that is what constitutes not something mutual but an asymmetrical block, an a-parallel evolution, parties, always `outside' and `between'... to produce all the phenomena of double capture, to show what the conjunction AND is, not a reunion, nor a juxtaposition, but the birth of a stammering, the trace of a broken line which always goes by adjacency, a sort of active and creative line of flight? AND... AND... AND..."[14]

# Drawing parallels

Architecture and cinema work with similar conditions although these conditions are not equivalent because they have different valences, powers and potentialities in each domain. Both work with space for example— creating space *works* (French: *œuvre*) through working (*œuvrer*) and opening it up (*ouvrir*) or spacing it out. But the space and spatiality of cinema are different from the space and spatiality of architecture. The same is true of time, sound, light, atmosphere, narrative, composition and

so forth. Nevertheless the two track each other across parallel terrain.
Maybe what is critical in this parallelism is the radical differences between
the two rather than their similarities. It may be that in their encounter, the
site of production is not a field of mutual commonalities, but precisely that
which takes each of them outside itself towards other fields, other
assemblages and other terrains. It may be that each only begins to be itself
and pursue its proper destiny when it eclipses the propriety of its
boundaries, when it becomes improprietous, delinquent and unseemly. For
Deleuze, what constitutes a style in literature is the moment when
language, through the stuttering that unsettles it from within, begins to
imply other conditions—that of music for example.[15] In her dialogue with
Deleuze, Claire Parnet implies that for cinema, an exemplary instance is
the potential of the fixed shot to convey "absolute speed, which makes us
see everything at the same time, maybe the character of slowness or even
of immobility. Immanence. It is the contrary of development, where the
transcendent principle which determines and structures never directly
appears in a perceptible relationship with a process, with a becoming."[16]
The conveyance of a sense of immobility, of time passing so slowly that
its passage passes unnoticed, or so that we literally undergo and suffer that
passage existentially, would then constitute what is proper to cinema and
at the same time what is least kinematic.

As we will see, cinematographers manage to achieve this quality in
very different ways—for example, Tarkovsky (*Mirror*) by intensifying the
material conditions of the image and the time it takes to pass; Nicholas
Roeg (*Bad Timing*) by switching between multiple timeframes with great
velocity; Carlos Reygadas (*Silent Light*) by persistently remaining with the
ambience of existential duration and Jean-Luc Godard (*Histoire(s) du
Cinéma*) by montage which juxtaposes, multiplies and densifies narrative
texture. In every case, the strategies and techniques of manipulating
temporality are deployed entirely within the fundamental limits of
cinematic production—the 24p frame rate limit of image projection—
rather than by adopting practices that lie outside the tectonics of cinema.
This suggests that a work will persuasively engage with the real only by
intensively working its fundamental limits, rather than by eliminating or
escaping them. What implications might there be for architecture of this
cinematic eclipse of time within time itself? How might the agency of
cinema allow architecture to conceptualise a parallel eclipsing of space
within space itself, and how might this open to the strange and unfamiliar
within architecture. What conditions would the deterritorialisation of
architecture through a working of its fundamental limits bring about, and
towards what other domains and conditions might architecture become
transposed as a result?

If the ultimate deterritorialisation for language is music, if a deterritorialised language is a "becoming-musical," then the ultimate deterritorialisation for cinema is for it to eclipse one of its fundamental limiting conditions. That is, to eclipse time and temporality by a "becoming-immobile" or a-temporal. This would manifest itself in a sense of absolute immanence—a simultaneous presence *at* all times and *of* all times. Another term for this is aeviternity, literally "ever-being." By implication, the ultimate deterritorialisation for architecture would be for it to eclipse its fundamental condition of embodied spatiality by a "becoming-mobile" and a-spatial. This would manifest itself in a sense of absolute ubiquity, a simultaneous presence *in* all places and *of* all places. Another term for this is infinity or "ever-presence." In both cases, the suppression of the interval—between now and then in time, between here and there in space—brings something extraordinary and uncanny to the conditions and experiences of time and space. It does not lead to an impoverishment of existential conditions, but to their amplification and transformation.

In this book, the general approach to mapping a parallel terrain between cinema and architecture employs the motif of *drawing*—drawing implications *from* cinema *for* architecture. Drawing can be thought of in three different ways. The first is to make a drawing *of* something that exists—for example, a face, an orange, a tree, a building, a street or a city. This is drawing's descriptive, indexical or *representational* function. Drawing an existing object or landscape is easier to conceive than drawing a film, a piece of music or a text. Nevertheless, these too can be drawn— by using storyboards in cinema, notational diagrams in music or metaphorical diagrams and ideational mapping in philosophy.

The second way is to draw-out *from* something—for example by drawing strength from being in a team, or drawing ideas from a certain philosopher. This is drawing's *interpretative* or *presentational* function. A face, a site, a piece or music, a text or a film sequence is investigated in terms of what can be pulled out or literally stretched out of it. These things are to a great extent concealed in the original. For example, concealed emotions in a face or concealed intentions in a countenance; obscured topographical or climatic conditions in a site; unexpressed subtexts in a narrative; unframable, unframed or out of frame presences in cinema. Drawing *draws* these occluded conditions *out of* the work and presents them foregrounded over and above what is visible, discernable, audible or perceptible. This presentational kind of drawing is also creative or productive. To use the Greek term, it is a *poietic* form of drawing.

The third is to draw-towards or *for* something. This is drawing's *instrumental* function. It has a futural, directing or destining objective according to which it also takes on a presentational character—since what is drawn out of one, for another, is destined to become a new production, a new presence. What is pulled out of something by drawing has a *clinamen*, it tends towards or defers to conditions and possibilities beyond the thing itself. Such drawing transfers something from one domain, which may have no spatial connotations—for example, a figure of thought, a sound, an atmosphere—into spatial diagrams which have two or three dimensional characteristics.

How a film has been made, how the camera moves, how actors move, how scenes are set-up and framed, how sequences are organised, how montage is constructed—these can all be diagrammed to convey a kind of structure or process, which can then initiate spatial investigations with implications and therefore applications beyond cinema. Instrumental drawing transfers qualities or techniques from one domain into something useful in another domain of application. These qualities and techniques are potentialities or virtualities that make possible what does not yet exist, what has yet to present itself. They become tools and apparatuses for releasing and mobilising new constructions and new possibilities that are not explicitly there in what is being investigated. With this kind of drawing the focus is not on accuracy of representation but on dispositional efficacy. Its purpose is draw *out* whatever might have transferable and operative value within a given domain *into* another domain where it can take hold and mobilise agency.

It is this third strategy of drawing—drawing *from* cinema *for* architecture in an instrumental manner—that will predominate in this book. Drawing in this way involves a double gesture, a double trajectory—extraction and projection. In the sense that it is directed at convoking new assemblages, this form of drawing is provisional. Eventually, by application of what is drawn into the new domain, instrumental drawing becomes presentational drawing. What might be outlined in relation to an existing film being analysed for its transferable conditions remains static and analytically derived. However once the instrumentality of the drawing begins to be directed to its applications in architecture, the drawing becomes projective, interpretative, innovative, futural and presentational. This conversion from an instrumental to a presentational orientation is not determined temporally, as a moment in time when one kind of drawing gives way to another. Rather, the presentational dimension of drawing remains latent within the instrumental and actualises itself within and at the same time as the instrumental process of drawing. The futural is implied in the present as something infolded and susceptible of being deployed and unfurled through this kind of drawing *for*.

Hence the many precedents used in the process are dealt with in ways that will open them up, even fracture them, so they can begin to circulate within different sites of assemblage and agency. A precedent must, through this drawing practice, cede, yield or give-up. It must give-way and deliver what it holds back or conceals, what keeps it to its limit and gathers it to itself as something incorruptible and unassailable. The precedent precedes, it goes (Latin: *-cedere*) before (*prae-*), it gives up the ghost and deceases. But this going-before is also a ceding, sedition, insurrection, mutiny, dissention, secession, a going-apart or away, a withdrawing of oneself from others.[17] A precedent precedes design in two senses. It comes before it (*prae-*) as an influence on design and it cedes itself, gives-way and yields *for* design, in advance of it. The question of how to trigger the decease of a precedent, how to open it up so that it unfolds its latent propensities for agency and for circulating amongst assemblages, becomes a critical condition of instrumental and presentational drawing. This very circulation through the etymological ambience of the word *precedent* shows how a singular entity might yield to multiple concatenations and implications of sense, how this multiplicity might be mapped by attending to resonances, how the resonant multiplicity might constitute an assemblage and how the resonances themselves, in the way they send and defer one to another, represent a circuit of agencies producing within the milieu. The process does not aim to conclude and close off meaning, to determine a final definition for the word, a terminal sense to terminate the process. Instead, its aim is to use the resonant potential implied and folded within the word to initiate circuits of vibratory, semantic and metaphorical associations. It is to blow-open the constraining limits of meaning so that sense can begin to multiply and proliferate. These multiple alignments and filiations are not geared to uncover some original meaning of the word, some original language before the Fall or pre-Babel. The *balbutiement* (stammering, babbling, blabbering) that Deleuze evokes in relation to the *and* does not refer to a fallen state of language, corrupted or otherwise abandoned to nonsense. Rather, it is language *per se*, in itself and *for* itself.

Deleuze's non-mimetic, a-parallel evolution that takes place between the terms of an encounter—here between cinema and architecture—operates much like the proliferation of ideas that were made to circulate in the etymological ambiance of the word *precedent*. The parallels do not have the status or function of types, patterns and models to be translated and applied from one to the other. They do not constitute solutions to problems or procedural methods. Their role is simply to produce an assemblage, a field of encounter and terrain of thought in which the thematic conditions of an architectural project might be articulated, investigated, elaborated and worked—conceptually, contextually, architectonically and technically. The parallels might prompt specific processes and types of exploration, diagramming and modelling. But these have the value of a necessary and sustained preparatory work—a kind of provisional training that produces a readiness for action and decision.

The work of drawing from cinema will proceed analytically, by dividing and isolating a whole film or scene or moment, in order to examine and comment upon it. The same generally applies to places, buildings and spaces. This methodology has substantial limits and will only yield a limited range of insights with limited application. More synthetic modes of cinematic and architectural reception will yield very different perspectives. Walking through a place, a building or a room without stopping to isolate a particular shape, assembly or detail; allowing a film to play itself out without focussing on a particular frame, sound, illumination or narrative turn. These continuous and seamlessly engaged experiences deliver a more holistic and less sharply defined sense of what a film might be about or how a building feels. They are genuine and important modes of reception, but less useful in this case, since what they produce is an overall ambiance with little detail, delineated implications or sufficient transferability to enable specific thematics and tectonic possibilities to emerge. In the process of drawing *from* cinema *for* architecture, the general approach to films and buildings will be neither encyclopaedic nor systematic. While I have sought close readings of both, I have not aimed to uncover internal consistency within a cinematographic or architectural work. I come to a film, or more often to a scene or sequence in that film, with a view to developing its usefulness for the architectural design process. Even then, the scope is limited to tectonic and formal concerns of spatial organisation, volumetric composition, tempo and duration, materiality, spatial experience and the phenomenological condition of architecture—in short, to a concern for the way the film has been "made" and constructed. For example, I am more interested in Roeg's manipulation of time in a specific scene or sequence in terms of how this might have resonances for how and in what ways the dimension of time might be broached in architecture, rather than how this might indicate a tendency in his work as a whole, a stylistic consistency across his films or a theory of time that might apply to cinema as a distinct discipline. Likewise, I am more likely to focus on a particular aspect, moment or detail in a specific building for similar reasons, rather than to discern some recurrent motif in an architect's work.

The example and the instance are in that respect radically autonomous and independent of any kind of internally coherent system that might be posited for a movement, a school or an author. The key concern relates to the usefulness and productiveness of the example and the instance, to their ability to trigger or unclench something in the parallel discipline. In that sense this is neither a work of criticism or theory. It is more than anything a work about the tectonics of production, the way things are composed and assembled, the way the assemblage affords some agency in further production, in further invention or in furthering the ambit of a creative practice. The ambition of the work is to multiply the armoury of architectural production—its "equipmentality," to use Heidegger's term. The same will hold true of my approach and use of *theory* or *philosophy*. This is not a work of philosophy. There is no attempt to carry out systematic readings of Deleuze, Heidegger, Nancy, Agamben or any of the other key thinkers whose work—but more specifically whose writings— have evidently influenced my own. The intent is to show how theory might be broached and worked through an analysis of issues or themes presenting themselves in certain works of cinema and architecture, or rather in certain fragments and moments of certain buildings and films. It is not a question of assigning intentionality on the part of a designer, an architect or a cinematographer. Neither is it to lay claim to the veracity or plausibility of a particular interpretation ventured in the process of analysing, drawing parallels and suggesting implications across the two disciplines and practices.[18]

The range of films and built works selected for analysis is in many ways fortuitous. They are simply projects that happen to be around, projects I have ready access to, that am familiar with and that I have seen or visited several times. I return to them because of their accessibility and familiarity, but also because of their depth of evocation. They have a thickness and complexity that can sustain several iterations of unravelling. Most are evidently situated within a distinct historical period—in terms of cinema, from Italian Neorealism to the apogee of European modernist cinema. In terms of architecture, the spread is very broad and syncretic— stretching from medieval exemplars in India, the Middle East and Europe to late modern projects persisting into the present century; and from significant examples of sacred architecture to apparently insignificant makeshift, adaptable structures and environments that would never make it into glossy monographs. While for both cinema and architecture the overall scope might appear constrained within the 1960s and 1970s, there are contemporary projects reviewed. In any case the scope of works dealt with is not contrived in advance as a set, selected for reasons of comprehensiveness of coverage; representativeness of a certain style, period or auteur; a desire to make up for lacunae in the coverage of marginal or marginalised genres or practitioners; the apparent cult status of certain works; an adherence to canons of cinema or architecture; or for any other such reason. There will be almost no treatment of films or buildings that attempt to comprehend the totality of a project—a whole film, in all of its dramatic, narrative, technical, aesthetic, philosophical or political dimensions; a whole building in all of its sociocultural, symbolic, political, programmatic, contextual, circulational, formal, technical or material conditions. Precedents are always dealt with syncretically and as infinitely fragmentable assemblages that are open to numerous iterations of analysis and interpretation.

Like the many choices made preparing this work, writing it and dealing with precedents, the general approach is fragmentary and makeshift—working with whatever happens to be at hand, whatever one comes upon, what is immediately available or suggests itself at a particular moment. Whatever presents itself in turn suggests themes and ideas that can be opened up through analysis to reveal implications for the work, as well as for the tectonics of cinema and architecture. There is no attempt at any kind of authoritativeness in the selection of precedents for study, nor in the methods used to deal with them or to write about them. The analyses, too, are fragmentary and makeshift. It might be that apparently minor aspects of a film sequence are foregrounded, or that a peripheral moment in the spatial event of a building becomes the focus for an extended discussion. If the disposition to observation, analysis and textuality is fragmentary, then the work's own rhythm will be fragmentary. If the work coheres, this will be through resonance between parts which barely communicate, rather than by any kind of formal coordination or totalising construction. Likewise, it should come as no surprise that the works selected for analysis lend themselves to foregrounding the fragmentary, the heterogeneous, the ambiguous, the unresolved and the irresolvable. In that sense, the selection of works, the method of working and the textuality of the work are fundamentally personal and make no attempt at objectivity.

The question of validity then arises. The observations ventured in relation to a film, building or place are construed in relation to what presents itself at any moment as perceivable in the work, rather than in relation to an overarching structure of intentionality on the part of the cinematographer or architect. Authorial intent is irrelevant to the extent that once a work exists any intentionality can have no purchase on the work's reception. Once released a work is freed of intentionality and at once delivered over to the thoroughly undeterminable and indefinite potentialities of interpretation. At the same time, what someone reads in a work, however fantastical that reading might be, is never totally without foundation. If reading is conceived less as reading *into* the intention that directs or inheres in the work and more as reading *for* potential associations, alignments and resonances that traverse the work, then in a sense, anything goes. The more layered and potentially resonant a work is, the more susceptible it will be to multiple readings. On the other hand, the more singular is the work's assemblage and construction, the less potential readings it will yield.

The issue with intentionality is that no intention is ever singular. Intentions are always collectives, assemblages and groups of ideas that may not always be explicitly foregrounded. Texts always comprise sub-texts. Within any assemblage some components will be sharply delineated, others less so and yet others will remain virtual, unarticulated or unidentified. Components within assemblages are never isolated but always interact with one another. These interactions produce configurations or delineations at various scales and to various degrees of resolution. The most apparent configurations might mask the less apparent, so that one is always dealing with multiplicities in states of heterogeneity and fluxion. Each defined contour is crossed by occluding edges and overlays, by uncertainties and ambiguities. Irrespective of purpose and intention, choosing to work with a certain assemblage is also choosing to work with the indiscernible, implied or potential components of that assemblage. Working with Heidegger's idea of boredom in relation to time, as I do here, implies also working with Jakob von Uexküll's idea of captivation in physiology, cybernetics and biosemiology. Working with an apparently rational geometrical system like the square implies also working with irrational ratios and proportions involving the square roots of 2, 3 and 5 and the Golden Section—all of which form part of the order of the square, whether declared or not. Working with Platonic *mimesis* in artistic production implies working with particular ethical dispositions having substantial political, sociocultural and environmental implications. It also means working with the inescapable fact of forgery, dissimulation and failure which haunt mimetic practice. All this means that any declared intentions can never exhaust the actual multiplicities inherent in and always exceeding the assemblages which form part of such intentions. There is always an internal logic or consistency working within assemblages. The more hybrid the assemblage, the more internal logics it has explicitly or implicitly engaged with, the more difficult the landscape of consistency is to map out and the more likely will be the potential of the accidental and the unexpected to surface.

Assemblages are fielded by design according to the choices made and the decisions taken. From that moment, their components are free to circulate and interact, to reinforce or cancel each other out, to augment or confuse, to transduce or stabilise, to transform or destroy. This applies in the design or creative processes of filmmaking and architectural production. Design is an opportunity to collect, mobilise and direct such diverse assemblages, assuming they and their components have been properly identified. If only a portion of the components have been recognised and worked with, the rest still remain and will influence the processes and outcomes of design. In architecture, such assemblages might be conceptual—for example, where certain philosophical ideas or theoretical conditions are taken up to frame the design process. They might be contextual—for example, where a site delivers aesthetic, thematic or theoretical content which eclipse its purely physical or sociocultural conditions. They might also be technological—for example, where choices of particular structural, constructional or environmental strategies and systems, or the use of a particular material, contribute formatively to the metaphorical or symbolic content of a building. Similar possibilities—theoretical, contextual and technical—exist for cinema. In both cases, the declared ideas, settings and means of execution or know-how used will have explicit dimensions, but they will also harbour implicit conditions that the design or production processes will release, and whose effects, if the implicit is not properly articulated and mobilised, might surprise. This element of surprise might constitute something catastrophic in the work, in the sense that some components of the assemblages, put into play either by design or inadvertently, might contradict and unsettle others, causing ambiguity, uncertainty, impoverishment or ultimately a radical disassemblage of the work. The surprise might also lead the implicit or hidden components to cause fortuitous amplification, reinforcement or elaboration of the internal logic or explicit intentions within the work, so that it emerges stronger, more persuasive and enriched. The effectiveness of the creative process is therefore a function of the degree of identification and mobilisation of components within the assemblages that it declares, articulates and operates. The more explicit the components are, the greater the opportunity to bring more of them into productive relationship, to conjugate them and allow them to resonate.

Once fielded, such assemblages and the components that constitute them, become available to multiple receptions and readings. There are as many readings as readers. Some will limit themselves to explicit content that can be shown to be part of a designer's or a filmmaker's declared intentions. But there will always be many other readings that are sensitive and receptive to implicit content and implied conditions—conditions that are unarticulated, if not unarticulable or inarticulate within the work. It is not the verifiability of a reading which drives the analyses in this book, but its creative efficacy, its ability to open up new perspectives, its viability in mobilising the potentialities inherent in the assemblage that the work fields and its capacity to keep the process of unravelling moving. The question of reading then touches on the issue of communication, and whether cinema and architecture—or works of art generally—are modes of communication, or whether they are something else altogether. This requires a certain loose fit in the intentionality of the work—a condition which brings about the common unwillingness if not inability of an author to explicity articulate their intentions or to venture a reading of their own work. The loose fit is something which maintains the work in a state of suspension, a condition of associative uncertainty and ambiguity whereby relationships between parts and components within assemblages are maintained in states of flux so that they might be interminably disassembled and reassembled to form multiple configurations, giving rise to multiple readings. This loose fit is not however sloppy or unthought. The looseness has to be calibrated to the organisational potential of the assemblage so that the configurational and receptional multiplicity can have some measure of rigor. Loose fit allows adjustability, hence reorganisational capacity within the work. In terms of receptivity, adjustability allows reading for manifold potential rather than for singularity.

This then leads on to the question of adaptability—a central question for sustainability in the sense of the longevity, endurance and perdurance of works, particularly within conditions of crisis. The adaptable is fundamentally open rather than closed to recombination. It therefore harbours a futural dimension and will always be oriented to a capacity of becoming and emergence rather than permanent being. It will always be available for modification and change. As qualified by the open, the adaptable is an aspect of potentiality, of capacity, capability and aptitude—that is, of disposition-*towards* and fitness-*for*. In any case, it is a question of receptivity—the ability to receive, to house, to harbour, to contain. The adaptable is receptive in the sense of being capable of holding much, of being copiously-apt or fit for multiple purposes. Like the apprentice, the adept is one able to grasp, but also one captivated or seized by what has been apprehended, yet remaining apprehensive towards it—that is, open to and anticipating both the possibilities and the implications of captivation. The adaptable is therefore an apparatus open to multiple joints, connections or housings which bring elements into proximity—be they spaces, construction elements or materials in architecture; or temporalities, characters, images, narratives and sounds in cinema. The arrangement and composition of parts is fundamentally a question of adjustment, of bringing the like and unlike components of an assemblage into juxtaposition, proximity and neighbourhood. This foregrounds the idea that wholes are characterised by the way parts are combined and fitted-together as a constellation or collective—that is, by the relational constitution and disposition which the Greeks called *sophrosyne* and the Romans *temperentia*, paralleling the Pythagorean *harmonia* which referred to the fitting together of parts within a whole. Adjustment is a question of both tempering and tampering, of mixing, regulating, moderating and modulating parts in relation to each other.

In the case of this book, reading works of cinema and architecture is less a matter of determining authorial purpose by analysing for meaning or verifiable intentionality, than a matter of reading for the proliferation of sense—that is, for the way in which a work not only makes it possible for it to be read in multiple ways, but in the way it actively *produces* sense through the resonant potential of its assemblage. These multiplicities of sense need not be predicted in advance. Many will well-up as a function of the unpredictable interaction of components within the assemblage. The components and dimensions of a work, and the way they are assembled to form distinctive clusters which resonate across differences, constitute the main focus for analysis. Works present components and assemblies that are intentional and unintentional, implicit and explicit, articulated and unarticulated, solid and transparent, coherent and inchoate. These are all made available by a work to be read in multiple ways. Such readings eclipse any purely communicational or informational content in the work. They initiate interminable acts of creative reception, combination and concoction which ultimately supplant authorial intentionality, taking the work into other worlds and into other lives.

Every reading that seeks to map and conjugate resonances between the elements found in a work is genuine and authoritative to the extent that it represents a distinctive creative trajectory which makes it available to rejuvenated constructions of sense. The reading is therefore not instrumental. It is not directed at determining meaning. Rather it is solely directed at a process of making oneself *ready*. That is, of making oneself receptive to the opportunities and latent potential available within a work, as well as to the capacity of that latency to be unfurled and produce. It is a question of reading as a preparation for "making" in the most general sense. Like drawing, one does not only read some-*thing*, one reads-*for* and in relation to a situation.

By strange turns of etymology, the word "read" and related words—such as red, road, ready, rhythm, rod, right and reed—are worth mapping out. To be ready means to make oneself fit or right for something, for some purpose, adjusting oneself to a circumstance, being at hand.[19] It is also to be *for the sake of*—to be in the neighbourhood of, to wake and watch over,[20] to be geared up and well furnished or equipped with an apparatus for doing so.[21] While being ready implies a readiness to ride, to take up a road, to move or act, it also requires one to remain behind, to rest—in the sense of waiting for the arrival of decision and in the sense of the ease which accomplishes the decisive act. This readiness to act is a being in potential, a preparedness for production and increase. It is a mode of being between passion and impassive readiness, gathered at the point of acting and assuming that point as pivot of action. To read is to make oneself ready for decisive enactment and conveyance.[22] The art of rhetoric (*rhetorike techne*) is founded on making oneself ready in just that way. It is an agency of productive utterance and advent. This taking place is an architectonic event—maybe *the* architectonic event. In the Hebrew, the word "read" is *qara* and also means "to erect timbers for floors or roofs, to establish (a place) and bring it about; to set up flooring, a pavement, a platform, an enclosure, walls, a city." It derives from the etymon *KR/*KIYR, meaning "what is incisive, penetrant, trenchant, what engraves, digs"—therefore something like a script, character, graphic or sign which serves to mark, record or conserve the memory of things; and a lecture, oration, speech which serves to evoke, convoke and bring about or produce. To read then means to call out and name, and in doing so, to create and build.[23]

## Framing the look

It may be that the image has always been about pointing out that things are not what they seem, that the seeming is always riddled with seams, that the very trope of representing the world seamlessly is the contested field that the image ceaselessly works and transforms. There is a sense in which the image can only effectively convey the real by allowing something of the unreal to surface in its midst—that is, by literally weighing on or *in* the surface of representation so as to magnify the power of the real and produce it as presence.[24] In his *The Future of the Image*, Jacques Rancière contends that there are multiple regimes of the image, each engaging a different dynamic between the image and what it images, all of them interconnected in their operation and all of them effecting an alteration of resemblance. For him, the image has two registers:

> "There is the simple relation that produces the likeness of an original: not necessarily its faithful copy, but simply what suffices to stand in for it. And there is the interplay of operations that produces what we call art: or precisely an alteration of resemblance. This alteration can take on a myriad of forms. It might be the visibility given to brush-strokes that are

superfluous when it come to revealing who is represented by the portrait; an elongation of bodies that expresses their motion at the expense of their proportions; a turn of language that accentuates the expression of a feeling … a word or a shot in place of the ones that seem bound to follow; and so on… The images of art are operations that produce a discrepancy, a dissemblance… the commonest regime of the image is one that presents a relationship between the sayable and the visible, a relationship which plays on both the analogy and the dissemblance between them."[25]

The key factor is the "combinatory capacity of the sign, open to being combined with any element from a different sequence to compose new sentence-images *ad infinitum.*" Rancière uses Barthes' distinction between the *punctum* and the *studium* to distinguish between the semantic dimension of the image and its power as pure presence, between "the unfolding of inscriptions carried by bodies and the interruptive function of their naked, non-signifying presence":

"The *studium* makes the photograph a material to be decoded and explained. The *punctum* immediately strikes us with the affective power of the *that was: that*—i.e. the entity which was unquestionably in front of the aperture of the camera obscura, whose body has emitted radiation… the utter self-evidence of the photograph, consigning the decoding of messages to the platitude of the *studium*… (But both attitudes to the image) base themselves on the same principle: a principle of reversible equivalence between the silence of images and what they say. The former (Barthes the semiologist) demonstrated that the image was in fact a vehicle for a silent discourse which he endeavoured to translate into sentences. The latter tells us that the image speaks to us precisely when it is silent, when it no longer transmits any message to us… the contrast between the *studium* and the *punctum* arbitrarily separates the polarity that causes the aesthetic image constantly to gravitate between hieroglyph and senseless naked presence."

Rancière proposes three forms of "imageness": the *naked* image, whose artless resemblance "excludes the prestige of dissemblance and the rhetoric of exegeses"; the *ostensive* image, which asserts sheer presence but without signification, positing "presence as the peculiarity of art faced with the media circulation of imagery, but also with the powers of meaning that alter this presence: the discourses that present and comment on it, the institutions that display it, the forms of knowledge that historicise it"; and the *metaphorical* image, opposed to the ostensive image, which fields an excess of signification but without presence, and in whose logic "it is impossible to delimit a specific sphere of presence isolating artistic operations and products from forms of circulation of social and commercial imagery and from operations interpreting this imagery. The images of art possess no peculiar nature of their own that separates them in a stable fashion from the negotiation of resemblances and the discursiveness of symptoms."

"Naked image, ostensive image, metaphorical image: three forms of `imageness,' three ways of coupling or uncoupling the power of showing and the power of signifying, the attestation of presence and the testimony of history; three ways, too, of sealing or refusing the relationship between art and image. Yet it is remarkable that none of these three forms thus defined can function within the confines of its own logic. Each of them encounters a point of undecidability in its functioning that compels it to borrow something from the others."

This brings Rancière to a concept of imaging that is conscious of and explicitly works the distinction between presence and signification:

"The labour of art thus involves playing on the ambiguity of resemblances and the instability of dissemblances, bringing about a local reorganisation, a singular rearrangement of circulating images... This art is led to query the radicalism of its powers... It aims to play with the forms and products of imagery, rather than carry out their demystification... This oscillation between two attitudes... (is) a double metamorphosis, corresponding to the dual nature of the aesthetic image: the image as cipher of history and the image as interruption."

In *The Evidence of Film,* Jean-Luc Nancy notes that cinema's long established status as an art of the imaginary, or a semiology, have prevented it from developing a character distinct from painting, photography, theatre or the circus. For Nancy, cinema is fundamentally *an art of looking,* the "taking-place of a relation to the sense of the world":

"We are dealing neither with formalistic (let us say, tentatively, `symbolic') nor with narcissistic (let us say `imaginary') vision. We are not dealing with sight—seeing or voyeuristic, fantasising or hallucinating, ideative or intuitive—but solely with looking: it is a matter of opening the seeing to something real, towards which the look carries itself and which, in turn, the look allows to be carried back to itself... Cinema's proposition here is quite far from a vision that is merely 'sighting' (that looks in order merely to `see'): what is evident imposes itself as the setting up of a look."[26]

This way of looking is not focussed on images as representations of ideas, places, times, things, people, spectacles or worlds. The cinematic image is not significant because it engenders a fascination for images as such, but only because it constructs a way of opening onto and accessing a world, and of enabling that world to cast its look, to appear and present itself to a looking. These images are not "on the surface" in the way they might be for painting or photography. They do not conform to the metaphor of Plato's cave where projected images are counterfeit and discredited imitations or mutations of an external reality, or else ciphers for archetypes and ideas that cannot be imagined, let alone imaged. The cinematic image is not "on" the wall or "in" the space of projection. It does not reflect an outside but "opens an inside onto itself." The image on the screen does not depict or represent an idea. It "is itself the idea."[27]

The cinematic image is therefore a manner of penetrating space. It constitutes the way in which a look perforates and advances into a space. That space is then an apparatus—"a looking site or device, a looking-box—or rather: a box that is or acts as an aperture or peephole made for looking, as we say in French 'un regard' when referring to an opening in that it is meant to allow an observation or an inspection (such as in a pipe system or machine). Here the look is an entry into a space, it is a penetration before being a consideration or a contemplation." What cinema invites is an attunement of the viewing gaze with the kind of cinematic looking mobilised by the film. It is:

"an education in looking at the world, with a look at this world where cinema dwells: a look taken by the hand and led away on a journey that is not an initiation, that does not drive to any secret, but that amounts to making the gaze more, stirring it up, or even shaking it up, in order to make it carry further, closer, more accurately. All of art is set in motion, and one consequently finds oneself very far from that which shaped the idea of a supernumerary art, and close to the kinematics that put at stake again a whole way of relating to the world:... Cinema becomes the motion of what is real, much more than its representation. It will have taken long for the illusion of reality that held the ambiguous prestige and glamour of films—as if they had done nothing but carry to the extreme the old mimetic drive of the Western world—to disappear, at least in tendency, from an awareness of cinema (or from its self-awareness) and for a mobilised way of looking to take its place."[28]

The nature of this motion can be cast in terms of Deleuze's definition of it as what "only occurs if the whole is neither given nor giveable":

"Motion is not a displacing or a transferring, which may occur between given places in a totality which is itself given. On the contrary, it is what takes place when a body is in a situation and a state that compel it to find its place, a place it consequently has not had or no longer has. I move (in matter or mind) when I am not—ontologically—where I am—locally...

Motion is not the opposite of immobility, and motionlessness is not static. It is the opening of the motionless, it is presence in so far as it is truly present, that is to say, coming forward, introducing itself, offered, available, a site for waiting and thinking, presence itself becomes a passage toward or inside presence."[29]

Such considerations imply that the motion of cinema (Greek: *kinesis*) is not directed to the resolution of discrepancy, the fulfilment of lack or the realisation of potentiality. Motion does not seek to bridge or erase an interval of difference. Rather, it is peripatetic. Directed to the maintenance and prolongation of a relay, it interminably weaves trajectories and circuits of deferral. As the mobilisation of a way of looking, cinema enables an attentiveness, a certain animated vigilance that constitutes a disposition to the world, to ways of looking upon it and engaging with it, as well as to watching and witnessing the manner in which that world—the look of that world in both its appearance and the gaze it returns—presents itself. For this reason, the cinematic gaze entails an exchange of looks, an "opening of one look onto another: the picture's and the onlooker's. This opening provides a space, a distance both necessary and respectful, and at the same time it works as a relation. The film is not a representation, it is an attraction for a look, it is a traction all along its movement."[30] This space of exchange involves a fundamentally *ethical* condition,[31] a condition of care, of regarding and having regard for what takes place. "Guarding calls for watching and waiting, for observing, for tending attentively and overseeing. We look after what is ahead and after the way it presents itself: we let it present itself—and thus we also leave open the field for its withdrawal, where presence is in reserve, where presence keeps itself preserved."[32] The look of cinema, the look it gives and the looking it calls for are both a giving-back, a return of the gaze: "Images (then) define a world where the given must be given again: it must be received and recreated to be what it is… But to give again the real to realise it is genuinely to look at it."[33]

"In one way or another, film carries us away: we are carried in this transport, it is our existence, and this cinematographic gaze becomes a condition much more than a representation. It is the condition of a permanent transformation or an indefinite and continual variation. In a sense, an invariant is what is actually varying or supporting the variation. But just as the material support is a diaphanous and receptive membrane, this invariant is the unit of variation, the form of the transformation… The invariant is thus the engine of the variation; the form is metamorphic or anamorphic. And in a similar fashion the true motor of cinema is photographic immobility. The support, or the substance, or the subject, is not carrying but is itself carried in this transport, driven or thrown, rather

than led, by a force or a motive remaining inexhaustible in its reasons or
its effects... It is a transport authorising itself: not a narrative delivering a
genesis or a maturation, an unconcealment or a denouement, but at the
most a chronicle of incidents in a journey that is truly neither of being nor
of becoming—and which one could just as well characterise as a slow
distending of what is motionless.... Cinema—its screen, its sensitive
membrane—stretches and hangs between a world in which representation
was in charge of the signs of truth, of the heralding of a meaning, or of the
warrant of a presence to come; and another world that opens onto its own
presence through a voiding where its thoughtful evidence *realises*
itself."[34]

Architecture has always been caught up in representational regimes. In
the arrangement of traditional Nias villages in Indonesia, axial symmetry,
geometric forms and layering function as spatial correlates of socio-
cultural hierarchy. The sacred architecture of India, Mesoamerica and
Christianity is organised to correlate with stellar and cosmological
symbolism. The form and ornamental programmes of civic buildings
inscribe the ethical, pedagogical and political dimensions of a city. The
distressed interstitial spatiality and metaphors of the Romantic Sublime in
Daniel Libeskind's Jewish Museum; the foregrounding of materiality in
Herzog and de Meuron; the tectonics of gesture captured through Frank O
Gehry's crumpled paper architecture—these are all instances of
architecture's enduring interest in directly translating and representing
concepts through the tectonics of built form. It works at every scale—from
the room to the street, from the house to the city, from the garden to the
wilderness. The fundamental act of architecture is a foundational act of
installation accompanied by an irrevocable violence directed at several
scales. By installing a world, architecture also enables the installation and
operation of a corresponding authority, power and rule of law—whether
the installation is Albert Speer's plans for Berlin, the virtual construction
of a city of bits, the erection of a studio in a suburban back yard or the
laying out of an allotment outside a provincial village.

The same question returns again and again in this book. What would
be left for architecture were it to abandon an adherence to tectonic regimes
of representation, mimesis and metaphor? In such abandon, what would
architecture need to surrender and what would it gain? In the case of
cinema, the abandonment of representation appears to bring it into
proximity with something essential to the core of its *kinematic* condition.
In ceasing to deal with the indexical classification and representation of
worlds and beings, cinema begins to map, track and *produce* worlds as
eventuating, arriving and presenting themselves to view. It does this in
strangely contradictory ways by working its kinematic core to the limit in

the immobile, wherein it returns as a kind of statics of the image. To do this it must weigh on all of the conditions and all of the technologies that environ and enable its conceptualisation, its production and arrival—place, space, time, materiality and narrative. The same is true for architecture. Surrendering its representational regime does not imply surrendering its foundational condition as a tectonic practice invested in the production of place. It would be, paraphrasing Deleuze, a question of exiting architecture *through* architecture. This means that architecture, in its representational mode, must withdraw in order for it to return to itself. If in the past architecture engaged with place representationally—for example by housing the deity of a locale within an enclosure calibrated to the cosmos—then a non-mimetic and by implication a non-signifying regime of architectural engagement might involve framing place to enable a way of looking, a way of seeing that things are not the way they seem, a way then of witnessing the manner in which place takes place, the way it happens and eventuates.

Architecture might then become an enabling infrastructure or apparatus, both triggering and affording the attentiveness and waiting which watch over the interminable arrival of place. It might become an empty armature that nevertheless points to, suggests, prompts and welcomes such looking, together with the spaces and the times necessary for it. Emptied of its representation function, architecture would then frame and defer to what takes place in and about it. It would become fundamentally *about* place, in the midst of it, in favour of it, having regard *for* it, taking care of the way it comes into being. Such a disposition to place would constitute architecture's capacity for an engaged rather than symbolic ethics. Its concern would no longer be to construct a regime of exclusion, compliance and disempowerment, or to concretise the representation of a particular political or metaphysical structure, but precisely to open onto to the ethical as such. Doing so, it would articulate frameworks for deferral to and relational awareness of other spaces, times, places, people, activities, climates, seasons, materials and so forth. In the sense that its primary function would be to open onto such dispositions, architecture would then become radically unstructured and makeshift, without in doing so becoming chaotic or indeterminate. It would simply develop different kinds of structures and frames, with their own operational and systemic rigor, accurately calibrated to the capacities of place but at the same time indefinitely enabling and open to what comes.[35]

## User's manual

The purpose of this book, through the numerous themes broached by way of analyses of films and built environments, is not to proffer motifs that can be literally translated between cinema and architecture. Rather, the aim is to extend architectural thinking beyond representational regimes operating within normative disciplinary and practice limits. The assumption is that a designer or maker—a cinematographer, painter or architect—will possess sufficiently developed know-how, skills and vocabulary within their own discipline to engage those themes in parallel and indirect yet resonant ways. For an architect this might mean working with the immanent potential of spatial tectonics, organisation, materiality, technology and ambiance, in ways and towards ends that might be unfamiliar and unexpected. For example, the sound character of David Lynch's films might initiate an investigation of the potential of acoustics to deliver spaces that are remote from their context in an auditory sense while remaining intensely connected with it visually. From this disjunction might emerge an ambiance of ambiguous engagement that is simultaneously proximate and distant, possibly conveying a sense of the unreality of the real or of the existential uncanny. In turn, this experiential quality within a space might so magnify the character of an environment as to highlight our disengagement from it, prompting reflections on the implications of how we relate to and deal with the ambient world. Another example might be to consider Carl Dreyer's dynamic angular framing in *The Passion of Joan of Arc*. This might initiate an investigation of how, within a single prospect from a particular space, the juxtaposition of several geometric framings, spatial alignments or volumetric orientations might contest the apparent hegemony of a single orthogonal system within a building. In turn, this might convey an unsettling or apprehensive quality to a particular space, sequence of spaces or places within an ensemble—something that we will see at play in the work of Sigurd Lewerentz for example. The dilated and disengaged landscapes of Michelangelo Antonioni's cinema might trigger an architectural investigation of landscapes which are devoid of content, yet sufficiently charged because of the way they are framed to foreground and heighten the presence of human beings whose comings, goings and processes take place in their midst.

In all of these cases the goal would not be to literally translate from cinema to building. It would be to build thematic and tectonic repertoire, to take up these themes spatially and architectonically, to investigate them through the process of spatial exploration and design, so as to see where such investigation might lead and what properly architectural propositions might emerge during the process. To that end, this book aims to help mobilise practices of thinking and investigation and to keep these interminably moving, shifting and reforming. The key gesture is not representation or literal translation, but thematic and tectonic transfer into different orders and contexts of practice. The examples above might arm a process of developing an architectural narrative consisting of different sequences, degrees and extent of environmental engagement. This might then foreground issues of sustainability by putting into question and enabling reflection on the manner in which we confront and deal with the world, the ways in which we are predisposed towards it, the subtexts of regimes that determine how we frame and regard it, visualise it, use and exploit it, how we distance ourselves from it, objectify and calculate it, receive and consume it. All of these conditions are open to tectonic and architectonic implication, manipulation and expression. They might prompt us to think differently and in a richer, more nuanced way about how a space is shaped, scaled, orientated, fenestrated, lined, lit and furnished in relation to the context in which it is situated, with which it is collocated and related.

Evidently, such transfers have no value in themselves. The proposition of this book is not to promote purely metaphorical, thematic or tectonic bases for architectural practice. The elaboration and investigation of thematic registers—drawn from music, film, philosophy, religion or gastronomy—must follow from and be calibrated to a thorough understanding of the human, contextual and programmatic dimensions of a project. The thematic scope must be drawn out of this understanding so that any thematic exploration can add value to the significance of the project at every level. Themes will also emerge during the process of design. In fact some themes might be unimaginable at the outset and only present themselves once the design context has begun to establish its ambiance, agency and pace. Themes arise within contexts of engagement because of the resonances made possible in the way a project is framed and assembled. As themes arise, they demand to be investigated, tested and exploited to gauge their propensity and usefulness to the undertaking. At this point, a process of research can take place so that themes might be clarified, opened up, elaborated and related to others in order to test their resonant potential. This is where parallels in other disciplines might be brought into the process—particularly in cases where the solely architectural context of investigation has stalled or become unproductive. This dimension of the design endeavour will be more fully explored in a future book. The cinematic parallels that are developed here should be regarded as having strategic rather than generative value to the architectural design process. Their function is to trigger, unclench and mobilise design thinking and tectonic opportunity, but always within an assemblage that has been provisionally mapped out in relation to a project's conceptual, contextual, programmatic and technical dimensions.

Five main themes of cinema will be investigated because of their most direct parallel to architecture. These themes are common conditions in both domains, although they are taken up and exploited in distinctive ways by each practice. The first theme concerns *place and setting*. Films and buildings are always located and situated in some place, which they frame in particular ways. They engage with and use places to construct worlds, each with distinctive characteristics and opportunities. In cinema, settings play a major part in the dynamic unfolding of narrative action. They not only background the action but interact with it, with the actors and the camera. They provide atmosphere and take on narrative value. They may be framed in such a way as to take on equivalence with actors and action, or to supplant them in becoming themselves the subject of a film. Likewise in architecture, contexts might serve as surrounding environments that situate formal and sculptural concerns. They might be given equal weight to those concerns so that form and context maintain a symmetrical and parallel presence. Or they might directly interact with the volumes and spaces created, transforming purely geometric and tectonic values into complex, variable and unexpected settings for inhabitation and circumstantial engagement. Here settings and contexts take on a formative role in determining cinematic and architectural quality, allure and ambience, rather than serving to simply background narrative, expressive or representational concerns. Beyond matters of arrangement and composition, place then takes up a critical role in the establishment of toponymic, sociocultural and existential identity. Places are inherent in the constitution of subjectivites and in the relationships that human beings develop with the world. They are spatial and temporal constructs that incorporate and are defined by distinctive spatialities and temporalities belonging to particular situations and settings, which in turn contribute to topological and sociocultural identity. Place is intrinsic to memory and to the mnemonic character of situated existence. Environments that do not or that cannot contribute to the development of individual and collective memory are by definition placeless. On the other hand, the conjugation of spatial, environmental, sociocultural and kinaesthetic dimensions allows human beings to develop enduring and formative relationships to places. What is most revealing is the way that films and buildings construct particular conditions of reception and engagement with the settings in which they take place—in particular with natural settings, with Nature or the "natural." Such conditions might perpetuate a kind of survey and dominion over the setting which effectively neutralises it, or they might enable significant interaction, engagement and exchange through which both what is situated and the situation itself are mutually revealed and transformed.

The second theme in the book concerns *space*. The common notion of space as *khora,* an abstract context and setting for the contents of existence, is contrasted with the notion of place as *topos*, which is situated, acculturated and topical space, tied to the events that take place there. Each notion implies different spatialities and spatial practices— khorographic and topological for example. Abstract space is structured by a set of constitutive formal qualities and tendencies such as centrality, expansion, layering, proportion, shape and so forth. These are a context of potentiality that cinema and architecture can exploit tectonically—that is, in the way that films and buildings are organised and composed, or in the way that they use and mobilise patterns, rhythms, tensions and energies for narrative, semantic, pragmatic or expressive ends. The manipulation of spatial potential establishes frames with static and dynamic geometric and relational dimensions and potential. Such frames allow cinema and architecture to look out at a world and to gather together world and humans into distinctive relationships. In that sense, spatial frames are *world-forming*. They selectively collate aspects of the world and bring them together into fields or assemblages of components whose potentialities and features can be conjugated and strategically deployed. At the same time, spatial frames function as limits which create boundaries of exclusion and control. These boundaries do not totally erase the conditions applying before the frame was put into operation. There will always be residues that belong neither to the outside nor the inside but which nevertheless persist and threaten the stability of the frame. Every frame is also an apparatus for looking. This brings the frame into the ambit of an ethics of the gaze. The look can be one of appropriation, power and control which neutralises, violates, obliterates or otherwise dis-empowers the framed, or it can enable an attentiveness and care whose function is to allow the framed to come into its own, into its own power and potential. This applies to the narrative conditions of cinema as much as to the formal, contextual and human conditions of architecture. Films and buildings can frame a looking towards the predetermined and designed, or they can open out to the unprogrammed, the makeshift, the "whatever spaces" and "whatever beings" that might just happen to pass by or take place in the midst.

The third theme concerns *time*, which is evidently a fundamental condition of cinema. The way time is constructed in a film; the way it is sped up or slowed down; the way cinema engages with past, present and

future; the distinctive temporalities that it sets up; a film's durational
structure and texture, its rhythm and pacing—all of these are critical
aspects of its construction, reception and experience. Cinema manipulates
chronological time to develop existential or subjective temporalities. Its
orientation to past, present and future; its engagement with the conditions
that characterise a particular duration or moment; its attentiveness to the
passage of time, to its continuities and discontinuities, to its
commensurabilities and incommensurabilities—are pivotal in the
conception, articulation and experience of film. Clearly time is not
available in the same way in architectural production or experience. A
built environment cannot explicitly manipulate time in the way that
cinema does. Even if taken purely in terms of chronology and duration,
architecture rarely foregrounds time. But because time structures processes
of design, construction and spatial experience, it persists even by default in
architecture. Architectural settings do imply particular temporalities. They
do this in many ways. Religious, civic and residential buildings create very
different patterns of spatial movement which promote different processes
and rhythms of use and experience. Architecture has engaged with time in
diverse ways. In some cases, buildings and spaces might function literally
as time pieces to indicate the measures of diurnal, seasonal and lunar
cycles. In others, such as might be found in Hindu, Buddhist, Christian
and Mesoamerican sacred architecture, they might engage with broader
cycles such as the precession of the equinoxes, or with stellar and
astronomical phenomena. Beyond such symbolic registers, examples
abound of architecture which makes time, and in particular the experience
of time's passage, a fundamental condition of experience. To do this
architecture needs to create conjunctions between static geometric and
formal components of its fabric and certain dynamic conditions in the
ambient world such as the movement of people, climatic variations,
diurnal rhythms and elemental conditions that are conveyed by sound,
light, air, water, earth and so forth.

The fourth theme concerns the *materiality* of cinema—the character,
weight, presence and transition of the image; the conditions of light and
sound, but also the means and know-how which produce a film, including
the apparatuses, materials and technologies of film and film making. Light
and sound are the formative materiality of cinema. Beyond making images
visible and conveying narrative, light and sound are constitutive of the
look, timbre, allure and tone of a film, but also of the web of signification
that it constructs. They can function to establish a neutral setting for the
narrative to take place. They can reinforce and amplify the narrative or
they can create fractures, disjunctions and trajectories which displace the
film, its setting and narrative into other registers, other dimensions and

other significations that lie outside its explicit framework. For its part, architecture operates as a receptor, modifier and transmitter of light and sound. The materiality of architecture is significant here. Materials absorb, reflect and transmit light, or modify the spectrum of white light in different ways. Tied to time and the seasons, light can make these palpable within architectural space depending on how it is received, modified and transmitted. Natural light, and particularly sunlight, also confers formative qualities to spaces. Diurnal and seasonal variations, the directionality of light, how and when it is admitted into the spaces of buildings, all have significant effects on the quality of space. Beyond the pragmatic need to adequately illuminate for use, these effects can contribute to the constitutive character of spaces, their potential to refer to realities beyond the utilitarian, and their capacity to signify and connect architecture to broader levels of meaning—symbolic, aesthetic, emotional, existential, socio-cultural and so forth. Sound contributes to architectural experience in two major ways. Because of their dimensions, their manner of assembly and their material conditions, spaces and buildings have inherent acoustic characteristics. Reverberant or absorbent, hollow or viscous, perforated or self-contained, the acoustic qualities of a space contribute not only to its functionality but also to broader registers and capacities of making sense. The second way in which sound affects architectural space relates to the framing of ambient sound. Irrespective of context—whether next to a busy road, the ocean or a primary school—a building might exclude or include ambient sound to various degrees. These sounds will enter into a space and form part of it. They will contribute to the character and quality of a space, connect it to events, to other beings, to diurnal, nocturnal, solar, lunar, seasonal and other cycles. They may relate to present events but also evoke the past, subjecting space to the operation of memory which invests places with significance. Because it is time-based, sound will also animate or activate space. It will contest space's formal permanence and stability and connect it to a wider world of mutation, change and transformation. Sound brings into space aspects of the circumstantial, the conditional and the contextual. It opens architecture to its milieu, expanding and deterritorialising space, exposing it to what is outside and radically other, to what might threaten its constitutive firmness, order and consistency.

The last theme of the book concerns *assemblage* and *agency*. The work of Gilbert Simondon on individuation, and Gilles Deleuze on *agencement* are used to develop a notion of tectonics which extends cinema and architecture beyond concerns of composition, form and aesthetics. The way films and buildings are conceived, designed, produced, received and experienced involve fielding multiple, overlaid systems which are then worked and conjugated to produce complex productive interrelationships.

These make possible and deliver the cinematic and architectural artefacts that we experience and inhabit. Such fields engage multiple registers. At the very least they will have something to say about place and placemaking; spatiality, geometrical organisation and composition; temporality and the orientation to duration and time; materiality and a perspective on light, sound, texture and timbre, materials and their technological disposition and arrangement. In the conceptualisation, existentiation and experience of films and buildings, these fields function as assemblages with specific agency. Following Simondon and Deleuze, the fields are neither stable nor unstable but *metastable*. They are not configurations and ensembles but dynamic systems with energetic and potential dimensions that play out interminable processes of stabilisation and destabilisation, resolution and irresolution, territorialisation and deterritorialisation. The multiple layers of such metastable assemblages evolve and devolve in patterns that disperse and cohere, dilate and become consistent. Ideas overlap, juxtapose or interpenetrate. The complex layers of place remain suspended and distinct or fold into consistent networks. Space forms into disjunct and decentred regions or interconnecting, gathered and folded zones. It develops into legible geometric volumes, patterns and sequences, or into overlaid systems that maintain disconnections and incommensurabilties, causing it to waiver and become ambiguous. Temporality follows continuous chronological and existential conditions or complexifies into multiple superimposed and coexisting phases—past, future and present; fast and slow—that stabilise, accelerate or decelerate the tempo of time. The material constitution of films and buildings might reinforce the existential conditions of a world—ambient light and sound, weight and gravity, the mass and immobility of the physical. Or it might be worked in such a way as to relieve, mobilise and volatise the material presence of place, space, time and narrative. Working with such assemblages in the conceptualisation, design and reception of films is not an inductive or deductive but *transductive* process. Transduction proceeds by mapping out, managing and directing potential according to an open disposition to what comes, rather than by determining closed ensembles in advance according to predetermined designs, whose net effect is to institutionalise stability, permanence, predictability and control. Thinking of films and buildings as metastable systems of potential available for indefinite transductive conjugation leaves them open to emergence, to genuinely participative encounter and to indefinitely creative engagement.

The analyses in the following chapters will investigate different ways in which cinematographers use the five themes of setting, space, time, materiality, assemblage and agency for dramatic, formal, semantic and expressive ends. The aim is to interpret the strategic value that these themes have and the role that they play in the composition, dramatic character and significance of films. On the basis of these interpretations, parallels will be drawn with architectural projects to show how the same themes influence the conceptual, semantic and experiential qualities of places and buildings. The objective of these analyses, interpretations and parallels is to broaden the conceptual base of architectural thinking and practice, to render it more reflective and critical, to venture different registers that it might engage and to reorient the architectural endeavour to the semantic and expressive potential of its tectonic and technical dimensions. The major contention of this book is that any inter- or trans-disciplinary parallels and perspectives on architectural design will only be valuable, productive and sustainable if they manage to reintroduce architectural practice to its proper milieu and trajectory—that is, in the broadest sense, to its *ergon*, to its proper "work" of constructing and articulating multivalent, engaging and enduring places for human beings.

# CHAPTER ONE

# PLACE AND SETTING

"Man is that inability to remain and is yet unable to leave his place. In projecting, the Dasein in him constantly throws him into possibilities and thereby keeps him subjected to what is actual. Thus thrown into this throw, man is a transition, transition as the fundamental essence of occurrence. Man is history, or better, history is man. Man is enraptured in this transition and therefore essentially 'absent.' Absent in a fundamental sense—never simply at hand, but absent in his essence, in his essentially being away, removed into essential having been and future—essentially absenting and never at hand, yet existent in his essential absence. Transposed into the possible, he must constantly be mistaken concerning what is actual. And only because he is thus mistaken and transposed can he become seized by terror. And only where there is the perilousness of being seized by terror do we find the bliss of astonishment—being torn away in that wakeful manner that is the breath of all philosophising, and which the greats among philosophers called enthousiasmos."[1]

## Setting

Architecture and cinema are always situated within a context—a site, a landscape, a room, a time. Consequently they are always framed by that context and set among the circumstances that environ them. Whether situated within natural or urban contexts, in a wilderness or suburb, in deserted spaces of abandonment or in a vibrant city, architecture and cinema always take place in a milieu, in relation to themes and ideas, objects and spaces, times and occasions, people and communities. They are always set within literary, cultural, intellectual or symbolic circumstances and always in relationship to an outside or to an Other that surpasses them. A fundamental condition for both is therefore the manner in which they conceive and engage with otherness—with what is excluded by the frame, outside the narrative or beyond the building. In some cases, the setting will contribute a great deal to the intrinsic value of a building or a film, in others, it will remain indifferent. By a curious doubling, both architecture and cinema also and necessarily frame the environment in which they take place. For example, by the way spaces, actions and volumes are co-located within a setting, and the way architectural openings and the cinematic frame selectively delineate that setting, including some and excluding other aspects of what environs them.

These two framings are also two phases of unsettling. What is framed displaces or dislocates what frames it, and visa versa. There is therefore always ambiguity between the framing and framed character of a setting. The slippage between delineating and being delineated threatens normative distinctions between inside and outside, container and contained. In other words, it is the limit and boundary between things which finds itself indeterminate as a result of this play between interiority and exteriority. The slippage is not a failure of the limit to maintain its containing function. Rather, the indeterminacy is constitutive of the boundary as such, since the concept of the limit is cognate with that of the residue—the *leimma* which is over and above or which exceeds the border.[2] At the limit, the withholding power of the boundary wavers so that interior and exterior interminably interpenetrate, vacillate and alternate their status and function.[3]

The classical reading of the relationship between a work and its setting is hierarchical. The work corresponds to essence—in Platonic terms, to the *eidos*, idea or form. This essential component initiates production, providing all that is causally necessary to its achievement. The setting corresponds to substance or matter, whose function is one of resource or support. The idea mobilises and makes use of what is available to it in the context of its setting. Form in-forms and directs receptive matter. In this conception the idea is superior to the context in every respect—the latter serving only to enable its foregrounding and achievement as the *telos* or end of a process of becoming. Other conceptions might privilege context over idea or develop an interactive relationship in which both terms of the duality have equivalent value in determining the work. There are three basic types of engagement between a work and its setting: *indifferent*, *aesthetic* or *productive*. With *indifference*, the setting is obliterated, modified, ignored or at best remains neutral. The engagement is minimal, although each may suffer greatly at the expense of the other. In architecture, contextual indifference is carried by the motif of the *tabula rasa*. The building exists in spite of its context—it could be anywhere. The context might be factually or metaphorically ignored, or it might be virtually or actually erased. Otherwise, it might be fundamentally modified or reconstructed to provide an altered setting. With *aesthetics*, the setting serves a representational function to locate the work within a codified framework or condition of reception and experience—for example, within formal, pictorial or symbolic registers. The engagement here is greater, but the work and its setting maintain a fundamental difference and disconnectedness. With *productivity*, work and setting are more fundamentally and reciprocally active so that each draws from the other and is changed in the process. Such interactivities create resonances not present before the two have come into relation. Something new is produced between them. The engagement here is radical to the extent that the respective status of work and setting begin to waver, to become ambiguous and undecidable. In cinema, this would mean that the setting takes up a genuine dramatic role in the narrative. It ceases to operate as mere background in favour of more complex interconnectivity and inter-agency which sees it foregrounded in relation to the characters and the action.

There is a fourth, more radical reading of the relationship between a work and its context. That reading does not depend on a dichotomous, antinomical or complementary relationship between the two, but on an identity that makes each a phase or aspect of the other. Here the work and its setting emerge simultaneously in the one phenomenon and in a single process. They are indistinguishable from each other such that any cause-effect relation becomes inoperative. Consequently the very idea of relationality shifts from differential identity (the work and its context are different yet related entities) to one of valence or power. Work and context become differentiated degrees or states, dimensions or powers, scales or harmonics of an indivisible singularity. They take place as variations on a theme or as impressions of a single condition. In cinema this would mean that narrative and context are not set over against each other, but appear interchangeably as aspects or phases of an event that does not so much take place in a given space and at a given time, but that conveys the taking place of place itself. In architecture this would imply that a building does not sit within or over against its site, but emerges as an articulation of the milieu in which it is set. This milieu is an assemblage or a setup which the building interacts with and operates—in the sense of the building working the milieu so as to release dispositions, configurations and conditions that are already-there, that are already present within the setting in nascent or latent states. Architecture might highlight or foreground these conditions, bringing them into palpable experience. In this way a context is revealed and brought to mind. Architecture and its context function instrumentally to convey, carry or deliver each other, to make each other available to each other and to otherness, to render each other noticeable in mutual concern for conjugation and production.

Asplund and Lewerentz' *Woodland Crematorium* (Skogskyrkogården, Stockholm, 1935-40) is an example of this fourth mode of relating a work and its setting. The project is organised according to two key frames of reference: the Picturesque, whereby a series of disjunct spatial sequences progressively reveal a narrative, and a conjugation of several symbolic motifs echoing particular Nordic traditions, but with wider symbolist resonances—grove, forest, clearing, hill, field, path, peregrination, temple, burial mound, cave, and so forth.

A constant play and juxtaposition of different scales from the gigantic to the miniature is mobilised to engage with ideas drawn from the Romantic Sublime, where fractures and contrasts keep spatial sequences moving, opening and closing, revealing and occluding, and where extreme juxtapositions create experiential and aesthetic shock. This relates to the project's function as a place of mourning and remembrance, where an encounter with the irrevocable limit condition of death gives way to reflection on life and care. A particularly moving instance of this juxtaposition of scale is developed around the monumental cross that pins the spatial, formal and visual composition. From the entrance gate, an asymmetrical perspective is created by the folded rising ground plane, the cross, the path, the main chapel, the side garden and the open field leading up to a knoll on the right. The formal and experiential emphasis is on procession and ascent. Yet the ascent is environed and sheltered by a distinct, distant border of ground and trees, which balance the severity of its exposure. The path is kept to one side, following a low wall and canopy above, which protect and direct the view up to the cross and across the field to the knoll. Groups of trees on the horizon close the scene, except for a breach which allows the cross to read silhouetted against the sky. This breach also signifies spatial continuity to the remainder of the site beyond the chapel. The overall scale is heroic and monumental. The

composition is as much a framing of sky and earth as it is a framing of
memory and memorialisation.

This framing intensifies the expanse of sky, but it is also calibrated to
the human scale and to the scale of human experience. The low wall and
memorial garden to the left have a tempering presence. They reflect the
pace and rhythm of walking, they shelter and encompass, they maintain a
familiar and secure scale in contrast to the widening expanse of field and
sky to the right. Along the path, the cross section is zoned from the low
scale, protected and raised memorial garden to the left, the boundary wall,
the grass border, the path and the lawns up to the knoll. Rising along the
path, the cross increases in scale and stature, becoming more substantial
the closer one approaches. The cross acts as a focus, a destination and then
a pivot for turning into the open terrace in front of the chapel. From a
distance, it appears indefinitely far and unattainable. In proximity, its
gravity and physical presence increase, but its unattainability turns to
inscrutability. It remains a foreign presence.

At the same time, the memorial garden works as a refuge from this
ceremonial sequence. The garden is more enclosed, with a high wall to the
left and a low wall facing the field. Gravestones signify its reflective
character. The dense canopy filters light, fractures the expanse of sky and
lowers the scale of the space. Read against and between the thick trunks,
through and between fragments of canopy, the cross still looms large, even
monstrously. But the fact that it is read together with other elements that
frame it, the cross becomes more proximate, nearer, more intimate, more
approachable. It is now numbered as one amongst rather than solitary, as
existential rather than transcendent. Yet it also maintains its distance. It is
both near and far, present and absent, forwarding and withdrawing into the
space of the memorial garden. Clearly these spatial conditions engage
particular theological conditions and their religious correlates as human
experience. God is both central and peripheral, absent and present,
proximate and distant. The same holds for the departed, who have

definitely left, but who nevertheless leave their traces. In a remarkable way this place, and the space and the places it makes available for mourning, is woven of such traces.

The mosque of Cordoba ($7^{th}$-$8^{th}$ C) frames nature in rather more stylised, metaphorical and symbolic ways. The site is organised into two complementary zones—an open walled garden of orange trees and the roofed mosque alongside the garden. The orange trees are planted in a regular grid. Inside, the structure of columns, the superimposed vaults and domes convey a crystalline parallel.

The grid of columns mimics the trees outside to create a crystalline double. Inside and outside are two versions or modulations of the same forested configuration—one petrified and inanimate, the other dynamic and organic, albeit domesticated and appropriated within the *domus*. Light comes through layers of arches to reach the ground in soft patterns, like dappled light in a grove of trees. The walled garden and its architectural double are manifestation of Paradise or the Garden of Eden—a reference explicitly conveyed by the etymology of the word from the Latin *paradisus*, Greek: *paradeiso* = enclosed park, from *para/peri* = round about, and the etymons *DEIGH/*DEIK = to build or form-up, to point out or indicate. In a second register, the gridded space, because of its homogeneity and lack of directional hierarchy, is endowed with a democratic character which does not privilege any specific orientation. Every individual has equivalent freedom of access and no position has precedence over any other—exactly as it would be in a forest, wood or glade. Because of this, and unlike the orthogonal and hierarchical spatial organisation of the Christian church, the individual is gathered within a community which does not necessarily totalise into an identifiable corporation. Within the intercolumnated space each person, like every column, remains distinct and solitary while at the same time deferring to others within an ensemble or collective. While the grid of columns maintains an evident rigidity and regularity at an abstract level, this orthogonal rigidity fades through actual spatial occupation and experience. The continuity of the ground plane and the multiple equivalent orientations made possible by the grid—orthogonal and diagonal for example— generate a space without constraint, affording multiple sequences of infiltration. In these ways the spatial and tectonic organisation of the garden and mosque are configured to engage metaphorical, symbolic, religious and sociocultural dimensions at the same time. The layering of these dimensions constructs the space as an assemblage of diverse registers which together mobilise an agency supportive of programmatic intention, amplifying the individual and collective experiences of worship and situating this worship within an existential landscape of significant symbolic power.

# Place

Individual and collective human identity and subjectivity are founded on engaging and forming enduring relationships with place and locale. For Jeff Malpas, the incapacity to engage with, form and maintain such relationships constitutes a crisis in the human being.[4] The relationship between person and place, self and environment is fundamental to human *being* as such, as well as to human existence and experience.[5] Embodied engagement with spaces, times, people and things is not something that takes place *in* place.[6] Rather, it is constitutive of place, of the taking-place of place. In that sense, place is marked with the traces and memories of human existence, of human beings "having-world" and "being-in-the-world" to use Heidegger's phrasing.

One of the fundamental ways that human beings express relationship to places is through naming or toponymy. The foundational character of naming is central in this respect. To name is to bring into existence, to recall. Topography and toponymy coincide in itineraries and narratives of place—whether symbolic, literary, aesthetic, political or pragmatic. Place is therefore intricately tied to language and to linguistic tropes. In Australian Aboriginal culture, the recollection of place, which is also a declaration of place attachment, belonging and identity, is enacted by pronouncing a litany of place names. This practice establishes a speaker's credentials, provenance and responsibilities—physical and metaphysical, social, cultural, environmental and spiritual. In the landscape tradition of China, the naming of places in a garden not only establishes the garden as a place within the literary tradition—that is, within a specific *being-in-the-world*. Naming is also fundamental to establishing the garden's identity and ensuring its proper functioning. The unnamed that consequently has no place within a tradition is literally inoperative and dysfunctional.

Malpas defines place as "an open region within which a variety of elements are brought to light through their mutual interrelation and juxtaposition within that region."[7] It is "inextricably bound up with notions of both dimensionality or extension and of locale or environing situation."[8] This idea of space aligns with Deleuze's framework for philosophy as the "creation of concepts" within a "plane of immanence" whose potential alignments and trajectories are reiteratively assembled and disassembled, combined and conjugated to produce configurations of ideas. Deleuze's notion of philosophy is of a practice that *works* a context or a place. It does not merely operate within a conceptual milieu, but makes that milieu work and produce relationally by enabling a shuttling between its constitutive elements. The concepts which emerge through that shuttling represent a kind of "individuation," focalisation or accretion of the field. In that sense, field and focus, milieu and concept, locale and locus, place and person are not disjunct realities but mutually engendering conditions, emerging by a kind of phasing or modulation of the milieu.

In *L'Individuation Psychique et Collective*, Gilbert Simondon contrasts two types of individuation. They are each processes by which individual existence is constituted, takes place and takes *its* place within a collective. In the "monistic" and "substantialist" type of individuation, the individual is self-consistent in its unity, self-founded, unengendered and resistant to what lies beyond its limits. In the second "bipolar" and "hylemorphic" type, the individual is engendered by an encounter between form and matter. Both types assume an anterior and individualisable principle of individuation, and are fundamentally ontological in character. The process of individuation operates according to temporal sequences as a becoming which is radically other than the individual whose becoming it is. Simondon then shifts focus away from the formal characteristics of the individual, and from the form-matter dichotomy, to suggest thinking both the individual and its individuation primordially in terms of the individualising operation "from which the individual comes to exist and whose unfolding, regime and modalities it reflects in its characteristics. The individual would then be grasped as a relative reality," a pre-individual phase of being whose extensive potential the individual will never exhaust.

Hence "what individuation causes to appear is not only the individual but the couple individual-milieu."[9] This milieu, context or environment is not necessarily simple, homogenous or uniform. It may be fundamentally heterogenous, inconsistent, racked with tensions and energetic potentialities that are then mediated by individuals as they come to be.[10] There is also a fundamental rethinking of "becoming" in Simondon. Contrary to classical thought, becoming is not something that a being undergoes or suffers in its individuation, something it must needs go through which remains external to it. Rather, becoming is *constitutive* of the being, it is a dimension of being, a capacity that the being has to *dephase* itself, to resolve itself in its dephasing. Becoming is the phasing or the phrasing and modulation of being. It is not "a frame in which the being exists; it is a dimension of being, mode of resolution of an initial incompatibility, rich in potential... Individuation ...is not a consequence deposited at the border of becoming and isolated, but the very train of this operation accomplishing itself... To think individuation, we must consider the being not as a substance, or material, or form, but as a system under tension."[11]

Simondon then suggests the idea of *metastability* to describe the condition of a milieu under tension in which individuation takes place. Ancient thought posited only stability and instability and the classic conception of being assumes a state of stable equilibrium. Yet stable equilibrium excludes becoming, as it corresponds to the lowest possible state of potential energy achieved once a system has exhausted or actualised all of its transformative potential. For Simondon, individuation takes place as a function of the resolution of a metastable state:

"Individuation is not the encounter of an available form and material existing as separate pre-constituted terms, but a surging resolution in the midst of a metastable system rich in potentiality: form, matter and energy pre-exist within the system. Neither form nor matter suffice. The true principle of individuation is mediation, generally presupposing original dualities of scale and initial absence of interactive communication between them, followed by communication between scales and stabilisation."[12]

Unlike processes of crystallisation in physics, where individuation takes place instantaneously, quantically, suddenly and definitively, leaving behind a duality of individual (the crystal) and milieu (the context in which the crystal subsists), human individuation is *perpetually* taking place. The living being is not the result of an individuation but a theatre of individuation, of amplification which sees the individual as an interminable adaption and modification of relationships with its milieu. "The living individual is a system of individuation, an individuating system and a system individuating itself."[13]

"The being does not possess a unity of identity, which is that of the stable state in which no transformation is possible; the being possesses a transductive unity, that is to say that it can dephase itself in relation to itself, overflow itself on both sides of its centre.... By transduction we understand a physical, biological, mental, social operation by which an activity propagates itself step by step within the interior of a domain, basing this propagation on a structuration of the domain enacted from place to place: each constituted structural region serves for the subsequent region as principle, model and constitutive primer... a crystal which, beginning with a very small germ, grows and extends itself in all directions in its supersaturated liquid medium provides the simplest image of the transductive operation: each molecular layer already constituted serves as a structuring base to the layer in the process of formation; the result being an amplifying reticulated structure."[14]

The limits or formal terms of this transductive process are not predetermined but emergent. Within the process, invention is neither deductive nor inductive but transductive. Transduction, unlike the former processes, does not seek a principle to resolve the problem of a domain elsewhere, but draws the resolving structure from the tensions within that domain. Unlike dialectics for example, transduction does not presuppose an available temporality as framework within which genesis unfolds. Rather, it emerges out of the pre-individual like the other dimensions which mobilise the process of individuation.[15] A useful motif is that of weaving. Weaving takes place in a setup constituted of warp, weft and shuttle. The warp is the vertical structure of threads. The material of the warp is traditionally stronger than the weft and works like a skeleton or armature within the cloth. When the warp is threaded on the loom before weaving begins, it is done according to a structure that will predetermine the possibilities of patterning the cloth. In that sense, the warp is a kind of genetic framework that holds the potential of what might be produced. The weft is the horizontal structure of threads carried by the shuttle and threaded-through the warp. These threads are beaten down to compact the texture of the cloth as it is being woven. It is the weft that actualises the potential pattern held virtually in the configuration of the warp. The shuttle functions diacritically to select threading sequences and patterns out of an indefinite set of possibilities.

Plato referred to the shuttle as having a discriminating function. The shuttle "decides" between one or another of the multiple threading options and in doing so produces the cloth. Hence the relationship, in Plato, between discrimination and creation or production—a sense conveyed in both words trough the etymon *KR. The shuttle works the potentialities setup within the warp and weft structure, discriminating between them and bringing them to visibility in the cloth as it produces it. The warp structures are like latent typologies of patterns, codified and handed down within families, communities and ethnic groups. In a society where weaving assumes an important role, particular weaving patterns traditionally "belong" to particular groups or families. They convey a complex assemblage of name, identity, affiliation, history and locale. They are emblems of ethnic, topological and toponymic associations. Because an *ethnos* will be always associated with an *ethos*—that is, a place of provenance with a manner of being in that place—the patterns also represent an *ethos* of *topos* or an ethical topography, embedded in the very fabric of the cloth. Here, the transductive processes of weaving and of what might be called *ethotopological* practices of placemaking and individuation or subjectivation appear to coincide in a mutually productive coupling of focus and field, being and milieu, meaning and means.

Malpas underlines the critical connections in the experience of place between human subjectivity and the specific conditions of space and time within which subjectivities are worked out:

"The binding of memory to place, and so to particular places, can itself be seen as a function of the way in which subjectivity is necessarily embedded in place, and in spatialised, embodied activity... the very identity of subjects, both in terms of their self-definition and their identity as grasped by others, is inextricably bound to the particular places in which they find themselves and in which others find them, while, in a more general sense, it is only within the more overarching structure of place as such that subjectivity as such is possible... Inasmuch as our subjectivity is inseparably tied to place, so our self identity and self-conceptualisation (and our conceptualisation of others) is something that can only be worked out in relation to place and to our active engagement in place."[16]

The constitution of place is both spatial and temporal. It takes place in relation to names, spaces and times that have been enunciated, dwelled-in and lived. Hence an embodied sense of the past attends every experience of place:

"To have a sense of the past is always, then, to have a sense of the way in which present and future conditions are embedded within complex `history;' that is articulated only with respect to particular individuals and concrete objects as they interact within specific spaces and with respect to particular locations... We understand a particular space through being able to grasp the sorts of `narratives of action' that are possible within that space; we understand a place and a landscape through the historical and personal narratives that are marked out within it and that give that place a particular unity and establish a particular set or possibilities within it."[17]

If there is a constitutive affinity between memory, place, subjectivity and the body[18]—if place is constituted of situated memories, of events that have taken place in particular spaces and at particular times (virtual or concrete) for a particular subject—then an individual who has no place, or who cannot form enduring relationships with place, is also someone who has no memory, someone who has forgotten who they are, someone whose individuation and subjectivation cannot take place. They are also someone incapable of experiencing loss, since they have no world and therefore nothing to lose. This is one possible reading of the dislocation of characters in the cinema of Michelangelo Antonioni—alienated beings incapable of developing enduring relationships to place or to each other, and consequently incapable of determining their individual identity and subjectivity. Referring to the work of Anthony Giddens, Jean-Yves Trépos summarises three principal aspects of modernity which constitute its radical break from the pre-modern condition:

"The separation of time and space (which furnishes the means of a precise spatio-temporal carving-up [decoupage], and breaks the links between activities and their localisation in a particular context of presence); the development of mechanisms of delocalisation (together with the creation of symbolic forfeits [gages] such as money, the establishment of systems-experts and the installation of relationships of trust and dependence [confiance]) and finally the reflexive appropriation of knowledge (the production of a systematic knowledge impacting on social life becomes an integral part of the system)."[19]

Dislocation and displacement are fundamental conditions of modernity. They resist every level and every regime of potential engagement—social, environmental, urban, aesthetic. But as Benoît Goetz argues, dislocation is above all a fundamental condition of existence as standing-outside, of space as divergence (ecartement)—if not disorientation and straying (egarement)—and of architecture as foundationally spacing and spacing-out an inside in relation to an outside.[20] Through modernity this fundamental dislocation becomes an inevitable predilection for antinomical spatiality.[21] In the opening sequence of Antonioni's L'Eclisse, the apartment in which a couple spend their last moments together becomes a cipher of modernity and modernist space. The room is crammed with mementos and emblems of intellectual and artistic sophistication, empty of all but exchange value—objects d'art, oriental tapestries, depictions of lost worlds, abstract paintings, empty frames, literary and philosophical books, piles of papers and innumerable works in progress. The entirely aestheticising disposition of the characters becomes clear when the woman shifts an ashtray so as to remove it from the field of an empty picture frame and repositions a small sculpture centrally in the same frame, before disinterestedly moving away.

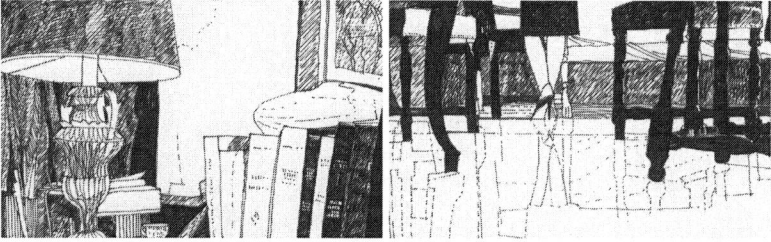

The deathly stillness of the interior, unconnected to the outside world except for the pictorial artifice of window frames, is broken only by the dumb rhythm of a fan giving some movement to the woman's hair or the man's shirt and tie. The body's sensuality is rendered thoroughly artificial. Human presence is repeatedly objectified—the man's elbow indiscernible from a pile of books, the woman's legs and shoes lost in a reflective field of table and chair legs that dematerialises the ground and dissolves the boundary between the real and its image.

The space is constitutive of the characters' worldly orientation, made possible by technologies of reproduction, displacement and communication. And yet the scene is fundamentally about the *aporia* of inter-personal communication; about two characters whose relationship and whose world are in the process of disassembling. The apartment is set within two contexts, seen through large windows once curtains are eventually drawn back to relieve the scene's early claustrophobia. In one direction, a dense forest of foliage and heavy trunks and in the other, an ominous mushroom-shaped water tower set within a *terrain vague*. The outside world is rendered purely emblematic as disengaged pictorial "landscapes," rather than as her abstract spaces or concrete places. The worldliness of the apartment straddles nature or the past—from which its ornaments and furniture have been appropriated; and technology or the future—the threatening conditions for which have been triggered by this appropriation. Between them, a dysfunctional relationship plays itself out in the pointless clumsy pacing and alienated gaze of the characters.

The film's settings foreground the dislocated condition of human being. The apartment is situated in a liminal zone of the EUR, still under development when the film was made in 1962. The context is filmed selectively by Antonioni to show mounds of rubble and vacant land under overgrown weeds. Remnants of a hilly grove of pines frame a view to Rome in the distance. The scenes unfurl on the outskirts of a city itself in historical ruin and suffering the ruination of development. In their sharp dark suit, black cocktail dress and high heels, the couple are out of place in this pulverised landscape of rubble, empty footpaths and roads, arched steel street lights and stark orthogonal built form. Elsewhere, the settings of modern architecture by their materials and propensity to weather badly, their abstract geometric patterns and textures, alienate and demean the human being, frame the body in negative ways, serve as poor backgrounds to the emotions of a face, the profile of a dress, folds of hair, or rhythms of footfall. Both person and place are mutually closed off to each other. In their demeanour, disposition and countenance these people find themselves alienated in a disabling milieu that makes no place for them.

## Taking place

The etymology of the word *place* opens up several interconnected registers which do not totalise into a single meaning.[22] Firstly, it refers to a portion of open, spread out and extended ground. Secondly, to space that is signed or marked in some way. Thirdly, to something that wells-up, arises or crowns. Fourthly, to an ordination, nomination or institutionalisation of territory which claims space—not in order to appropriate or control it, but rather to claim it for the opportunities it harbours and that arise, spring-forth, surface or appear in it. Finally, to space that is populated, inhabited and frames the possibility of dwelling— understood as the coming-to-be or taking place of *whatever-being*, whoever it might be. Place settles and steadies before it is about siting or settlement.[23] It stabilises the extension and extenuation of existence, operating as a stabilising ground for the multiple trajectories of being. Place therefore always combines two gestures—extensivity seeking separation or sedition and intensivity seeking conjunction and sedimentation. The first is a gesture of deterritorialisation and disorientation, the second of territorialisation and orientation. The double bind of simultaneous locatedness and disclocatedness was made a paradigm of what it means to philosophise, to *be-situated-in-philosophy*, by Heidegger's contention that the fundamental condition of philosophising, of maintaining a productive disposition to the open, is to be "at home in homelessness."[24]

The social, cultural and political conditions in which Heidegger's thinking moves and articulates itself demand a foregrounding of the notion of Being as Being-in (*Insein*) through stable dwelling, implying a sedentary association with place through the motifs of home and homeland (*Heimat*). Yet Heidegger's privileging of the condition of homelessness (*Heimatlosigkeit*) is also a privileging of abandonment and oblivion, of being at home as dwelling in disorientation, as being out of one's country and one's familiar place. Further, Heidegger foregrounds the disposition of wonder as foundational and necessary to proper thinking. This disposition, because it takes us out of the familiar, is closely allied to the uncanny, the unhomely (*Unheimlichkeit*). These two conditions—one privileging home and dwelling, the other homelessness and disorientation—while radically different, do not constitute a conflict or lacuna. Rather, the experience of their simultaneity—of *being at home in homelessness*—is the necessary and constitutive character of *Dasein*, of being-there or more accurately of being-the-there and the proper thinking that attends to such being. The implication may be that only one who dwells, who is at home or in place, who is *the* there that being is, can have the possibility of experiencing the disquieting condition of wonder and the uncanny. To make place for this disposition would mean to make room for the homeless, the unexpected, the alien and foreign—in short, for the Other, for *whatever being*, for *any-space-whatever,*[25] for spaces of pure potentiality. This can only take place as the spacing-out of an interval and an opening, of an in-between, a midst and milieu.

To *take* place can mean two things. Firstly, to *take up* a place or location, to appropriate a position in spatial extension—that is, to be somewhere and not nowhere, here and not there. Secondly, to *take place*, to happen, to come to be—that is, to be an event that occurs at some time not anytime, now and not then. We are accustomed to keeping these two meanings distinct so that what takes place concretely—say, taking a seat or a place in a theatre; and what takes place existentially as taking place or happening—say, the event of a performance, are kept distinct logically, spatially and temporally. By contrast, the Hebrew word for place, *makuwm*, means *the measure of what arises*, what is performed, accomplished or constituted and established as existing. It is a condition of existence as much as the factuality of an existing thing or being. In that sense, place becomes *the manner in which something issues-forth*, takes place, springs into place and into manifest measure. The conjugations of subject and object, existential and concrete, process and product, means and meaning, imply that what takes place is *the taking place of place itself.* Place arrives together *with* and *as* its arrival. It is not something *in* place, but place itself as the inside and outside of taking place as such.[26] This taking-place of place—the way place makes room for its own taking-place, the way this taking-place is the place itself—becomes a *gesture of arrival* rather than a defined spatial position, extension, form, pattern or enclosure. Taking-place would then be a certain dispositional inclination and openness; the tendency to a certain kind of sharing and arranging; a manner of operating or working-towards; a means of enabling the tarrying necessary for attending to whatever comes and the furnishing and fitting out of this milieu that renders it enabling and operative.

In the Western Desert of Australia, the term *landscape* has no purchase. The preferred words are land or country. Land has universal and juridical sense, while country refers to specific, acculturated places identified in terms of particular alignments between people, history, language and location. Nancy put it with uncanny precision: "the country and the people refer to one another. Perhaps the people are the country that speaks, and perhaps the country is a language when it is set outside of meaning."[27] For the *Ngaanyatjarra* people of the Gibson Desert, the land is marked by various stories of *Tjukurpa* (law) and acts of ancestors (*Tjukuritja*). *Tjukurpa* is a pattern of relations which registers and binds together people, their language, their country, the plants and animals which populate them and the protocols and responsibilities of care. Country is therefore a narrated topography—an inter-textual setting available to be read, mapped and enunciated interactively. The indigenous experiences of country contest picturesque notions of landscape, and the privileged status of visuality. Instead, country is experienced kinaesthetically and dialectically as a resonance or shuttling between body and memory.[28] Walking initiates a remembrance of genealogical, mythical and geographical networks of inheritance and descent,[29] and announces that experience through narration. In practice, these networks weave itineraries of adventure which narrative recollects and presents. In this context, narrative carries or conveys country. It does not merely refer to, register or report on country, but actualises country as an event and advent of narration. In this walking, moving is not simply moving-*through*. It is also moving *with* the configurations and processes of place, being awake to various speeds and shapes of movement, and to the various constitutive systems and networks which operate in and constitute the place. Walking country is therefore a process of reading, in great detail, its current state and condition—its ecology, geology, meteorology, astronomy, and so on. This prepares a caring for country through various adjustments made in terms of cultural and environmental practices, behaviours and protocols necessary for sustainment—ranging from ceremonial activities, to hunting and gathering and fire management.

In terms of spatial practice, country is not experienced through detached visual survey but through engaged walking which traces specific itineraries. Particularly in desert country, this engagement involves constantly shifting perspectives of displacement and interrupted views framed against the tilted edges of undulating terrain and intermittent vegetation. The prospect is never complete, panoptic or totalising. There is no build-up to a generalised monumental configuration, vista, or moment of survey. Any visual sense of the whole is eluded and constantly deferred by attending to the multiple registers and resonances produced between various elements and their settings. Rather than disassembling, this multiplicity achieves consistency and alignment the longer country is walked and traversed.[30] The rhythms of walking play-out a negotiation of position and trajectory. They affect the pace and disposition of movement and experience. The direction, density and viscosity of movement change according to the body's relationship to the contours and the trail being followed. Space pulses between dilation and contraction. It fields networks of spatial dynamics experienced in terms of relative speed and shape of movement, rather than in terms of proportion and geometric configurations. In this temporal, gestural, peripatetic and pulsational practice, landscape and body are assimilated to choreography and chorography, simultaneously traversing, performing and articulating space.

This place-specific kinaesthetic functions as a way of construing and actualising country by recreating and remembering, orchestrating and reconstituting its fractal parts in relation to the body. The experience is always one of *moving in-between*, through and with the land—rather than from, towards or against a destination. The journey is always an itinerary—an enumeration of places traversed along the way, a geography and genealogy of place, a conjunction of familial lineage and topography, an expression of filiation and affiliation.[31] Social and cultural interaction and negotiation—in other words, social practices—are analogous to the relational character of environmental systems and processes. Hence *ethos* and *topos* conjoin in an an ethics of place—one's mode of being in *a* place, being *placed* and *being* place. One's affiliation to country is therefore always performed as an affiliation to a way of walking and a way of speaking—that is, to a distinctive style which identifies that practice in terms of a distinctive community and its distinctive region. One's position and trajectory, one's orientation, comportment and disposition, one's narrative voice—these are always given and understood in relation to another's, and therefore in terms of a shuttling-between these singular others who gather and disperse in communities of difference.

Gregory Burgess' *Uluṟu-Kata Tjuṯa* Cultural Centre (1995) is organised around two serpentine buildings that evoke the mythical snakes *Liru* and *Kuniya,* watching each other warily across the open field of a battleground. The buildings arc around a desert oak in a natural clearing oriented to the southern face of *Uluṟu.* They do not so much contain or close off *Uluṟu* as frame and open it up to significant readings in relation to country.

For the *Anangu* people of Central Australia, *Uluṟu* is marked by the lore and the law of *Tjukurpa. Anangu* country is principally known by being walked, danced and spoken or sung, rather than looked at and visually surveyed. The kinaesthetic of walking this dune country is characterised by meandering contours and undulations of surprising scale which change continuously—building up and releasing, quickening and slowing down, revealing and occluding. Without horizon or vantage, perspectives shift so that the process becomes one of constant orientation and disorientation—not only to the country but more importantly to the topographical and cultural memory that subtends it and brings it to resonance and sense.

To arrive at this building visitors walk from a carpark on the west around the *inma* danceground to skim the southern wall, before turning and entering an arrival space located at the "head" of one of the serpents.

This space is a cool, quiet and luminous reorientation from the desert heat and glare. There follows a pentagonal exhibition area poised around a massive column with branched struts and a skylit lattice. This winds around to the third major area of the southern building. Between them is a yard where *Anangu* work on handcrafts below a traditional shelter (*wiltja*). In the northern building are an exhibition, performance and meeting place, public facilities and service areas. Between the two buildings is the open *inma* around a desert oak and further to the north-east, a larger area with the southern face of *Uluṟu* closing the vista beyond. The experience of arrival and of walking around the building is entirely conditioned by a series of overlapping circuits that weave between enclosed and open spaces.

The question of the boundary between inside and outside, between architecture and its site, is here constantly deferred by a play of complements—solid and void, shaded and unshaded, enclosed and open, hidden and revealed, as well as resulting spatial dynamics—which keeps space in motion and delays decision. In this fluctuation, space is repeatedly brought to closure—which means that it never effectively closes but plays indefinitely at the limits of enclosure. Consequently, the country can never be surveyed as a whole from any vantage point but has to be engaged through circuitous walking. Glimpsed in shifting perspective and partial angles of view through tilted or segmented edges, a sense of the country slowly builds by deferral of parts to each other. The experience is relational and communal, subject to a shuttling, alternating rhythm between different spaces as one moves about, between people seen across spaces or seen crossing spaces, people seen advancing and withdrawing into shadow, shade and strong sun or slipping into furrowed walls and wandering against the rhythms of solid, void, and bright, framed landscape. The in-between pervades in permanence. One is always in passing, always infiltrating trajectories which are never fully known and whose pacing is reflexive and quiet. This framing iterates the cadences of moving among dunes, listening to the enunciation and singing of *Tjukurpa,* sliding between landscape and narrative, renegotiating position and trajectory. Engaged in framing and being framed, one's relation to country is always open. One is always outside, or rather one is always about the wavering limit of an interminable deference.

The rhythms articulated by closure, and by the negotiation of position and trajectory affect the pace and character of experience. They articulate threshold, pause and procession. The floor, walls and roof of the centre swell and undulate about fluid and tidal spaces characterised more by energy than shape. Direction and density of movement change according to the body's relationship to an architecture and a materiality that resist. Space pulses between dilation and concentration. It fields a network of spatial dynamics experienced in terms of speed rather than proportion—that is to say, in terms of a distinctive temporality. The centre installs both a chorography and a choreography specific to place. Space and movement are orchestrated in a setting that frames for the body and the landscape a poetic of appearance and disappearance, a narrative of presence and absence, an aesthetic of view and review. Playing on the limits of such ambivalences, these rhythms pace for visitors an *Anangu* reading of *Uluṟu*.

The buildings are configured in shadow as skin, carapace and crust. An arbour stretched over frame and earth wall, a backbone through taut skin, bones under skin like lapped scales, then draped and hanging—this is above all an architecture of peeling skin and pelts. Space is made in shade by tensing apart earth and sky, by lifting up the skin of dunes and pegging territory. Independent elements of the building's two and three-dimensional assembly—frame, surface, mass—slide or shear against each other. Columns hug or part away from walls to open up interstices, folds, places of confluence and conveyance. The buildings breathe and open to breezes, cooled and quickened by passage through shaded and open spaces, perforated curved walls and the undulating skirt of eaves.

The centre resists uniformity and the systematics of prefabrication. It contests the metaphor of seamless and effortless craft. Its remarkable body shows the stages of an extremely labour-intensive construction. It registers effort and struggle in the roughness of its bush technology and site-specific assembly. Materiality is taken to excess of bulk and to saturation of chromatic and textural value. Earth walls and timber soffits receive light from the dune floor and return it to deeply shaded spaces that glow red and purple, swelling and receding with the passage of time. As skin peels back and reveals bone and sinew, space is flayed and exposed or turned inside-out. Shedding skin, the building reveals *Uluṟu* as elemental incandescence and as the interminable refractions of *Tjukurpa*.

Numerous metaphors code the centre. The two serpentine buildings represent *Liru* and *Kuniya*, *Anangu* and non-Indigenous organisations working together, two dune forms and *Uluṟu*. The centre is entered through a serpent's mouth. Snake motifs multiply in the plan and layout of buildings and low walls, in breezeways, blocks and curved cladding profiles, in roof ridges and the massing of "heads" and "tails," in ornamental schemes on floor and wall, and in slit-eye skylights. The profiles of *Uluṟu* and the dune topography are registered in segmented undulations of roofs read against ground, sky and the rock itself. Displays and videos reinforce this multiple coding by producing shifting and overlaid narratives. They tell not one story but the confluence of numerous stories, of different parts of stories and of numerous versions. They resist a linear reading, inviting instead a resonant listening that attends to difference, to the specific and particular rather than to any generic "central Australian Aboriginal dreaming".

Likewise, tectonics and spatial experience are constructed around numerous superimposed systems with multiple resonances. For example, in one spot on the entry sequence where *Uluru* comes into full view before one turns and heads up into the entry space, there are at least eight elements, each following a different alignment: curved earth wall, inner and outer columns of the veranda, segmented outer ring beams, radiating rafters, battens, the edge of shingle eaves and the inclined, compacted earth floor. These differences are clearly sensed by reading inclined horizontals and verticals of columns and wall surfaces against each other, against people and against the landscape. In these allusions, systems slide over each other and no one system dominates. There is no build-up to a generalised monumental configuration, vista or moment of survey. Any visual sense of the whole is elusive and constantly deferred by the representations made and the resonances produced between buildings and their setting. Rather than disaggregating, this multiplicity tends to a kind of suspended coherence the longer its landscape is walked and traversed. The building initiates a physical and cultural experience of the *Uluru* landscape in which spatial sequence, temporal rhythm and materiality draw on and bring to existential presence an *Anangu* practice of understanding place and constructing dwelling.

The way that place or landscape is portrayed in cinema is always indicative of a particular perspective on the world. Two instances of portraying the Australian "Outback" can help foreground the way place is constructed, the formal tactics used to setup and frame such a construction and the implications this might have on the way architecture also frames

and constructs place in significant ways. In Werner Herzog's *Where the
Green Ants Dream* (1984) the country around Cooper Pedy in South
Australia is conveyed as a wasteland disturbed by the actions of miners, on
which indigenous and non-indigenous people alike have tenuous purchase.
Herzog preludes the film with low visual resolution sequences of
tornadoes in North America to a soundtrack of Faure's *Requiem*. The
opening sets up a highly charged field in which images of powerful natural
destructive forces are conjugated by an intensely lyrical musical reflection
on death and grief. The graininess and slow tempo of the images, together
with the distance of the shot, removes the sequence from realistic
depiction into highly abstracted patterns of flux that solicit fascination
rather than dread. The harmonics and dynamics of the music raise the
power, scale and register of the sequence into a truly operatic and tragic
ground for the whole film. There is then a cut to a prefabricated metal shed
in a dust storm of intense haze and glare in Coober Pedy where the
remainder of the film will be set. Herzog performs here a double
dislocation. Firstly he excises the images of tornadoes from their
existential setting and from reality by a control of materiality, light, time
and sound. Secondly, he excises the actual setting of the film (Coober
Pedy) from the heroic and sublime setting (North America) provided by
the opening sequence.

It then becomes clear that the miners who are staking a claim to
indigenous land are equivalently excised from it, living a tenuous life in
makeshift accommodation that only barely manages to remain grounded.
There are further circumstantial and unplanned dislocations which have no
less impact on the overall sense of deterritorialisation that pervades the
film. The indigenous actors were flown in from Queensland and had no
connection with the particular country in which the film is set, in spite of
the land rights focus of the narrative. They are twice excised—once from
their own country and again from their cultural personae and identities in
order to perform as "actors." The Green Ants of the title refer to a fictional
"dreamtime" story scripted by Herzog and not to any *Tjukurpa*—local or
otherwise. The ubiquitous piles of sand that give the landscape its
otherworldly tenor were not made by mythical Green Ants but by opal
miners. The sum of these dislocations has a profound effect on the
character and efficacy of the film. The country depicted is a desolate
oblivion—hence in a sense excised from itself and abandoned to the
wasteland that it has in fact become. The miners are excised from land
they deal with contemptuously and purely in terms of Heidegger's
concepts of "enframing" and "standing reserve." They make no enduring
relationships with each other or with the place. They are—albeit

parodistically and recklessly—the only true nomads of the scenario. The indigenous people are dislocated from themselves and their country, as well as from the country that they now find themselves in and must speak for on screen.

In such a heightened context of dislocation and excision, everything on screen is pure and irrevocable displacement, placelessness and non-belonging. Yet aspects of the film that have been read as substantive flaws (the acting is wooden, the narrative doesn't ring true, the indigenous participants are romanticised or disrespected, the country is misrepresented, the politics are facile, the aesthetics of the sublime is misplaced) are in many ways produced by the sequences of displacement that underlie the film's conception and execution. The film may not be a *realistic* depiction of a concrete state of affairs. But what it does—by multiplying and conjugating these networks of displacement and non-belonging—is to achieve an intensively *real* portrayal of the irremediable disconnection and loss that haunts the modernist subject.

In an extraordinary sequence of shot/reverse shot, Herzog summarises the whole conceptual matter of the film. The two elders (custodians of the Green Ant dreaming story and the country they are "guarding") stand with back to camera, each to an each edge of the frame. Their spears divide the frame into 3 panels. In the centre panel, the miner leans out of his vehicle, demanding to be let through. The spatial disposition is clear enough.

The elders are stable, upright and guard the way. The miner is agitated, asymmetrical, protected by the windscreen of his vehicle, in control of the wheel, fully expressing the deterritorialisation he stands for. The impasse he faces is amplified by the way Herzog has set up the framing. The countershot shows the two elders again occupying either side of the frame, but this time more loosely positioned so that the background landscape envelops them. The two are markedly different in intensity and countenance, in contrast with the previous shot where they appeared more alike. The curve of the track between them reinforces the symmetry of the frame, as does their position on either side of the two spears. The angle of the camera in relation to the ground distorts and flattens depth. In these shots the camera is still and persistent in its gaze, with only the ambient sound of the wind relieving the strict geometry. The set up is highly artificial as is the intensity, quality and direction of the lighting. This foregrounds the elders—particularly in the second frame—in a way that would not be the case in ambient light. Consequently they loom, dislocated out of the frame as much as from the surrounding landscape.

The resolute frontality of these shots, the spatial setup and the lighting all conspire to flatten the perspective and set up an impassable dichotomy between the elders and the miner, between indigenous and non-indigenous law. This is magnified in a later reverse shot showing one of the elders staring down a mining foreman who has demanded they leave. The elder's face is almost entirely absorbed into shadow, his eyes two small bright pinpoints of light. Again the camera stays persistently with the shot for a long moment to amplify the standoff. The effect is troubling and mesmerising. Herzog has transformed the elder into a cipher of otherworldly presence and unyielding authority, but he has also displaced if not erased the elder's subjectivity and identity so that he now comes to stand in for a collective and abstract idea.

A series of documentary films made in 1965 by anthropologist and filmmaker Ian Dunlop for the Australian Institute of Aboriginal and Islander Studies provides an interesting contrast. *People of the Western Desert* features footage of the so-called "last surviving traditional indigenous people," who had had no contact with white people when they "came out of the desert" shortly before they were filmed. The project was ostensibly ethnographic, although the factuality that one would expect of such a project remains contestable. The setting is the country around Patjarr, Western Australia, about 800kms northwest of Uluru.[32] The objective was clearly to depict the *Ngaanyatjarra* people in a realistic way, to describe their country and their daily lives.

The film is in black and white and has no ambient soundtrack, only a voiceover which attempts a factual commentary of what is seen on screen.[33] The intense heat of the desert is conveyed by the bright glare and washed out tones of the film. Trees are threadbare and shadows patchy on dry ground. The constant wind characterising this country is visible only in its effects on grass and foliage. The lively conversation of the adults, the laughter of children, the sounds of moving through the bush, hunting, digging, winnowing and so forth are not registered. The silence which backgrounds the commentary has a surprisingly deadening effect, isolating the figures from their environment and the viewer from the film's subject matter. It lends an unreality to the experience of watching the film, particularly for anyone familiar with the place. Dunlop attempts a minimal representation of the landscape as it is, without making any kind of narrative of it. However, because of the setup, because it frames its subject matter in very particular ways and comes to the viewer already mediated by the ethnographic gaze, the film cannot avoid constructing something over and above the factuality that it seeks to capture. Whether through technical constraints or aesthetic predilection—these two not necessarily mutually exclusive in the circumstances—the setup intensifies the isolation of the people. It shows them in dark silhouette against broad horizons, shooting from below with exaggerated perspective so that people appear to loom up against an expansive sky, and framing scenes to as to convey the formal emptiness and featurelessness of the country.

To non-indigenous eyes there is nothing there. The lack of distinctive geographical features, the solitariness of the figures whether individual or in small family groups, the absence of ambient sound, the relentless slow pace of the activities depicted and the relative immobility of the camera, make the people appear ghostly, their environment desolate and their condition desperate. The facility with which the people move around their country and go about their business is certainly carefully observed and fondly conveyed. But the absence of any contextualisation of these people and their place within a specific cultural, ritual and mythical framework makes them appear entirely subject to circumstance, of limited or no ambition and occupied only with day to day physical survival. The fact of indigenous identity being an alignment and mutual co-dependence between person, community and place is not given voice. The isolation, the remoteness and the people themselves are consequently depicted as dislocated entities in a dislocated and dislocating environment. This might serve ethnographic and aesthetic ends but it does not convey the full story.

Such abstraction renders people and place as observable subjects within the voyeuristic frame of a tightly edited calculating gaze, while also rendering them subject to a dislocating and entirely visual aesthetic register—patterns of light and shadow, trajectories of motion, dark silhouettes against light surfaces, textures, parts of bodies and faces, the brightness of teeth, the lustre of dark skin, the iridescence of outlines.

In *Dreams: Sunshine Through the Rain* (1990) Akira Kurosawa takes up a traditional Japanese legend to develop an idea of place as the site of potential emergence and monstration of incorporeal beings, in this case of *kitsune* (fox-spirits)—magical beings who can assume human form. In this particular dream, against his mother's strict instructions, a child ventures into a forest to witness the wedding procession of *kitsune*—an event that takes place at times of sunshine through rain. The opening scenes establish a dichotomy between the family house as interiority and refuge and the forest as exteriority and danger. The dichotomy is mediated by a gatehouse which functions as a threshold of transgression. Once in the forest, concealing himself behind the trunks of trees the boy follows the foxes' slow and measured dance until he is noticed—a moment which breaches the spell of the event and frightens him away. The child's transgression (it is forbidden to see this procession) leads to his banishment from home and his initiation into adulthood.

Kurosawa uses the massive trunks of trees to frame the animals' viscous rhythmic pace, moving as a single coordinated mass. Their deliberate footfall, mechanical swaying and deliberate choreographed gestures contrast with the diaphanous and foliate light that pervades the interspace of the forest. The boy follows their movement as they come in and out of frame, in and out of sight between the trunks. The atmosphere created by luminous colour, dappled sunlight and shade, mist and slow rippling of foliage against the rhythmic beat of the procession and the furtive glances of the child, create a texture of time radically different to that outside the forest. The procession of *kitsune* appears to manifest itself out of the very substance of the forest, rather than being *in* it. The foxes are conveyed as an animate form of the forest—its *anima*, or soul-body. At the outset, they are occluded and harboured by it, and by the mist that pervades the scene. Eventually they present themselves out of the forest's structure, as the breath and rhythmic impulse of its geometry and substance. In this way Kurosawa depicts nature not as a neutral and abstract space in which beings and events come to be situated or take place; or as a container for life that would come from elsewhere to lodge itself within its bounds. Rather, nature is always-already inhabited. It is fundamentally harbouring and occluding. It is always-already the pure potentiality of eventuation and foundational ground of presentation.

In *Throne of Blood* (1957), two samurai on horses find themselves disoriented in Cobweb Forest—a place radically other than the one depicted in *Dreams*. The latter is bright and hopeful. This one is dismal. Both have darkness—but the darkness in *Dreams* is a luminous chromatic gloom, a gloaming replete with possibility. The darkness and light of Cobweb Forest are about destitution, decay, mould, charcoal and ash. The trees, branches and foliage have no discernable form. They interlace in dense masses, leaving little in the way of interspace. Unlike the open texture and deliberately geometric ranks of trunks in *Dreams*, the environment they create is dense and clammy. The forest becomes a snare, a trap in which the two become snagged. Galloping with what they imagine is great purpose, the samurai soon realise that they are going around in circles. Arrogance and hubris gives way to nervous confusion, panic and fear. They eventually confront a spirit of uncertain gender, old and wizen, white as a ghost, spinning yarn, singing. These tropes are classic interpretations of symbolic forms. Forest and clearing represent a site of disorientation, initiation and transformation. They are both a trap and a space of opportunity. The spirit of the place spins yarns—that is, tells stories, narrates lives, plots and exploits. Destiny is woven, much like the setup of warp and weft that predetermine the pattern of a fabric. Kurosawa's take on the tragic condition of human beings is exhilarating. The men meet the *aporia* of their condition in the guise of a spirit who weaves time and destiny. They come to know who they are and what they are to do. And they do this in a place set apart from the everyday world in which they exercise their rule and execute their power. This place is a space of exception located not outside but folded within and harboured by the everyday—a place inherent in the spatial and temporal texture of nature, needing only the opportune trigger of crisis to become operative.

Both settings convey something of an awaited, impending event. The mysterious character of the places is manifest by two very different spatial configurations. In *Dreams*, the forest consists of spaced out, fairly regularly positioned trunks. A diaphanous canopy hovers above, doubling a blue sky. The canopy appears separated from the trunks, suspended some way beyond and mostly out of frame. Yet its effects are palpable on screen. It filters streams of sunlight in dappled patterns that reach to the forest floor. The mist that hangs in the forest's midspace receives and condenses that light, giving it substance, making of it an additional instrument of occultation. The forest's thick undergrowth and mist envelop the *kitsune*, leaving only the sway of torsos—as if their bodies were somehow folded into the substance of the forest. The trunks create a vertical banding within the frame, conveying an open spaced-out texture to the setting and creating a space of tension, since the edges of the forest are not visible. In this charged portion of indefinite extension, framed by the offset trunks, there is a sense of something about to take place, of beings about to appear. It is a space of waiting and watching, which is precisely what the boy does. He of course represents pre-rational non-judgemental awareness, open and available to whatever comes, even anticipating it. Yet his anticipation is not specific. He has been told that *kitsune* appear at times of sunshine through rain, but he is not certain of what will take place. He is entirely given over to the transgressive possibility of advent, emergence and eventuation.

Because of a framing which plays between visibility and invisibility, one is never sure what is likely to appear. Once apparent, Kurosawa sets the *kitsune* and their swaying rhythm against the immobile structure of trunks so that they come successively into and out of view. Being out of view does not mean that they are not there. On the contrary, the point is that they have always-already been there. The fact of their visibility is triggered by a readiness in the one looking to make himself available to the already there, to be open to whatever comes, to await its taking place. This is made possible by the field of spatial tension that Kurosawa constructs through a play of geometric framing, dilated intercolumnation, layering, density and atmosphere. The boundaries of the forest are not given by any perceivable or even possible end, beyond which there might be a rural clearing, village or city. Rather, the limits of the space are rendered by the increasing close-packed pattern of converging trunks and canopy in perspective. The edge of the forest is not a boundary line, but a condition of conjugated density; not the extraneous imposition of a periphery, but an inherent change of state in the very substance of the place.

By contrast, the space of Cobweb Forest has a compacted or felted texture, fulled of knotted and gnarled branches, bushes and twigs. Its structure has no grain or geometric consistency and is of a much drier thorny substance. Unlike the forest of *Dreams*—where rain and sunlight, elementally water and fire, shimmer and imply progenerative moisture and spring—here the climate is arid and the foliage drained and dry. The setting rustles rather than shimmers; the blacks are carboniferous and the whites calcinated. The materiality of the forest is more like gunpowder, or earth and fire as a kind of pulverised matter ready to explode. In this context, the spirit does not emerge as a monstration or foregrounding of the already there. Rather, it arrives through a sudden and unexpected rupture in the material and spatio-temporal fabric of the forest. Nevertheless, both the spirit and the two samurai are depicted as almost transparent to the forested background. The intricate profile of their armour and their wild gestures and facial expressions double the convoluted knotted veil of branches and leaves, so that at times they seem to disappear into the background; whereas in *Dreams* both the boy and the *kitsune* are drawn in clear profile and in stains of colour against the green background and dark trunks.

In *Bad Timing* (1980), Nicholas Roeg frames the narrative within predominantly interior spaces that are sensitive to the psychological conditions of the characters; and to the past, present and future events that take place in them. The characters witness events in accordance with their disposition. The young woman, a free spirit, dwells entirely in the present. She is subject to the machinations of her partner who is haunted by the future, and a detective whose quest to confirm the man's crime of ravishment turns his gaze towards the past. The two men exist in an indiscernible condition between past and future, and experience the spaces of the world in terms of their opposed trajectories. These spaces harbour traces of past events but also traces of things that might potentially happen. The same holds for the various objects that Roeg foregrounds. Leafing through reproductions of Egon Shiele's paintings, the detective assigned to solve the crime reads an identity between the man, Shiele's emaciated male subjects, and the sexual transgression implied by the depictions. He "sees" the man naked and preening himself through the veil of these images and the ambiance of the empty apartment. Later, looking for clues amongst the woman's belongings, he picks up a shell that holds sand from the couple's trip to North Africa. Emptying it triggers a jump cut from the woman's apartment to that earlier time in the desert of Ouarzazate. Objects, images and spaces function as repositories of other times, spaces and people, of traces left inscribed by events that have taken place and as premonitory emblems of those that might or will eventuate.

The objects, spaces and rooms of the film are marked by trajectories of the characters' subjectivities and by the traces and implications of their actions. The places that Roeg constructs are inseparable in their ambiance and materiality from the human beings that inhabit them, the events that are latent or that take place in them and the circulation of memories that crisscross and weave them into what they are. These settings also double the psychological states of the two characters. The man's apartment is orthogonally arranged, rendered in severe hues of grey and blue, the walls are lined in books, and the technologies of surveillance and scientific enquiry—answering machines, photocopier, typewriter—populate the frame. By contrast, the woman's apartment is makeshift, bright, colourful and filled with mementos. The aspect of the former conveys a space of regulated order where the protagonist deliberates and works methodically and systematically. The latter conveys a space of constant variation, much like a tapestry woven of past experiences out of which the present is interminably being made. Places and objects have no abstract existence outside their situatedness within particular worlds that are inhabited and brought into existence by particular people, nor outside of the goings on that they have harboured and been a part of.

Roeg flashes backwards and forwards to undermine any sense of linear time. In doing so, he concatenates and conjugates the times of past and future events with the concrete experience of spaces in which these events have or will take place. The anachronistic texture of the film parallels an "anatopical" framework, where the spatial and temporal outside continually interrupt and presents themselves in the midst and in the moment. Spaces, times and events external to the narrative's present are given equivalent value, presence and substance; building a spatial and temporal structure in which here and there, now and then coexist without distinction. The off-screen is brought palpably into the frame which it interminably threatens and overcodes. This is reinforced by Roeg's complex soundtrack, which intersperses conversations and sounds from past and future with the ambient sounds of the present. Most notably, Roeg overlays the ringing of an unanswered and possibly unanswerable telephone in several scenes. The dysfunctional relationship and communication between the two protagonists, and the asymmetrical dependence of the woman on the man's attention and time, is paralleled by this call to answer which can never take place.

## Framing place

The landscape as a type in painting, literature, photography, cinema and architecture is always already artificial. Landscapes are produced by and reproduce specific regimes of visuality, representing specific conceptual and philosophical attitudes to the world and to the human being's condition, presence and role in that world. The landscape is always made in the image of such regimes. It is made *up*, contrived or concocted in relation to their coordinate systems and regulatory frameworks. A landscape is therefore never "natural"—if by nature is meant what arrives unmediated as pure auto-production. Interpreting Aristotle, Heidegger defines nature (Greek: *phusis*, Latin: *natura*) primarily in terms of emergence (*Aufgang*).[34] It is "that which lets something originate from itself."[35] *Phusis* is un-mediated self-movement and self-production; unlike cinema, art and architecture, rhetoric and philosophy, which require mediators and intermediaries to mobilise, motivate and bridge between incorporeal ideas and their manifestation into concrete, perceptible, audible and comprehensible experience. The unmediated self-production of nature is fundamentally profuse and excessive. It always overflows or at least threatens to breach the limits which keep it in check. "Left to itself, *this* `nature,' through the passions, brings about the total destruction of the human being. For this reason `nature' must be *suppressed*. It is in a certain sense what should not be."[36] The exemplary apparatus of suppression is the city:

> "The city conceives and constructs itself as an ordered and geometric clearing in the midst of a forest of branching and fleeing signs which continue to carry a dimension of dread. The end of dispersion and the open spaces that structure it constitute at best an enclave that loses its efficacy the further away from it one is. Greek religion can be understood in its ensemble and in its contrasts as the effort to render compatible these two distinct universes, that of the city entirely given to measure, and that of a world sensed as immense, dangerous and unmapped (*inarpenté*)."[37]

Jean-Christophe Bailly investigates the propensity in Greek thought to fix and arrest flux, to counter chaos and hubris and answer the *horror vacuui*—this terror that emptiness might become flooded with the unimpeded excess and monstrous profusion, or *monstration* of natural, aesthetic and semantic production. Flux is the wayward, unpredictable trajectory of dispersion—in other words everything that the city and civic virtue establish as counterpoints and safeguards against the troubling and pullulating incontinence of nature. The labyrinth is the figure of such pullulation, as it is of nature itself—labyrinthine, rhyzomatic, cancerous; and the city is the apparatus which dissimulates its presence and influence:

> "The labyrinth, in all of its possible states, is in any case the place where one is led astray, the very place in which and by which space is scrambled and where all possibility of orientation is destroyed. Elsewhere it is also, in the Cretan case which interests us, the dwelling of a monster, intended and conceived for it. Now the city, all that it will become, all that it is in its earliest phase, is entirely directed by the effort of separating itself from the monstrous, and that is why we can say that the genesis of the city (*poléogenèse*) is essentially anti-labyrinthine; because it dispenses with the monstrous and what originally has to do with the monstrous, but also because it dispenses with space without measure or landmarks, seeking rather to establish by way of spacings and voids the clarity of a visible and

legible harmony: the city that Greece seeks to give consistency to is drawn within a confused and toustled universe as the space where one does not get lost, where one cannot feel lost. It is as such opposed to the labyrinth, which, as we know, often serves as reflexive image of today's metropolis or of the great city in general."[38]

This propensity to bring the threat of unregulated flow to a standstill is implemented by the exercise of power through technologies of control, which Giorgio Agamben, following Michel Foucault, calls *dispositifs*— apparatuses or machines which function to organise and regulate the production of predictable order. All that the *polis* is symbolically, politically, economically, culturally, environmentally, architecturally, conspires to keep unfettered abundance at bay, to safeguard the *politeia* from excess, to resist incontinence of all kinds: telluric daemons, natural processes, emotional fluxions, political dissention, semantic pullulation, geometrical chaos.[39] The city is a *dispositif* for a *techne* of limitation, boundary setting and exclusion. This is why in the city, and on behalf of the city, nature must be tamed and acculturated as landscape, garden, *hortus conclusus*; or else domesticated, dominated and brought under the dominion of the home or *domus*.[40] In this context architecture becomes *the* instrument of a toponymy of control: *agora, acropolis, temenos, theos, oikos, oikonomia, templum, sanctum, deus, intervallum, impluvium*. In mathematics and geometry, control aims to counter the incommensurable by way of the orthogonal; in the natural sciences, to counter the surfeit of production by way of classification; in music, to counter discord by way of modulated harmony; in philosophy, to counter linguistic and semantic ambiguity by the determination of fixed meaning; in architecture, to counter nature by way of grounded appropriation, installation, orientation and survey. This standstill and stabilisation of flow has a negative and excluding function—the prevention, closure and shutting-down of potential, the stabilisation of flux and the exclusion of altereity in favour of the planned, the predictable, the calculable and the homogeneous. And yet the stabilisation of flow is not necessarily a gesture applied from without. Flow always-already includes a condition of restraint. It is always-already an alternating flexion, a double gesture of retreat and advance, withdrawal and presence that constrains and affords. The apparatus of this double gesture, which brings fluxion to the brink, is rhythm.

For Aristotle, nature (*phusis*) is *arche kineseos*—the originary ordering of movedness or change.[41] Movedness is not necessarily displacement "in space," since static beings can also be in movedness. Rather, it is a case of alteration (*metabole*)—a change through which something "hidden and absent comes into appearance" and emerges "into presenting."[42] Aristotle distinguishes between natural things and artefacts (*poioumema*), which are things made and measured-out by *poiesis* or artful production. The *arche* of art is *techne*—the know-how of dealing with things, the familiarity with what grounds every act of producing towards the achievement of a goal or completion that is not an "end," but a "finite perfectedness" (*telos*). The *arche* of the movedness of artefacts does not rest in the artefacts themselves but in the *architecton*, the one who controls the *techne* as *arche*. "The origin of the `making' is outside the thing made." In his gloss of Aristotle's text, Heidegger gives an architectural example:

> "A house has the origin and ordering of its being a house, i.e., something constructed, in the constructor's prior intention to build, which is given concrete form in the architect's blueprint. This blueprint—in Greek terms, the house's appearance as envisioned beforehand or, literally, the idea— orders each step of the actual constructing and governs the choice and use of materials. Even when the house `is standing,' it stands on the foundation that has been *laid* for it; however it never stands *from out of itself*, but always as a mere *construction*. As long as it stands there—in Greek terms, as long as it stands forth into the open and unhidden—the *house*, due to its way of standing, can never place itself back into its *arche*."[43]

This contrasts with nature-beings (*phusei onta*), which have the *arche* of their movedness not in another being but in themselves. This movedness is not only outwards. "Something determined by *phusis* not only stays within itself in its movedness but precisely goes back into itself even as it unfolds in accordance with the movedness (the change)." "The act of self-unfolding emergence is inherently a going-back-into-itself. This kind of becoming present is *phusis*."[44] There are two critical aspects to the unmediated self-production of nature. Firstly, it is a twofold phase of externalisation and internalisation—a double gesture of simultaneous departure and return, radiation and occlusion, appearance and disappearance, remembrance and forgetfulness, presence and absence. Secondly, the kinetics or *kinematics* of production pivots on rest (*kineseo stasis*).[45] "The purest manifestation of the essence of movedness is to be found where rest does not mean the breaking off and cessation of movement, but rather where movedness is gathered up into *standing-still*, and where this ingathering, far from excluding movedness, includes and for the first time discloses it."[46]

Heidegger now ventures a fundamental characteristic of kinematics— being is always already *being-towards-death*. The motif Heidegger turns to is the Greek term *steresis*—privation. The standing-still and ingathering accompanying production, which Heidegger calls "the self-presencing into the appearance," is a kind of absenting which is itself an appearance. However,

> "*steresis* is not simply absentness. Rather, as absencing, *steresis* is precisely *steresis* for presencing... in *steresis* is hidden the essence of *phusis*... *morphe* as *genesis* is *odos*, the being-on-the-way of a 'not yet' to a 'no more.' The self-placing into the appearance always lets something be present in such a way that in the presencing an absencing simultaneously become present... in essentially 'being-on-the-way,' each being that is *produced* or put *forth* (excluding artefacts) is also put *away*, as the blossom is put away by the fruit... With its very coming-to-life every living thing already begins to die, and conversely, dying is but a kind of living, because only a living being has the ability to die. Indeed, dying *can* be the highest act of living... Unlike *techne*, *phusis* does not first require a supervening *poiesis* that takes just something lying around (e.g., wood) and brings it into the appearance of 'table.' Such a product is never, of and by itself, on-the-way and never can be on-the-way to a table. *Phusis* on the other hand, is the presencing of the absencing of itself, one that is on-the-way from itself and unto itself. As such an absencing, *phusis* remains a going-back-into-itself, but this going-back is only the going of a going-forth."[47]

Heidegger then recalls Fragment 123 of Heraclitus—*phusis kruptesthai philei*, nature loves to hide itself, or to *encrypt* itself—which he translates as "being loves to hide itself":

> "self-hiding belongs to the predilection (*Vor-liebe*) of being... the essence of being is to unconceal itself, to emerge, to come out into the unhidden—*phusis*. Only what in its very essence unconceals and must unconceal itself, can love to conceal itself. Only what is unconcealing can be concealing. And therefore the *kruptesthai* of *phusis* is not to be overcome, not to be stripped from *phusis*. Rather, the task is the much more difficult one of allowing to *phusis*, in all the purity of its essence, the *kruptesthai* that belongs to it. Being is the self-concealing revealing, *phusis* in the original sense... *Phusis* is *aletheia*, unconcealing, and therefore *kruptesthai philei*."[48]

The critical issue here is both ethical and tectonic. It is the idea of preserving, for whatever it is that presents itself in this "self-presencing into the appearance," the *right* to concealment. There is implied the notion that whatever advances and shows itself also shows itself in occlusion, in privation and in retreat. Heidegger elaborates using Heraclitus' Fragment 93 on the Oracle of Delphi. The oracle neither conceals nor unconceals but points out or indicates. "This means: it unconceals while it conceals, and it conceals while it unconceals." In this sense, privation is not lack or denial but preservation. It is witholding the "*kruptesthai* that belongs to it"—that is, encrypting what is proper to it. This means revealing, unconcealing and bringing into presence *without betrayal*, without exposing the being or thing to a bare nudity that would violate, exhaust and render it inoperative.[50] Rather, it is a question of revealing while at the same time maintaining the being in potential, preserving a state of latent efficacious power, capacity and capability. It is to keep it in a state of pure and interminable potential of delivery and transformation. Ultimately it is a question of limits and of the wavering condition of the limit (*peras*), which simultaneously holds and releases, conceals and shows. For Heidegger, the limit is not a term but a threshold—"*peras* in Greek philosophy is not `limit' in the sense of the outer boundary, the point where something ends. The limit is always what limits, defines, gives footing and stability, that by which and in which something begins and is."[51] This is why nature, *phusis*, is fundamentally arrhythmic (*aruthmiston proton*). It is "the primarily and intrinsically unformed" which *techne*, in its multiple dimensions and disciplines must bring into formal and logical control by opposing *kruptein* (concealment) with *legein* (*logos*, order)[52] through the imposition of rhythm.

The condition of late modernity privileges a distinctive perspective on nature. The impacts of war, the collapse of the military-industrial complex and consequent social, political, epistemological and environmental degradation shift the concept of nature from an idealised setting to the exhausted and devastated sites of abandonment. Such sites now proliferate. They are the remnant zones of evacuated industrial production with their attendant machinery and apparatuses, serving as reliquaries for post industrial urban, landscape and architectural intervention. As in the Ruhr Valley and across the innumerable post-industrial cites of Europe, the trope of urban and regional regeneration is in the process of appropriating traces of this toxic past in order to convert *terrains vague* into new sites and regimes of inhabitation, founded on reconfigured strategies for wealth creation and socio-cultural recreation. In this scenario, how is nature regarded, what looks frame its appearance and how does it return the look?

In *Germany 90* (1991), Godard extends his recurrent theme of the "death of cinema"—the focus of his monumental *Histoire(s) du Cinema* project (1988-1998)—with a reflection on the "death of Germany" after the fall of the Berlin wall. The tone of the film is autumnal, melancholic and elegiac. In it, nature is depicted as an evacuated and evanescent landscape, on the verge of extinction. Several tropes converge in this metaphor—the collapse of socialism and human subjectivity, the ubiquity of industrial capitalism and its nefarious effects on human and natural worlds, the hegemony of commercialism, and in particular of commercial (a-political and non-critical) cinema. While the character of Lemmy Caution—a spent detective wandering through this desolate landscape—manifests disillusionment, disappointment and contempt for the situation in which he finds himself, the film maintains a quiet anticipation and hope. This is largely communicated by the way Godard constructs and renders the natural setting of the film, particularly in opposition to built form, industrial structures and the gaudy environments of the commercial world. In its autumnal state nature holds something in reserve and promises something to come. It appears alternately as incorruptible and fragile, impenetrable and perforate. It weeps elemental fluids and mist. Invariably it just exists, alongside human beings and machines, waiting for things to work themselves out, or to efface themselves in awaiting oblivion. The tone and ambiance of the film parallel Maurice Blanchot's reflection on the time of waiting:

> "Since when had he begun to wait? Since he freed himself for waiting by losing the desire for particular things, even the desire for the end of things. Waiting begins when there is no longer anything to wait for, not even the end of waiting. Waiting ignores and destroys everything it waits for. Waiting waits for nothing."[53]

On first reading, the natural world appears to have surrendered to the enframing power of technology. The whole film is suffused with a wasted post-apocalyptic light. All is trace, remnant and residue: the rubble of civility, the detritus of ideology and propaganda, the faded cosmetics of culture and habitus and the remainders of a fractured picturesque landscape. The earth gives up its minerals. The environments of post industrial non-places, of woods, lakes and sky, appear toxic. Nature remains silent. It offers no resistance but persists in a state of dematerialisation with no purchase on the fact of its eventual erasure. And yet Godard depicts the natural precisely as persisting and enduring in quiet suffering. In its exhausted watching over what is taking place, nature maintains a presence of deep lustre—a gloaming that is simultaneously gloom and gleam, ravishment and ravishing sublime beauty. This persistence is what will outlive the irreversible march of events and the catastrophe to come, which Godard describes in terms of a "final struggle between money and blood." The scene of an impending apocalypse, to be enacted on the burning ground of nature itself, will here not lead to a new heaven and a new earth, but to a permanent state of exhausted quiet perdurance.

By contrast, Tarkovsky renders the landscape through a conjugation of sound and image in such a way that sound effectively unclenches a dematerialisation of the image, a de-figuration of representation, a deformation of configuration and a pulverisation of boundary. The image is not erased or supplanted but brought to a state of vibration that is at the same time a change of state and a change of register. This *other* register may be *an* other register (narrative or metaphorical, figurative or symbolic), or simply the register of otherness and alterity as such. In *Stalker* (1979), Tarkovsky thickens space to such an extent that the intervals of difference which constitute it are displaced and become uncrossable. This affects the countenance of the characters, their disposition and rhythm of walking, their attitude to each other, the places they traverse, their prospect or destiny and the spatio-temporal fabric of the world they find themselves consigned to. In that world, an "opaque transparency" pervades:

> "We are within a *principle of the incompleteness of elements* where the environment composes itself while incessantly decomposing… everything is in a process of deformation, even the formless. To the extent that the shot is a translation of the parts of an ensemble into space, or the transformation of a whole into time. In this movement of decomposition and recomposition, the originary pulsional world, appears in an informal guise. From there one could undertake a study of the *informal* in landscape within cinema, or photography, to the extent that the *pleasures* (jouissances) *of matter* take us beyond the constraints of form, at least momentarily. The *precipitation towards a stain* at the heart of the image-landscape translates chaotically the versatility of a shimmering (*chatoyant*) space, of proliferating matter."[54]

The fluid state of the image's materiality demands interminable adjustment, configuration and reconfiguration. This is doubled by the turbulent deconstitution and reconstitution of space, time and materiality in the montage and narrative. Individuals and collectives, living beings and things, places and occasions, facts and recollections are all subjected to fundamental stresses that effect changes of state, scale, volume, density, outline and sense. They exist in constant processes of transformation and becoming—becoming-body, becoming-memory, becoming-stain, becoming-slur, becoming-molecular, becoming-calorific, becoming-moist, becoming-toxic, becoming-abject:

"Chaos can appear only in transitory forms, in contours that flee on every side. The informal certainly evokes the idea of *abjection*, of the viscous, the monstrous, of a distancing of nature. And the chaotic dispersions, the detritus, the spongy substances of Tarkovsky's image confirm this *troubling abjection* of the world."[55]

These transgressions of form (subjective, psychsomatic, representational, built, spatial, temporal, material) are inherent in form *forming* itself, in form taking itself to an excess of signification whereby it vaporises sense. Such transgressions weigh on the spatiality and temporality of place and experience. They affect spatial and temporal proximity and distance. They concatenate the virtual spaces and times of memory and dreams with the concrete and contingent circumstances of the everyday. They stretch or compact, dilate or condense the fabric of space-time, rendering it tenuous and porous, thick or distended, capable or incapable of supporting presence, capable of conveying appearance or powerless to resist its disappearance. In these scenarios place is shown in the midst of its un-becoming and undoing, leaving only the barest traces and indices. And yet place retains an abiding presence—if not as a particular extent of space and time, then as the faintest potential of a possible taking place. The image of the Tree of Life that opens and closes Tarkovsky's *Sacrifice* (1986) is a cipher of this enduring power of renewal. That power persists in and drives every turbulent conflagration of memory, individuality and community, and every instance of desolation and waste that recur in Tarkovsky thematic cinema.

## Displacement

In the essay *Uncanny Landscape*, Jean-Luc Nancy reads three senses in the idea of landscape, or more properly *countryside* (*paysage*)—location (*pays*: country), occupation (*paysan*: peasant/countryman) and representation (*paysage*: landscape/countryside). These are three dimensions of a single reality, indicated by the Latin term "*pays*: *pacus* or *pagus*, the canton, that is, again—and this time in conformity with the word canton itself—a `corner' of land." This cantonment by cornering and crossing constitutes a geometric, cadastral opening in the crux of the two axialities which produce the angle. The consequent quadratic articulation of space involves "partitions, divisions, delimitations of cultures or of passages, of circulations and sojourns. There is no need for the immediate invocation of property as an imperious act of takeover or extortion (`this is mine'); that will come later. For the moment we can imagine that the proper or the appropriated, though not yet the possessed or the exploited, is confused with what is occupied by the occupation… it is perhaps not so easy to disentangle the proper itself from all its appropriations, expropriations, a depropriations, although they cannot simply be collapsed together."[56]

The spacing out and cadastral crossing of landscape is a quadrature of the stars, a manner of capturing and fixing celestial influences, of replicating cosmic patterns and their sacral presence within a terrestrial cadre.[57] This is the primary function of the frame as an apparatus of appropriation. Once captivated, the patterns can be stored and made available—in Heiddeger's terms *enframed* by technology and quantified as standing reserve—in order to be mobilised to calculated application. But Nancy's main purpose is to treat the condition of divine presence and absence in terms of a landscape from which divinity has departed:

> "When the country is transformed in such a way that its land and occupation become urban and industrial, even in the countryside—in its cultures and its exchanges—then the divine withdraws from presence. Meaning is no longer a matter of presence but of another regime, suspended between pure absence and infinite distancing. A general estrangement occurs, in which pagans and peasants can find themselves unsettled, straying and lost. It is this that we encounter in the question of landscape, that is, of the representation of the country and the peasant, but perhaps also of estrangement and uncannyness… The landscape opens onto the unknown. It is, properly speaking, place as the opening onto a talking place of the unknown. It is not so much the imitative representation of a given location as the presentation of a given absence of presence… instead of depicting a `land' as a `location (*endroit*),' it depicts it as `dislocation (*envers*)': what presents itself there is the announcement of what is not there; more exactly, it is the announcement that, `there,' there is no presence, and yet that there is no access to an `elsewhere' that is not itself `here,' in the angle opened onto a land occupied only with opening in itself."[58]

Nancy makes the point that the spacing out of an interval is never simply the production of an empty or fully exposed exteriority. Spacing also effects an involution, a space *in* itself that is also destined *for* itself. As possibly the first open enclosure, the garden "is also a disclosure, opened to a capacity… it is not simply closed: it is also opened, and the opening as such lays out the edges, the demarcations that it needs." The landscape "is not a garden, for the garden belongs to a presupposed, pre-existing space, which is the space of a dwelling. The garden is domanial; it belongs to the order of the courtyard: the house and its outbuildings open onto it, but it does not open onto anything… In the garden there cannot be any landscape (in the sense of countryside). There can only be the positing of reminders, citations of certain types of landscape (that is one of the principles of the Chinese garden). This is not merely a question of scale; it is a question of the relation to what is far and near, in a sense that is not simply that of measurable spatial distance... The landscape begins with a notion, however vague or confused, of distancing and of a loss of sight (*une perte de vue*), for both the physical eye and the eye of the mind."[59] In the depiction of landscape this distantiation is tied to the articulation of a register and of coordinates of indeterminacy at the heart of nature. The landscape, in contrast to the garden, is what constantly flees its boundaries, or else it is the place in which the ravelling and unravelling of boundaries is constantly being played out from near to far, *ad infinitum*. The single god, his "penetration" into nature "along with the unbounded enlargement that accompanies it, also constitutes a withdrawal of all divine presence and thereby of all presence in general: what is henceforth present is the immensity itself, the limitless opening of place as a taking place of what no longer has any determined place"[60]:

"This feeling is that of an absence:... because here, in this `here' of the landscape, it does not consist of itself but of its opening... an affirmation that the divine, if it presents itself in some way, certainly does not present itself as a presence or as a representation, nor as an absence hidden behind or within the depths of nature (another form of presence), but as the withdrawal of the divine itself.... The landscape is the space of strangeness or estrangement and of the disappearance of the gods. It is, in truth, the opening of the space in which this absenting takes place... It neither hides nor reveals nor evokes the invisible as an over-visible that it would be necessary to divine by squinting into the light of the sun. For it opens onto itself... all landscape painting paints a horizon: it paints the one-dimensionality of its line as at once closure of space, a flight into infinity, and an arabesque laid out and multiplied in the lines of trees, clouds, hills and paths, branches and vaults, loops and angles, so many fractals of a single horizon, which never stops drawing back and renewing the partition of its elements."[61]

Here, Nancy turns to the Heideggerian theme of the *uncanny district*—the *topos* in which the *daimon* originarily came to presence:

"*Topos* is the Greek for 'place,' although not as mere position in a manifold of points, everywhere homogenous. The essence of the place consists in holding gathered, as the present 'where,' the circumference of what is in its nexus, what pertains to it and is 'of' it, of the place. The place is the originally gathering holding of what belongs together and is thus for the most part a manifold of places reciprocally related by belonging together, which we call a settlement or a district. In the extended domain of the district there are thus roads, passages and paths. A *daimonios topos* is an 'uncanny district.' That now means: a 'where' in whose squares and alleys the uncanny shines explicitly and the sense of Being comes to presence in an eminent sense."[62]

But now that the gods have withdrawn—whether by a human devaluation of the sacred or by an effective retreat and estrangement of divinity: the two are not mutually exclusive—place can only subsist emptied of presence, yet indefinitely open to pure *taking place*:

"Uncanny estrangement occurs in the suspension of presence: the imminence of a departure or arrival, neither good nor evil, only a wide space (*largeur*) and a generosity (*largesse*) that allows this suspension to be thought and to pass. For this suspension is always a question of a passage or a passing on. A landscape is always a landscape of time (*temps*)... time of year (a season) and a time of day (morning, noon or evening), as well as a kind of weather (*un temps*), rain or snow, sun or mist. In the presentation of this time, which unfolds with every image, the present of representation can do nothing other than render infinitely sensible the passing of time, the fleeting instability of what is shown...A landscape is always the suspension of a passage, and this passage occurs as a separation, an emptying out of the scene or of being: not even a passage from one point to another or from one moment to another, but the step (*le pas*) of the opening itself. This site is the immobilisation in which forward movement is grasped as a basis or a 'footing,' a span of the hand, the marking out of a measure according to which a world can be laid out.... The gaze does not discover presences within an already formed and given order, like that of religion, which populates the forests and the fields. It discovers the place without the god, the place that is only a place of taking place and a taking place for which nothing is given, nothing is played out in advance... What is contemplated is a *templum*... When it is sacred, the temple defines a place for presences... When it is the temple of the landscape... it cuts out a place for the withdrawal of presence, for the thought of presence as withdrawn from itself: estranged and unsettled presence, from which all the gods have departed and the humans are always still to come."[63]

Henceforth, landscape can no longer be confused with a ground that "contains" presences. It can now only operate as a pure surface of presentation and production of sense:

"A landscape contains no presence: it is itself the entire presence. But that is also why it is not a view of nature distinguished from culture but is presented together with culture in a given relationship (of work or rest, of opposition or transformation, etc.). It is a representation of the land as the possibility of a taking place of sense, a localisation or a locality of sense, which makes sense only by being occupied with itself, making 'itself' and this corner, this angle opened onto an area opposite or onto a spectacle already laid out; but it is an angle opened onto itself, creating an opening and thus a view, not as the perspective of a gaze upon an object (or as vision) but as a springing up or a surging forth, the opening and presentation of a sense that refers to nothing but this presentation."[64]

In the work of Antonioni, the landscape is such a field of estrangement and abandonment. Yet while it constitutes an empty frame, this emptiness is not without character. It represents neither lack nor neutral ground, neither *tabula rasa* nor receptacle of becoming. It does not function as a milieu in which the divine is dissimulated, a ground or source out of which forms and actions are drawn or a background over and against which they advance. Nevertheless it is there, it has a presence, it has a situated spatiality and temporality in which narratives unfold. It maintains a palpable, brooding demeanour, but always indistinct and evasive. Evacuated, it is above all *indifferent* to what takes place, to what goes on within it and around it. And yet, it does intervene—not directly or with the formative force of an idea or purpose, but wholly as a *resistance* which tests the places, the characters and the character of what takes place. The primary function of settings in Antonioni is to fundamentally displace and dislocate. They are always literally or metaphorically deserts and wastelands—in the etymological sense of places undone and unbound, disassembled and abandoned to oblivion.[65] At the same time, they themselves undo and unbind subjectivities, relationships, narratives, places, spaces and times.

Whether natural (*L'Avventura*, *The Passenger*), industrial (*Red Desert*), cultural (*Zabriskie Point*) or urban (*L'Eclisse*), the desert in Antonioni is not a wilderness in which nature presents itself as unmediated auto-production and pure *phusis*. Rather, it is place forsaken and exhausted, in which only residues of past worlds remain as more or less erased traces. The landscape is the archetype of the ungodly, of place from which the gods have indefinitely if not effectively withdrawn. Evacuated but not vacant, it is marked by the smears and elisions of divinity in withdrawal, of the sacred whose disappearing tracks trace and entreat its texture, its density, its consistency and its propensity to gather and disperse, remember and forget what has taken or is about to take place. In that sense, the landscape is a cipher for the condition of modernity as such, its very *eidos*. There is henceforth no other space possible, and every space that seeks to repeal it always finds itself destined to repeat it. This is why the space of modernity is always tragic. It cannot-not present the constitutive abjection that both produces and abandons it.

Antonioni's landscapes play out a revolution in representation and perspectival vision,[66] coinciding with a crisis of narrative syntax, of the status of the character and more generally of the centrality of the subject in modernity, together with its subjection of the object. Subjects are given no pre-eminence amongst the places and objects which equivalently populate the visual field. This works at the narrative as well as aesthetic level. In classical cinema, the gaze trains across a landscape that it seeks to comprehend, to tame and domesticate.[67] Whether it be the gaze of the camera which "captures" a visual field in order to appropriate and enframe it, the gaze of characters who scan a landscape in order to build an existence within it, or the gaze of spectators who witness these two gestures of visualisation and depiction. With Antonioni, the purpose of framing is to observe the factuality of the world, the incidental moments and events in the life of a character or a setting that appear peripheral but in time, little by little, serve to clarify.[68] As Barthes observed, it is a vigilant, careful watching and scanning of the world for which meaning is never prescribed or unproblematically imposed but indefinitely deferred and fundamentally vacillating.[69] In this approach, the landscape becomes the site of a narrative search amid traces and residues, or amid the shadows and ruins of a world consisting of the dregs of past stories as well as the potential for new assemblages. "My work," writes Antonioni, "is like digging, it is archaeological research among the arid material of our times."[70]

The landscape harbours and conceals these dregs, or else it operates as a framework onto which they may be projected; in the same way that desire comes to be projected beyond the self into the world and onto others. Nothing is as it seems and everything is either much less or much more than it seems. The search takes place for both characters and spectators. It takes place for the camera itself, whose scanning seems independent of characters and actors. At the same time, this search is not pro-active. Camera and characters function simply to let be, to let appear. The seeking is passive, disengaged, even disinterested. Characters appear foreign and alien to the places they find themselves in, uncertain of their place, their position and role in the narratives they wander through. They are fugitives with nothing to flee and no homeland to claim exile from. In Antonioni, the classic hierarchy of roles—author, character, reader or spectator—is recast. Space, the landscape or cinematic setting are no longer contexts in which, or backgrounds over and against which action develops and takes place. Rather it is place itself that becomes paramount as it takes up an active, subjective role in the narrative. It becomes itself a protagonist.[71]

To depict certain conditions of spiritual aridity, moral coldness and the empty existence of the upper-middle classes, Antonioni develops cinematic techniques based on dislocation and displacement. A key characteristic of these conditions is the lack of desire and the inability to establish enduring relationships beyond the self, with others or with the world. To convey this Antonioni uses multiple viewpoints and disengaged trajectories of looking.[72] Contexts are filmed using uncoordinated field/counterfield and shot/countershot setups which disturb the continuity and therefore the legibility and logic of the setting. Characters are shown looking upon a world in which they have become peripheral. This is not because of an erasure of the centre but on the contrary because of the centre's proliferation, causing a multiplication of points of view, perspectives and visual frames into which both the characters and spectators are dissolved: "the act of seeing is differentiated from the act of looking, and the act of looking from that of narrating. The landscape... has a determining function in this; it is a veritable chemical reagent, before which the subject is decomposed: character and spectator learn that their identity is a fragile, precarious and nevertheless necessary construction."[73] Person and place are given equivalent value, even though people are never fully confortable where they happen to be, not least because of the indifference towards them that the settings communicate. In this way, the aesthetic condition of the crisis of representation conveys its ethical face.[74] The ethical dimension of looking, of the gaze and of the visual frame is a key characteristic of Antonioni's cinema. Of course the alliance between ethics and place is fundamental to classical Greek thought. It was Plato who defined place as a conjunction of *ethos* and *topos*, a way of being place, of being placed and of taking place. But with Antonioni the alliance is not felicitous. Sandro Bernardi has commented on the political dimension of Antonioni's landscape:

"The bourgeoisie... cannot bear the sense of infinity and of nature, it must make fun of what it does not understand... (it) symbolises *homo oeconomicus* who, closed up in his purely quantitative space-time, is in the process of destroying the world after having destroyed the landscape... (it is) a representation of modern man who extends to the entire world his incapacity to look."[75]

In addition, the landscape plays a central role in the creative process. Antonioni seeks to convey the "collision" that takes place between a setting and an artistic intention:

"The most direct way to recreate a scene is to enter into a rapport with the environment itself; it's the simplest way to let the environment suggest something to us… its only a matter of organising and arranging the sequence, adapting it to the characteristic details of the surrounding environment… improvisation comes directly from the rapport that is established between the environment and ourselves."[76]

Classical linear narratives follow a course towards predestined conclusions and are constructed within synthetic, symbolic spaces with homogenous texture and consistent structure. Against this, Antonioni builds labyrinthine and concatenated narratives and spaces that are fundamentally unstable and disorientated and that in turn disorient and destabilise the gaze and purpose of the characters that operate within them. Yet this is not done by abandoning classical cinematic space and setup, but by establishing the image or sign of that setup before undermining or abandoning it during the course of the narrative. This subversive radicalisation first develops the expectation of a stable perspectival frame in conformity with which the action will unfold, then challenges that structure from within, turning it inside-out so to speak. Because of this, the trajectories followed by characters and the very structure of cinematic space privilege deviation and detour rather than the straight and direct. As a result, a constant possibility of precariousness and disorientation is foregrounded, giving design no purchase and suggesting the precariousness of all design, of all purposing and intentionality. Unable to construct a framework for destining and decision, characters and spectators subsist in a state of limbo—a liminal condition in which they encounter a foundational *aporia* and sense their own disablement and disconnectedness.[77]

But this aporetic and liminal condition is also a condition of excess. By implication, narratives do not resolve themselves. Rather, their potential to produce multiple possibilities of sense thicken the dramatic texture and make it impossible to settle on singularities of meaning. Hence the uncertain identity and alienation of subjects and places that is often cited as characteristic of Antonioni. In that sense Antonioni takes up the motif of classical tragedy, wherein human beings are irrevocably abandoned to their own devices and to hubris by the Gods whose withdrawal leaves only oblivion. Bernardi notes the radical difference between the tragic, epic and mythic registers in the landscapes of Luchino Visconti, which are settings lacking myth and centre.[78] *L'Avventura* may also be read as a metaphor for disorientation and the experience of loss in a world abandoned by the sacred, devoid of all coordinates and bearings. And yet the characters never admit to, nor have any intimation of the sacred, which is either lost to them, or which they have long forgotten. And not only they but also the landscape itself, which nevertheless preserves the memories, vestiges and dregs of archetypal sacred sites—desert, sea, wood, garden.

The "adventure" of *L'Avventura* takes up the trope of a quest for the sacred, with the key exception that the travellers are unaware of the sacrality that has both withdrawn and which confronts them. The sacred is not lodged in anything concrete, waiting to be discovered, but in the fault lines of a context that threatens to unravel. "For Antonioni nature is there, facing us, close but inaccessible, desacralised and yet still mysterious and terrible, absent but always present, by its deafening silence. The experience of nature (is) the experience of the sacred in a desacralised world."[79] The characters, though, do not see beyond the narrative line of a mundane disappearance—that of Anna's. But this disappearance is coded in multiple ways. At a metaphoric level she simply leaves the island and leaves them to it. She leaves her "friends" to themselves and to their own eventual forgetting of her. Yet Antonioni also includes a faint sequence in distant shot showing a motor boat returning to the mainland—an event unseen by the group who are resting at the time. The boat emerges from behind the looming outline of the island and disappears, in a straight line following the horizon, to the right of the screen. There may well be a mystery, but Anna's disappearance is primarily into the folds of the frame, absorbed and occluded by the landscape:

> "These interstices open into the visible are the fault lines through which the mystery, the unknown, represented by the extremely ambiguous and uncertain concept of `nature,' are introduced into the film... nature is the multiplicity of viewpoints, it is the sacred as resistance of the world to the centrality of perspective that human beings wish to impose... This *polytropic* look... underlines the crisis that afflicts representation, *the weakening of form in perspective and in montage which assure a correspondence between different shots and fields*, the lack of correlation between seen and seeing, between object and subject."[80]

The lack of correlation is worked through strategies that conjugate what is in and out of the frame, what is seen and unseen. And yet the out of frame and the absent will often carry considerable narrative and semantic weight. They are in fact integral to the texture of the everyday. They are present in the midst of what is depicted as its other face and as the other face of the subject. For Antonioni, existence is fundamentally marginal and the spaces in which existence is played out are likewise marginal, peripheral borderlines and *terrains vague*. At one level they are empty fields evacuated of content. They represent the loss or erasure of the landscape. At another they are replete with potential content, narratives, histories and trajectories. Or else they manifest a palpable resistance to the comings and goings that traverse them. "The camera looks, studies and interrogates the sites of innumerable possible stories without ever dwelling on any one of them... it limits itself to furnishing, in a semiotic fashion, a series of `indicial' signs of a world that lies outside the film, without these signs ever transforming themselves into a discourse."[81] Such indices remain discrete and unconnected. They do not point towards any unifying or totalising scheme but remain like the traces or residues of possible schema, of other "truths," each one equally plausible. The connectedness of these indices is never fully sketched out, giving the film a fractured texture of gaps and fault lines.

But these are not a sign of structural failure. Rather, the wavering between included and excluded, seen and unseen, framed and unframed represents the constitutive pattern of the cinematic fabric. What is in frame for the viewer might be out of frame for the characters—for example, in the case of the implied return of Anna to the mainland. The alternative also applies as characters become preoccupied with conditions and events which are out of frame and withdrawn from the viewer—objects, people, emotions, a face. The out of frame might be marked by what is only suggested or sensed through effect rather than presence—for example, the sound of wind, the emotional agitation and discomfiture of the characters, their peripatetic gaze, their interminable deterritorialisation into and out of the frame.[82] The frame never assumes the perspective of any individual character and yet it is neither objective nor neutral. There is a palpable sense of the landscape's own gaze—what Bernardi calls "subjective views without subject."[83] This notion of the landscape or setting throwing back the gaze, possessed of its own looking and its own face, gives it an equivalent presence to that of the characters. More critically, it denotes the setting's capacity and propensity to unframe and dislocate the narrative, suspending the image's representative function and causing its status as evidence to vacillate and disperse.

The pivotal site of Antonioni's *Blow Up* (1966) is an urban park in which the protagonist photographer captures images that he believes, through successive enlargement, inadvertently register evidence of a crime. The park is clearly an emblem of acculturated and domesticated nature. It is in every sense a garden in which the forces of nature have been civilised. Yet this garden is subject to a persistent tousling wind. It is also framed as an interior within an outside devoid of prospects beyond the surrounding foliage that masks the background and horizon. The garden therefore occludes in a double sense.

It dissimulates the evidence of a possible crime and it conceals its own situation within the existential space of the city. It is therefore twice removed, which amplifies its potency as a place-apart, a site of danger and disorientation, of hidden mysteries and trickery. In this sequestered space—set somewhere between the *hortus conclusus* of Italianate gardens where nature is excluded in favour of an acculturated landscape, and the English Picturesque where boundaries are occluded to present the simulation of an unlimited natural expanse or countryside—Antonioni dramatises the ambiguous relationships between nature and culture, the real and the virtual, potentiality and actuality, presence and absence.

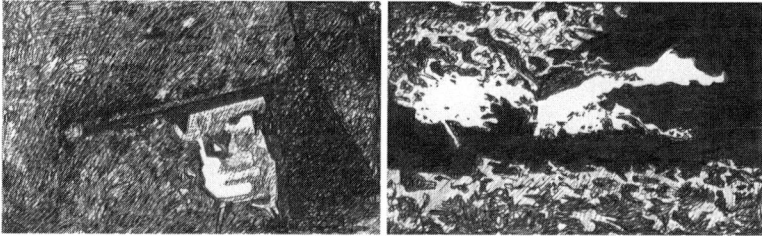

The site is also a framework for concealment in two phases—concealment of narrative detail (the signs of a crime), and concealment of an unstable wilderness that perpetually threatens the false tranquility of the park. This is doubled by the effects of wind and by the luminous sombre greens of canopy and wooded midground that convey an enigmatic darkness harbouring all manner of possibilities. The place threatens the protagonist's desire to evidence the sequence of events leading to the assumed murder. It also calls into question what representation can and cannot convey, what it discloses and what it keeps concealed. The multiple viewpoints adopted by the camera, and the multiple disconnected takes develop this still further, to the point where the reality sought by the camera proves to be as evasive, fugitive and unrepresentable as the evidence sought by the protagonist.[84]

This leads to an unframing of representation and its total dislocation. A fact doubled by the increasing scale of the photographer's fanatical enlargements, each showing a more advanced state of the degradation, dematerialisation and evanescence of the image, inversely proportional to its capacity of producing sense. Ultimately what is at stake is the crisis at the core of the modern subject whose place and whose taking place become destined to irremediable displacement and infinite estrangement.[85]

# CHAPTER TWO

# SPATIALITY

"By drawing lines, arranging words or distributing surfaces, one also designs divisions of communal space. It is the way in which, by assembling words or forms, people define not merely various forms of art, but certain configurations of what can be seen and what can be thought, certain forms of inhabiting the material world. These configurations, which are at once symbolic and material, cross the boundaries between arts, genres and epochs. They cut across the categories of an autonomous history of technique, art or politics."[1]

## Setup

Architectural and cinematic space can be read in two ways. The first concerns *abstract* space as pure measure, disposition, geometry and dynamics. This is the way built environments and films construct two and three dimensional settings for framing and conjugating sense, such as static geometric patterns and the dynamics implied by related articulations of lines, surfaces, depths and volumes. The second concerns space as *ethically* constituted. Here, the framework shifts from space to *place*. That is, from abstract to existential, populated, inhabited, furnished and acculturated environments. In both architecture and cinema, spatial framing establishes regimes which convey specific perspectives on people, place and world. Embedded in every framing system is an attitude to the face, to the body, to faces and bodies in community, to embodiments in spatial and temporal settings and to the conditions and opportunities they afford or exclude. The framing of space constitutes a *setup* that brings into relation different elements within an interactive field. The implications of these relations are aesthetic, political, philosophical, ethical, narrative and dramatic. They develop in terms of spatial patterns, forms, lines, dispositions, orientations, energies, trajectories and tendencies made available for articulation within the arrangement.

In relation to abstract space, the geometric frame can be considered according to a classical and orthogonal order comprising a centre, three dimensions and the six directions of space—up and down, left and right, front and back; sky, earth and underground; north, south east and west. Such an order implies a regime of related spatial qualities such as enclosure and exposure, layering, symmetry, scale, proportion and rhythm; as well as spatial energies such as contraction and expansion, centrifugal and centripetal forces, rotation, shear, torsion and so forth. In such a system the setup implies a whole logic of causality and hierarchy. The centre is original and transcendent in relation to a marginal periphery; the inside occults and encrypts transcendent presence; the sky relates to heaven and the underground to hell; up can only take you higher; right is privileged over a sinister left; the back (the rear, the past) is overlooked in favour of the front (evolution, the future, the avant garde); development is preferable to conservation; every axis is eschatological and meaningless without an origin and an end; centralised stability is preferable to situations where the "centre cannot hold"; revolution, chaos and catastrophe are conditions of crisis and centrifugal disassemblage that are best avoided; and so forth. However, every spatial organisation and form that appear configurationally stable and static include rhythmic dimensions that constitute foundational kinetic patterns of production and formation. A cube for example is apparently a static form of rational proportion (1:1:1), but the configuration hinges on a complex of incommensurable values (1:$\sqrt{2}$, 1:$\sqrt{3}$, 1:$\sqrt{5}$) without which the cube could not exist as a structured entity and a structuring force or system. A delineated cube can therefore be read as a momentary state in the kinematic reflux of a system produced by rhythmic diagonal iterations and repartitions across its three dimensions. These systemic and rhythmic dimensions of geometric form and the architectural settings that result from them may be invisible or unmanifest. Nevertheless, to the extent that they provide the spatial and structural tensions necessary to keep forms from collapsing, they retain a necessary and unavoidable presence.

As Pierre Sauvanet notes, the Greeks conceived of rhythm in terms of arrest rather than flow.[2] This is clear in the etymology of the word *ruthmos*, from *rheo-* = flow + *thmos* = standing. The arresting character of rhythm manifests as partitioning, iteration, pulsation and beat, which measure and give shape to continuous flow in space and time. This is why, from Democritus to Aristotle, rhythm is fundamentally a question of form and configuration (*skhema, morphe, eidos*), before it is applied by analogy to the *forms of movement*, to the temporal rhythms of music and dance and from there to the ethical dispositions and moral rhythms necessary to ensure temperance and harmony in the soul.[3] Rhythm is "form at the instant that it is assumed by what is moving, mobile, fluid, the form of what has no organic consistency." It is "the form of flux, or the fluxion of form"[4]—that is, a "particular manner of flowing," a distinctive process of "formation," which yields proportionate configurations and dispositions.[5] If both Plato and Aristotle defined rhythm as the "order of movement" (*kineseos taxis*)[6] it was primarily, according to Sauvanet, in order to contest the Presocratic and Heraclitean *panta rei* ("everything is in flux"). Plato's logocentric political and ethical philosophy privileges the proportional and harmonic coordination of parts to whole by rhythmic and eurhythmic articulations that counter the arrhythmic tendencies of Heraclitean cosmology:[7]

> "How should we join in a single analysis the two senses of *rheo* as unceasing `flow,' in all continuity and irreversibility (Fragment 134 (91): `we can and cannot enter twice into the same river'), and of *metra* as measure, as discontinuity and reversibility? No doubt, in Hericlitean thought, each thing is only what it becomes: such is the paradigm of rhythm which is itself only when it becomes other. In other words, the double opposition between continuity and discontinuity, between irreversibility and reversibility, is only apparent: it necessarily resolves itself in movement. Each being takes up a form, but this form is fluid."[8]

Aristotle considered material nature or substance to be fundamentally arrhythmic (*arrhuthmiston*). Rhythm (*rhuthmos*) is then what produces the distinctive form, figure or configuration (*schema, morphe*) of beings, imprinted into a malleable substantial ground (*hule*). This ground is matter, what of itself lacks structure, the formless, what is without-figure. The absence of *skhema* and the privation of form signified defective being.[9] On the other hand, for the Sophist orator Antiphon, it was the presence of form, contour and limit which signified defective existence, since only the formless endures and persists unchanged. For the latter, *arrhuthmiston* would mean *freed of rhythm*, rather than formless. For the Atomists, manifest difference is produced according to three modalities— *rhusmos* or proportion, *diathike* or contact and *trope* or turning. These three correspond respectively to *skhema* or figure, *taxis* or order and *thesis* or position. Rhythm then becomes a mode of differentiating potential by combining, configuring and conjugating unchanging atoms. Vitruvius elaborates an architectural corollary of these atomistic ideas. For him, architecture consists of order (*taxis*) and disposition (*diasthein*) which determine composition; eurhythmy and symmetry which determine proportional harmonics and finally convenience and distribution which are the properly domestic conditions of buildings as households (*oikonomia*).[10] Eurhythmics is carried in architectural tectonics by proportion, which constitutes the distinctive figure and shape (*skhema*), or type (*tupos*) and character, imprinted in arrhythmic substance. Eurhythmics is the multiple proportioning of parts within a unique ensemble. *Skhema* refers to fixed form while *rhuthmos* refers to form in so far as it is motion, in so far as it is *in formation* and in the process of distinctively configuring itself.[11] Critical here is the notion that space and the configurations that develop in space are not only stable and formal but also rhythmic and dynamic. This is because they carry traces of their formation and also because they include multiple components and dimensions in various states of virtuality and actuality.

Spatial frames which contribute to cinematic and architectural setups are therefore never merely static, closed structures and grids but assemblages, ensembles and systems consisting of fields of potential that can be mobilised precisely because they are charged and in flux. Architecture and cinema have adopted and worked with spatial frames and regimes in different ways at different times depending on the characteristic theoretical, aesthetic, technical and visual predisposition of the people who implement them. But geometric frameworks in cinema and architecture are never purely abstract neutral systems of organization and repartition. As Rancière writes, particular ways of articulating space involve distinctive world views with corresponding conceptual and political regimes.[12] The geometric frame and the space of cinema that it sets up can consequently take up a mirroring of the space of the world (up, down; west, east; north south), which in turn parallels the spatial constitution of the human being in whose corporeal frame such a structure is embedded (head, feet; left right; front, back). The same is true of architecture, which constructs a spatial field or situation in which the conjugation of cosmic, tectonic and human coordinates can be played out.

These scales of doubling are projected into the spatial body of a film or a building. The setup has a centre and a periphery with parallel layers of space deploying in horizontal and vertical zones. The framework can be internally consistent, systematic and hierarchical or it may be riddled with ambiguities and internally contested. There may be multiple centres and multiple peripheries. Boundaries between spatial zones may be indeterminate. There may be emphasis on foreground and frontality, iconographic symmetry and *stasis*. There may be a mirroring of deep experiential space and its excess. Or there may be iconoclastic asymmetry and turbulent fields of fluxion. The geometric setup might pre-exist and pre-determine a work, which then complies with its regulating pattern. The framework might exist independently and indifferent to what goes on within and around it. Or else it might be considered as an emergent rather than pre-established framework, in which case the work will develop to adapt itself in relation to indefinitely negotiated indeterminacies. How the spatial setup is established, maintained and then worked-with will substantially influence the semantic content, look, experience and affect of films and buildings.

Because the frame engages spatial depth, breadth and height, it will invariably involve layering. Foreground, mid-ground and background, left and right, up and down, imply hierarchy—at least potentially. Layering establishes densities within the frame. There are zones and boundaries of more or less depth and thickness, compaction and aeration, consolidation and definition, transparency and opacity, singularity and conjugation. There are thresholds and gaps, interstitial fields and intervals, continuities and ruptures between the layers. There are then hierarchies overlaid according to narrative, filmic or thematic demands. Layers may be differently weighted so as to unsettle expectations for dramatic, aesthetic, political and other ends. In cinema this might play out by giving greater import to what takes place in the background of off-screen, while the foreground on-screen action remains incidental or irrelevant. The cinematic frame can foreground a background and screen an off-screen, allowing them to advance even as they retreat to the farthest reaches of the frame. Spatial regimes, and their associated strategies of framing visual and narrative possibilities in depth, change in relation to theoretical, political and aesthetic predilections. Deleuze has commented on the shift between classical regimes where spatial layers remain orthogonal and self-sufficient, and modernist regimes where they become oblique, inseparably intermingled and inter-reactive, causing abrupt modifications of scale:

"Depth is no longer conceived, in the manner of the 'primitive' cinema, as a superimposition of parallel slices each of which is self-sufficient, all of them merely traversed by a single moving body. On the contrary, in Renoir and Welles, the set of movements is distributed in depth in such a way as to establish liaisons, actions and reactions, which never develop one beside the other, in a single shot, but are spaced out at different distances, and from one shot to the next. The unity of the shot is produced here by the direct liaison between elements caught in the multiplicity of superimposed shots which can no longer be separated. It is the relationship of near and distant parts which produces the unity. The same evolution appears in the history of painting between the sixteenth and seventeenth centuries: a superimposition of planes each of which is occupied by a specific scene and where characters meet side by side is replaced by a completely different vision of depth, where characters meet obliquely and summon each other from one plane to the other, where the elements of a plane act and react on the elements of another plane, where no form, no colour is restricted to a single plane, where the dimensions of the foreground are abnormally enlarged in order to enter directly in a relationship with the background by an abrupt reduction in size."[13]

The relationship of point of view to the action and the places in which it unfolds will also set up systems of spatial dynamics that have semantic value for the narrative. Camera position and movement in relation to place and action are critical in this respect. A still camera set frontally and normal to the action that moves parallel to its picture plane will convey a very different regime of visuality and looking than one set high, shooting obliquely at an acute angle and moving diagonally in relationship to the setting and action. Further complexities can be introduced by disassociating camera, place and action so that each has a different position, coordinate, orientation and trajectory of movement. The geometries set up by and within the frame in purely spatial terms (centrality, axiality, symmetry, decentralisation, dispersion, asymmetry, shooting from below, above or level with the coordinates of the place or action, and so forth) are necessarily conjugated by energies and tendencies that develop between differentiated component and layers of the space (expansion, contraction, rotation, torsion, tangential release, linear displacement, shearing, spiral devolution, and so forth). The conjugation of spatial coordinates, orientation, disposition, energy, tension and trajectories of motion which are applied to camera, place and action both singly and in combination produce very complex assemblages of possibilities that can be mobilised for dramatic and narrative ends.

The same applies to architectural space which is always and more explicitly set up within such contexts of geometrical structure and dynamic potential. In both cases the spatial setup contributes fundamentally to the character, reception and experiential affect of a building. Geometries of framing involve articulating lineaments, setting boundaries and borders. But these are never simple divisions. Every line always implies and defers to another line—its mirror, shadow or double. Between them there is a zone of indiscernibility traversed only by interminable deterritorialisation. This is another way of saying that in the three dimensions of existential spatiality there is nothing one-dimensional or two-dimensional. These are in fact subsets or sections of a three dimensional reality. A line always has thickness and thickness is not a question of intrinsic property but of extrinsic and relational association. In an architectural plan, the line of a wall represents the double faces of a material and the multiple skins and zones that constitute an assembly—rainscreen, membrane, external lining of external skin, frame, insulation, internal lining of external skin, cavity, external lining of internal skin, frame, insulation, internal lining of internal skin. In terms of macro and micro planning—that is in terms of the strategic and tactical patterning of space—geometric organisation mobilises multiple overlaid zones, latent or virtual, but in both cases experiential: wilderness, countryside, rural, regional, infrastructural, suburban, urban, service, sporting, recreational, entertainment, commercial, administrative, parkland, cultural, local, residential, road, street, footpath, yard, step, porch, threshold, door, hall, corridor, living, study, sleeping, bathroom, courtyard, garden, fountain. There are no clear lines of demarcation, only zones that interminably fluctuate, overlap, oscillate, interpenetrate, concatenate, mutate and defer one to the other.

In the cinematic setup, the relative disposition, geometric organisation and motion of camera, frame, actor and setting constitute a dynamic field of symmetries, asymmetries, orthogonals and diagonals that can be equally conjugated to create interactions and combinations of compositional and dynamic potential. This organisation is fundamentally strategic. The field constituted by the frame is able to gather elements within and outside it so as to interplay potential conjugations. The frame enables the development of patterns with narrative, formal and dramatic registers that are not available to the singular elements alone. It *communalises* singularities, but without necessarily resuming or unifying them and without making of them an identifiable collective. In other words, the frame mobilises singularities in their otherness to each other and to what is other or beyond the frame itself. The containment it offers opens access to what singularities might *become* through deferring to each other, passing past each other, being juxtaposed and conjugated.

Evidently the frame includes and excludes, setting up tensions between withholding and releasing. But the excluded is not the non-existent. Rather, it subsists, or properly *ex-sists*. That is, it stands outside the boundaries of the included, it waits on and weighs on that boundary and does so critically and productively. What the frame excludes—for example the invisible which takes place off-screen or out-of-field—might carry greater narrative or strategic weight. It may be more significant and have greater presence than what is visible on-screen. The excluded exists in a state of tension; or rather it works tensions at the core of the included, challenging the boundaries and limits of the frame. That is to say, it *insinuates* itself. This tension opens the included to what lies outside it, exposing it and allowing it to communicate with or become subject to an alien presence. The out-of-field makes transgression possible and operates by terrorism. This is its only proper *modus operandi*, since its banishment is also its abandonment by the frame. The off-screen, out-of-field and out-of-frame are all instances of the *parergon*—literally what is outside (*par-*)

the work (*ergon*); or as Derrida has it, the *hors-d'œuvre*. But the *parergon* is also what takes place *through* (per-) the work, what the work bears and produces, as well as its carriage, its bearing and its forbearance.[14] This gives the out-of-frame at least an influencing if not constitutive role in the setup established by the frame. Because the frame essentially frames a distinction between an inside and an outside, it also frames a metaphysics of presence founded on the interface of a limit:[15]

> "These strictures of framing (*Einfassung*), these effects of margins and borders are chemically precipitated in the notion of parergon, of hors-d'oeuvre. With Plato, the word *parerga* indicates what is supplementary, but according to Derrida the *parerga* cooperate, `from a certain outside into the inside of the operation. Neither simply outside nor simply inside,' in the manner of a signature... In brief, the logic of *parergon* reveals itself more powerful than that of analytics and the `chiasmatic invagination of borders' powerfully dislocates the internal/external margins."[16]

The frame articulates fields of inclusion-exclusion and trajectories of tension that reinforce and challenge the limit of the frame at the same time. With the limit we are also in the ambit of the remainder and the residue—the *leimma*.[17] Absent yet palpably present as trace, remainder and *reminder*, the excluded disturbs and haunts the field delimited by the frame, causing it to waver and to become an ambiguous and undecidable neighbourhood. The current lexicon of architecture is full of such liminal references to transparency, opacity, ambiguity, blurring of the boundary, undecidability between interior and exterior, diaphanous screens and frames. The glossary, or rather glossolalia, inevitably mobilises glass as the pre-eminent material of liminality.

Already with Mies van der Rohe's *Barcelona Pavilion*, and Jacques Tati's *Playtime* (1968), glass becomes a means of returning the gaze and with that, of erasing the interval which makes space possible. Mr Hulot is disorientated because the environment he finds himself in makes no room for him precisely because it is a zone of the pure deferral of space through interminable inter-reflection. With Jean Nouvel's *Fondation Cartier* (1994) and *Quai Branly* (2006), the effect is taken to its limit. Here nature and architecture are cast within a refracted landscape of utter undecidability. Not only does the distinction between inside and outside waver, but the status of nature as contexture and setting for architecture—emblematised at *Cartier* by a remnant garden and at *Branly* by a horticultural "Grand Tour" equal to the superannuated museological programme of the building—is thoroughly sabotaged. It is never clear which—nature or architecture—is in which. This condition is largely played out through the reflective and refractive character of several layers of enormous sheet glass walls, each layer reflecting what is in front of it, and transparent to the inter-reflections and inter-transparencies of subsequent layers.

Clearly the trope is one of flattening out all sense of perspectival depth and hierarchy, of obliterating the sequential, chronological or "cinematic" apprehension of three dimensional space. In this way space is turned into the fractalised two dimensional screen of digital interface on which all information appears to simultaneously present itself from all directions at the same time. Paul Virilio critically referred to this tendency as marking the "lost dimension" of architecture which leaves only the condition in which everything has always-already arrived without ever having to depart.[18] But one can also read the effect in terms of Roland Barthes' notion of the relay and free-fall of signification at the limit of intertextual overcoding, which manifest as eroticism and *jouissance*:[19]

"Is not the most erotic place of the body there where the vestment yawns? In the perversion (which is the regime of textual pleasure) there are no `erogenous zones' (an annoying expression anyway). It is intermittence, as psychoanalysis said it well, that is erotic: that of skin scintillating between two garments (the trouser and the jumper), between two borders (the open shirt, the glove and the sleeve); it is the scintillation itself which seduces, or even: the staging of an appearance-disappearance."[20]

The extreme condition of radical reflectivity might be taken to erase the architectural, to deny it its presence, bulk and materiality or its part of logocentrism and monumentality. Miralles Tagliabue's *Torre de Gas Natural* (Barcelonetta, 2007) is a striking and by no means unproblematic example. The deconstructed fractured volumes and dazzling fragments of reflection make the building's overall form elusive and indeterminate. Its exterior registers the multiple layers of the context because of a diverse faceted surface. In that sense it presents nothing but extreme deferral. Yet the building has considerable weight and presence at the ground and on the skyline because of its imbrication of disparate reflections, its heroic scale and looming centrifugal geometry. The tower therefore plays out two simultaneous gestures—disappearance or erasure of singularity and identity through extreme reflectivity and formal deconstitution, and appearance or intensification of singularity and identity by the same reflectivity taken to extreme and ponderous bulk. The ambiguity of this gesture is amplified by the materiality of the skin which implies transparency and lightness yet delivers only the blind spot of a dark and sinister presence, all the time sparkling, shimmering and endlessly transforming in response to its setting.

There are then two possibilities for the frame. It can operate as an intensive framework for inclusion-exclusion, in which case it will always be concerned with delineation and closure. Or it can operate as an extensive and excessive field that both delimits content and harbours its transgression—a setting that enables this *mise en scène* of appearance-disappearance to take place because of its openness to the unframed and the out-of-field:

"The out-of-field fulfils its other function which is that of introducing the transspatial and the spiritual into the system which is never perfectly closed... there are always simultaneously the two aspects of the out-of-field: the actualisable relation with other sets, and the virtual relation with the whole... It is not because the notion of the whole is devoid of sense; but it is not a set and does not have parts. It is rather that which prevents each set, however big it is, from closing in on itself, and that which forces it to extend itself into a larger set...Thus the whole is the Open, and relates back to time or even to spirit rather than to content and to space."[21]

For Deleuze, "all framing determines an out-of-field."[22] The out-of-field [hors-champ] "is not a negation; neither is it sufficient to define it by the non-coincidence between two frames, one visual and the other sound (for example, in Bresson, when the sound testifies to what is not seen, and 'relays' the visual instead of duplicating it)." In Hitchcock, the frame "confines all the components," and acts as a frame for a tapestry rather than one for a picture or a play. "In one case, the out-of-field designates that which exists elsewhere, to one side or around; in the other case, the out-of-field testifies to a more disturbing presence, one which cannot even be said to exist, but rather to 'insist' or 'subsist', a more radical Elsewhere, outside homogenous space and time."[23] This is how Deleuze summarises his thinking of the cinematic frame:

"Framing is the art of choosing the parts of all kinds which become part of a set. This set is a closed system, relatively and artificially closed. The closed system determined by the frame can be considered in relation to the data that it communicates to the spectators: it is 'informatic', and saturated or rarefied. Considered in itself and as limitation, it is geometric or dynamic-physical. Considered in the nature of its parts, it is still geometric or physical or dynamic. It is an optical system when it is considered in relation to the point of view, to the angle of framing: it is then pragmatically justified, or lays claim to a higher justification. Finally, it determines an out-of-field, sometimes in the form of a larger set which extends it, sometimes in the form of a whole into which it is integrated."[24]

With Sergei Paradjanov's Sayat Nova (1969), the montage is flat and symmetrical, the narrative is driven by a series of "living tableaux," and the absence of camera motion immobilises the frame. This does not mean that space and motion are inexistent. Rather, Paradjanov frames a constantly unfolding indefinite non-place between movement and pause, between the infinite and the finite, between ubiquitous generalised presence and specific concrete existence. He suspends the narrative somewhere between heaven and earth, in the vicinity of the angelic. This framing parallels the rarefied space of iconography—settings for as-yet un-actualised yet eternally valid potentialities; or in Platonic terms for the

archetypal and unmanifest entities that exists as transcendent ideas in the
world of forms. Parajanov extends the boundaries of filmic space by
compressing it into a surface with little depth. By camera angles shooting
downwards so the ground plane fills the screen, by masking depth through
shallow screens behind actors that erase the horizon and by "sliding shots
opposed to the volume of deep images,"[25] Paradjanov fills the frame,
creating symmetrical tableaux in spaces without perspective. Movement
tends to take place orthogonally and normal to the screen.

   Because the space of the film is concentrated and strictly delimited, or
generally framed by a landscape or buildings that mask depth, the intensity
and limits of the frame are amplified. If we were able to see beyond the
controlled space, the energy of each scene would leak and dissipate.
Keeping the setup and movement orthogonal and symmetrical, keeping the
depth shallow and the background concealed, preserving the energy within
the frame, allowing the energy to circulate and trigger geometrical and
gestural dynamics, registering no off-screen or out-of-field, maintaining
the energy of containment and limitation so as to focus attention entirely
onto narrative and metaphorical or symbolic content—these strategies
allow Paradjanov to set the scenes in an abstract world dislocated from
existential coordinates. Such intensity of framing is constitutive of the
other-worldliness of the images, amplified by the spatial and temporal
setups    and    shifts    that    are    unfamiliar    to    existential    experience.
Manipulating relative spatial scale, disposition, dimension, foreground and
background layering and articulation, diachronic and synchronic rhythms,
Paradjanov severs the filmic texture from the everyday, making it
susceptible to the unexpected, the ambiguous and the alien. And yet the
montage is highly charged both semantically and aesthetically. Each
element within the frame is highly symbolic—a red hand, a death helmet,
signs of the poet's impending death, scenes of medieval minstrels, iconic
religious artefacts. Typically, characters, objects and qualities are rendered
primarily in terms of their materiality, their substance and physicality—

feathers, blood, dye, milk. These elements are combined by juxtaposition or sequence to generate conjugations and concatenations of semantic content and to build the signifying texture of the film.

In *Baby Doll* (1956), Elia Kazan uses the armature of a swinging garden seat to frame a pivotal scene between Vaccaro and Baby Doll. The man visits Baby Doll to confirm a suspicion that her husband is responsible for burning down his cotton mill. She is underage and has not yet consummated the marriage. Vaccaro's presence is therefore doubly provocative and threatening. He is there to seduce from her the fact of her husband's culpability. At the same time, abandoned to a ruinous mansion in the heat of summer, Baby Doll manifests a pure state of becoming-sexual. This narrative setup is accommodated by the swing frame which houses the couple spatially, but also provides an apparatus that will mobilise and heighten dramatic tension. Kazan shoots the scene tightly against a frame that constrains action within strict zones and boundaries. A vertical pole divides the screen in two. To the left is a diagonal brace hard against the edge of the screen. Vaccaro occupies the zone to the right of the vertical. His space is unconstrained and he is free to leave it at any time. Baby Doll is positioned to the left, between the vertical pole and the diagonal brace. Her space is one of entrapment. Vaccaro is dressed in black. His figure looms large and fills the screen. She is dressed lightly and portrayed as diminutive and fragile. He claims dominance over her space by grasping the vertical pole. He looks directly at her. His hand and arm form another diagonal, focussing on her face which is looking off-screen left.

The spatial frame is divided by series of contiguous vertical and diagonal lines which zigzag through the actors' bodies and gaze. They shift the screen's centre of gravity to the left, towards the woman and the impossibility of escape from the frame. Black and white, evil and good, strong and weak, violator and virgin are conveyed at one level by the actors' clothing and disposition and by the geometric setup. At another level, this is simultaneously unsettled since Vaccaro is after the truth—therefore honourable in spite of his opportunism, whereas Baby Doll's frustration and naivety compel her to recklessness. The two characters are disposed along a diagonal line from Vaccaro's head top right to Baby Doll bottom left, hard against the diagonal brace against which she is forced to shrink away from him.

The vertical pole of the swing functions as a threshold that Vaccaro first threatens then breaches (in the plane of the screen, from right to left). Baby Doll retreats away from this vertical demarcation against the diagonal brace left of screen. When Vaccaro crosses the vertical line into *her* space, she is forced by him against this diagonal, before pushing away towards him, crossing the vertical into *his* space, squeezing herself out of the frame and finally extricating herself from the entire setup (across and out of the plane of the screen, from left to right and back to front). The entire power of the scene, its suspense and erotics, depends on the spatial setup of the screen. It is not only a question of geometric demarcation but also of a charged, dynamic field of vertical, horizontal and diagonal forces operating across and through the surface of the screen. The extraordinary ways in which the actors work that framing so as to manipulate and mobilise the tensions embedded in it enable them to play out their scene of coy seduction and violation.

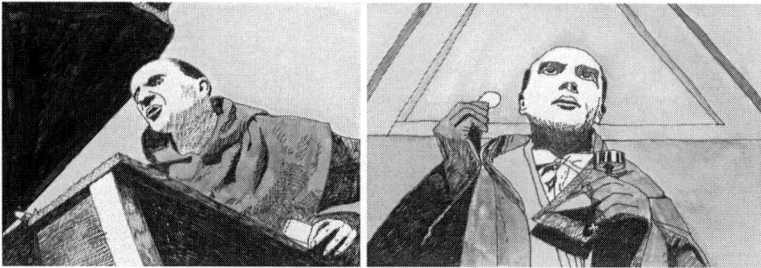

In *The Passion of Joan of Arc* (1928), Carl Dreyer constructs a spatial setup of extreme opposites and exaggerated perspectives. Settings feature backgrounds and borders beyond which there is nothing but an evenly illuminated white sky. There is little delineation of a horizon and no palpable sense of the ground. Only faint references are made to any an ambient world beyond the boundaries of the frame. The action appears to be taking place high up in a rarefied world where existential spatial coordinates have no purchase. Dislocating the setting allows Dreyer to abstract and amplify the power of the spatial setup. The framing shifts from hierarchical, axial and symmetrical geometries to turbulent diagonal and formless setups. In one scene of a priest dispensing communion, the spatial setup of geometries accentuates the vertical dimension that represents religious delegated authority. The priest is shot from below. The hierarchical geometry is reinforced by the priest's triangular cloak, his upward gaze, the vertically vanishing lines of the architectural background, the bright light descending from above and darkness rising from below.

In another, the spatial setup amplifies the divisive and inexorable executive power of the Church. Here, a priest berates the accused from his pulpit. He is again shot from below, sandwiched between furniture positioned at severe acute angles to the frame, a black palanquin hovering above, the dark corner of the pulpit and an even sky behind. The combination of sermon (power of the Word) and palanquin (symbolic presence of divinity) establish the priest's delegated power and the intractability of instituted religious authority. At the same time, the whole film functions as a sequence that spatially doubles the deconstitution of that authority. Dreyer shifts from angular to fluid dynamic geometries and directions. He translates orthogonal and diagonal spatial orders into organic, fluid and reversible systems, converting a legible network into a completely irreparable illegibility, disorientation and overturning of coordinates.

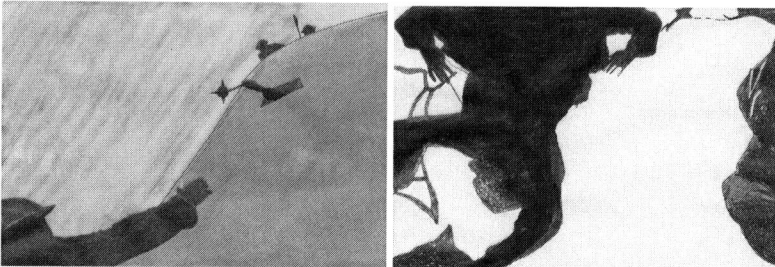

To do this, Dreyer systematically increases the extreme angularity of the framing, uses inverted camera angles and frantic action that moves helter skelter across the surface of the screen, and dematerialises physicality by returning it to a conflagration of writhing forms and thick smoke. The final sequence of Joan's burning at the stake is cast as a total rupture in the spatial and temporal fabric of the world. The turbulent unravelling of the filmic space doubles a breakdown in the authority of the Church and in the capacity of the Church and the *polis* to deal with the crisis and catastrophic implications of the event.

## Looking away

In representing three dimensional space the cinematic frame can take up two distinct functions, each associated with a different kind of looking as much as a different look. In mainstream narrative film the frame invites a looking that has to do with capture and appropriation, with hemming-in and binding. The frame is part of a visual regime that organises a way of looking as much as it collects a set of elements to be looked at.[26] It functions as an apparatus of the gaze. It looks upon a world in such a way that the character and disposition of its looking are defined by two conditions—a formal condition calibrated to spatial phenomena, and an ethical condition calibrated to the being-in-common that the frame gathers into the filmic image. The gaze, space, ethics and the image itself thereby determine the primary cinematic setup.

According to Heidegger, Plato conceived Being "in terms of the 'sight' and 'look' in which something shows itself, in terms of the 'countenance' that at any time 'a thing' or, in general a being 'takes on.' The 'countenances' things take on, their 'outward look,' is in Greek *eidos* or idea. Being—idea—is what in all beings shows itself and what looks out through them."[27] A species is also a species of appearance, a manifest and surfacing speculation.[28] Heidegger distinguished between a looking "which makes presence possible... (and) at the same time shelters and hides something undisclosed," and "the look of a being that advances by calculating, i.e., by conquering, outwitting and attacking... the look of the predatory animal: glaring.... But the basic feature of this grasping look is not glaring, by means of which beings are, so to say, impaled and become in this way first and foremost objects of conquest."[29] The implication is a call for a kind of looking that does not "lock" onto a subject in order to incarcerate or eliminate it. On the contrary, this looking proceeds by way of attentiveness and *care* towards the arrival of whatever manifests itself in a given situation. It is not a matter of closing down but of unlocking and releasing. The word itself harbours both meanings from the complex etymons *LEUQ/*LEG, which denote on the one hand to behold, mark, collect, legislate, locate, lock, enclose, cover; and on the other to shine, send, delegate, extend, emit. The overall but ambiguous sense is of a double simultaneous gesture of restriction and extension, of a radiant containment, of a halo that rings darkness or a realisation that every recollection also recollects its own forgetfulness and erasure.[30]

For Bernard Stiegler, the frame can engender attentiveness or it can destroy attention—as is the case for what he calls the "cognitive and cultural industries" which have developed:

"to capture attention by every means (given the complicity of media), leading in reality to the destruction of systems which produce attention— for example primary identification in the child. The destruction of attention can be particularly observed in the research that American psychiatry and paediatrics are undertaking on attention deficit disorder, from which many American children suffer often treated with Ritalin (derived from cocaine) or Prozac (an antidepressant). These children are less and less able to concentrate on anything whatsoever. They are destroyed by technologies of attention capture that ruin their capacities of retention and pretension. No one escapes this cognitive and affective saturation, in other words this disaffection and decognition, which is a 'loss of knowledge,' a sort of social epilepsy."[31]

Stiegler refers to Katherine Hayles' distinction between deep attention, hyper attention and attention deficit. Hyper attention is characterised by the rapid oscillation between different tasks, the flow of multiple information and a high level of stimulation, paralleled by a low tolerance for boredom. By contrast, deep attention is attention capable of focussing on a single object for a long time.[32] Each form of attention has a distinctive temporality and a distinctive manner of looking—rapid, darting, oscillating, dispersed and dilated for hyper attention; slow, focussed, profound and thick for deep attention. Evidently the disposition that accompanies deep attention is more attuned to Heidegger's looking "which makes presence possible."

The frame can be thought of as a setup that enables this attentiveness, this ethical disposition of looking that is responsive to the milieu and to the otherness which arises within it. Strategies that overdetermine what the frame conveys, or that saturate the frame with an excess of conveyance, produce parallel situations in which there is no space for looking, no enablement of attentiveness and no space for care. Equally, frameworks that predetermine singular or closed meanings have no capacity to trigger and engender a production of sense. The central question concerns the openness of the frame and its capacity for *poietic* engagement by those attending to it, or paying attention to what it frames and how it looks. This condition of openness is only possible if the components assembled by the frame have a marked propensity for deferral, deterritorialisation, ambiguity and oscillation, based on their dislocation and distraction from each other.[33] It is only possible if the purpose of that framing is not to totalise and subsume the components it assembles, to domesticate and familiarise them or to erase their strangeness to each other. Maintaining the potential and agency of the assemblage is entirely a question of preserving the mutual unfamiliarity, the radical difference and the uncanniness of the components that constitute the ensemble. Such distantiations, discontinuities and incommensurabilities are precisely what make possible the tensions and temptations that mobilise desire—in particular the desire for sense, to *make* sense and to produce sense.[34]

The theme of care is fundamental to Heidegger's philosophy and plays a pivotal role in his *Being and Time*.[35] Here, only the barest outline of themes will be made to help develop what might be called an *ethics of the frame*—that is, a manner of framing that is attentive to the Other who is encountered and gathered into its field. What Heidegger calls a "structure of care" is constitutive of *Dasein*. It is the manner in which being is and beings are (there) in the world. Being is always being-with (*Mitsein*) and being-there-with (*Mitdasein*) others. The others that being encounters in the world are other *beings* as well as *things*. These latter make up the *equipmentality* of the world. The equipmental (*Zuhandenheit*) consists of those things that are "ready to hand" and "round about us." Such things are not isolated entities but form part of assemblages within regions or contexts that have particular spatial characteristics. This regional spatiality is fundamentally relational since the things that are ready to hand are always implicated with one another within an "equipmental system" or "equipmental spatiality."[36]

Space is thus conceived as a field or milieu in which the ready to hand can be encountered in its presence. In that sense, being's engagement with the equipmental system of things doubles the being-with-others of *Mitsein*. In both cases, the authentic manner of encounter—that is, the proper manner for being to *be* in the world, to *take place* and to have its place or its *there*—requires an attentiveness towards things and others that is characterised by care (*Sorgen*), concern (*Besorgen*) and solicitude (*Fürsorge*). Care is the foundational disposition of Dasein in its dwelling and its being-with-others. As Stiegler notes, "*the self is indissociable from care* (*soin*) in as much it has a double dimension that is *psychic and social*, so that to take care *of oneself* is always already to take care *of the other and of others*."[37] The solicitude which characterises care is a *caring-for* in the sense of having regard for the welfare of the Other. This is not a question of *leaping in* for the other so as to take over their concern or disburden them of care. Such a leap would dominate and make the Other dependent. Rather it is a question of *leaping ahead* of the Other, "not in order to take away his 'care' but rather to give it back to him authentically as such for the first time." Care is therefore a liberating process, pertaining "to the existence of the Other, not to a 'what' with which he is concerned; it helps the other to become transparent to himself in his care and to become free for it." Carer and cared-for are thereby "authentically bound together, and this makes possible the right kind of objectivity [*die rechte Sachlichkeit*], which frees the Other in his freedom for himself."[38]

It is in the foundational nature of the frame to *frame*—that is, to betray by a gathering or a looking which captures, captivates and locks or shuts down. That is the sense of *cadre* and *encadrement*—a quadrature that squares-off but also double-crosses; that frames by enframing and entrapment. This is the *careless* potential of the frame; and it is why framing is always a question of ethics. Heidegger's conceptualisation of care counters the danger he considers posed by the technological, insofar as it "enframes" human beings and nature, converting them into "standing reserve."[39] Instead, care enables the foregrounding of concern and solicitude as operational objectives of the frame and of framing, so that framing becomes a fundamentally preservatory and salvatory act. The looking mobilised by frameworks of enablement and care would not look at, or even towards the Other. Rather, it would look around or about, within an interval of distraction and deferral, in the space or milieu retained between frame and framed. It would be a looking-out for the look of the other—that is, a looking-out for the becoming-subject or the individuation of the other. The frame would attend not only to the otherness of the Other but to their *becoming-Other*, to the unfamiliarity which might, in whatever space and at whatever time emerge slowly and incrementally, or surge suddenly from the being—but always unexpectedly and without programme. A framing of care or concern would be a framing for the other, yet not for them as such but for the preservation of their capacity to interminably become-other both to us and to themselves. It would mean being-with, beside and alongside them so as to accompany their suffering, their passage and their undergoing with forbearance. Solicitation is a suffering because through it a being is shaken, hastened and summoned into presence.[40] It is a caring which excites and incites, triggers and unclenches, frees and releases. The kind of framing appropriate to care involves creating a space of distantiation, a spacing-out and leavening that leaves room enough for the Other to take place.

The look that Dreyer throws towards *Joan of Arc* is a remarkable instance of care and proliferation. Here, the cinematic screen doubles the face as pure materiality, as pure surface of modulation, production and surfeit of emotion. The face becomes a turbulent map or topography of passion on which a staggering discontinuous sequence of subjectivities is drawn out—resolute and wavering faith, certainty and doubt, despair, grief, love, longing, guilt, joy, compassion, contempt, ecstasy, realisation, pain, dying. The unfathomable perturbation of the face shows the subject in its wholly open permeability and radical surrender to the migration of affections.

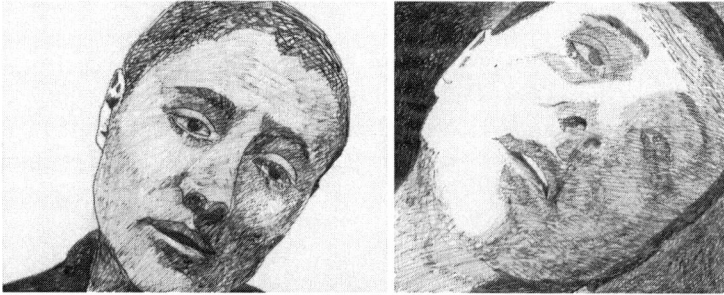

    The frame has a surfactant materiality that neither neutralises nor hypostasises but liquidises the emotional capacity of the subject, enabling it to well up in excessive monstration. It maintains the multiplicity of emotions in a state of volatility and possibility, while at the same time materialising them not on but *as the surface itself.* At no time do the emotions become iconic, emblematic or symbolic. The face is never totalised or objectified. Dreyer's framing of Mlle Falconetti's face is still and very close. Yet it constructs a conceptual distance that preserves the irreconcilability between the look, the looking and the Other who is being looked-at. It is in fact a looking out for the look of the Other which subverts the violating and captivating power of the gaze. This distance safeguards the Other within an enabling space of deferral and respect. It makes room for the other's subjectivation, their individuation and becoming. The irreconcilability of this distance, and the persistent attentiveness of the look that stays with the face, is what allows the presence of the Other to take place in utter incomprehensibility and wonder.
    This kind of surface and the looking which frames it could well function as a paradigm for the cinematic screen and the architectonic ground. The normative concept of the frame is of a neutral apparatus that by locating and arranging its contents effectively neutralises and reconditions or recast them into a new regime. Likewise, the surface is generally conceptualised and idealised as a polished mirror or undisturbed homogenous plane of reflection that is erased or that withdraws at the moment of reflection. This is the paradigm of the selfless artist whose individuality is erased in the work. It is integral to Platonic *mimesis* where the transfer of paradigmatic form in matter must be an unimpeded reflection of the original, unaffected by the artist's mediation. The perfect

surface is thus a perfected mirror that enables absolute reflectivity with no blemish. In other words, the perfect surface erases all resistance, all materiality and texture, every grain and timbre. Here on the contrary framework and surface are intensely materialised and this materiality fundamentally conditions the character of what becomes, surfaces or co-appears with the frame.[41]

In his reading of Abbas Kiarostami's *And Life Goes On* (1992), Nancy calls the director a "filmmaker of the shot" rather than a "filmmaker of narration." Central in this is a critique of the notion of interiority as a foundational condition of the subject, which Kiarostami pursues by an ethical disposition in his framing of the cinematic gaze. For Nancy,

"The entire film is… inscribed in an avoidance of interiority… Interiority is avoided, it is voided: the locus of the gaze is not a subjectivity, it is the locus of the camera as *camera obscura* which is not, this time, an apparatus of reproduction, but a locus without a real *inside* (the tollboth at the beginning and, then, the inside of the car, with the framing through its windows or windshield—or the inverse, the same car shot from the outside, be it from close up or far away). The image, then, is not the rejection of a subject, it is neither its 'representation,' nor its 'phantasm': but it is this outside of the world where the gaze loses itself in order to found itself as *gaze* (regard), that is, first and foremost as *respect* (*égard*) for what is there, for what takes place and continues to take place. For once, *sight* is not the capturing of a subject: to the contrary, it is its deliverance, its sending forth ahead of itself (*envoi devant soi*)… Here cinema plays simultaneously, inextricably on two registers (but perhaps there is no cinema worthy of its name that does not play on these two registers). The first is a register of uninterrupted continuation, of movement (after all, that is what *cinema* means: continuous movement, not representation animated with mobility, but mobility as essence of presence and presence as a coming, coming and passage), of displacement, of continuation, of perseverance, of the more or less errant and uncertain pursuit… The other register is that of the passage through the image, or to the image: cinema itself, television, the soccer game on television, the image hanging on the wall, the gaze in general: not the gaze as point of view… only the gaze as carrying forward, a forgetting of the self, or rather: (de-)monstration that there will never have been a *self* fixed in a position of spectator, because a subject is never anything but the acute and tenuous point of a forward movement (*avancée*) that precedes itself indefinitely."[42]

In Nancy's account, the central concern of cinema is not to represent a world or a subject, nor to tell a story, but to pay attention to the world, to care-for it and call it forth. The way the camera locates, frames or positions an actor in the landscape will set into play various spatial setups. A long shot, mid-shot or close up will each present different opportunities for relational dynamics. These can operate and communicate at several levels—aesthetic, political, symbolic, and so forth. In Pier Paolo Pasolini's *The Gospel According to St Matthew* (1964), the close-up has such a political function. The faces are uncoupled from their context. They fill the frame, occluding mid- and back-ground. Depth of field and distance, which are normally used to communicate the genus or the type, are erased. Variously drained of emotion, puzzled, blank or suffering the affects of a narrative that escapes them, these faces are disembodied, without community beyond the mob, distended in a landscape that deserts them, devoid of a place or homeland. In this way, Pasolini focuses on the specificity and singularity of the person, right here and now, rather than using people as icons or types, as emblems of realities beyond the everyday. The camera wanders between faces with uncertainty, rather than setting up static archetypal tableaux. At the same time, he uses compositional devices common to the iconography of Medieval and Renaisance painting—the ruin, frontality, symmetry, desolate liminal landscapes of abandonment that emulate arcane mythic settings. These multiple kinds of framing, references and registers develop an ambiguity within the image, which doubles the wavering hold that the characters have on their condition and destiny.

But this mythological dimension does not open to a sacred realm, or provide an iconographic dimension. Instead, it foregrounds the oblivion of the singular being, subject not to the will of God but to a scriptural narrative that arrives from elsewhere to stretch and tear the fabric of the everyday. Pasolini himself remarked on the purpose of this framing technique. Speaking of Neorealism, he noted the predominance of sequence shots, wide shots or mid shots and the scarcity of close ups:

"The ideological characteristic of this stylistic phenomenon is hope for the future. In Italy, it is a characteristic of the Marxist Cultural Revolution after the Resistance. And this hope justifies a certain unconditional love for the middle class man, the Italian middle class man (de Sica, and Rosellini too). In my films... there aren't any sequence shots, never. There are very few wide shots or mid shots. There has never been a conjunction, a montage (*attacco*), cutting from a wide shot to another wide shot, of a mid shot to another mid shot, which is characteristic of a typical Neorealist film. In my films there is a third thing, the predominance of close ups, which are full frontal close ups, independent of expressive vivacity, but dependent, I would say, on their spiritual nature. And the ideological characteristic of this stylistic structure is not hope but despair."[43]

In the work of Antonioni—particularly *The Passenger* (1975)—the frame is there simply to look, not to capture. Evidently Antonioni deliberately constructed and predetermined the montage. Scenes were either tightly scripted and enacted or loosely improvised within thematic limits. The issue does not hinge on the degree of artifice but on its purpose. The motivation for strict control is to create precisely the opposite effect—an effect of accidental rather than premeditated capture. The camera might wander, characters and elements might come in and out of frame, or begin a trajectory off screen then describe a portion of it in frame only to conclude it again off screen. What happens to be in the frame is thereby given the character of a part or fragment, of an incidental event. In Antonioni, montage seems to consist entirely of accidentals which nevertheless provide the film's inner consistency. The overall sense is of a disassociation between a camera that indifferently looks and a subject indifferent to being looked at. It is a relationship constantly on the verge of faltering and collapsing. Nevertheless this looking is neither immaterial nor passive. In attending to what arrives, to what comes in and out of it, this frame might in fact resist the gesture of capture and remain wholly outside and alien to the action taking place. Alternatively the frame might only admit a restricted band of a much larger indiscernible totality. The focus of the film, what is properly inside it, what it properly contains, what it is *about* is precisely this incapacity of the frame to hold the events that slide in and out of its cadre.

There is then something of the indeterminate, the unplanned and the unpredictable in such moments. What the frame does is enable what Agamben has called *whatever being—Quodlibet ens*, "not 'being, it does not matter which,' but rather 'being such that it always matters.'"[44] The frame does not capture to prevent escape but to allow and set free a coming and going of whatever happens to be taking place. It does not insist on consistency of place, character or narrative. It does not construct a unitive structure or any sense of accountable content. Rather the frame is disinvested of its attachment to the events it frames. This disinvestment is also a debilitation. The contents will always overflow the frame, which must indefinitely defer any totalisation or teleology. In Antonioni, all the frame can do is watch over the interminable constitution and deconstitution of multiple and simultaneous events with different degrees of alignment or consistency, but whose coexistence, co-appearance and common passage across the frame constitute the filmic texture. Agamben's *whatever being* parallels Deleuze's *any-space-whatever*. Referring to the cinema of Antonioni, Deleuze typifies *any-space-whatever* as a setting that has no "coordinates, it is a pure potential, it shows only pure Powers and Qualities, independently of the states of things or milieu which actualises them."[45] Deleuze correlates *whatever space* to a fundamental displacement of spatiality in modernity and to its representation in the cinema of modernity—the work of Antonioni for example. It is radically different to pre-modern space which is particularised according to its dimensions, location, qualities and socio-cultural associations. Pre-modern space is first and foremost *determined* space—*this* space *here* and *now*. By contrast, the *whatever space* of modernity is in a sense nowhere and no-when. That is, it is not *placed* in any way and cannot constitute any kind of *place*.

It would be incorrect, however, to read Deleuze's *whatever space* as *non-place*—neither in Augé's sense of the placelessness of airports and shopping centres, nor in terms of the abandoned, desolate and irremediable oblivion of *terrains vague*.[46] *Whatever space* is not an abstract universal which holds for all times and all places. It is neither the pure unqualified receptivity of Platonic *Khora*, nor the bare Euclidian space in which anything can happen. Rather, it is deconstituted space, space which has lost its homogeneity, space in which the metrical relationships or connections between parts have become inefficacious. Consequently, in *whatever space*, these relationships and connections, while inoperative, remain open to indefinite reconstitution and reestablishment in multiple ways. *Whatever space* is not empty but teeming with combinational potential. It is a space of virtual conjunction and conjugation grasped as a pure site of the possible and as a milieu open to whatever comes.

Such a concept of space corresponds to Deleuze's notions of assemblage and the plan(e) of consistency or immanence. These are figures of potentiality. They are frames, ensembles and milieux which bring together components with the capacity to mutually resonate and conjugate new assemblies. Within these milieux, components have agency. They possess the capability to operate, cooperate and produce. They harbour immanent potential, susceptible of being mobilised and put to work. Milieux, assemblages and planes of immanence can be thought of in multiple ways. They can be thematic fields for the invention of philosophical concepts, literary fields for the development of narrative figures and by implication, spatial, temporal and other fields for the development of cinematic and architectural possibilities. In that sense, *whatever space* can be thought of in parallel with a notion of the *makeshift*.

At the island of Elephanta, near Bombay, there is a path along a sea wall linking the boat wharf to the caves of *Gharapuri*. Along this path a woman has set up a makeshift tea stall. Before the woman arrived, before she conceived of and constructed her stall, this was a kind of *whatever space*. It was not defined or named; there was no sign reading "build a tea stall here"; it had not been allocated a functional purpose. The tea stall had not been designed *into* the breakwater. It was neither predicted nor programmed in advance. The space was simply part of a pathway along a sea wall. And yet fortuitously, the space had been sufficiently defined in such a way that the tea stall was implicit in it and could be incited or solicited from it. The potential of organising a structure of shade, windbreak, counter, shelves, tables and chairs, was an immanent capacity of its position, orientation, dimensions, materiality and cross section. The rocks forming the sea wall were of such a size and profile that the gaps between them allowed makeshift poles made of scavenged local scantlings to be firmly wedged in. These in turn could provide vertical support for a wind break and shade structure, stabilised against updraft by the poles. A network of ropes could be tied and tensioned to the poles, and a patchwork of canvas stretched around and overhead. The orientation of the structure meant that the shade produced fell onto the correct side of the path at the correct time to attract passing tourists. The manner of its assemblage enabled shade cloth and windbreak to be simply relocated as required.

The particular spatial setup of this place provided a suitable infrastructure that implied certain possibilities without any of them being

explicitly named or manifest. In that sense it enabled definite latent
possibilities while remaining programmatically indefinite. Until the
woman came along with her resourcefulness and her care, no-one had
thought of a tea stall in this place. The woman's resourcefulness
constituted her design creativity in the most fundamental sense. Not
creativity as the invention of fantastical forms, but as the capability to read
the propensities of a given situation, then to act so as to exploit and profit
from that situational capacity. *Whatever space* is this very space of
situational capacity, of multiple relational possibilities that can be made
available and enabled through design. Design—in particular the design of
space in architecture—then becomes a question of how unplanned,
unpredictable and unprogrammed yet highly specific conditions might be
accounted for and incorporated into setups and frameworks, which have
the capacity to solicit and incite the emergent latent potential of fields,
milieux and settings.

## Narrative frames

The Other is such an unexpected emergent potential whose otherness
framing has in its sights. It is not only a person but anything whose
immanence or impending arrival might become subject to the frame—a
face or landscape, an aspect or prospect, an activity or encounter, a
narrative turn. Geometric systems that frame and determine architectural
form also frame the patterns of life that take place in the interstices and
folds of form. But an architectural plan is not merely a prescription or
generator for spatial, geometric and formal configuration. Conceptually
and effectively it is a certain *look* at organisational opportunity and
potential. The plan frames actual, virtual and latent patterns and
trajectories of spacing, occupation and inhabitation; of exposure and
shelter; of orientation, disorientation and peregrination; of territorialisation
and deterritorialisation; of ambulation, and perambulation. It collates such
potentialities within assemblage and zones, delineations and boundaries,
which are never clear cut but always overlapped, juxtaposed, ambiguous
and wavering. The plan is a management of the in-between, the interval
and interstice. It gathers agencies and tendencies that will eventually be
taken up in the desires and temptations of those who infiltrate the spaces it
fields.

The plan also frames particular dispositions to a site, a landscape, a
city and a world. It frames an attitude to the elements, substances and
materials of that world. If this frame were about care, concern and
solicitude, it would in each case attend to the emergent potential of form,

site and matter. This means that the geometric frame would need to accommodate the potential of itself becoming other, of dislocating and displacing itself, of becoming multiple, ambiguous and foreign to itself. Such framing would have concern for the instability that lays at the core of every stable form, for the incommensurable systems that not only subsist in but define form—for example the proportional system of irrationals inherent in the cube, or the capacities of regular systems to skew and double themselves, to iterate or fold. In the same way that care cares-for and solicits the Other's freedom without betrayal, the frame would solicit multiple formal and spatial potential not through the destitution and collapse of form, but in the midst of its sameness and apparent singularity. Likewise, in making room for and disposing of activities, functions and life patterns, the frame would have concern for the programmatic instability that haunts every brief, for the multiple potential configurations and rhythms of use that always remain unpredictable and unprogrammable. Architecture's framing of site, landscape and setting would likewise attend to the manner in which that framing promotes a certain looking and looking-after its milieu. Here there is implied a whole range of strategies and structures of care—the kind and degree of interference with the ground; orientation to the cardinal directions; engagement with topography; how aspects and prospects are literally framed, occluded and dissimulated within an orchestration and dramatisation of the gaze; the manner in which a building might bring into relief or amplify the overlooked, latent or erased conditions of its urban context; how a disposition of spaces in relationship to a particular quality of light might prompt certain lines of reflection and enquiry; the manner in which a view is framed to enable a conveyance of the landscape's uncanny dimension—that is, its becoming-other-to-itself.

In all of this, the implication is not to mobilise signification in explicit, literal and representational ways—for example by translating ideas directly into built form or by explication through interpretative signage, naming and labelling. Rather, it is a call to work at the very materiality of architecture in an elemental and substantial way. It is to work with, to work and *put to work* all the themes, tropes and components of architecture—static and dynamic geometric order; spatial forces such as expansion, contraction, radiation, layering, sequencing, rotation, torsion, shear, fluxion and oscillation; fundamental architectural motifs such as the floor, wall, ceiling and roof; skin, frame and mass; door, gate, hinge, latch, window, threshold, sill, lintel and mullion; step, stair and ramp; ledge, shelf, bench, alcove; reveal, skirting, cornice, batten, scotia. It is to regard these in such a way that what is latent in them, what haunts and is dissimulated in them is called-forth to unfold through solicitous framing.

There is a rarely explored and interminable resource for foundational inquiry and radical tectonic investigation into these architectural fundaments, in this basic tectonic lexicon—for example, that the door *reveals;* that passage under the lintel is a sublime and liminal *ex-perience;* that the window is an eye to the wind; that door and death are cognate figures; that the scotia harbours an articulating darkness. Such inquiry would unfold and map out potentialities of sense, then investigate the proliferation of such diversities of sense through architectonic manoeuvre, manipulation and expression. Critical to the undertaking is the maintenance of a prerequisite *multiplicity* rather than unity of sense, and a prerequisite *disjunction* between multiple registers of sense. In this way, the incommensurability of sense functions to keep a charged and resonant space between different registers, thereby enabling and mobilising them to interact, conjugate and produce.

Le Corbusier's *Villa Savoye* (1929) is commonly cited as an example of the *architectural promenade*—a narrative spatial organisation and framing tied to the Picturesque and to tactics of sequentially unravelling spatial experience and order. It is much like a story slowly revealing itself through its reading, or the way in which dramatic tension and suspense are mobilised and sustained in cinema. In this case the various parts of spatial configuration and their explicit relationships appear to be disjunct, although the space itself remains continuous. Over time, as one moves about, through and between the spaces, an order eventually clarifies and reveals itself. This movement sets up continuous and discontinuous relationships to spaces and prospects that are seen and unseen, expected and unexpected. Spaces lead into each other in fluid sequences, despite there being distinct folds and ruptures in the geometry of movement and infiltration, and between the spaces and zones of the house and its setting.

This kind of spatial system has been called *cinematic* because of the sense of an unfolding suspense, rendered palpable as previously withheld but anticipated spaces come into view and into availability for use. These previously withheld spaces are in fact latent zones, volumes and locations, projected in advance within the design without being fully declared at the outset. This creates a tension between where one is and what one knows, what one becomes aware of but without seeing, and the desire that this tension mobilises which keeps one constantly moving and discovering.

The strategy used conjugates actual, evident and occluded spaces as well as latent forms, geometries, directions and tensions, to orchestrate an iterating narrative of anticipation, desire and resolution that impels and sustains the journey. Throughout, a sense of spatial continuity prevails. The denouement is inevitable, and the predestined goal, in this case the integrated zone of internal living room and external terrace, is eventually reached. While the spatial sequence shifts, staggers and folds in two and three dimensions, the overall narrative is a linear one. Or at least it is maintained by a predominant linear circuit with several sub-circuits peeling away in sideways loops to service areas and adjoining rooms.

Another narrative for the *Villa Savoye* can be gleaned from Corbusier's *Five Points*, which outline his vision for a new architecture: raising the building on a structural grid of columns (*pilotis*) to free it from the damp ground; a designed *free façade* unencumbered by any loadbearing function; a *free plan* of non loadbearing partitions; *horizontal* windows to provide even illumination and ventilation and a *roof terrace* which converts the occupied land area into a raised private garden. At least that is the pretext. For each of the five points and for the vision as a whole there are several non tectonic and non spatial subtexts. Raising the building off the ground responds to a distaste of the earth and the moist. By implication it also answers to a perceived lack of hygiene in the historical city, to its putrefaction and rottenness—hence the gesture of *tabula rasa* that the siting strategy demonstrates. Eliminating the loadbearing function of the façade answers to impatience with stylistic and compositional limits imposed on artistic freedom. Ribbon windows provide a continuous visual sequence, calibrated to the horizontalising tendencies of modernity. They respond to distaste for the vertical dimension of hierarchy and transcendence, but also to a taste for techniques of framing and montage drawn from contemporaneous developments in photography and cinema. The roof terrace represents an appropriation and privatisation of nature, together with an overarching desire to command and survey the territories obtained. The overall vision suggests a desire to disconnect the processes of dwelling from any concrete engagement with the earth and the ground, while establishing a strictly visual regime of engagement with the world. In short, the vision is one which radically abstracts, rarifies and aestheticises the relationship of human beings and the world.

Naturally this is not a narrative that Le Corbusier would have ventured or subscribed to. It is nevertheless plausible and has substantial sociocultural, political and ethical implications for the way human beings using such buildings are conducted to think about, encounter and deal with a world they are no longer part of but interminably confront. While the lineage of this narrative is long—the confrontation is an integral part of Greek tragedy for example—its exclusively aesthetic and non-symbolic register marks it out as a unique disposition to the world that is characteristic of modernity and that pervades contemporary architectural thinking and practice.

By contrast, Louis Kahn's residential projects employ a much more compartmented sense of space. Individual rooms generally maintain their geometric identity and coherence within a more disjunct spatial arrangement. In Corbusier, the wall is aesthetically and technically freed of structural function. Its space defining function is provisional and contingent on particular circumstance. It operates more like a screen and has a more active role in defining and mobilising movement—whether this is the kinaesthetic movement of the body in space or the purely visual movement of a peripatetic gaze. In Kahn's domestic work the wall retains at least its geometric, if not structural function as the principal definer of form. It maintains the geometric integrity and coherence of forms within an overall configuration. This means that rooms are not linked by the circulation of a continuous and pervasive abstract space, but by clefts, perforations, doors and gates within walls. In Kahn's work, the editing or montage of space is more discontinuous and juxtapositional. The same conjunctional technique is used in other ways—for example in the way Kahn frames the environment around the house, and in a broader sense, the way he frames nature. In a corner of the dining room in the *Korman House* (1971-1973),[47] Kahn juxtaposes four elements: a brick wall, a timber framework set forward from the wall, a fireplace and a high window. The window frames a partial view of tree canopies against the sky—a snapshot of nature. The fire place frames a log fire—a snapshot of human beings' appropriation and domestication of natural resources. The brick fireplace is massive and corresponds to the earth and ground. The timber wall is lightweight and corresponds to the forest. Both, like the fire, are products of human ingenuity and technology. A reading of the conjunctions could be ventured using Heidegger's motif of enframing. The wall *frames* nature, in the sense of betraying it and conveying it into standing reserve through technology. It does this in two ways. Firstly into the fuel that warms the domestic hearth, which subjects nature to human domination through the technological. Secondly into a rarefied emblem or icon that capitalises Nature and subjects its contents to a regime of transcendent signification. Architecture is then implicated in a technical or machinic apparatus of enframing.

This is unlikely to have been Kahn's reading of the scene. Rather, he may have wished to convey a transformation of the natural into its archetypal referends and to gather an assemblage of symbols into dialectical resonance—for example the outside (Wilderness), the inside (Civilisation), the tree (Nature), the fire (Hearth), the brick and timber walls (architecture's primary and didactic role of framing so as to reveal the verisimilitude of the world). In any case what is more relevant here is Kahn's strategies of disjunctive and discontinuous spatial assemblage—strategies that parallel a cinematic montage of juxtaposition and jump cut in which the whole narrative is not delivered through the smooth and continuous articulation of a sequence, but through the conjunction *and*. That is, through an overlay of multiple instances, each of which preserves its singular differential identity whilst simultaneously contributing to a deferential collective network and affect.

The approach to Burgess' *Hackford House* (Traralgon, Victoria, 1983; destroyed by bushfires in 2008) begins at some distance, when the natural valley in which the house is sited is revealed. At first undulating and irregular, the approach becomes more orthogonal as the vertical axis of the composition is evidenced. The first threshold yields a strongly symmetrical arrangement of masses and volumes, with the major horizontal axis of the composition dominating. The second threshold embodies a division. This occurs in the forecourt, above a large circular pool and fountain. At this point, the roof directs the eye downwards towards the earth and water whilst at the same time revealing a lookout tower at the trop of the house through an oval aperture in the ridge. The oval shape reinforces the linear emphasis of the axis that extends through to the third threshold at the front door.

This ordered sequence previews the geometric order of the house itself and makes explicit a three dimensional cross around which the house is organised. Burgess summarised the geometric *parti* through a theme of transformation: "in the heart of the house, gravity and light are connected by stairs, a floor window opening to the gully below and a tower pushing through a quatrefoil roof light opening to the sky emphasise this relationship. Opposing forces are at play; integrating energy is apparent. This house is a vehicle for approaching wholeness."[48]

From the lowest level of the central space a stair rises up to a lookout in a sequence of alternating contraction and expansion around a central column. Strongly contained by surrounding walls of dark timber, the stair grounds and stabilises the centre. This concentration is released at the first level through horizontal dilation and expansion of space towards the landscape. At this level an awareness of the vertical axis is established through lower windows that reveal the gully and fernery below the house, and by an increasing sense of the luminous space above. The central stair now rises within a square shaft bounded by four columns supporting the lookout. The upper level walls are built of lighter Tasmanian Oak and translate the density of the lower area into a glowing space that spirals upwards to the summit. A bridge and platform now cross the void, leading to a spiral stair built around the column.

This discontinuity marks a change of function, spatial quality and engagement with the world outside. Rising up this stair the space is concentrated within an area of lattice between the columns until a further discontinuous shift is made into a more intimate space of increased containment. Before the final threshold into the lookout, accessible this time by a ladder, spatial concentration is relieved by four circular windows in the four cardinal directions. At this level the house and its landscape are seen from a position of survey and disengagement. The whole sequence is articulated by a set of disjunctions. Three different kinds of stair prompting three different kinds of displacement (orthogonal and centralised, spiral, linear and vertical) are juxtaposed in three spatial zones with different degrees of density, containment and relationship to the landscape. At the same time, the sequence maintains continuity through each shift. The centre of the house conveys a theme of transformation at several registers—experiential, conceptual, spatial and symbolic. The constant alternation between centre and periphery in space and geometry double an equivalent rhythm between occlusion and disclosure of the landscape. The same tensions of concentration towards the centre and release to the boundary are orchestrated in the peripheral spaces. The life pattern of the house takes place as a continuously intertwined or knitted kinaesthetic engagement with this rhythm of centripetal and centrifugal displacement. There is also a transformative rhythm in the materiality of the house—from dark materials and darkly lit spaces below, near the centre, to lighter materials and spaces above and on the periphery. The whole composition is a dramatisation of spatial tensions conjugated around a rhythmic alternation of energies, providing spaces of variable stability, resolution and degrees of containment or release. At any time, orientation to the house and the landscape is calibrated in relation to the spatial structure which is based on a three dimensional cross installed into its central vertical spine. Externally the house reveals itself initially as a stable composition massed about a vertical axis. But the balance and symmetry of the composition shift constantly in relation one's alignment with its spatial coordinates. The alternation between static and dynamic, symmetrical and asymmetrical, orthogonal and fluid, endows the building with a palpable vitality. This vitality is not merely geometrical or experiential. It also points to a critical dimension in Burgess' design process and his work of over thirty years. The architect is charged with *taking care of buildings*, in the sense of having concern for their carriage or bearing, for the manner of bringing them into being. Design is then not about the imposition of form on materials and sites. Rather, it is fundamentally about a duty of care—an attentiveness and tending to the coming into being of buildings through gesture. For Burgess, buildings are *ways of becoming*. Buildings, as *beings*, call for care and solicitude. The calling of design is to a watching over the building-up and the up-building of buildings as beings that are *on the way*.[49] The tracing of such gestures of care is what produces architecture and also what remains embedded in buildings as the traces of their thinking, making and becoming.

Interestingly, Burgess' work does not fit the mainstream predilection for seamless, *careful* resolution and detailing. It is common for connections and joints to be rough and jarring—which is to say that there is an element of the unsettled and unsettling in the work. In a palpable way, buildings appear discomfited and deprived of a comfortable aesthetic resolution. They seem to be not-yet-finished and not-yet-ready. The concept of care at work here is therefore not one that seeks conclusive resolution and relational or aesthetic closure. Rather, it is one that attends to a kind of difficult and infinite finishing. In this way it longs for and never ceases seeking this not-yet—a resolution that will always already be denied it. This roughness is human; it is the clumsy way in which we question the deeds of another, an awkward stuttering in search for words, a whispered admission of uncertainty: "I don't yet know, I'm not yet sure." In Burgess' work an apparent carelessness, which is not without care, functions to keep a level of irreconcilability moving within the fabric of the architecture. This takes place between site and buildings, forms and masses, spaces, rooms and corridors, components, colours and materials. The parts tend towards each other, meet and connect but without ever fusing seamlessly. If they touch, they do so in passing—unsuspecting, almost by accident, according to a gesture essentially beyond them. The parts meet in difference and indifferent to each other—and yet they defer one to the other in coming to meet up but not-quite-yet meeting. There are evident gestures of reconciliation at work—in the geometry, in formal composition, in detailing. But the parts, masses, rooms, spaces and materials keep apart from these gestures. They are never fully identified with them nor ever relieved of their singularity and otherness—both to each other and to a whole that remains in emergent reconciliation. In this way a gap or difference is preserved between the gestural intention and the factual reality of the architecture. The gap maintains tension, the tension maintains desire and the desire keeps the arrangement in ceaseless unpredictability, ambiguity and transformation. In other words, the work is intentionally and necessarily incomplete.

If for Aristotle the function of art is to perfect, fulfil or finish Nature, here it is to maintain configurations of incompleteness. The work is not yet there, it has not quite yet arrived. In that sense it desires and longs for consummation but without resolving that longing in any kind of tectonically perfected end. Rather, it wishes to show the difficult and untidy means of transformation and completion in its very undergoing. This tension of incompleteness is critical to Burgess' architecture. Seen as a total opus, his various projects seem to be parts of an interminable process of subjectivation or deployment of potentialities. Every building represents a particular stage of this process and every other building is the arrested development of this same process at a different stage. Following a sort of embryology, each building contains all the others in potential. Burgess has spoken of his buildings as "evolving organisms"—where evolution parallels the "intuitive exploration of relationships (between people and place, and towards) a sense of the whole."[50] In this lies the fascination and discomfiture, the delight and unease of the work, since as interminable mutation it can never rest easy but must always be out of sorts. This restlessness is an "instability of becoming," "at once anxiety and exultation, the risk and the transport of relation."[51]

The metaphor of formal, spatial, tectonic and material transformation in the work as geometries develop into others, spatial sequences lead from containment to release, horizontal spaces are gathered into the vertical, is a metaphor of personal transformation. The building becoming itself mirrors or parallels an individual being becoming itself. Hence the recurrent metaphors of evolution, gestural transformation and auto-production that lead to improvement, in the sense that William Blake made of it: "improve[me]nt makes straight roads, but the crooked roads without Improvement, are roads of Genius."[52] The unimproved crooked roads, the roads of excess which lead "to the palace of wisdom," are a paradigm for the formal program of Burgess' work. Blake may well have intended to compare Nature and Artifice, but here, if the work is crook its crookedness is a question of suffering and undergoing. Its restlessness shows two things. Firstly, it presents the designer looking for the work through design in a disposition of care and solicitude. Secondly, it presents the work itself looking for itself, being the looking that it is. In both cases there is a kind of desire and *extasis* of longing that finds its trace manifest in the "look of open resolve" that characterises every gesture of the designer and every articulation of the architecture.[53]

In parallel ways, Peter Zumthor's *Sumvigt Chapel* (1986) brings into proximity several referends and registers that align and reinforce a consistent narrative, in spite of being effectively latent or disjunct. In this narrative the majority of tectonic moves conforms to the symbolic syntax of Christian church buildings. Some moves however do not conform, giving the building an edge that contests metaphors and meanings intrinsic to that syntax. The plan of the building is unusually leaf-shaped, with the entrance located near the point and the altar near the flattened curve. It has axial symmetry in only one direction and follows a hybrid typology conjugating a centralized circular plan with the stretched axiality and one-fold symmetry of a basilica. The aisles form a circuit around the walls, with the seats central in the space and staggered in length to take up the variable width. There are no eye-level windows and the interior is visually disconnected from its context. The space is illuminated by a continuous highlight between the walls and the roof. The roof appears flat but is in fact pitched to a ridge beam arching slightly along the main axis of the space.

In common with church typologies, the space broadens out towards the altar. This is achieved through the expanding plan shape and the luminosity of the upper part of the space rather than through an increase in the scale and verticality of space around the crossing and the altar. The roof is lifted away from the continuous surface of the wall, which is in turn pulled away from the columns that support the roof structure. The columns are spaced out from the wall with fine, barely readable brackets. Consequently the wall appears more connected the floor, and with it forms a contiguous base that grounds the space and gives it gravity. The colour of the walls—a silvery green-grey contrasting with the blond timber columns and roof framing—reinforce this quality. The slight arch in the ridge beam together with the curved walls give the space an indiscernible bulge, so that it seems held and suspended between constraint and release. At its simplest level, the space serves a reflective, contemplative function by turning inwards rather than outwards. It works as a *temenos, templum* or *sanctum* that is cut off from the everyday, but that simultaneously transforms the everyday into something extraordinary and unexpected. The room conveys the idea of a clearing in a wood, lit from above and stretched or poised between sky and earth.

However the apparent simplicity of the space conceals several levels of complexity and several simultaneous narratives. While the overall story is maintained in the general experience of the space, Zumthor makes a number of surprising tectonic moves, all with significant technical implications. These disrupt an expected logic in the structure and component assembly of the architecture, creating disturbances between various dimensions and narratives. The effect of these disturbances is not to sabotage the room's symbolic, social or cultural registers, but to heighten or intensify their effectiveness. The room's floor is a surface of timber boards arranged in a symmetrical herringbone pattern that reinforces the longitudinal axis. The edge of this surface is pulled away from both the wall and the columns which continue below the floor. The space of the recess into which the wall and columns terminate is relatively dark. This allows the edge of the floor to read as a continuously suspended independent line.

The gap or negative joint is a common modernist trope that disconnects parts of an assembly which are normally mediated by a third element, such as a skirting or coving which covers or otherwise conceals the actual connection while ornamenting the junction. Yet the negative joint which connects by separating also has classical roots in the Greek notion of the *skotos* (darkness, shadow), which gives the word *scotia*—an architectural shadow mould that multiplies re-entrant angles by successive folds. The concept of darkness is also in the word *connection* through Latin *nectere* = to bind, and the etymon *NOK = darkness; as well as in other words associated with connection like *knot, neck, nexus, night* and the negative *not*. A connection is therefore literally a darkening-together, a ligature that tightens, constricts and consigns to forgetfulness, oblivion and absence. The idea can apply to construction detailing as much as to the composition of larger surfaces, volumes and districts within an architectural or urban assembly. Carlo Scarpa used it to articulate new interventions within the old fabric of buildings across various scales. At the *Villa Savoye*, Le Corbusier shifted the external columns back from the edge of the main facade to express the independence of the first floor living areas from the recessed lower floor and the site, thereby establishing the function of the house as one of surveillance based on dislocation. The separation of component parts sets them up as autonomous elements only related to each other by an unstable proximity. The joints then become interfaces of distraction and fault lines of the potential disaggregation of the assembly. At *Sumvigt*, pulling the wall surface away from the columns allows these to stand freely in the space. Together they read as a screen in front of the wall, with the wall appearing as the main loadbearing element because of its colour and uncertain thickness. In fact the reverse is true. The wall is supported by the columns and floor, but the support connections are not immediately visible.

A noteworthy example of this kind of disjunctive connection is the cathedral of Strasbourg (12th-15th C). Here the external wall's multiple functions—to enclose space, to modify the climate, to admit light and to express certain civic and symbolic values—are separated from each other. The wall is in two parts—a solid inner leaf which does the pragmatic work, and a diaphanous web of fine columns and vaults spaced away from the inner leaf. This extraordinary screen appears to have no structural function beyond supporting itself. Its major role is resolutely metaphorical and symbolic, although it also serves aesthetically to modulate the scale of the façade and historically to valorise and locate the building within a particular tradition. The screen's predominant tectonic and metaphorical values conjoin in the way that it veils the whole building and dematerialises its mass by a play of solid and void, light and shadow.

The first Judaic tabernacle or tent of meeting was conceived as hanging from heaven and stretched across the earth like the sky or like a cloud. Its function was to represent the shadow of God cast onto the earth, protecting the people of Israel and indicating to them an itinerary of peregrination towards a permanent land. This is the origin of architectural configurations such as the stretched fabric over the altar in the Dome of the Rock in Jerusalem and the parasol or baldachin—whether mobile, or permanent as at St Peters, Rome. The night sky was likewise conceived as a perforated veil stretched across the world, through which the light of heavenly shone. The tabernacle (Hebrew: *mishkan*) was a pavilion (*shekina*)[54] or tent (Greek: *skene*), associated with the human body (*skenos*) and likened to a cloud (*skia*) or sky-cover (*skephas*)—all from the etymon *SQEU = to cover or hover-over, as in *skull, skin, scale*. The metaphors extend seamlessly into nautical referends. The *skene* is a landing-boat (Greek:

*skeuos* = vessel; *skaphe* = dug-out/skiff, sailed by a *skipper*); or a covering vestment (shirt/skirt) that roofs the ancient Greek *tholos*—a vaulted chamber that doubles the cosmos.[55]

The veil at Strasbourg is then an image of the *skene*—the gossamer screen of an *iconostasis* through which the presence of divinity advances and retreats. At *Sumvigt* this is reversed. The external wall presents an opaque surface to its environment. By contrast, the interior relieves the mass and contiguity of wall and floor to create a series of independent suspended layers. The separation of timber columns from the wall, and their uncertain termination under the floor, allows them to read more firmly connected to the roof structure. The columns are tapered. They are thicker and broader near the floor—that is, more square in cross section, compared to a rectangular profile near the ceiling. They are made of the same material as the ceiling structure and continue the same geometry down to the floor. Reinforcing this identity of roof and columns is the evident isolation of the floor by means of the *scotia*. The whole floor appears to be a single floating surface or disc, since the means of its structural support is not shown. Freed from the walls and any obvious substructure, the floor seems to have a variable indeterminate location and capacity to slide up or down within the space. The net result is that the columns appear to hang from the ceiling; and because of their tapering profile, to have been stretched in the process, thereby amplifying the tension between roof and floor. It follows that the columns begin to read as aerial ribs or cables in tension rather than as struts in compression, grounded in the earth. The superstructure of the space works like a strung canopy—an idea explicitly pursued in certain medieval church buildings.[56] Except that here all structural elements seem to have been formed in such a way as to deny the visual logic of their structural function—the floor floats, the columns are not anchored, the roof levitates, the ridge arches. The whole tectonic strategy is geared to dematerialising the carrying capacity of the building fabric. It lends to the space—essentially a suspended interstice stretched between floor and roof—a lightness and lack of gravity amplified by its disengagement with the earth.

The hanging columns extend from a ribbed roof structure that evokes the framed carcass of a ship or the skeleton of a fish. A main ridge follows the axis of the plan (keel) with ribs radiating to a ring beam above the wall (hull). There is no central aisle, so the whole space reads as a nave. Nautical symbolism abounds in Christian doctrine and architecture. Nordic churches feature prominently displayed scale models of timber boats. The word *nave* links etymologically to both *navel*—in the sense of *umbilicus*, centre of the body—and *naval*, in the sense of a ship or vessel. The church building is metaphorically a vessel that conveys the faithful to "yonder shore." The nave leads the believer to the altar, which is metaphorically the navel or centre of the world—an *umbilicus mundi* that also functions as a door between earth and heaven. The word *vessel* is from the etymon *VAS, meaning interval, space, bladder, belly or womb—in the sense of a sheltering, generative enclosure, but also one which is about to breach its withholding limit. Words associated with dwelling (*Vesta* or *Hestia*, goddess of the hearth) and clothing or apparel (vestment) are connected; as is the geometric motif of the *vesica pisces* (literally "bladder of a fish"), out of which all polygons can be developed by subdivision. In Vedic manuals of architecture, the Hindu temple is elaborated out of a figure called the *Vastupurushamandala* (literally "diagram of the indwelling deity"), again by proportional subdivision and repartition. The domestic space of ancient Greece is delimited by the protective and enclosing shadow (*skia*) of a cosmic tree and bough, which expands into the form of a tent (*skene*). This mythic paradigm served to pattern the ritual *skiades*—a domical hut built of branches and leaves erected by the Spartans; the *skiron*—a large parasol used in Athenian festivals called *Skirophories*; and later, the domed *tholoi*.[57]

The proliferation of such a multiple network of referends in relation to a fairly modest space are likely to be unintended by Zumthor. They may unjustifiably complicate what is a simple and legible architectural arrangement. Nevertheless, these readings only become possible because of the specific elements and themes that Zumthor has gathered and brought into proximity within the spatial and tectonic assemblage of the building. They are implicated and complicated within the setup, irrespective of intentionality or provenance. Frames, assemblages and setups always comprise actual and potential components and capacities. In conjugation these can promote multiple readings, multiple tectonic effects and multiple spatial narratives. The potential conditions that develop in the interstices and adjacencies of the frame, but which were neither conceived nor declared as such, give rise to complexes of sense developing as emergent phenomena in the arrangement. They may be read and experienced in the architecture independently of a designer's explicit programme. In many cases, they come with the territory in the same way that the $\sqrt{5}$ comes with the cube and a sense of autumnal lethargy comes with the temporality of late afternoon.

# CHAPTER THREE

# TEMPORALITY

"In fact the only time that can be called present is an instant, if we can conceive of such, that cannot be divided even into the most minute fractions, and a point of time as small as this passes so rapidly from the future to the past that its duration is without length. For if its duration were prolonged, it could be divided into past and future. When it is present it has no duration."[1]

## Time

At the most basic level, architecture might be defined as the organisation of forms in space and cinema as the composition or montage of images in time. These are problematic abstractions, but of provisional use in developing possible parallels. Assuming these definitions, the implication is that time does not play a foundational role in architecture. Nevertheless time remains a constitutive condition of architecture and placemaking. It takes time to design, build and experience buildings and their settings. Architecture is conceived, produced and situated as much in particular places as it is in particular times. It has a history and it is set within implicit and explicit temporalities of numerous dimensions and scales—socio-cultural, political, commercial, institutional, technological, environmental and so forth. Architecture surrounds and make place for the life patterns of human beings which manifest in time and which in turn condition it's conceptual, formal and experiential reality. So while time may not have the status of an immediate material reality in architectural design it does play a part, however latent.

Like space, time is a fundamental condition of existence. There are concrete and abstract, subjective and existential dimensions to space and time. These may be foregrounded or backgrounded, aligned or unaligned, in concord or discord. Nevertheless we always exist somewhere and at some time. What we do and the events we experience are always set and articulated in relationship to spatial and temporal contexts. Not only are these situated in space and time but they also *construct* the space and time of their setting. The activities we carry out, the way we move and our gestural being delineate shapes and forms that are locatable; that have conditions of relative distance, orientation and adjacency; that express particular geometric patterns with intrinsic measure and scale; that have intensity and thickness, and so on. Likewise, beings and events express particular rhythms, phases, pulsations, gestures, cycles—in other words, an entire system of mobile, dynamic and kinaesthetic practices and trajectories. The relationship between these two spatial and temporal systems is not clear cut. Space and time are not independent or mutually exclusive conditions of existence. They maintain an ambiguous correlation that makes them fundamentally interdependent. Nor are they mere containers *in* which we exist and *during* which we exist. Space is inconceivable without the time it takes to traverse it and time is inconceivable without the space between one moment and another. Erasing either one of these conditions erases the other by annulling the distinction between one space and another, one instant and another. Such distinctions are made possible by intervals of difference. The interval is therefore existentially foundational. We can only be, we can only have room enough to dwell and breathe, because of the interval. However, we can only physically be in one place at one time, at least at the minute. Without space there would be no difference between here and there, above and below, left and right. Everything would revert to a single *point* and be concurrent at all times. This is the classical notion of *aeon*—ever-being. Also, we can only be in one place at one time. Without time there would be no difference between now and then, past and future. Everything would revert to a single *instant* and be everywhere and ubiquitous. Ubiquitous ever-being may well constitute an enduring longing of human beings, if not an undeclared programme for everything from religion to technoscience. But it also happens, in all probability not fortuitously, to be an enduring description of divinity—*the being whose centre is everywhere and whose circumference is nowhere*. Be that as it may, the instant and the point appear to be originating and limit conditions of space and time.

Space and time are therefore made possible by difference, by the division or distension of a singularity to produces an interval of separation. The interval is the expression of difference in the same way that in music a solid sound or tone is in fact the physical manifestation of a void—the space or interval which distinguishes one tone, frequency or state of vibration from another. The interval is necessary to differentiate between here and there, up and down, left and right, front and back, now and then, past and future. In space the centre is expressed by an undivided point, and in time by an undivided instant. Both are singularities or unities which exclude intervals. Hence they represent radical presence, manifest by the spaceless ubiquity of the centre in space and the timeless everpresence of the instant in time. Neither point nor instant are extended, yet they operate as origin and principle of extended concrete existence. They constitute the opening of an interval through which and as which beings develop their indefinite potential by passing from virtuality to actuality. The centre is therefore a limit condition. It works as an orifice, threshold and aperture, if not apparatus of differentiated existence. In terms of space, the centre is a door or gate, and in terms of time it is an occasion or opportunity. The threshold permits passage in two phases or directions. In one direction the world is produced by the multiplication and conjugation of difference and altereity. In the other direction the world is resumed into the oneness and singularity of the same.

According to Plato, the one is not in time[2], nor in space.[3] It has no shape, no bounds, is nowhere, is not in anything[4], is neither stationary (*hestanai*) nor in motion (*kineisthai*):[5]

"If the one has no relation to time (*khronou*), it has never become, never was becoming, never was; you cannot say of it that it has now become, is now becoming, or now is, or that it will become, or will be hereafter [therefore] the one has no connection with being at all [consequently] the one is not at all."[6]

Like space, time is not atomic. It is not constituted of an indefinite number of instants. Spatial and temporal movement progress by indivisible bonds and entire measures. They are continuous phenomena which do not add up to an agglomeration of discontinuous entities. Therefore they cannot be calculated except by approximation through discontinuous arithmetic.[7] Since in continuity "there is no unit,"[8] neither the point not the instant has extension. The line is not a sum of discontinuous points, nor is it indefinitely divisible since it is by definition a continuous entity. Likewise, duration is not a sum of discontinuous moments but a continuity that observes the conditions of a different regime with different rules. A geometric parallel might be the series of polygons of increasing sides developed out of the division a circumscribing circle (triangle, square, pentagon, hexagon, heptagon, octagon, decagon...). The series produces distinct configurations, each with different characteristics and propensities, and yet it clearly tends towards the circle which constitutes the origin and term of the series but which is defined by a radically different order.[9]

Time is "the order of motion" (*kineseos taxis*)—"a moving production of eternity (*kinoton tina aionos poiesai*) that abides in unity," an "everlasting likeness moving according to number" (*arithmon iousan aionion eikona*).[10] In terms of the circle or wheel of time, the centre conveys the presence of eternity in the midst of temporal flux. It is "always with the one, throughout its whole existence; at any moment when it is, it is now."[11] "Between motion and rest there is located this paradoxical entity, the instant, which occupies no time whatsoever; into this and out of this the moving passes towards rest, and the rest towards movement."[12] The word *instant* derives from a prolonged form of Greek: *staoreo*—meaning to stand firm, to exist, to be extant.[13] The etymon *STA in words like history, stance, instant, existence and so forth, indicates a prolific complex of meanings and registers—cosmogonic and cosmological (establish, install); spatial (stump, stake, staff, stage, story, station, stance, distance), temporal (solstice, instant) and legislative (constitute, institute, status, standard). Notably, Plato defines history (*historeo*) through *STA as the arrest (*histesi*) of flow (*reo*).[14] The consistent sense is of a vertical axis or pillar (Greek: *stauros*, Sanscrit: *sthamba*) whose installation establishes the world by arresting the flux of becoming. The same sense is preserved in weaving where the vertical warp is an originating stable framework on which the horizontal weft is threaded by an alternating shuttle. The rhythmic conjugation of these two—vertical and horizontal, frame and lattice, order and variation, stasis and dynamics—produce the fabric's pattern.[15] This is why rhythm, defined as the arrest of flow, is such a foundational theme for cinema and architecture; as it is for art generally where the primary concern is to delineate and articulate configurations of all kinds—conceptual, narrative, locational, spatial, temporal, acoustic, formal and so forth.

In the Hindu Vedas it is the sun that "opens" space (*akasa*) and time. The primary existential sense we have of time and the interval come to us from natural diurnal and seasonal cycles. These are made possible by several concatenating differentiations—the separation of sun and earth giving light and dark, the rotation of the earth giving day and night, the inclination of the earth's rotational axis giving the seasons and the rotation of that same axis giving the *precession of the equinoxes*.[16] The conjugation of diurnal and seasonal cycles produces four annual pivotal moments—the summer and winter solstices when the sun is at its highest and lowest respectively, and the autumn and spring equinoxes when the sun rises and sets dues east and west. The solstices are moments when, at noon, the sun appears to stand still (Latin: *sol stitium*) between its ascending and descending phases.[17] Reaching the limit points of its cycle, the sun appears suspended between contrary tendencies and in this hovering, begins to tremble and shimmer. These points are thresholds of contraflexure—limit conditions or terminals that mark a turning in the sun's course. They are more accurately tropes, "turning circles" (Greek: *tropikos kuklos*) or nodes, which suspend and impel its motion at the same time. In that sense they are not *in* time but are dilations in or exceptions within the fabric of time. Also suspended is the moment of twilight which belongs neither to the day nor the night. It is not a measurable extent of time and has no definite duration. It is not sensed as a third entity between day and night, but precisely as the advancing-withdrawal of one in and of the other—the becoming-night of day at dusk and the becoming-day of night at dawn. Visibility and clarity of discernment at twilight is difficult as the extremes touch their limit, become confused and ambivalent and start to waver. The question is not to decide between them but rather to encounter undecidability as such; undecidability as the erasure of duality, poised on this turning point that is both auspicious—since it unveils an opportunity, and dangerous—since every passage harbours a kind of death.[18] Passage through the door is always at a price and every entrance is also entrancement.[19]

In Book Eleven of the Confessions, St Augustine agonises over the threefold nature of time. Future, past and present seem not to exist and yet we have a palpable sense of them. The future is not yet, the past is no longer, and the present has not yet passed. While fundamentally elusive, it is the instant alone which is capable of representing stability and endurance in the inconstancy and fluctuations of time. Yet the instant has no definite existence since, while ever-being, it never becomes. In that sense the instant exists as a stand-in for eternity in the midst of existential time. In as much as time flows or pulses between past and future, the *standing* of time can only be situated in the present or instant. In the same way that in space the consummation of the six directions can only be situated in the centre or point. Neither not-yet nor no-longer, temporally unlocatable because always passing, the present is this fugitive existent that cannot-not be lived. As such it is the centre of time, belonging to neither past nor future, yet conditioning both as the hinge on which they turn and return one into and out of the other. At that moment without duration, the instant's poise is neither pause nor rest but contraflexure, inflexion and limit of inversion—like the gloaming of twilight in which day and night become indistinguishable; the slack sea at high tide when waters appear to swell and become heavy; the moment before a torrential storm; sweat in sweltering heat; flushed cheeks; laughter; the instant tears well up. Each one of these is a limit condition which threatens to breach a boundary. But each is also an opportunity, a threshold between worlds, an opportune time (*kairos*) rather than a moment in time (*khronos*). Or else it corresponds to the motif of *wu wei* in Chinese philosophy—action without action. At these moments, time and space are taken to a limit of potentiality and undecidability. The dimensions of space compress. Past and future withdraw into their common presence and hinge in the instant of time, leaving only ubiquitous presence.

Cinema does not only take place in time. It also constructs temporalities. Godard's juxtapositional montage in *Germany 90* conjugates scenes from different situations and times and incorporates slow and rapid motion sequences to create a multivalent and heterogeneous temporal fabric. But he also surrounds the film in a reflective autumnal aura that sets up a kind of memorialisation. He does this by filming at the onset of a European winter, saturating images in deep burnt orange, setting shots up in low sunlight, directing actors towards a general disposition of fatigue, compliance, resignation, disinterested undergoing or internalised melancholia. These conjunctions of filmic and performative conditions create an assemblage which gives the film a distinct existential temporality—a viscous and exhausted pace that makes time's passing a cipher of endings, forgetting and oblivion. In this time frame, the peripatetic and disillusioned Lemmy Caution wanders through the catastrophic landscape of a violated Nature and a spent communist ideal, in which the only future prospects are the jerky signs of contemptuous capitalism. Godard's juxtapositions are not only imagistic. They are also assemblages of temporalities, of different time frames and durations attaching to those images and referring them to extra-imagistic registers—political, philosophical, ethical, historical, aesthetic and so forth.

This parallels the characteristically different temporalities of distinctive landscapes. Walking through desert, tropical rainforest, managed pine plantations, moor land or sand dunes are experiences strongly conditioned by the kinaesthetic rhythms created by place-specific topography, the form and pattern of trees, open and occluded vistas, flora and fauna, colour and light and so forth. Places have characteristic rhythm, tempo and durational potential which affect the disposition and orientation of the body, its disposition, countenance, footfall, pace, prospect and mood. For example, the Ngaanyatjarra desert lands of Western Australia are featureless from a classical perspective which looks for distinctive geographical landforms. But the quiet ecology of the place, revealed only after sustained walking and attunement, is no less striking. The place promotes its own rhythms of inhabitation, reception and appreciation. It builds narratives through kinaesthetic rather than visual engagement, and it requires reiterated experiences of extended duration to properly convey those narratives. The desert here is characterised by the small scale, the quiet, the fleeting, the folded, the fragment and the incremental. There can be no totalising representative image drawn and no archetypal form or essence conceived. The biological, climatic, cultural, historical, spatial, temporal complexities will not present themselves in rapid time frames of reception. The required slowness of experiential investment is characteristic not only of its aesthetic dimensions, but also of its *terroir* and the ethical topography that it manifests. A managed plantation is radically different. The regularity of the grid, the evenness of the trees' girth and canopy density, the pervasive silence and withdrawal of life on the forest floor, the darkness above and below and the axial and diagonal prospects promoted by its form and layout all convey a distinctive spatiality and ambit of experience. But they also promote a distinctive temporality, strangely disjunct from the ambient temporality outside its boundaries. The resulting kinaesthetic experience will have its own regular mechanical rhythm and pace.

In the opening sequence of Ingmar Bergman's *Cries and Whispers* (1973) at least three kinds of duration are overlapped and juxtaposed; just as there are several clocks shown, each beating a slightly different rhythm. The film is a meditation on waiting and on awaiting the arrival of a passing away. Two women and a nurse watch over the last hours of their dying sister. The film depicts multiple temporalities—distinct temporalities for each sister, another for the nurse, some related to the house itself, to its severe interiors and to interiority as such; others referring to chronological time, to the mechanical times of clocks, each beating its own rhythm; yet others to the seasonal and diurnal rhythms outside the house. External times are paralleled by the dying woman's internal time, by the pace of her breathing, the pulsations of her pain and her slow extinguishment. These multiple times are overlaid and conjugated, or they come into conflict. They pass and trace their respective passage. They coexist simultaneously, but are also radically other—which means they that they maintain their differences and fundamental irreconcilability. Some mark the time of the woman's passing away. Others are oblivious: she has already been forgotten by her sisters and by the autumnal landscape that surrounds the house. On one occasion, momentarily relieved of her pain, the dying woman seeks to inhabit a different time: to write into her diary, to be relieved of her condition, her sickness and her sisters. She is interrupted and returns to bed, knowing that the space of time she needs for this will not eventuate. There is the outside world, the world of the house, the world of each woman, and the world and time of the one who is dying. There are furtive times and places harboured within and between these others. The time of the outside world surrounds the house and goes on independently of the characters. The clock time is mirrored by the formality of the house and the way it is furnished; by the sisters and how they are dressed.

Because places are inhabited spaces forming part of complex sociocultural registers, they are always located somewhere and experienced by someone at sometime. They are therefore conditioned by the time of their existence and the time of their reception. Because time is a constitutive dimension of experience, it cannot-not be engaged with in architecture. The division and repartition of temporal intervals then becomes a central parallel concern for the arts of space and time. The division of space yields different typologies and patterns of spatial organisation, while the division of time yields different durational and rhythmic patterns of temporal organisation. Particular spatial patterns have proportional characteristics based on the numerical and geometrical systems deployed to generate them. These also have corresponding rhythmic and dynamic characteristics which are equally constitutive of the spaces and become palpable in the experience of those spaces. Regular orthogonal spatial grids imply equivalent temporal conditions that will influence how spaces framed by those grids will be kinaesthetically experienced. The organisation of rooms along a corridor will create an iterative rhythm of use characterised by repetitive alternation, while a series of interconnected rooms that must be traversed to cross a building will create a more continuous and fluid rhythm of movement. In architecture, spatial patterns have temporal implications and construct specific temporalities.

Elías Torres' study *Zenithal Light*[20] is a remarkable compendium of the tectonic and experiential implications of light directed downwards into the spaces and volumes of architecture, which in turn affects the temporality of those spaces. Calibrating the orientation, fenestration and materiality of rooms and volumes to the motion of the sun and moon, to the direction of winds prevailing in summer and winter, to prospects, to geological and biological specificities of a site, are a way of constructing an assemblage with dynamic agency and potential for architecture. Such architecture then becomes a receptive infrastructure or enabling framework that brings various static and dynamic, spatial and temporal components into adjacency, overlay, alignment and conjunction, or into contrast and opposition. To these can be added less concrete referends. For example the associational layers that attach to places and occasions, be they individual or collective. Memories of past events, of experiences undergone, of insights gained, of people encountered, of books read, will all attach to particular locations and seasons. Such memories are recollectable and triggered by peculiar conjunctions—for example, a window oriented to catch the gathering warmth of summer in a northeast breeze in Sydney, 2003, might bring to mind an afternoon spent swimming Redbank Gorge in the Northern Territory, 1989. Such recollections are evidently subjective and highly individualised, yet they might also become transferable evocative components of architectural atmosphere. The outcome of conjunctions that trigger memories are not predictable or programmable in advance. They cannot be designated, designed or named. However the degree and complexity of receptivity and propensity for conjugation that an enabling framework makes possible *are* mappable and programmable in advance. That infrastructure then simply lies in wait— literally and figuratively. It makes itself available to receive and frame the multiple conditions of a setting. It has the capacity to allow these conditions to be interrelated in multiple ways. It enables juxtapositions and conjugations. And it waits on those who happen to be there to avail themselves of its potential to produce.

## Limit, *caesura*

Two possibilities or two moments present themselves at every limit— passage and impasse. These two combine in the *aporetic* condition or *limbo* that haunts every threshold. The limit resists passage, or at least it presents decisiveness with the undecidability that attends every decision. This *aporia* of passage, which blocks or defers the way through, is an experience of the superabundance and fullness that the limit represents. At the limit, the limited wells up in superabundance; so that as well as being a zone of prevention, a liminal site is also a site of profusion harboured in the undecidability of potential and its potential production. This double phase is constitutive of every limit condition because the limit is not a periphery or horizon of closure but a pivot of actualisation—much like the trope of contraflexure around which the twilights and tides turn. Heidegger's reading of the limit in terms of Greek *horizmos*, *horos*, and *peras*, is well enough known: the boundary is not an end but "that from which something begins its presencing."[21] In and as the limit, potential comes to present itself as a threshold of promise. For Agamben, this liminal condition is the interminable dwelling *in potentia* that Melville's Bartleby, the scrivener who has ceased to write, conveys through his "I would prefer not to." It is a potential not annulled in actuality, in the instant in which it passes into act, but preserved and remaining in it.[22] And in it there is neither action nor non-action, *intus* nor *extus*, inside nor outside, but only ebb and flow—only the "still sea (*mer étale*)[23] that has completed one of its tides, its rising or descending flux, and which remains suspended for around an hour before being taken over by an inverse motion.... The slack sea composes or deposes a moment of equilibrium and of uncertainty. There is produced at the same time an appeasement and a wavering. The moving water amasses, but its mass remains slack (*demeure labile*).[24] The motion of conquering or of retreat, the ascent or descent have reached a limit, and on this limit they tremble, as is the law of the limit in general."[25] This trembling registers the potential of the limit—whether it be at the interface of distinct atmospheric layers, ecological systems, historical epochs, philosophies or concepts, narrative or representational figures, social or cultural communities, urban or suburban districts, at the edges of buildings meeting a street, between the rooms of a dwelling or between materials in a construction assembly. Culturally, such conjunctions have always been sites and opportunities of significant ceremony. In architecture, they have always been a locus of ornamentation and decoration. In any case, they are always sites where things well up, where the monstrous and abject take place—like tears at the borders of emotion, weeds in the crevices of industrial wastelands, or the riotous conurbations of the global city.

The word limit is from the Latin *limitem*—to assign a boundary or threshold (*limen*), which obliquely (*limus*) constrains and restricts (*limne*)—like a harbour or haven (Greek: *limen*), like the borders of hell (*limbus*), or like the place of interstitial abandonment that is neither here nor there (*limbo*). The idea of binding and constraining are curiously related, through the etymological root *LEM, to notions of a breach or break, of a brink about to be *but not yet* broached. The Hebrew etymon *LM parallels this sense of the generative productivity of boundaries—as if the limit would be a state of being, or the state of a being *on the verge* of bursting and losing the withholding capacity of its borders.[26] The Hebrew word for limit is *gebul*—from the root *GABL, literally meaning enlargement causing inundation; or metaphorically, a swelling river about to burst its banks.[27] In Greek, the limit—the *horos* or arising horizon of restraint[28]—is *peras*: what presses, passes or travels-through. The word is allied to bear[29]—that is, to the experience of passage, of ferrying and bearing, of carrying a burden but also *how* one carries it, one's *bearing*. It is related to the notion of making, conveyed through the Latin: *ferre*—to make, to produce. Every encounter with and experience of the periphery is a burdensome and perilous undertaking, a proof one endures, a trial one passes through while nevertheless having to press on and produce.[30]

In every sense, all making is forebearance and conveyance; bearing-through and carrying-across from potentiality to actuality. Liminal states are consequently not states of defined closure, integrated stability or formal cohesion. They are unstable states poised on the breach, or potentialities of the open to manifest itself as fervent and effusive fecundity. It is in this sense that the limit is what wavers or shivers so as to touch its own incandescence. This condition of excess that is both withheld and promised by the limit—and which is both the excess of the limit and the limit of excess—is the remainder. It is because something always remains over and above what a limit might define that the boundary is precisely what is always destined to break. The limit separates and connects two "sides" around an interval of incommensurability corresponding to the residue. Yet the residue is also a space of interpenetration in which the antinomies begin to fold and *interfere* with each other—that is, within which they begin to inter-fabricate. Heidegger characteristically works antinomies like movement and rest, concealment and unconcealment, absencing and presencing, by way of a simultaneously twofold gesture. One of the antinomies retreats for the advance of the other, one is the becoming other of the other. For example, the inside is not a separate condition to the outside; rather, inside is the condition of "becoming-outside." Likewise, darkness is the condition of "becoming light," of a gathering luminosity that does not occlude darkness but shows it as such. Rest, too, is not cessation of movement but an ingathering of the potential for movement.[31]

This double gesture might operate as a foundational strategic motif in every kind of liminal practice. Between apparent opposites and at the limes of borders and margins a residue remains to mobilise and return opposites into each other, to render them present one to the other and working one through the other. In architecture, this might apply at a number of levels and scales—for example, in how the social and the techtonic might be thought; in how radically different theoretical contexts might be overlaid and animated; in how relationships between a building and a site might be played out; in how the borders of inside and outside might be worked volumetrically in a facade; in how the connection between a column and a beam might be assembled, or the frames of a window might be modelled. In every instance, strategies and tactics might engage one or another of the opposites but not in terms of their opposition, not even in terms of their complementarity. Rather, they might do this in terms of their presence to each other and their yielding one to the other— that is, in terms of the wavering undecidability that attends the rhythms of their becoming-one-another. In this wavering, nothing is as it seems, everything interminably defers and certainty is abandoned to vaccilation. But this state of things is far from terminal because it is only in such a state of play that the potentiality of the undecidable as such is triggered, begins to fluctuate and pullulate.

The coursing of time is brought to a standstill in the instant. This impalpable yet lived moment is where the figures and trajectories of past and future overlap, where an incommensurable discrepancy at the heart of time opens up a breach, break and *caesura* through which time undergoes both seizure and liberation. Like the empty felly of a wheel or the eye of a storm, this instant has no substance and suffers no change. Yet it constitutes the strength of the wheel and the pivot of movement. In the Hindu mythic dance of *Siva Nataraja*, the god is imaged poised as a mobile section through the whorl of a cosmic dance which produces, preserves and destroys the world. Siva's whirling stance is a manifestation of *shakti*—his consort and the potential that is not actualised but preserved in his embodied flexional topography. Siva appears at a standstill. But what is stilled in this everpresent readiness to act is the full but unimplemented force of production, maintained in the instant of an absent presence. The arrest of flow and its suspended fluxion is a collected intensification, welling up to a limit of potential and mass. In its evident groundedness the figure is heavy and grave, yet it gathers the telluric into an aerial promise. Siva is shown not at the moment of action but just before it, like an offbeat that holds his rhythmic transport on just this side of a calamitous or felicitous rift.

The *caesura* of time is palpable in Hieronymus Bosch's *Triptico de Los Improperios* (1510-1515). The triptych shows Christ mocked at three different moments of the Passion. The cloaking, crowning and flagellation (Matthew 27: 28-31) are here presented simultaneously. In addition to its narrative and discursive function, the work conveys the idea that events in chronological time are manifestation of potentialities preserved in an un-manifest non-time where past and future coalesce.

The triptych shows these three events as phases of a-temporality in which history and destiny overlap. More remarkable and shocking is the treatment of the gaze of Christ. In the first panel, he is shown looking down, with his head lowered, fully caught up in the existential conditions of the moment. The composition preserves the authority of the frame which conveys the properly artificial character of depiction and keeps the various gazes within the limits of the frame. The second panel breaches this rule. It shows Christ looking directly at the viewer, beyond the confine of the frame. This gaze is that of the past looking towards the present, towards the *nunc* or the now when two looks *lock*. This *nunc stans* is untensed or standing time, the instant outside of time's fluxion. The instant of the gaze sends the past forth into the present, while recalling that moment to itself as past. This exchange across two times, across two spaces and across the spatial rules of framing and depiction mobilises the interval, making of it a conduit and relay. The moment represented signifies a presencing of the past in the midst of the everyday. It also conveys a subjectivation or individualisation of the look. Christ sees and sees *into* not only the present, but also into the *person*. He sees the person looking and makes this knowledge known. The person he is looking at is absolutely singular—the I that I am in my looking beyond myself. His gaze is simultaneously single and multiple. It is singular for each person and at the same time common to all—since each one will see and be seen seeing. The instant of the look violates the existential framework and setup. It deconstructs the pictorial rules of representation by transgressing the excluding and rarefying functions of the frame. It violates the person by exposing the interiority of the subject. It violates space by making here and elsewhere contiguous. It violates time by conflating past and future.

The countenance of each look is extremely potent. In the first panel, Christ is caught up in the moment of his resignation and acceptance of what is taking place. In the second, the look is one mixing apprehension, contempt and betrayal, but not towards what is taking place or towards those who are enacting the scene. Rather, the look points to and unveils the viewer's logically impossible yet real complicity in the event. At once proximate and distant, confrontational and aloof, questioning and judgemental, the look draws the viewer into the machinations of chronology. Present and past exchange normal causal relationships, as the present and the singularity of the person become causal in relation to the past. The viewer is thereby drawn into the grotesque community of mockery, into the spaces and into the time of the frame, into times and spaces that are not there and then but here and now. In the third panel, apprehensiveness and contempt give way to compassion and understanding. Beyond the theological content (the Kingdom of God is at hand) and the religious content (each is to blame, yet salvation is in that knowledge), there is a further dimension. The work conveys something crucial about time as such—that the future is radically implicated in the past, that it places the past under stress and pulls it forth into the present.

Agamben's investigation of messianic time in the Gospel of St Paul—the time of now (*ho nun kairos*) which Christ inaugurates—is instructive.[32] Messianic time is not eschatological; it is not the time of the apocalypse, the time of the end of time. Rather, it represents time contracting, time beginning to end, or the time remaining between time and its end. *Ho nun kairos* is situated between two temporalities (*aiones*) or two worlds (*kosmoi*)—this world, which is a world-duration stretching from creation until its end, and the world to come, or eternity outside time that will follow the end of creation. The first is *khronos*, the actual "profane" time of past, present and future. The second is *akhronos*—immanent non time. The time that remains is a *caesura* introduced at the limit between these two temporalities, a residue (*leimma*) that constitutes the incommensurable zone or limbo which exceeds them both. *Leimma* signifies the impossibility for a whole and its parts to coincide with each other—or what amounts to the same, for a whole to coincide with itself. It is what remains between whole and part as irreconcilable *lacuna* and incommensurability which prevents the system from closing.[33] It is "at the same time an excess of the whole in relation to the part and of the part in relation to the whole."[34] In the dimension of time, this lacuna is *kairos*—a kind of ulterior time that exceeds chronological time but which is neither supplementary to nor outside of it, "a time internal to time—not ulterior but interior."[35] *Ho nun kairos* is then "*the time that time takes to end*":

"It is therefore neither the line of chronological time—representable but unthinkable, nor the instant of its end—likewise unthinkable; but neither is it a simple segment deducted from chronological time, and which would go from the resurrection to the end of time: it is rather operative time which grows inside chronological time, which works it and transforms it from the inside; it is the time that we need to make time end—in this sense: *the time that remains to us*. Since our representation of chronological time, as that time *in which* we are, separates us from what we are and transforms us into impotent spectators of ourselves—spectators who look without time at the time that flees and their proper and infinite absence from themselves, on the contrary, messianic time, as that operative time in which we seize and achieve our proper representation of time, is the time *that* we ourselves are; for that reason, it is the only real time, the only time that we have."[36]

The time *in which* we are and the time *that* we ourselves are. This is another way of distinguishing between chronological time—*khronos*, an abstract quantitative time within which we exist, and *kairos*—a state or condition of exception within *khronos* that does not contain but rather constitutes our proper, qualitative and existential being-in-the-world. *Khronos* is time as homogenous mechanism of duration, while *kairos* is not only occasion but opportunity—that is, a portal, gateway, door or site of access hollowed out of the fabric of time. In that sense, *kairos* is the instant of time which belongs neither to the past nor to the future. It connects, relates and binds them together; but it also functions to release them from their bonds. The distinction between *khronos* and *kairos* corresponds to that between space and place. Space is *khora*—the quantitative abstract container *in which* we exist; while place is *topos*—the qualitative existential condition *that we are*, a conjunction of space, person and event. Like *kairos*, place is an opportunity produced in the midst of space which is both an exception to it and something that permits its limiting conditions to be exceeded. *Kairos* is *within khronos* but not subject to it. It is not *another* time but a contraction and abbreviation of time; a scission within the fabric of time; a delay, deceleration or retrogradation of its tempo; a knot or inconsistency that troubles the homogeneity of duration and causes it to interminably defer:

> "The two extremities... contract within each other to face each other, and this contraction is messianic time—and nothing else. Again, with Paul, the messianic is not a third *aeon* between the two times, but rather a *caesura* which divides the division between the times and introduces between them a remainder, a zone of unassignable indifference inside of which the past is displaced into the present and the present extended into the past... Messianic time is neither the achieved, nor the unachieved, neither the past nor the future, but their inversion... (this converse movement) is a field of tension in which the two times enter into a constellation that the apostle calls *ho nun kairos*, where the past (the achieved) rediscovers its actuality and becomes unachieved, while the present (unachieved) acquires a kind of achievement."[37]

This to and fro alternation between past and future, achieved and unachieved is read by Agamben in terms of a motif of recapitulation (*anakephalaiosis*). The rhythmic fluxion between past and future, which stand facing each other across an interval of difference, traverses and successively contracts or densifies their disjunction. It does so by conjugating and intertwining potentialities within the interval, or the possible figures and schemes that time can assume. This fluxion does not take place *in* time but in effect *weaves* the fabric, structure and ambiance of times. It takes the intervening space to a state of amplified plenitude, which represents an eschatological completion or fullness—what Heidegger refers to as the advent of the "last god," prepared for by "those who are on the way back (and who) are the true forerunners of those who are to come. (But those who are on the way back are also totally other than the many who only `re-act,' whose `action' is consumed solely by the blind clinging to the heretofore [the past], briefly seen by them. What has been as it reaches over into the futural, as well as the futural in its call to what has been—this has never been mentioned to them."[38]

For Heidegger, "the eternal is not what ceaselessly lasts, but rather that which can withdraw in the moment, in order to return once again. That which can return, not as the same but as what transforms unto the new, the one-only, be-ing, such that in this manifestation it is at first not recognised as the same." To illustrate this process of a double overarching fluxion or inflection between past and future, Agamben cites the example of rime and the sextine metrical rhythm of Romance Poetry. This rime proceeds by repetition, alternating inversion, turning and returning of strophes, each time shifted or displaced—"the last word-rime of a stanza becoming the first of the next, the first sliding to second place, the next to last to third place and the second to fourth place, etc." As a "temporal machine tending from the first towards its proper end," the materiality of the poem consists of a temporal fabric in the process of being woven and in an alternation which successively compresses and drives it forward. The poem concludes with a recapitulating *tornada,* which returns it to the beginning:

"Across this complex coming and going, turned at the same time towards the front and the rear, the chronological sequence of homogenous linear time transforms itself completely to articulate itself in rhythmic constellations which are themselves in motion. There is however no other time which, arriving from who knows where, would substitute itself for chronological time; on the contrary, it is the same time which, by its proper more or less secret internal pulsations, organises itself in order to give place to the poem. And this until the moment of the end, when the retrograde and crossed motion completes itself and until the poem seems condemned to start again: but the *tornada* takes up and recapitulates the word-rimes in a new sequence which exposes all at once their singularity and their secret connection... The sextine—and, in that sense, every poem—is a soteriological machine which, through the sophisticated *mechane* of initiation and repetition of the word-rimes (which correspond to the typological relationships between past and present), transform chronological time into messianic time. And as well, this latter is not another time in relation to chronological time and eternity, but the transformation that time undergoes in giving itself as remainder... as the time that the poem takes to end."[39]

## Other times

According to Marcel Martin,[40] time is the pre-eminent condition and materiality of film, but it is *duration* that is privileged in his analyses. Duration is not time as an abstract sequence of instants. It is the subjective *experience* of time, and it is this aspect that is the proper concern of cinema. Duration might stress the flow, flight or passage of time. It might suggest an indeterminate time; fast or slow, directed towards the past or the future. It might express the permanence of time, its lasting a long time, and the boredom that ensues during which nothing much happens but where duration as such is intensely felt. Cinema manipulates time in such a way as to convey different kinds, rhythms and configurations of duration. It does this in four fundamental ways: by *accelerating*, *decelerating*, *arresting* or *reversing* time. Cinematic montage introduces three types of time: the time of *projection* and duration of the film, the time of *action* within the film and the time of *perception* or the subjective impression of duration experienced by the viewer. These three may or may not coincide according to how time is manipulated and therefore how duration is configured.

By *acceleration*, time is condensed and materialised while simultaneously the slow is rendered in extreme rapidity, allowing the normally imperceptible to be sensed. In this way the fabric of time is stretched and perforated, and in its speed converted to a line of flight which dematerialises and deterritorialises the moment. Occurring simultaneously, compression and dilation give to acceleration the power to convey something strange and uncanny because unfamiliar, impossible and yet present. By the *deceleration* of what is equally imperceptible—the partial moments or the *inside* of rapid motion—the fast is rendered in extreme slowness, time is rarefied and dematerialised. But the extreme slowness also compresses duration, conveying a sense of its weight and gravity, of a potentiality or power held in reserve. This again is an uncanny experience since it expresses something of the extraordinary intensity of the moment, condensed in a kind of stasis of presence. In both cases—time accelerated or decelerated—there is a sense in which we are looking into the substance and matter of gesture, into an unfolding of the instant or the present. This condensation of time gives the impression of a lived plenitude. The *arrest* of time transforms mobile duration to the instant of the image. It has the effect of transfixing and eternalising the moment but may also convey a

condition of crisis in duration and a breakdown of the temporal setting—
particularly when the arrested image persists in the space-time of narrative
action that continues to unfold.[41] These simultaneous moments—one
effectively withdrawn from time and leaving only a trace, the other
abandoned to time's flux—create disjunction and disengagement which
put duration at risk and convey a kind of terror at the core of experience.
The *inversion* of time—leaving aside its comedic function as a literal
rewind—likewise conveys a crisis within duration and the mechanism of
time. It is amplified when the inversion forms part of a continuous
alternation between forward and rewind and is even more striking when
the intervals of alternation are microseconds. The net effect is to transfer
attention away from the narrative setting towards the machinations of
gestural production, the materiality of the image and the machinery of
projection.

Manipulating duration affects the temporal texture of a film but it can
also install several simultaneous temporalities within a unique filmic
space. This conveys a coexistence of different beings, states and
conditions of being, of memories and recollections, and so forth. Different
rhythms of time can correspond to different verb tenses which refer to the
way actions, events and states of being *are* or *exist*—for example, the
imperfect (it used to happen), past continuous (it was happening), present
simple (it happens), present (it is happening), present perfect (it has
happened), pluperfect (it had happened), future (it will happen), future
perfect (it will have happened), conditional (it would happen), subjunctive
(it were to happen) and so forth. Cinema then becomes a means of tensing
time then conjugating those tensions, allowing them to inflect each other
so as to produce multiple complexes of duration.

The coexistence of different temporalities can put into play different
possibilities of resisting the chronological and the abstract in favour of
specific, heterogenous, non-linear and existential experiences of time—for
example, the presence of people or events that have passed; the emergence
of oneiric, imagined or real states; the altered tempos of memory and
dreams. Accentuating the duration of time by long sequences, slow motion
and slow tracking shots can intensify the experience of attending to the
passage of time, to its viscosity and materiality. There is then the moment
of a return to the past—a flashback which unsettles the structure of time
by introducing either the sudden intrusion of or the transitional passage
into a different temporality. Similarly, the fabric of time might be
unsettled by the welling up of subconscious or subliminal dimensions—for
example dreams or alternative interpretations of an event carried by
different characters. Alternating between past and present, real and virtual

within the forward motion of duration folds time so that these now face each other and enclose or bind the narrative. Returning to the past puts the viewer in the position of knowing something about the film's unfolding, destiny and denouement. This is the fundamental trope of classical tragedy where prior knowledge of destiny colours reception of the narrative from the outset and amplifies its dramatic implications. In cinema, it puts into relief aspects of the film's narrative which are not related to the story and how it will *turn out*—for example its aesthetic or emotional content, its settings, and so forth. But it does not necessarily erase drama or suspense.

A classic example is Billy Wilder's *Double Indemnity* (1944). Here the fact of the protagonist's fate is presented at the outset. But the details of how and why he got to where we find him is revealed episodically and sequentially, only now and then returning by flashforward to his office, where he began to recount the story. The time of the film is therefore woven in broad relays between present and past. Each pass of the relay shortens in duration by a kind of exponential narrowing. This fulls, thickens and felts the fabric of time, successively concentrating it so that the end rejoins the beginning before moving forward at the last to an ultimate denouement. The film first opens then closes time by turning it in on itself, by making of it the inside of a fold, with no seam and no possibility of recollecting the past or elaborating the future.

A parallel manipulation of time frame is used by Alejandro Gonzalez Inarritu in *21 Grams* (2002). Here the narrative develops episodically. The sequential order of scenes is fractured and reconfigured by a non-linear montage which creates ambiguous time lines and requires the viewer to reconstitute the story from the fragments shown. However, the temporal disjunctions have a substantial role to play in building suspense and elaborating the dramatic content and affect of the story. They do this through a juxtaposition of the intensive character of the episodes. Placed in sequence, these episodes—which have no common measure of time and are made to alternate between present, future and past—begin to condition and mutually inform each other. Scenes involving different characters, or the same characters in different scenarios which seem narratively or temporally unrelated, then begin to carry weight and implications for each other. Juxtaposed scenes may have equivalent or radically different tonalities and pace (the woman breaks down on learning that her family has died in a car accident, a group of friends are in the midst of a boisterous party), but their conjunction builds tension and suspense. Out of this rhythmic alternation of times and intensities, Inarritu slowly weaves the narrative through a process of reassembly. This is carried by the way uncertain gaps or durations between different scenes are made to narrow successively or overlap as the film develops. Each instance of flashback and flashforward contributes links that join previously unrelated facts, events and emotions. The dynamics of this montage technique is something like darning holes in threadbare cloth, or assembling a patchwork fabric. The film does not open at the temporal beginning of the story, nor close at its end. The fabric of time is distorted and folded so that the story builds its own time frame as well as the narrative. Scenes do contextualise each other temporally but always indirectly and allusively (the opening sequence anticipates the protagonist's desire to meet the unknown woman who now lies beside him, the dying man's handling of a jar containing his diseased heart after an operation anticipates the donation of a heart by the woman's husband who is killed in a car accident; the title *21 Grams* refers to the supposed weight of the soul which "departs" the body at death, and so forth).

In Antonioni's *The Passenger* (1975), reporter David Locke is doctoring a passport in his attempt to exchange identities with a man—an arms dealer who has just died in the adjoining hotel room. He is listening to a recording of a conversation with his counterpart from some days before. He turns his head towards a terrace outside the room. Framing him from behind, the camera slowly pans across to the terrace where the exchange took place. A man walks into the frame, delineated by the doorway, his back to the camera, the desert in front of him. He is wearing the same blue shirt that Locke wears while he works on the passport. What was a tape recording is now a real-time conversation. The smooth transition reinforced by the recorded conversation brings two moments into the sequence of a single shot. Two different times and two different places are made to coexist in the one seamless event. We are unsure whether the man is Locke or his counterpart. Locke then enters the frame and the fact of the flashback is established. Later, the camera will continue its anticlockwise pan from the counterpart (in the past) back to Locke working on the passport (in the present). Again the camera will pan from a space made available to the narrative through being framed by an architectural structure of openings, across a series of surfaces that flatten out and erase the depth of the image, into another framing indicating a different time in the same place.

By filming such sequences in a single, slowly panning shot, Antonioni establishes apparent continuities in space and across time, as well as an ambiguous continuity in the narrative. He then superimposes several discontinuities. Events that have taken place in different rooms and at different times now seem to share the same pictorial space and the same narrative presence. Past and present coexist interchangeably within the

same setup, which now gives to space and to architectural settings
something akin to a memory. The architecture seems to work as a neutral
frame that brings into proximity different dimensions and phases of space
and time, as well as different worlds that the two men inhabit. The
architectural setting of doors, windows, columns, edges, reveals, surfaces
and volumes is used by Antonioni to double the camera's framing. Scenes
take place within multiple spatial frames, operating as overlaid armatures
into and out of which the characters move and through which their worlds
are juxtaposed. These frames become an apparatus through which specific
assemblages and agencies can be mobilised. The masking of characters as
they enter and leave a scene, or as they move within it, allows Antonioni
to shift from one space to another and from one time to another. As
characters leave the framed visual field they might be moving to another
segment of the same space depicted, or into other spaces and other times
that are properly out of frame.

Staying with the moment, filming the slow pace of the everyday and
employing the shot to dwell with the tempo of the ordinary is a recurrent
trope in Antonioni's work. There is a predilection for manipulating regular
chronological time by working its pace and tempo, by thickening and
slowing it down, by focusing on a time of watching rather than on a time
of doing:

> "Time agglutinates, duration is uncertain, it seems very long or very
> short... Light is inconsistent in sequences of shot-reverse shot, where skies
> or backgrounds do not coordinate in terms of real time... the use of an
> empty field at the beginning of the framing... disorients our perception of
> time, since ordinarily an empty field marks an interval of time, its use in
> continuity within the same scene renders the line of chronology
> uncertain."[42]

In both filming and montage, Antonioni privileges a radical suspension
of movement and time in order to construct durational and indeterminate
frames open to whatever comes.[43] In the last sequence of *L'eclisse* (1962)
he abandons the narrative and the protagonists in favor of an extended
meditation on the uneventful. What has also abandoned its role of
following the narrative is the camera itself, which now becomes an
autonomous agent of pure perception. Set in the EUR district of Rome,
amid *terrains vague* and new residential apartments, Antonioni turns his
camera towards the mundane—empty streets, building sites and hoardings,
sprinklers, close ups of water on shimmering leaves or seeping from drains
and burst pipes, insects teeming through undergrowth, rustling foliage and
so forth. Overall nothing happens and yet the sequence maintains an

unbearable density of eventuation. It is a whole world, a *mundus* in which human beings have no purchase. The occasional characters moving about resemble the protagonists but are more like types into which the protagonists have by now been erased. Largely disengaged, they are shown looking out or up towards the sky for something undefined. The spaces depicted have uncertain boundaries, dispositions and orientations. The urban context shown is not reducible to a single district but is composed of fragmentary places that show no contiguity between them. The tempo of the scenes combines an open time of watching and waiting with the ambient rhythm of the places and events shown. Dilating space and time in this way brings about a state of tension and premonitory suspension, implying an impending event to come, the moment of something *just about* to happen. At one level this might be nuclear catastrophe; at another, a narrative catastrophe whereby the previous solidities of image, place and occasion, of characters' subjectivities and dramatic interactions are all reabsorbed into a milieu of oblivion that abandons, forgets and supercedes them.

In a similar vein, the urban park in *Blow Up* (1966) is a meticulously executed framework for unraveling the film's fundamental question regarding the verisimilitude of the image. The park has two important characteristics—its propensity to simultaneously occlude and reveal, resist and afford. The protagonist enters the park as if entering a zone of indistinction or a rupture within the city. The park establishes its own place by the continuity and breadth of its grassy slopes, the absence of horizon and background which annexes it from the surrounding built environment, and the tree trunks, canopies and plants which create a constantly varying patchwork frame through which the action is seen. It also establishes its own tempo by a disconnection from the chronological structure of the world outside, the decelerated and dilated rhythm of activities taking place there and the effects of wind animating and rustling the background foliage of trees. Together, these qualities convey the park's autonomous spatio-temporal and material existence and its general disinterest in the inconsequential characters and events that take place within it. There is a mild element of foreboding and objection, if not resistance to those events by the park. The rustle of foliage seems phased and calibrated to the narrative, increasing in intensity at particular critical moments. In that sense the park is given an animate dimension, equivalent to if not eclipsing that of the characters. In the penultimate scene the protagonist is there looking for clues to a murder, clues he was not able to capture on film on a previous occasion. Now armed with his camera, the clues have vanished, leaving him searching in vain within the occluding spaces of the undergrowth and the dilated time that nevertheless imposes a strange urgency. Whether what he saw was concretely there, whether it was only there for the seeing, or selectively projected into the images he had been enlarging is merely a circumstantial subtext. Of greater import are the palpable evanescence of factuality into fiction and the dislocation of instrumental seeing into a milieu of fabulation and *poiesis*.[44] These shifts are only enabled through the altereity of the place in which the protagonist now finds himself—a place whose spatiality and temporality are fundamentally seceded from one world in order to construct another with radically different propensities and opportunities.

In *Bad Timing* (1981), Roeg contests the hierarchical chain of cause and effect that is normally taken to motivate the intentions of human action unravelling in linear time. The chain is fundamentally undermined by placing the familiar chronological structure of time under severe stress. The characters appear to become subject to the push and pull of energies mobilised by an incessant slippage between past and future. These energies operate in the manner of unconscious drives that do not originate with the characters but in the circumstances and milieux in which they find themselves—milieux that are highly charged and whose fabrics are under great tension. The characters sense and encounter these tensions implicitly and subconsciously. The narrative unravels from the opening sequence in the Belvedere Museum, Vienna, where the two protagonists move between rooms, observing paintings. Her curiosity and attentiveness to the art works eclipse his supercilious, wandering gaze. While they have not yet met, the conditions for that meeting and for their story are already present and inexorably presenting themselves. Just before Roeg jump cuts forward in time to an ambulance carrying her to hospital after a drug overdose, the camera fixes on Gustav Klimt's *The Kiss*. The aesthetic control and elegance of the painting then gives way to a juxtaposition of Egon Schiele's premonitory embrace of a couple in *Death and the Maiden*—the man's dark eyes looking well beyond the scene, towards the observer but also towards a palpable sentiment of figurative and literal tragedy. The use of this painting is apposite. In it, the maiden conveys a frail tenderness that seems to be comforting the figure of death that looms above her. She appears to be the stronger figure in spite of her diagonally prostrate position, while death remains vertical. The look of death is troubled, as if carrying a terrible burden. His gaze extends towards the viewer, out of the spatial and temporal frame of the painting. In that way, death sees past the present to the implications of his role in the scene.

The soundtrack doubles the film's jump cut at this point, superimposing a wailing siren over Tom Waits' *Invitation to the Blues*, which had accompanied the characters' crossing choreography of observation in the museum. Characters, space, music and image conspire to depict a setting of extreme torsion. At the outset, this sequence establishes the tone and tenor of the denouement as well as the spatial and temporal dynamics of the whole film. Roeg then cuts to a scene taking place between these two moments, when the woman separates from her husband at the border. The three moments—past, future and intermediate—establish a temporal rhythmic keynote for a film that will interminably shift in period and register. There are two significant effects. The viewer will not easily know where they are in the unfolding of the narrative. The characters, too, will become caught up in this ambiguous timeframe so that they themselves will not easily follow their own devices and drives. The penultimate scene—the "bad timing" of the title—refers to a missed opportunity that will prevent the detective from securing a confession from the man. That moment arises because of non-alignment in the timeframe of two events—the man's immanent exposure as the perpetrator, and the woman's unexpected recovery, reported too soon during the detective's questioning.

Entering the woman's empty apartment and seeing the unmade bed, the detective "sees" one of the couple's earlier sexual encounters. The man then turns from his entanglement, apparently sensing the detective's presence from the future, with a look that conveys his implicit guilt and as yet unconsummated crime of ravishment. In this way Roeg constructs the place of the apartment as perforate to the influences of past and future. The present is and is visible in the past as presentiment, as potentiality harboured in the very motivations and conditions that bring about events. The man is several times aware of the detective's ominous futural presence—a presence that brings to mind the implications of his present disposition and designs. Elsewhere, a soundtrack from events in the future is overlaid on a scene in the past, and a future scene is intercut to interrupt the flow of a sequence set in the past. This kind of temporal exchange gives to the present situation of a scene an orientation that is outside and beyond the moment—either to past conditions that have influenced it or to its future import. Two time frames coexisting in a state of tension, strain the film's temporal fabric, drawing it back or impelling it forward. No moment is without past or future. The shape of that moment, what it gives rise to, what it excludes and includes, how it is situated within a broader temporal structure and narrative—all of these do not exist absolutely, but always in a context of overlap and ambiguity that is constantly under stress and convocation from outside its bounds. The shifting temporal structure has a significant narrative function. Rather than explicitly presenting the key scene of ravishment at the outset, then showing how the story unfurls, Roeg begins with its after effects and over the length of the film reconstructs the incident out of overlapping fragments of past and future events that have conspired to bring it about. It is the detective's (and the director's) surgical work of reassembling the fragments that holds the narrative together. In beginning with the end and ending with the beginning, Roeg's montage subjects chronological linear time to the pressure of vacillating temporalities that suspend and reconstitute it into a non-linear, un-centred and heterogenous system of physiological and existential coordinates within which the narrative builds.

For Agamben, the fundamental conditions of cinema are repetition and arrest. Repetition is not a return of the same. It is the return *in potentiality* of what has already been actualised. Repetition restores the possibility of what has been in order to render it possible again—hence the proximity between repetition and memory:

> "Doesn't cinema always do this, transforming the real into the possible and the possible into the real? We can define the already seen as the fact of `perceiving something present as if it had already been,' and the inverse, the fact of perceiving as present something which has been. Cinema takes place in this zone of indifference. We then understand why working with images can have such an historic and messianic importance, because it is a way of projecting potential and possibility towards what is by definition impossible, towards the past."[45]

Cinema thereby operates in this zone of undecidability between the real and the possible. The second transcendental condition of cinema is arrest—the power to interrupt. Following Hölderlin, Agamben likens this arrest to the *caesura* in verse. By stopping the rhythm and unfolding of words and representations, the *caesura* causes them to appear and be exhibited as such, aside from their narrative function within the flux of meaning. Referring to the works of Debord and Valery, Agamben defines cinema as a "prolonged hesitation between image and sense. It isn't a question of arrest in the sense of a chronological pause, but a power of arrest which works the image itself, which subtracts it from its narrative power to expose it as such." Repetition and arrest are indissoluble transcendental conditions of montage, whose objective is to work that deep ground where images have such palpable presence that they become indiscernible:

> "Together, repetition and arrest realise the messianic task of cinema that we were speaking of. This task is essentially to be undertaken alongside

creation. But it is not a new creation after the first. We mustn't consider the task of the artist uniquely in terms of creation: on the contrary, at the heart of all creative act there is an act of de-creation. Deleuze said it one day, in relation to cinema, that every act of creation is always an act of resistance. But what does `to resist' signify? It is above all the power to de-create what exists, to de-create the real, to be stronger than the fact that is there. Every act of creation is also an act of thought, and an act of thought is a creative act, since thought is above all defined by its capacity to de-create the real."[46]

Agamben then asks: "What becomes of an image worked by the powers of repetition and arrest. What changes in the status of the image?" These questions weigh on the normative and Hegelian conception of the image's instrumental and expressive function, conveyed and realised by a medium which is destined to erasure in the final work: "The expressive act is accomplished once the means, the *medium*, is no longer perceived as such. The *medium* must disappear in what it gives us to see, in the absolute that shows itself resplendent in it. On the contrary, the image that has been worked by repetition and arrest is a means, a *medium* that does not disappear in what it gives us to see. It is what I would call a `pure means,' which shows itself as such."[47] The as-such of the image now shows itself as a zone of undecidability between truth and falsity:

"The image exposed as such is no longer an image of nothing, it is itself without image. The only thing that we cannot make an image of is, if you will, the being image of the image. The sign can signify anything, except the fact that it is in the process of signifying. Wittgenstein said that what cannot be signified or said in a discourse, what is in some way unsayable, that is what shows itself in the discourse. There are two ways of showing this relationship with the `without-image,' two ways of bringing to sight that there is no longer anything to see. One is porno and publicity which act as if there is always something to see, always more images behind the images. The other, in this image exposed as image, is what lets appear the `without-image,' which as Benjamin said is the refuge of every image. It is in this difference that a whole ethics and politics of cinema are played out."

Agamben's purpose is to reflect on how the manipulation of time and duration through rhythm and disjunction can affect not only the temporality of cinema but the very status and semantic potential of the image. By working the image through repetition and arrest, its instrumental function as a medium of representation is transformed into pure means, into pure presentation and advent. It is in the work of Tarkovsky that these two processes—manipulating duration to create altered temporalities and working the image so as to make of it a pure means—converge. In his *Sculpting in Time*, Tarkovsky recalls two conditions of time which determined the character of his films *Mirror* (1975) and *Stalker*:

"I felt it was very important that the film (*Stalker*) observe the three unities of time, space and action. If in *Mirror* I was interested in having shots of newsreel, dream, reality, hope, hypothesis and reminiscence all succeeding one another in that welter of situations which confronts the hero with the ineluctable problems of existence, in *Stalker* I wanted there to be no time lapse between the shots. I wanted time and its passing to be revealed, to have their existence, within each frame; for the articulations between the shots to be the continuation of the action and nothing more, to involve no dislocation of time, not to function as a mechanism for selecting and dramatically organising the material—I wanted it to be as if the whole film had been made in a single shot."[48]

For Tarkovsky, the fundamental condition of cinema is the expression of the coursing of time through rhythm. While montage and editing have the pragmatic function of assembling component parts into a whole, these parts and the style or technique of assemblage are not the major formative elements of a film. They are not a vehicle for cinematic expression. Tarkovsky critiques Eisenstein's practice of montage cinema since for him the film arises not in the process of editing but in the process of shooting:

"The idea of 'montage cinema'—that editing brings together two concepts and thus engenders a new, third one—again seems to me to be incompatible with the nature of cinema. Art can never have the interplay of concepts as its ultimate goal. The image is tied to the concrete and the material, yet reaches out along mysterious paths to regions beyond the spirit."[49]

Tarkovsky's poetics of cinema develops out of a sense of the *affective* rather than representational or intellectual capacity of the image. For example in *Stalker*, the Zone does not symbolise or stand in for a specific representative typological or archetypal space whose character can be decoded. It is at best a world, the environment in which the characters lead a life. This life consists in the interactions between people and the places they find themselves in, interactions that are mobilised by the internal constitution of the characters. In that sense the Zone is produced by the characters. Its affective features correspond to the psychological conditions of the people who are navigating it. The time-pressure, rhythm or tempo of the Zone likewise corresponds to the pace of the characters' affective interactions with their inner selves, conveyed by Tarkovsky through long slow tracking shots giving a palpable experience of the passage of time. The affective is pursued through a resolute concern for the *materiality* of the image—specifically the materiality of time expressed through rhythm. In its flux, its passage and coursing, time is not singular but multiple, not homogenous but heterogenous. It comprises different zones with specific densities appropriate to the dramatic character of the scene, or to its affective content and context. Each scene shot will have a specific rhythm and density of time—fast or slow, continuous or discontinuous, compact or dilated. Montage is then the process of joining and aligning, or otherwise structuring, sequencing and assembling such temporal materialities so as to mobilise affects. For Tarkovsky, montage determines structure but not rhythm. The process of editing as the montage of time-pressures is not one conceptually determined in advance. Rather it is an *emergent* process:

> "In a curious, retroactive process, a self-organising structure takes shape during editing because of the distinctive properties given the material during shooting. The essential nature of the filmed material comes out in the character of the editing... A prodigious amount of work went into editing *The Mirror*. There were some twenty or so variants. I don't just mean changes in the order of certain shots, but major alterations in the actual structure, in the sequence of the episodes... It was clear that the parts came together because of a propensity inherent in the material, which must have originated during filming."[50]

The time of the shot is not determined by the chronological time of the take or the editing, but by what Tarkovsky calls "the pressure of the time that runs through the shots." The aim is not to render an *exact* sense of chronological time but a sense of the existential character of the time proper to the affect being conveyed. Here Tarkovsky is close to Heidegger's distinction between exactitude and truth: "the exact is not yet the true, that is to say, that which shows us and preserves what is most proper to a thing."[51] The truth value of the cinematic image and sequence is sourced in a *manipulation* of realistic duration. Tarkovsky achieves this by stressing time, subjecting it to tension and pressure in order to dilate or intensify it into an altered time, closer to the temporality proper to the moment—and to do so with a comportment of *preservation* and *care* that is cinema's ethical responsibility. This time-pressure is not a vague sensibility but is physically "imprinted in the frame." It has material presence in the substance of the film and can therefore directly affect its reception and experience. Time-pressure refers to both an internal state of tension within duration, as well as to a specific tendency, dynamic or inclination that constitutes the duration's outward trajectory and relational potential—something Tarkovsky calls "operative pressure, or thrust."[52]

This idea corresponds in music to the inherent dynamics of a tone, given the mode or scale in which it is set. Individual tones and groups of tones, runs or chords, will manifest particular energies, kinetics, tendencies and propensities or "desires"—for example the tendency to repetition, to remain in suspense, to be resolved, to lean towards chaos, and so on. Music then becomes the management and assemblage of these propensities towards a given dramatic purpose. A good example is The Necks' performance of *Aether* (2001). Common in much of their music, the piece conveys a sense of interminable beginning and infinite finishing. The opening structure consists of four chords. The first three are repeated and harmonically open while the fourth is lower and harmonically closes the sequence. This motif is repeated with varying duration between the chords at each iteration, reducing over the length of the piece. Over and above the chords, multiple layers of sound are introduced—first wholly within the chord intervals, then overlapping and extending across chords until they develop continuity and extend across the repeating motifs. These layered sounds are piano notes, percussion beats and riffs, bells, organ and electronic sound textures whose eventual overlapping overtake the initial fourfold structure. The sound texture very slowly fills and densifies musical space, while the increasingly reducing duration between chords and beats compresses and accelerates time. The piece creates its own tempo and temporality. Because of its immersive character, and the psychosomatic affect of music, chronological succession is supplanted by a wholly other existential temporality that totally conditions its reception and experience.

Well into the piece, initially unconnected and suspended tones come to be linked into variations on a run of paired notes, unfolding into an assertive short and repeating melody that is doubled by multiple variations and echoes. In this way the music pivots on the interval between the initiation and termination of a melody that is interminably sought and endlessly deferred. This deferral is musical and temporal since it works both harmonic and durational material to create compressions and dilations, contractions and expansions, densifications and rarefactions of the tonal and temporal fabric. In deferring melody the dynamics of overlaid chords constantly point in its direction but also disperse into multiple retreats and detours without ever acceding to, declaring or setting upon it. The reiterative deferral being played out functions to preserve pure musical energy and to maintain rather than consume the melodic potential latent in the mode or scale in which the chords are set. At the same time, the piece builds in density, complexity and texture through figural overlay, instrumental timbre and rhythmic juxtaposition. The rhythmic pattern thickens to such an extent that it becomes pure and relentless beat, tending to but never reaching its limit in the single wavering and shimmering tone which opens, underlies and concludes the whole piece. What *Aether* performs is a process of intertwined envelopment and development of possibilities, articulated from pure acoustic and resonant material through a practice entirely founded on the kinetics of sound and time.

Another example might be Arvo Pärt's *Festina Lente* (1988-90), where the same melody is played simultaneously by three groups of instruments at three different time scales—slow, natural and fast. The instruments begin together but the disjunction in tempo causes the three streams to immediately diverge. During the piece, the three will develop radically different dynamic and harmonic relationships as they separate, cross-over and align with each other. This will range from resonance and concord to complete discord and chaotic deconstruction of the melody; from dynamic alignment, upgathering and amplification to an extreme opposition and cancellation of energy. *Festina Lente* is an investigation of music as the playing out of pure resonant time, which parallels Tarkovsky's contention that cinema is first and foremost a tectonics of time. The contradiction in the music's title—*festina lente* means "to hurry slowly"—also defines its ambit. By overlaying one melodic pattern with its accelerated and decelerated variations, Pärt constructs an image of time in the process of unravelling and decompressing—the present put into tension and stress by the antagonistic of a propellant future and a restraining past. The piece moves from stable regular organisation to irregular coagulations of multiple layers; then inexorably towards deconstitution as the texture of the piece disentangles into broad horizontal sheets of sound decreasing in proximity, separated by intervals growing in distance. Pärt effectively spatialises both sound and time through a texture that fades to an indefinite and infinitely finishing end.

The form in which time is imprinted by cinema is factual, concrete and material. Comparing the centrality of time in cinema and music, Tarkovsky writes of cinema as a tectonics of time:

> "Of course in music too the problem of time is central. Here, however, its solution is quite different: the life force of music is materialised on the brink of its own total disappearance. But the virtue of cinema is that it appropriates time, complete with that material reality to which it is

indissolubly bound... Time, printed in its factual forms and manifestations: such is the supreme idea of cinema as an art... What is the essence of a director's work? We could define it as sculpting in time."[53]

The factuality and materiality of time does not refer here to concrete chronological time, but to the particular time or duration—"the very *movement* of reality: factual, specific, within time and unique"—that attaches to events, objects and people interacting in particular situations and circumstances. Various time frames, rhythms or tempos are made to coexist within chronological time without necessarily following or being subject to it. This phenomenological, experiential and existential temporality—subjective at the core—parallels the existential spatiality that constitutes place as something exceeding concrete abstract space.[54] But the temporality and factuality of the cinematic image is not descriptive or documentary. Rather it "presents as an observation one's own perception of an object." Quoting Dostoyevski's precept—"life is more fantastic than any fiction"—Tarkovsky frames his discussion of the image in terms of Japanese *Haiku*, where succinct observation of particular moments conveys a simultaneously immanent and transcendent sensibility, eclipsing the circumstantial without disengaging it.

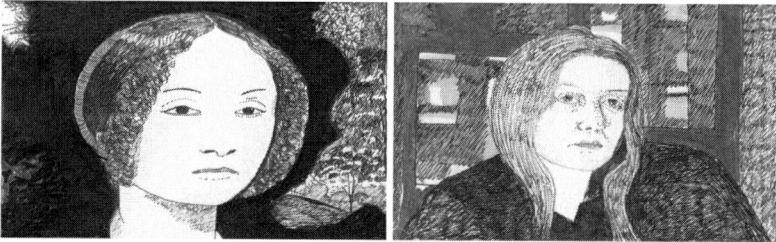

Analysing Leonardo da Vinci's *Young Lady with a Juniper*, Tarkovsky explains why the portrait was used in *Mirror*. The director wished to superimpose so as to relay different temporal registers, and to convey an ambiguous aspect of the female protagonist's character that is both specific and general:

"We needed the portrait in order to introduce a timeless element into the moments that are succeeding each other before our eyes, and at the same time to juxtapose the portrait with the heroine, to emphasise in her and in the actress, Margarita Terekhova, the same capacity at once to enchant and to repel... the emotional effect exercised on us by the woman in the picture is powerful precisely because it is impossible to find in her anything that we can definitely prefer, to single out any one detail from the whole, to prefer any one momentary impression to another, and make it our own, to achieve a balance in the way we look at the image presented to us. And so there opens up in us the possibility of interaction with infinity, for the great function of the artistic image is to be a kind of detector of infinity."[55]

For Tarkovsky, infinity is inherent in the very structure of the image. The image is not about a meaning but about a *world*. Images convoke and conjugate worlds. They do not symbolise or represent ideas outside life but embody and express life in its substance and materiality. Paralleling Agamben's treatment of the *example*,[56] Tarkovsky contends that it is the unique element in an image—its distinctive, individual, inimitable and idiosyncratic character—that transforms the particular into a general or universal type: "The general could be said to thrust the particular forward, and then to fall back and remain outside the ostensible framework of the reproduction... We are faced with a paradox: the image signifies the fullest possible expression of what is typical, and the more fully it expresses it, the more individual, the more original it becomes."[57] The critical condition for relaying an image from the general to the universal, or from the circumstantial the infinite, is therefore a quality of ambiguity and undecidability which makes it impossible to close the process of observation or terminate the relays of sense. To convey infinity, the meanings potential in the image should not be singularised or totalised. Rather, they should be preserved in their multiplicity and potential to interact and indefinitely exchange. Remaining elusive and thereby allusive, the components of the image become impossible to disassemble since the boundaries of sense are not defined or delineated. The indivisibility preserved within the labyrinthine heterogeneity of the image's semantic potential maintains the look—its fascination and desire.[58] This elusiveness is something that *aerates* the texture of the film, captivating and inviting engagement through a "deep intimate experience."[59] Images invoke the gaze and convey powerfully because of resonances mobilised by juxtaposition. Putting various modes and regimes of signification into inexhaustible allusive assemblages allows an image to move beyond the facticity of the seen into a state or degree of reality that would be *larger than life*.[60] The image then triggers perceptions that involve fundamental shifts in scale, fundamental changes of power or transforming conjugations which foreground or otherwise heighten the everyday without departing from it, and which preserve it in its being as such, immanent and without transcendence.

The ultimate cinema for Tarkovsky is the chronicle, presumably because it is in the chronicle that the facticity of events can be most directly imprinted on film by what he calls an *observation-image*, in which the element of time has a critical role to play:

"The cinema image, then, is basically observation of life's facts within time, organised according to the pattern of life itself, and observing its time laws... The image becomes authentically cinematic when (amongst other things) not only does it live within time, but time also lives within it, even within each separate frame... No other art can compare with cinema in the force, precision and starkness with which it conveys awareness of facts and aesthetic structures existing and changing within time."[61]

As Robert Bresson has said, "crude realism alone will not communicate reality."[62] In other words, the communication of facticity does not lie in the faithful and realistic capture of facts, events, emotions, places, colours and so forth. It lies in the *artefactualisation* of facts, not their reproduction. The real can only be properly conveyed through an intensification of particular aspects of the concrete and the everyday, manipulated through the artifice that cinema is, along with all other arts. It depends on a supplemental dimension of the image, something over and above its natural or descriptive registers—what Bazin has called "an asymptote of reality"[63]—according to which the image ceases to function representationally and begins to register verisimilitude.

Herzog parallels this concern for conveying the supplemental element of factuality and its potential to convey extraordinary otherness. His documentary work is always situated in a zone of indiscernability between fact and fiction: "all my documentaries are stylised. In the name of a more profound truth, a more ecstatic truth—the ecstasy of truth... they contain parts that are invented. I often say that it's a question of fictions in disguise."[64] One objective of this cinema is to foreground the absolute strangeness of the everyday, the unspeakable and unrepresentable character or the untellable story that evades every narrative and every event. His is a perpetual quest for the truth behind fiction—or rather the fictionable component, the fabricational and artefactual potential of every fact. This otherness constitutes a rupture in the time of factuality, in the time of the image and the tempo of its advent. Cinema's role is to convey this confabulational altereity, this parallel dimension that coheres within the image and the narrative; at the same time placing and threatening to displace them. The displacement creates a parallel simultaneous condition which brings about a certain wavering between the factual or documentary component and the fabulous otherness that scandalises it. The shock of this outrage may have moral and ethical registers and affects. More relevant however is the strategic dimension of the shock. Because of the displacement, two times and two narratives coexist and interpenetrate—the circumstantial or documentary, and something of an entirely different scale that troubles and unsettles it from within. The juxtaposition of these two, each with their own texture and tempo, violates the normality of the first. It breaches and exposes it to an excess of signification surpassing what is circumstantial in it; taking it and the viewer beyond the factual condition that it appears to convey.

In Tarkovsky, the supplemental dimension of the artificial involves a high level of discrimination, exclusion and exaggeration—in other words, of a fictionalisation that constitutes cinema's proper artisanship. The implication for framing and for the look is that the cinematographer must engage with a process of pure observation of facticity, with an eye to capturing the time-pressure or tempo of events, the psychological rhythm of people, the states of mind appropriate to an event, the intensive substantial presence of objects and processes. Capturing these in the materiality of film, then assembling and orchestrating their kinetic force through montage, would constitute the fundamental practice of cinema. This means that the image must bear a significance which eclipses communicative, representational or symbolic functions. It becomes a cross section through the time-pressure or intensivity which is not so much captured as captivated by it. The sequentiality of images is then a way of tracking the transformation of these kinetic relationships by way of what Deleuze, through a reading of Bergson's *Time and Memory*, has called direct time-images. "(1) There are not only instantaneous images, that is, immobile sections of movement; (2) there are movement-images which are mobile sections of duration; (3) there are, finally, time-images, that is, duration-images, change-images, relation-images, volume-images which are beyond movement itself."[65] Deleuze casts these three types in terms of a general history of the image, each produced after a crisis in the previous type. Instantaneous images refer to photography, movement-images—or mobile sections of duration—refer to the classical cinema of narrative action, while time-images refer to the direct imprint of the force of time as such:

"It is only when the sign opens directly onto time, when time provides the signaletic material itself, that the type, which has become temporal, coincides with the features of singularity separated from its motor associations. It is here that Tarkovsky's wish comes true: that `the cinematographer succeeds in fixing time in its indices [in its signs] perceptible by the senses.' And, in a sense, cinema has always done this; but, in another sense, it could only realise that it had in the course of its evolution, thanks to a crisis in the movement-image. To use a formula of

Nietzche's, it is never at the beginning that something new, a new art, is able to reveal its essence; what it was from the outset it can reveal only after a detour in its evolution."[66]

Tarkovsky's means of registering the materiality of experience comes with the idea of the *imprint*. The intensive character of the image, which conveys an event by configuring the kinetic power and pressure of its temporal conditions, is carried by a direct imprinting into its very *chemical* substance and texture as a physical and haptic presence, which in turn directly affects the viewer's perception and emotional disposition. This imprint transforms the image from a luminescent to a kind of photoluminescent presence which is not merely produced by projection, but which appears to emit its own light and produce itself. The reception, perception and affect of the image are thereby returned to the sensory motor schema and the habitus of a premodern sensibility. It requires a disposition—both in the making of the film and in the experience of it—of *staying with* the time of the shot, of remaining and tarrying or of watching over the fullness of its duration. The image thus endures and persists both psychologically or affectively and physically or retinally. In contrast, the time and the image in Roeg are fundamentally elusive and perdurable. The time of events—the simultaneity, overlap and interchange of past, present and future—is conveyed by rapid, blurred and evanescent traces of its passage. Instead of materialising in the photoluminescence and presence of the image, time and the event are dematerialised and deterritorialised to such an extent that any possibility of dwelling or remaining with the time of the event is interminably deferred.

## Time of the shot

In the opening of *Éloge de l'Amour* (2001), Godard films several casting sequences during which a director outlines the characters of a fictional narrative. The actors are in close up, reflecting on the characters' personae. The director explains: "do you understand it is not Eglantine's story, but a moment in the history, the great history and story (*la grande Histoire*) that passes through Eglantine, the moment of youth." The actors' faces are screens that register the scanning mobility of emotion, doubt, delight and discomfort. In these scenes, Godard cuts each sequence short. The shot does not stay or linger with the face beyond what appears to be an interrupted moment. It cuts to black a fraction of a second before a scene's expected end, just as the actors' eyes are being averted, just as they look down or away. This looking away is not to anything at the margins of the frame, to anything outside the frame or off-screen. Instead, the gaze looks beyond the setup itself, away from cinema and its artifice, back into the inner character and subjectivity of the person. And yet this inner gaze is directed outward, outside both the film's frame of reference and the actors' bodies.

This kind of gaze proliferates in the film. It clearly has a psychological register—individuals reflecting with some doubt if not despair on themselves, their world and their place in it. The actors are either searching for something tangible in the characters they are about to portray, or else they are looking into the emptiness and impossibility of portrayal as such. It is a looking fundamentally different to the gaze that violates the frame by looking the viewer in the eye. With the latter—for example in Bosch's *Triptico de Los Improperios* mentioned earlier—the gaze ruptures artifice itself. The frame and setup are momentarily annulled and the time of the scene, or the time of enchantment, is suspended in favour of a radically different but parallel time of concrete experience which undermines the constructed time of the film.

Here though, the gaze is a looking beyond the moment of the scene into other moments, potential within the setup but retained within its depths. These are moments and times that might be pocketed within the time of the shot—moments of a past that is suddenly and unexpectedly sensed, a kind of irruption of history within the story, an intimation of something to come, some impasse to be encountered or some experience about to be undergone. The look captured by these moments is directed outside the narrative, outside the frame and beyond the subjectivity of the characters. It is a look into the very conditions of cinema and artifice. For Godard this condition has a history, which he holds to be in a state of extinguishment within the crisis of the image, the cinema of mass consumption and the pervasiveness of telematics. The crisis parallels a condition of fragile and irrepressible erasure of the subject in the contemporary world.[67] The troubled gaze of the actors consequently sights into a threshold of oblivion. But Godard does not allow the trajectory of this peripheral gaze its full exposition in time, its full denouement or unravelling. By cutting to black just as the gaze becomes peripatetic, or else absents itself from both setup and subject, Godard amplifies its trangressive potential. The character is left at the borderline of a troubled acquiescence from where there can be no rescue. The cinematic moment is abandoned at the instant of its fullest potential eloquence. These disjunctions convey the film's preponderant motifs of melancholia and resignation. At the same time, the film's allusive registers and deep materiality—its lustrous visual tonality, colour, sound and timbre—produce an intimation of hope and ravishing beauty. This doubling of sadness and hope, melancholia and beauty are recurrent stylistic themes in Godard's late work. More significantly they show how a cinematic montage of radical contrast and disjunction is capable of not only mobilising multiple meanings, but of conveying the vaccilating indeterminacy that is foundational for sense and its production.

In *Stranger than Paradise* (1984), Jim Jarmusch also cuts to black; but these cuts take place after extended moments in which narrative tension is either suspended or allowed to dilate beyond expectation. This creates pauses in the fabric of the film, rests in the rhythmic transport of the narrative and a relaxation of dramatic tension. Such pauses articulate and shape the film through an episodic structure of short fragments that remain independent and are not necessarily connected logically or chronologically to an overarching story. They work like cross-sections taken through a larger form or a longer narrative that will never be fully outlined. The sense of time is extended and spread laterally rather than being driven linearly. The film follows the road movie genre, so there is a general sense of sequences unfolding in time. But the order of episodes is never explicitly chronological. The black pauses between them are generally not overlaid with voiceovers, so they work like *caesurae* and empty spaces into which the viewer can project or reflect. These edit cuts have an entirely different value to those used by Godard in *Éloge de l'Amour*. Jarmusch's rhythm of editing is more comic than tragic. The pauses have the character of the space of time left by a comedian just before or just after a punch line. Different kinds of laughter are prompted in each case, but the whole strategy depends on a particular timing that withholds as much as it delivers—a timing that reflects the off-beat and syncopation of Jazz.

In a different register, David Lynch's *Lost Highway* (1997) works two narratives across each other in parallel rather than episodic times and spaces. The events take place in the vicinity of disjunctions, overlaps and ruptures in the fabrics of space and time. The main characters look to be unaware of who they are, where they are and in what timeframe they exist.

Deeply troubled, they subsist in settings whose very structures are troubled
and on the verge of collapse. They move in spaces that have no distinct
edges, whose borders fade into an enveloping darkness and function like
the transitional zones of a constantly threatening mutation. People enter
into and emerge from gloom as if they were recurrent troubling memories
slipping in and out of forgetfulness. This darkness corresponds to a
psychic zone which conceals an indefinite potential of individuation and
characterisation. The multiple shifting subjects might correspond to
multiple narrative variations inherent within the story, or to the multiple
implicit possibilities of each character to exist differently in different
circumstances. The worlds they inhabit might be parallel dimensions or
variations and mutations of the same dimension, developed out of the
same circumstances by the differentiated play of possibilities offered
within the setup. The multiplication and concatenation of events—each
representing different points of view that are similar but non-identical to
each other—develops out of "the impossibility of knowing the infinity of
possible non-totalisable perspectives, like a vanishing point that one can
approach without ever reaching... Mulholland Drive does not present a
linear time that is real or effective but uniquely a succession of virtualities,
of times that oppose each other—therefore not a unique time, but different
temporalities that cross each other and sometimes meet each other without
ever being able to be truly unified."[68]

In *Sayat Nova*, Paradjanov frames cinematic sequence as hovering
potential or threshold of motion that is about to but has not yet fully
mobilised. The temporal field within which the action takes place is
twofold. It parallels familiar diurnal time since we are aware of sun, clouds
and so forth; but it is also uneven in rhythm, density and texture, and its
reparation is heterogeneous. It is not an abstract time of equal periods in
which actions of various kinds take place. Rather, the events themselves
create their own time—decelerated when a veil passes over a face or a
fruit is slashed; accelerated when a woman dances or a child runs across
the domed roof of a bath house; synchronic or diachronic in retelling the
poet's life; anachronistic in the film's Christic references and metaphors.
These uneven spatial and temporal frameworks bring an element of
ambiguity and instability to the structure of the film; a shivering and
shimmering character conveying iconic and epic sensibilities through
which formal and narrative textures of the film undergo a hypostasis.

For Deleuze there is never one world, constituted of a particular set of
possibilities which render all other possibilities incompossible—that is,
impossible to take place or to coexist. The world is not a *kosmos*—a
convergent, totalising, harmonious or harmonising *uni*-verse. Rather, it is a

*khaosmos*, characterised by disjunctions and heterogeneities, discontinuities and interminable bifurcations that make multiple incompossibles possible— at least virtually. For Lynch, this virtuality cannot remain concealed. Incompossibles constantly threaten to perturb the texture and tempo of actuality, to the extent that the actual itself becomes nothing other than a circulation of virtualties. In Lynch's work, the disruptive trigger to compossibility is released by way of particular events, objects, images or characters (a kiss in *Mulholland Drive*, a severed ear in *Blue Velvet*, a video image in *Lost Highway*, the neighbour in *Inland Empire*). These function like triggers that unclench an apparatus which releases, displaces or turns one world into another, interpenetrating their respective spaces, times and narratives. They cause dilations in the space-time continuum of a world, provoking thresholds and zones of passage between multiple incompossible worlds. Such events are the accidental and catastrophic conditions that loiter in the margins of every apparently benign and familiar incident or advent. They are accidental because they befall unexpectedly and catastrophic because they overturn the circumstantial conditions and coordinates of the milieux in which they take place.[69]

The diverse elements of a world—virtual or actual, foregrounded or backgrounded, occluded or visible—are thereby rearranged into different assemblages with their own dynamics, spatial constitutions and dispositions, durations, tempos and rhythms. Places show their other face; opportunities provide different events; characters undergo exchange or mutation; the familiar becomes uncanny and the unfamiliar stabilises. Such exchanges between incompossible worlds operate by interminable doubling and interpenetration, which are recurrent themes in Lynch's cinema. What is troubling is not the fact of incompossibility or the threat of other worlds breaching the existential logic of this one in becoming actualised. What is deeply unsettling is *this* world—the fact of its irrevocable wavering and flickering instability; the moments it harbours around which it begins to tremble and unravel; the propensity for it to dilate and become transparent to the otherness immanent within it.

This is why in Lynch the apparent solidity of the world is placed under constant stress to reveal its fundamentally unstable and fluxional character. There is nothing other than dreams and every dream irremediably threatens to overflow into nightmare. People, places, times, objects, images—these are all rendered in terms of an ever-present latent potential of becoming-other and elsewhere, rather than in terms of a stable, selfsame being-there. All are subject to the uncertainty of deformation, deterioration, dissolution and monstrous reconstitution. If there is a horizon where these multiple spaces, times and events converge, then it is maintained in a state of absolute withdrawal, persisting as an unimaginable, undepictable and unrepresentable future.

Both spatial and temporal setups double and reinforce this kind of transformative ontological potential. In *Lost Highway*, the spaces of the film's opening sequences are barely differentiated in relation to the darkness that pervades them, as well as to the spaces around and between them which appear to be dilations and condensations of that darkness. There are numerous moments when the camera's travelling enters an obscurity within the space, emerging later in a different space which may or may not be contiguous. It is never certain whether characters are coming in or out of rooms, whether they are arriving or departing into or out of different spatial and temporal zones. The spatial texture appears homogenous and continuous due to the actors' and the camera's fluid motion and the smooth montage. Yet space is clearly layered discontinuously. Between the layers are gaps allowing characters and the narrative to slip in and out. There are also violent and rough transitions— for example when a character's contours become ambiguous before undergoing a disfiguring shape-shifting transformation. This is amplified by the way personae are framed, decentred within and subordinated to the frame. Their restless movement across the frame or from room to room, filmed by a camera that remains more or less immobile, creates an instability within the shot that doubles the uncertain hold that characters have on themselves and on the world they traverse.[70] In Lynch's work it is never a question of inhabitation or dwelling. Everything is under constant threat of displacement and deterritorialisation—subjectivities, places, spaces, times, materials, flesh, emotions. In *Inland Empire* (2007) for example, there are several moments that trouble, reverse or shift the chronological dimension of the film: the protagonists watch a video of a scene that has yet to take place; a character claims to be present in two places simultaneously; people have regular intimations of the future implications of present experiences and events:

> "Different times interpenetrate so that what has already happened is also what will take place. 'Its a story that happened yesterday, but I know that its tomorrow,' says Nikki to Dewon, before telling him of a curious recollection which is precisely what we then see, in the next scene, as if it had taken place subsequently... Nikki... walks the length of a dark corridor which represents a bifurcation of time, reaching finally the threshold of a room. She observes curiously and we are shown what she sees, that is to say, but from another point of view, exactly the same scene that she had seen beforehand... We now understand that this curious noise, which had earlier disrupted the rehearsal, was none other than Nikki."[71]

The interiors which give *Lost Highway* its claustrophobic mood are barely contextualised. They are lit artificially in saturated colour that amplifies their theatricality, their remoteness from engaged experience and from the everyday rhythms and textures of space and time. External light is diffused through veils that prevent a clear sense of the outside or a definitive sense of whether it is night or day, although the predominant tone is nocturnal. Sources of light are generally hidden, or they are as multiple and indistinguishable as their coordinates. The chromatic quality is resolutely *chiaroscuro* and rendered in saturated colours, the quality of which is constantly on the verge of darkening. These characteristics make the setting uncertain, disorienting and creepy. They enable the time of the scene to become potentially anytime. They cause temporality and spatiality to waiver and hence to amplify the dramatic tension, anticipation and expectation of what might take place. The resulting liminal setting is a kind of limbo that hovers between wakefulness and sleep, reality and dream, consciousness and the unconscious.

Lynch makes this temporal ambiguity—as well as the uncertainty between actual and imagined—a central aspect of *Mulholland Drive* (2002). The interpenetration and folding of time and the unravelling of the narrative parallel a psychic unravelling of the characters. They play out several possibilities that the narrative holds by implication, but which can have no space within a linear account. A further reading is that the multiple narrative possibilities correlate with the multiple personalities that are potential in each character—an idea central to the *persona* in classical theatre. Narrative and physiological unravelling might also be read as instances of the breakdown of spatial and temporal structures in the world of the story, in its taking place and in the images that convey it. Here characters encounter an instability within the setting itself which begins to unravel around them. The fact that the story is recounted in flashback is not revealed until close to the end of the film. The revelation occurs during sequences of high tension so the viewer is given little space to make sense of the fact. The flashback is not a simple recounting of a series of past events. Rather, it is the playing out of a story in which fact and fiction, real and imaginary develop in unstable conjugations and combinations. Identities shift and wander between characters; settings for various events are swapped; personae are transported into parallel worlds; past and future overlap each other and premonitions of the future eclipse the present of recollected events. Likewise, with *Inland Empire* the protagonists' fusion of their actors' and characters' personae, together with the tragic history of the film they are shooting which becomes an inevitable destiny for them, create a network of potential narratives and personae that Lynch intertwines.

The characters become entirely subject to the inevitable crises which interminably transform the temporal and spatial structure of the film. Different settings are rendered as indistinguishable variations of a series of interior themes so that the actual location of any particular scene becomes unlocatable. The opulent house of the actress doubles an opulent Polish bourgeois apartment, which in turn doubles the staged apartment of the protagonist; while a ludicrously artificial set for a sitcom featuring rabbits doubles a gaudy motel room.

These films take on the nature of feverish nightmares in which space and time become porous, folded, dilated and unstrung. The pervading gloom takes on a sense of subconscious depth out of which the characters and events of the film are produced. Darkness operates much like the unmanifest potentiality that serves as a ground to the production of a world, as exemplified in Japanese *Noh* drama by the curtain *agemaku* and by the *skene* in ancient Greek theatre—the curtain or veil stretched between manifest and unmanifest worlds, through which characters advance and retreat. The dark spaces concocted by Lynch are always heterogeneous in texture. They conceal and occlude other times and spaces, other characters and beings, other worlds and opportunities that threaten to overflow their borders. Compared with Godard's cool detaching blacks, this darkness is hot and forms an integral part of the world of the film. It is entered into and traversed by the camera and the gaze. Otherwise it simply subsists alongside the visible as pure darkness, as a doorway of some sort, constituting an ever present potential for invasion and infection or purification and escape. In all these dark transitions we are not dealing with the same black—or rather, the same black is conditioned each time by a radically different setup. With *Éloge de l'Amour* the black is a threshold signifying rupture in the time of the scene; a moment when the subject encounters a troubling impasse. With *Stranger than Paradise* it coexists with the time of the scene, working to syncopate the narrative. In *Lost Highway* it subsists within the narrative and temporal structure of the film as a parallel but discontinuous zone of subconscious perturbation into and out of which the characters advance and recede.

In contrast to Godard's short-cutting of the shot. Herzog uses shots that linger well past the expected limits of a scene. In *Fata Morgana* (1970), the camera stays with the event, the landscape or the face to the point of exposing the subject to an excess of the gaze. Particularly with the face and the psychological comportment that it carries on screen, this becomes the limit condition of an unbearable experience. The discomfiture has strategic value. There is discomfort for the character suffering an excess of observation that has by now become objective and calculated. There is also discomfort for the viewer who is obliged to dwell with the discomforting gaze. Or else there is the vacuity of the character who is now out-of-character, whose performance has lapsed but who is still being observed.

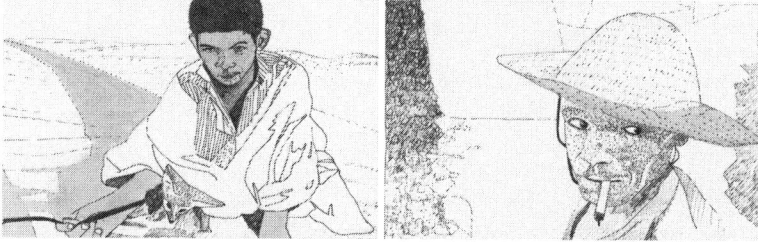

By remaining with the face, Herzog is able to scan emergent aspects of the character that could not be available during the frame of performance when the actor is "in character"; much as Antonioni claimed for his own work:

"Holding a shot past the normal time to capture peripheral moments and events, sequences of long shots, tracks and pans that followed the actors uninterruptedly... a few moments after they had completed their performance of the written scene... these moments were exactly those which offered me the best opportunity to select and utilise... certain spontaneous moments in their gestures and facial expressions that perhaps could not have been gotten in any other way."[72]

By filming the boundary between acting and non acting, or by filming around the moment of an ending in anticipation of a cut that never comes, Herzog depicts the fragile texture of time and being. The moment filmed is in fact the moment of the potential collapse of artifice, of the frame and the setup. It is a moment of the deconstruction of the gaze, when the power of the image as presence alternates with its frailty as evanescent passage. Framing itself collapses since the camera, still running, has ceased to run for anything in particular. It has ceased to look at anything specific. It just looks and its looking is a kind of vacuous, open but persistent gaze. This persistence has a violent dimension since the gaze violates the subject's potential—even their ethical *right* to maintain distance and disjunction between self and persona. The time of the shot is here a time simultaneously unbearable and unwatchable, a time of waiting over the deconstitution of the persona—the mask through-which (*per-*) the subject sounds (*sona*), or through which the subject encounters and engages with the world. This moment opens a zone of uncertainty and ambiguity for both character and observer. What was deliverable within the setup and by its agency is no longer possible since the moment has eclipsed the opportunity presented. What is now made possible is something other, wholly fugitive, illicit and in excess of the frame. This is not the out-of-frame or the off-screen, which would still be part of the setup. Rather it is something in excess of cinema itself—a moment of realisation for what is sighted by the frame, a moment that delivers the sighted to a sense of its objectification by the gaze and the *aporia* in which it now finds itself. No longer part of a narrative and unable to escape the frame, the sighted becomes trapped in a zone of oblivion between interminable capture and the impossibility of release.

Herzog's opening shot in *Fata Morgana* is a relentless sequence of landing aeroplanes, each landing doubling the last and repeating the same event for a series of different aeroplanes. The images are rendered shimmering and evanescent by the zoom lenses used and the thermal haze that saturates the scene. In nearly four minutes that seem like an eternity the effect is extraordinary. The experience moves from curiosity (what will this lead to?), to puzzlement (how many landings will there be?), to discomfort (how long will this last?), to boredom (can we move on to the next scene?), to surrender—and from there to something extremely disconcerting and moving. The persistence of the gaze and the iterations resist the flow of linear narrative time and causality.[73] By bringing time to indefinite repetition, its texture is densified and its constraining limits amplified. As a result it can no longer sustain any interval; and without interval time ossifies. It comes to a standstill and to a kind of unavoidable ever-presence. But this iterative densification also builds its own rhythm, eventually hypnotic, which perforates the condition of time altogether. It opens time to a beyond in which normative order and its conditions no longer hold. The repeating images double this by preventing any narrative sequence from unravelling. Through such rhythm, the gaze is carried beyond the factual images of relentlessly landing aeroplanes to an experience of the tragic condition of humanity irremediably confronting the power of technology and its own entrapment. On the other hand the machinic potential and power of technology conveyed by the aeroplanes is taken to such a level of excess by the interminable iteration of the images that this power returns as powerlessness and simultaneously excessive impotence. This is the remarkable tragic register of the sequence. The realisation of this *aporia* is a fundamental condition of classic tragedy and Herzog constructs the same heroic confrontation as a prelude to *Fata*

*Morgana*'s core message—the loss of the mythological, the consequent laying waste of nature, the consensual role of human beings in this waste and the longing for a sort of repatriation to originary and paradisiacal being. *Fata Morgana* means "mirage." Its landscape is the desert as wasteland—a waste ground for the detritus of the machineries and machinations of war and a limbo for the abandoned, the eccentric, the marginal and the lunatic.

*Lessons of Darkness* (1992) achieves a similar *ekstasis*.[74] Here, Herzog captures scenes of the burning oil wells of Kuwait following the Gulf War. The tempo of normal documentary coverage of events in the media at the time restricted images to short sequences. Here, Herzog films them in long sequences with persistent attention to the human, environmental and aesthetic tenor of events. In his own words, he films them according to "another *timing*, another patience, another insistence. I filmed them for the memory of the human race."[75] This determined gaze has its own determined tempo—a relentless dwelling-with the image that affects deeply the chronological dimension of the events, shifting them into a different temporal register. The already extraordinary scenes now become super-ordinary. That is, they begin to engage significance whose scale and dimension are outside the event, outside the image and the shot. The conjunction of the images' extreme graphic quality, the apocalyptic character of the soundtrack (Mahler's *Götterdämmerung*; Verdi's *Requiem*; Pärt's *Stabat Mater*), and Herzog's solemn voice over narrative combine to take the factuality of depiction into a heroic and sublime register.

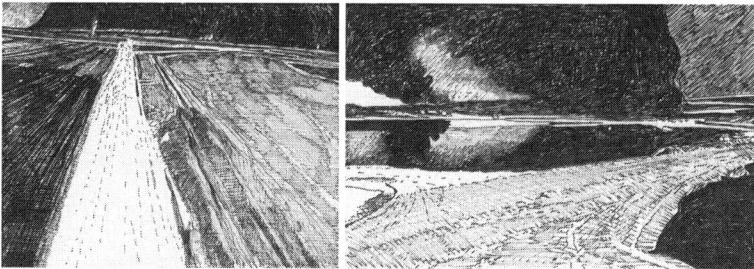

The double tempo of these scenes—the actual time of the events and the dramatic or heroic time of their significance—parallel a second doubling which is recurrent in Herzog's cinema. This second double is that between power and powerlessness—or rather, between power as outrageous excess of potentiality and its other face, the frailty of impotence. A further parallel is the doubling of the gigantic, associated with excessive power, and the miniature, associated with frailty; or again between the grotesque (chaos) and the admirable (order). In all cases, the pairs are not opposites, antinomies or complements. They are two faces of a single phenomenon alternating one in the other—powerlessness being only one aspect or moment of power.[76] What Herzog films is in fact the *hubris* that accompanies the degeneration of excessive power, or the moment of its catastrophic ruination. Hence the retributional, ethical and deeply human character of his cinema. At another level, Herzog's meditation on power and *hubris* can be read in terms of the cinematic image itself. The image imposes itself as pure presence, as a taking place of the power of the gaze and the gaze of power. Advancing into view, the image installs an *eidos*, a regime of seeing, a seeing and a being-seen. It conveys appearance as world-forming, showing-forth-through (*ap-per*) an occluding limit. This monstration is fundamentally a demonstration of power so that the arrival of every image is always-already the exercise of a corresponding appropriation. At the same time, every appearance is also an *aporia*, an encounter with the impenetrable materiality and resistance of the periphery, if not the grounds of representation. In that sense, every image preserves the traces and tracks of a difficult passage through the impasse of appearance. These traces are not contingent or accidental but constitutive of the image as such. They constitute its grain, its texture, its weight, the tempo of its age, the conditions of its arrival and the advent that it is.

## *"It is boring for one"*

Such instances of the dilated times of a shot can be usefully read through Heidegger's treatment of boredom (*Langeweile*). The tempo of a shot, the temporal structure of a film and the corresponding montage or editing which assembles images and sequences, form part of a film's setup. They constitute the properly technological condition of its production and reception. As such, and according to the alliance of *poiesis-techne* that Heidegger proposes, they also constitute a poetics of cinema—that is, a manner of making and of bringing to presence. In *The Fundamental Concepts of Metaphysics,* Heiddegger proposes the experience of boredom as a means of entering into a sense of attunement to philosophy and thinking. The theme of boredom is significant here because it plays out possible relationship between different kinds of temporality and moments of vision. As "fundamental attunement," boredom provides a kind of temporality that enables insight. As we saw with Tarkovsky, the "sculpting" of time and the engaged experience with time that is directly inscribed in the image sequence are fundamental to the perception of something essential in a scene. Tarkovsky manipulates duration in such a way as to make time a site and threshold of vision. Hence there is a prerequisite temporality for preparing the moment of vision and experiencing the verisimilitude of events depicted on screen. This is why Heidegger's treatment of boredom, and the temporalities associated with the three kinds of boredom that he foregrounds, is instructive for developing a perspective on the relationship between time and experience.

For Heidegger, boredom is the necessary disposition for philosophising. He elaborates three kinds of boredom. He does this sequentially even though there is no necessary logical relationship between them. First there is an ordinary kind of boredom, which he describes as the feeling we have when we get to a train station, we have missed the train and have to wait for the next train. We notice things around us but do not relate to them. We continually look at our watch and we get bored. He then moves on to another kind of boredom, which is not to do with the boredom of objects and events, but more with a state of mind in which time seems to have come to a standstill. We find ourselves suspended in a kind of limbo which time has vacated, leaving us empty and disengaged. There is finally the third kind of boredom, *profound boredom*, which prepares for a moment of vision. This vision is not directed outward but inward, into the one who sees, into the subjectivity that constitutes the being (*Dasein*) as being (*Sein*) there (*da*):

"At first it seems that what bores us are boring things and people and suchlike... In the second form of boredom, that which bores us manifests as time in its standing. It is now no longer the things surrounding us, nor one's own person that bores us. What bores us is time. It is what specifically leaves us empty and holds us in limbo. Certainly it is the time that we have left ourselves, the time which still remains fixed in the form in which we think we know it in the everyday, the time with which we reckon. Yet now in the third form of boredom what leaves us empty in the manner of entrancing us is the time of Dasein as such, and what holds us in limbo and impels us is this time in its possibility as moment of vision, the temporality of Dasein itself with reference to that which is essentially proper to it, and indeed in the sense of the making possible of Dasein in general: *horizon and moment of vision*. What bores us in profound boredom... what is solely and properly boring, is *temporality in a particular way of its temporalising*. What is boring is not things as such—whether individually or in a context—nor human beings as people we find before us and can ascertain, neither objects nor subjects, but *temporality as such*. Yet this temporality

does not stand alongside `objects' and `subjects,' but constitutes the ground
of the possibility of the subjectivity of subjects."[77]

The experience of boredom has more to do with the tempo of time than
its measurement. In boredom, time does not drag because it is too long but
because it is too slow, "too slow for us"—and because it "holds us in
limbo." The question of boredom is not the same as the question of time,
but boredom does conceal the essence of time. In this limbo we are held
by factical time, we are left empty. We want to overcome its vacillation, to
eliminate boredom by subverting time, doing something or being occupied
in some way so as to speed it up or eliminate its drag. We are left empty
because the things around us—the things at hand that constitute the
equipmentality of the place we are in—have nothing to offer us. They
"refuse" us and "abandon us to ourselves." Boredom arises out these two
conditions, these two "structural moments": "firstly being held in limbo by
time as it drags along, and then this coming to be left empty by things and
in general by the individual beings surrounding us."[78]

The second more profound kind of boredom does not involve simply
*becoming* bored by this or that, because in this case there is nothing
specific and no determinable context that we can become bored by. In fact,
it is the indeterminate that bores us. Time neither drags nor oppresses, we
do not find ourselves in limbo, "and yet we are bored. *It*—we know not
what—bores us." In this latter case, the experience of being left empty is
integral to and grows more profound from the depth of the situation. It is
essentially a comportment of seeking nothing from a situation or event and
of thereby obstructing something in ourselves, of allowing ourselves to
slip away from ourselves and from our circumstance in some manner
(*Sichzurücklassen*). In this casualness (*Lässigkeit*), through which we
abandon ourselves (*sich überlassen*) and leave ourselves empty
(*Leergelassenheit*), we give boredom leave to be (*seinlassen*), we let it be-
there (*da-sein*). In this second degree of boredom, the passing of time is
not something that occupies us and we do not find ourselves in limbo. It is
rather the converse—"time does not bind us to itself. It *abandons* us
entirely to *ourselves*, i.e, it leaves us free and lets us be entirely there,
alongside and part of things"[79]:

"Time does not bind us, it withdraws, as it were, and yet—by *abandoning*
us only for a period to our *being there and part of things, it does not release
us* entirely... It does not show itself as flowing away or as pressing and yet
it nevertheless shows itself—but how? In such a way that it seems as
though it were not there. It shows itself yet does not flow—it *stands*. Yet

> this doesn't not at all mean that it has vanished, rather this *standing of time is a more originary holding in limbo*, which is to say, *oppressing.*"[80]

In its standing, time "whiles" and endures, abandoning us but not releasing us, announcing itself as a more originary being in limbo. The enduring of duration "swallows up, as it were, the flowing sequence of nows and becomes a single stretched `now' which itself does not flow but stands." We let ourselves be entirely present to the situation, to whatever is happening, and in so doing, "we are cut off from our having-been and own future." These two, past and future, are not "factically removed" thereby. Rather, they suffer a modification, a "peculiar dissolution of the future and having-been into the mere present," which now subsists as a single stretched now, a standing time that endures, sealed off from the past and unbound from the future, with no memory of having-been and no futural horizon. This forgetting on the one hand and lack of prospect on the other compress the present into itself. They take away from the "now" any possibility of transition and fluxion "from not-yet to no-longer." All that remains for it is an abiding standing and persisting, whose experience of *"being held in limbo to time in its standing"* constitutes the second kind of boredom—"being bored with."[81]

Heidegger now aligns the two structural moments of boredom—being left empty and being held in limbo—to the fundamental condition or ground of being, of being-there (*Dasein*), of being-*the*-there, *in* which we are and *that* we are. Specifically, to the temporality proper to being, to the way the temporality of being temporalises itself. In the first kind of boredom, the conditions are imposed from the outside—it is the particular situation and circumstances in which we find ourselves that transpose us into boredom. In the second kind of boredom, the conditions are less "situation-bound." They arise from inside, *"from out of Dasein itself."*[82] Nevertheless both kinds of boredom arise relative to a particular situation. In the first we seek to pass the time so as not to engage with it and in the second we do not want to engage with it.

Heidegger then introduces the third and most profound kind of boredom. This boredom does not arise in relation to any particular situation or circumstance. It can occur "out of the blue."[83] The questions of passing the time or filling an emptiness which presented themselves in the first and second forms are not simply missing. Rather, they are "no longer permitted by us." This boredom overpowers us by our sense of its interiority in relation to our being, to our Dasein. In this way we are *attuned* to it and it compels us to engage with it—or in Heidegger's terms, to *listen* to it."[84] In this attunement we are *indifferent* to the circumstances in which we find ourselves. The indifference is not calculated or conscious. It is not the result of an abstraction or a generalised evaluation of ourselves, the people and objects around us, or the equipmental character of the circumstances. Rather, "all of a sudden everything is enveloped and embraced by this indifference." All the beings, objects and events that both populate and constitute it as a situation, as a place, "recede into an indifference."[85] "Being left empty in this third form of boredom is Dasein's being delivered over to beings' telling refusal of themselves as a whole... we find ourselves—as Dasein—somehow left entirely in the lurch, not only not occupied with this or that being, not only left standing by ourselves in this or that respect, but as a whole."[86] This being left in the lurch relates to a sense of possibilities or potentialities for being which are refused and left unexploited. The refusal refuses both prospect (future) and retrospect (past). The experience of this refusal is a third kind of being held in limbo. Each kind of boredom has a characteristic "time-structure." In the first, being held in limbo was characterised by a sense of time dragging; in the second by a sense of time standing. Now, in this third, it is characterised by a sense of timelessness; a remoteness from time or removal from its fluxion. At the same time, in this kind of boredom we become more aware of the weight of time and that "boredom can only be comprehended in terms of original temporality." Now Heidegger identifies this refusal of potentialities for being, for Dasein, as a *calling*, "which properly makes possible the Dasein in me"[87]:

> "It is boring for one. To such coming to be left in the lurch by beings' refusal of themselves as a whole there simultaneously belongs our being impelled towards this utmost extremity that properly makes possible Dasein as such. We have thereby determined the *specific being held in limbo of the third form: being impelled towards the originary making-possible of Dasein as such...* This *leaving empty that takes us into an expanse* together with a *holding us in limbo that intensifies extremity* is the originary manner in which the attunement that we call boredom attunes us."[88]

In this attunement Dasein is entranced within a surrounding "horizon of time" in which past, present and future are not articulated separately or severally. The time proper to this entrancing horizon is time *as a whole*.[89] In the emptiness of this entrancing time, the attunement produces an "undiminished leeway and space in which to play"—an opportunity in which the full situation of an action opens itself and keeps itself open. What is refused also becomes uncircumventable and therefore calls and impels Dasein to a "resolute self-disclosure" which is a "moment of vision" into "the fundamental possibility of Dasein's existence proper."[90]

Time is concealed since we have no experience of it as articulated chronology and yet it is also palpably present and impelling since we have the experience of it as a singular environing horizon.[91]

It is profound boredom which makes possible the "moment of vision of genuine action"[92] that ruptures the entrancement of time. The vision is not of a specific moment in time but a look into the three directions of past, present and future.[93] That moment distinguishes human Dasein from the animal's captivation and subjugation to their environing-world (*Umwelt*). It is the irruption of an in-between, a letting-be or letting-prevail, a projection that is the structural moment of world-formation. The moment represents an entrancement into something both distant and proximate, something "not merely initially ungraspable for conceptuality, but for our everyday experience as well... so ungraspable not because it lies in some remote and inaccessible realm which could only be reached by the highest speculation, but because it is so close to us that we have no distance from it that would allow us to catch sigh of it."[94] This is why profound boredom brings with it a state of suspension and dizziness which open to an experience of the uncanny.[95]

## Withholding potential

The state of entrancement and enrapture involves a double phase of being thrown and retained, being there and away. This withholding is read by Agamben as a "distress of reservedness," equivalent to impotentiality (*adynamia*) or passive potential that nevertheless constitutes originary openness. Agamben develops this theme in various analyses of the motifs of power (*potere*), potentiality (*dynamis*) and impotentiality in Aristotle, all of which are founded on the notion of privation:

"In its originary structure, *dynamis*, potentiality, maintains itself in relation to its own privation, its own *steresis*, its own non-Being. This relation constitutes the essence of potentiality. To be potential means: to be one's own lack, *to be in relation to one's own incapacity*. Beings that exist in the mode of potentiality *are capable of their own impotentiality*; and only in this way do they become potential. They *can be* because they are in relation to their own non-Being. In potentiality, sensation is in relation to anesthesia, knowledge to ignorance, vision to darkness... What is the potentiality of which, in the moment of actuality, there will be nothing impotential? It can be nothing other than *adynamia*, which, as we have seen, belongs to all *dynamis*: the potential to not-be. What Aristotle then says is: *if a potentiality to not-be originally belongs to all potentiality, then there is true potentiality only where the potentiality to not-be does not lag behind actuality but passes fully into it as such*. This does not mean that it disappears in actuality; on the contrary, it *preserves itself* as such in actuality... Contrary to the traditional idea of potentiality that is annulled in actuality, here we are confronted with a potentiality that conserves itself and saves itself in actuality. Here potentiality, so to speak, survives actuality and, in this way, *gives itself to itself.*"[96]

This experience of privation and impotentiality consists in withdrawal, concealment, occlusion and opacity. The occultation is constitutive of the originary disposition of Dasein's repression, retreat and evasive turning away—equivalent to the condition of profound boredom and its proper temporality. Agamben calls this the "passion of facticity." In that sense, profound boredom is identifiable with the Greek motif of *lethe*, conveying the fundamentally lethargic disposition whose withdrawal dilates into a moment of vision triggered within profound boredom itself and leading to an encounter with *a-letheia*—the "un-withdrawn," "un-concealed" and "un-disclosed."[97] And yet the point made by both Heidegger and Agamben is that concealment and unconcealment are by turns what prevents the being from full disclosure or exposure. They are a single gesture accomplished in two simultaneous phases of externalisation and internalisation, advance and retreat, such that potentiality is not erased in actuality but conserved in it as an enduring *dynamis*, a deferred or retained power of production.

By contrast, the normative idea of architecture promotes the full declaration and elaboration of potential. This is what Corbusier might have meant in his definition of architecture as "the masterful, correct and magnificent play of volumes brought together in light. Our eyes were made for seeing forms in light: shadows and light reveal forms; cubes, cones, spheres, cylinders, and pyramids are the great primary forms that light reveals well; the image is clear and tangible for us, without ambiguity. That is why these are *beautiful forms, the most beautiful forms.* Everyone is in agreement about this: children, savages and metaphysicians. It is the very condition of the plastic arts."[98] In this view, architecture is about articulating and giving full value to formal identity, differentiation and expression. It is a question of the legibility of formal relief, of foregrounding vertices, edges, profiles, surfaces and masses over against each other and against a backgrounding context. A parallel might be the detailed articulation of musculature in a Mr Universe—every muscle, sinew, cartilage, vein, joint, limb made distinctly legible or drawn forward out of flesh and body to stand-out individually and severally. Such a body is categorically not athletic because its state and capacities are not calibrated to any particular sport but to a kind of universalised image of athleticism and power that is factically good for nothing. Now and then this image has served as a model of beauty in architecture and elsewhere.[99] But there are clearly other registers in which the disassociation of parts and their radical differentiated expression is not as highly valued. Instead, as in certain kinds of early Greek and Buddhist sculptures, it is the undifferentiated and plump excess of flesh and the continuity of its materiality that are idiomatic. Fullness conceals the parts, withholding them in potential and expressing them only as the barest signs of a possible emergence and elaboration, or as the barest traces of a withdrawing monstration.

A key condition of architectural expression is the *degree of articulation* and elaboration played out in its formal programme. The simpler the overall form, the less articulated are its component parts, elements and assemblies. The more complex the form, the more differentiated and articulated they are. This does not mean that the simpler forms necessarily possess greater power or potentiality. So called *minimalist* architecture is in fact devoid of virtuality, since all potentiality has been effectively erased from it, to be supplanted by a single formal type—a cube, say, or a cylinder. At the other extreme—*maximalism* perhaps—the play of excessive differentiation and severance in the articulation of parts is taken to such a degree that equally nothing virtual remains. All potential has been exhausted in its being fully drawn out and actualised. In both cases nothing enduring is left and nothing remains to be drawn-out or imagined-into. In the first it is because of extreme poverty and in the second because of extreme saturation. Both are conditions of excess which exhaust potentiality. There is a radical difference between someone who says little because they have nothing to say and someone who says little because they hold silence and deferral to have strategic communicative value. The question is again one of potentiality, of maintaining action in virtuality, of storing and not expending power—at least until the opportune time.

An architecture of potential might then present itself, concerned with formal restraint and with quiet, slow elaboration calibrated to specific temporalities of engagement and emergence. It would be the architectural equivalent of dead time in cinema and slow food in gastronomy. Such architecture might not investigate the fully expressive mode of formal articulation but rather the inarticulate potentialities of forms occluded within the simple, the homogenous, and the smooth. Its temporality would not refer to the expressive diversity of multiple events, to any big event, to the articulation of significant moments, to speed or monumentality. Rather, it might simply frame a kind of waiting for what comes, a way of gathering the minuscule, the small scaled, the episodic, the fine grained, the quiet and the slow. It might frame the everyday in order to register and indicate such things as moments and phases of time, sunlight on soil or leaf, wind in foliage, clouds moving across the sky, sheets of snow and the sounds of human presence. It might be attentive and sensitive to the passage of time in its minutiae, the receptive character of places, the manner in which they gather memories of the past and projections of the future, the way that the "now" might not be experienced as a solid entity but as pure passage and trajectory. In short, an architecture of blandness rather than intense flavouring since, as Francois Jullien explains,[100] the bland (*la fadeur*) is not something without flavour but something in which flavour is enabled to grow and emerge in complex assemblages. Flavour is not imposed in advance, nor is it singular or differentiable. It develops in relationship and by inclination or declination. Emergent flavours defer one to another in a web of co-modulation. Individual flavours are never determinable as such, neither do they integrate seamlessly into blended singularities but maintain their incommensurability in relation to each other. Some advance leaving others to fade, or retreat leaving others foregrounded. Blandness is just this double movement—the advancing-withdrawal of flavours, their evanescent nascence. *Fadeur* is the flavour that interminably retreats and fades—like a half remembered dream on waking, where recollection advances with apparent certainty and palpable clarity while at the same time withdrawing inexorably into forgetfulness. The experience of this double gesture, which is also the *aporia* of a double bind, is something like the tension between potentiality and actuality, between the virtual and the real, between absence and presence and between retention and throwness in profound boredom. The entrancement of this horizon of contraflexure is also the threshold of entrance into vision.

The implication for cinema and architecture is to develop ways of working space and time at their core in such a way as to preserve and not expend potentiality. Maintaining a high degree of latent intensity and propensity within a work enables it to conserve its capacity for production, to remain adaptable and responsive, to keep itself available for the circumstantial and the unexpected, to never exhaust itself in bringing itself to light, to always leave open possibilities of reformulation and reconstitution. The manipulation of framing, space, time and narrative allow cinema to build the conditions and settings in which this scenario might be played out. But the possibility seems less immediately accessible in architecture—even more so since time, which provides the necessary dimension of change and mobilisation, is not generally accepted as an intrinsic dimension of architecture. In effect, the classical notion of architecture favours formal stability and stasis (order, *skhema*, *taxis*) over change and dynamics (*ruthmos*, *kinesis*). Architecture's enduring function is to convey permanence in the image of established symbolic, religious, political, epistemological, institutional and socio-cultural ideals. It does this by mobilising fundamental spatial qualities—such as centrality, hierarchy, axiality, symmetry, proportion and so forth—towards mimetic and representational ends. The spatial organisation of the cathedral or temple corresponds to customary beliefs about the structure and constitution of the world. A building might gather around a vertical axis which represents the link between earth and heaven. It might gather together the 4 directions of horizontal space and centralise them on an altar directly below a dome or spire. Its cross sectional and elevational fabric might be layered in a tripartite way—base, perforated wall and roof representing earth, humanity and heaven. The proportioning system used to determine a building's measure might be drawn from certain numerical or geometrical symbolisms associated with patrons, saints or gods; patterns corresponding to cosmic exemplars such as the golden section; periods, rhythms and cycles of times such as the solsticial cycle or the precession of the equinoxes; astronomical conditions such as the position of the pole star or mythical and ritual figures that engage sacred narratives or practices.

In all such cases, architecture is set up to serve both a mimetic and an instrumental function. By imitating divine patterns, a building establishes itself within a sequence of cosmic correspondences according to the hermeneutic formula *as above, so below*. Such correspondences also aim to institute alignments between human being, world and cosmos that are considered productive and beneficial. They make possible relays between sacred and secular with consequent potential to increase the benefits accruing from heaven. Buildings calibrated or "attuned" to cosmic order then operate as conduits or instruments to intensify and amplify the presence of the sacred in the everyday, in turn becoming apparatuses of redemption. In such architecture, if time and its passage feature at all it will be symbolic; and that symbolism will inscribe the associated dynamics of cycles, rhythms and motions into fixed arrangements that stabilise the flux of time in order to convey a sense of permanent eternity within the fabric of the building.

By any account, the five astronomical observatories (*Jantar Mantar*) of Jai Singh II, constructed between 1727 and 1735, are extraordinary examples of architecture where spatial organisation and form are conceived in direct relation to time.[101] The geometric and formal programs derive entirely from the astronomical, planetary, solar and lunar bodies, courses and trajectories which are manifest *inversely* by the three dimensional shapes, orientations, co-locations, scales and dimensions of the structures. The buildings are explicit apparatuses for the theoretical/scientific work of speculation and the religious/political work of control. They function by providing a fixed framework of lines, edges, surfaces and volumes whose shadows can be cast or against which moving bodies and constellations can be read. But they also work metaphorically as crystallisations and embodiments of temporality at various scales— diurnal, seasonal, annual, precessional, solar, lunar, planerary and so forth.

The structures formalise and bring the dynamic condition of mobile three dimensional spatial configurations of astrononomy to a standstill. They spatialise time. Their striking forms are not the product of imagination or design in terms of free plastic invention. Rather, they emerge directly from the precise, rigorous mapping of arithmetic and geometric patterns that are already there. And yet they strike us as inconceivably imaginative—almost as the unmediated autoproduction of the astronomical system itself. Nevertheless, the observatories of Jai Singh remain within architecture's primary role of the installation and institutionalisation of stability.

Apart from symbolic registers, architecture has the capacity to engage with time in more experiential ways. To know the time of day situates us within a chronological system and allows us to be oriented and to operate within that system. By contrast, not to know the time, not to be situated chronologically renders that situation ambiguous, uncertain and unstable. This might provoke experiences of wonder or anxiety, of ecstasy or distress. Even more troubling, it might furnish efficacious settings for the subjugation, institutionalisation, pacification and neutralisation of individuals and collectives. The widespread standardisation of built environments through planning, construction and environmental codes of compliance are causing the proliferation of homogenous buildings and spaces. Interiors required to comply with standard codes for space lighting result in spaces of evenly bright illumination that exclude the potential to reflect ambient conditions, diurnal and seasonal changes and other contextual variations. Because a sense of these is fundamental to maintaining a relationship with the ambient world, such spaces become effectively dislocated from their milieu and normalise that dislocation. Equally, environmental codes that legislate for maximum daylight and exclusion of eastern and western sunlight so as to reduce energy consumption promote a particular level of brightness together with an almost total lack of variation in ambient internal lighting conditions. The obvious results are sameness of spatial quality irrespective of functional programme, an extreme sense of isolation and disengagement from existential conditions and the lack of any sense of ambient temporality—or rather a smooth temporality that admits of no variation and therefore of no sense of time. The experience of disorientation, fatigue and other stress in airports, shopping centres, hospitals, libraries, museums, urban spaces and high density housing developments is not only due to a lack of formal distinctiveness and spatial wayfinding markers. It is likely to be more fundamentally due to a lack of temporal coordinates against which human beings locate and calibrate their activities and their life rhythms.

In its drive to install, represent and express a world or a state of affairs—cosmological, political, aesthetic, emotional—the normative register for architecture has always been a question of ontology and *being* rather than *becoming*; of product rather than process; of form rather than formation. The task it has always set itself is to be self consistent and conceptually coherent, rigorous and firm, clear in its conveyance of ideas, permanent in its standing and predictable in presence. When engaging matters of time and process it has always sought to translate fluctuations of all kind—ritual and mythological, cosmic and astronomical, musical and kinaesthetic, conceptual and tectonic, technical and material—into stable states of fixity, into embodiments and crystallisations of dynamic patterns. The *squaring of the circle*—which in geometry constitutes a steadying of the circle's indefinite mobility—is appropriated by architecture as a foundational strategy for arresting and spatialising time by calibrating it to the four directions of centralised existential space. Such cornering or entrapment of the mobile enables all manner of spatio-temporal correspondences to be ventured—for example alignments between morning, the east, spring and birth; and afternoon, the west, autumn and death—which are so fundamental to the organisation of the Christian church. The musical columns around the *mandapa* of the *Vithhala Temple* at Vijayanagar, South India, represent a spatialisation of music in a similar way to the Hindu Temple's spatialisation and localisation of ontological structures, mythical narratives, ritual processes and sacred presences. The ornamental programmes that encase civic decorum on the facades of innumerable town halls, libraries and theatres throughout Europe follow the same pattern in a different register. Recent developments in architecture—in spite of formal appearances and allegations to the contrary— mirror equivalent predilections. Whether exploiting the fantastical formal potentialities of parametric, genetic or biological modelling; informational, demographic, climatic or financial data flows; organic, geological and non-Euclidean evolutionary geometries; architecture invariably works the same terrain of metaphor, mimesis, translation and representation. The resulting buildings may be formally extraordinary and they may be extraordinarily well received. They will certainly conserve architecture's complicity in the manufacture and commodification of style; but what they cannot do is enable it to effectively displace its practices away from simulation and counterfeit. In the guise of dislocating architecture's logocentric foundations, or of being *relevant*, these approaches succeed only in replacing one kind of hegemony and representational regime with another. The double exhortation for architecture to conserve rather than eliminate potential, and to genuinely engage with processes of becoming and formation, is not deliverable within such regimes. A significant impediment is the recurrent sourcing of influences, knowledge, strategies and techniques from disciplines outside of the architectural, outside of the thematics and materialities that constitute architecture's proper tectonic ground. Instead of architecture literally building static simulations of concepts, temporalities, metamorphoses, transformations and other dynamic figures, it might become a framework or a setting that is accutely calibrated to the circumstantial dynamics active in every situation, receptive to the facticities of change and responsive to their patterns, capable of registering their fluxional traces and trajectories and enabling these to be sensed and experienced as they arrive and depart, present and absent themselves.

In this respect there are two potential dimensions of engagement. The first is related to the *architectural* as such and comprises both formal and programmatic aspects—that is, the geometric systems used to develop formal arrangements and the kinds of activities and processes that take place in and around a building. Both of these include aspects of potentiality and temporality. The geometric order of a building will have virtual and actual conditions to the extent that some aspects of the order might be explicitly articulated while others might remain latent. The relationships of tension between the explicit and the latent will characterise the propensity of a geometric system and the spaces developed out of it to retain mobilisational potential. Retaining potential means that geometries and spaces gain a *futural* aspect—a dimension of potential becoming that may or may not manifest but which nevertheless subsists as possibility. Likewise, the activities, events and occurrences that take place in buildings might to a large extent be programmatically determined according to a brief. However there will always be activities that remain unprogrammable because they are unpredictable and subject to the circumstantial conditions of occupation and use. These are in turn subject to opportunities and temporalities made possible by the human and environmental milieu. Both programmable and unprogrammable events bring with them characteristic temporalities and patterns of elaboration which will necessarily enter into relation with the temporalities and use patterns instituted by the building in accordance with its brief.

The unprogrammable represents a dimension of potentiality within buildings. To enable it to take place architecture must first acknowledge then build adaptive and transformative capacity within the programmatic, spatial and temporal structures that it fields. The simple trope for achieving this is *multivalency*—that nothing in a building (a space, a ledge, a column, a window, a threshold, a shelf, a garden, a public square, a wood, and so forth) should ever have a single register or a single use. This applies to all dimensions of the building—conceptual, functional, formal, technical, material, and so forth. It applies equally to all scales of endeavour, from public space to the fine grained articulation and furnishing of rooms. Implied in this is a shift from architecture as formal plastic expression to architecture as enabling infrastructure, as a framework rich in potential for adaptation, modification and transformation. The way to achieve this is not through the common tropes

of generalisation and flexibility, which erase rather than retain difference
and which invariably produce outcomes that are good for nothing in
particular. Rather, it is a question of designing for the unprogrammable in
direct, specific and quantitative ways. Firstly by elaborating multiple
possible scenarios, then by explicitly designing for these in detail and
finally by aligning and reincorporating the multiplicity of detailed designs,
each answering to a different scenario, into a lesser set of outcomes that
can function equally well in multiple ways.

The process is one of explicitation and elaboration of potential,
followed by implication, folding and withdrawing of that potential into
rarified figures in which it remains implicit yet open to indefinite
exfoliation. In that process, the issues of quantity and accuracy are
paramount. The notion of *loose fit* does not imply loose thinking or loose
measure. What makes a ledge good for sitting is a question of what kind of
sitting is meant and what kinds of dimensions pertain to that kind of
sitting—sitting to eat breakfast or dinner, sitting to read Plato or a fashion
magazine, sitting to gaze, lying down for a rest or to sleep, sitting alone or
with others, assisting in a seminar or lecture. Each of these is enabled by
very specific conditions of attention made possible by very specific
widths, heights and depths, degrees and kinds of enclosure, relationships
of aspect and prospect, light and acoustic conditions, timbre and
materiality of surrounding surfaces, and so forth. The design process
would account for multivalent facticity but then reabsorb that multivalency
into simpler articulations into which the multiplicity retreats. In the case of
a ledge for sitting, every ledge for every scenario can be drawn and
overlaid to suggest a range—that is, a multilayered *zone of potential,*
rather than a single average, which can serve to coordinate the options into
one solution accommodating all scenarios without compromise. The
example is basic, but the principle is clearly transferable across different
scales and degrees of design complexity.

In addition to building programmatic capacity, architecture can also
build multivalent adaptational capacity to incorporate dimensions of
potentiality and temporality. For example, the changing nature of building
occupation and use will prompt successive manipulations and changes to
spaces, sites and built form through processes of alteration, accretion,
maintenance and replacement. Generally these aspects remain uninflected
in the conceptualisation and production of buildings and are seldom
designed into them. Yet they are not inessential. In a very real way they
test the efficacy and fitness of architecture. Buildings that do not
incorporate adaptational potential can very quickly become inoperative
and unsustainable. Spaces and buildings which incorporate potentiality

and inflect temporality, which build adaptational and programmatic capacity, are responsive to circumstance and charged with possibilities. They provide clues and indications for initiating, mobilising and actualising inbuilt potential. Such spaces convey a palpable sense of their growing into *what they are becoming,* rather than conveying a permanent image of *what they are.* How then might architecture enable and support such unavoidable dynamic conditions? How might buildings be organised and made as resilient systems and frameworks for adaptation? How might such systems prompt and suggest the means and methods of adaptation? How might they not only accommodate inevitable modifications but allow these to become genuine and integral parts of an architecture of emergent rather than predetermined character.

Because places are inhabited and acculturated settings in which events have taken or will take place, they are also situations where specific spatialities and temporalities apply and can be experienced. Duration is never generic but always the duration *of* something specific, of a particular *occurrence.*[102] The moment we happen to be in a space will always be set within a double tension—simultaneously in relation to a space we have just been in and a space we are about to be in. There is always both recollection and projection. If the space we are in is definitively sequestered from others as in the case of cellular spatial organisation, or in spatial organisations that follow a linear and discontinuous narrative, then we will be cut off from both preceding and succeeding spaces. On the other hand, if the space we are in allows us to have a sense of the spaces we have been in and other spaces available to us then we will have an intimation of a having-been and a to-be in previous and future settings. In this case, the present moment of being in a space will be framed by and project both the past and the future. For example, looking from a dining room through into an external courtyard across into a study, beyond which the edges of trees define a hidden wood does not simply describe a literal, explicit itinerary. Looking from one space simultaneously into the several aligned spaces of an *enfilade* of rooms and spaces—each representing its own rhythm and pace, its own disposition to and framing of the world, its own associations of history and memory and its own projections into the past and the future—does not merely depict a utilitarian condition by way of a pragmatic perspectival gaze.

In both instances we are looking at spaces beyond severance and into the distinctive modes of being and the distinctive kinds of dwelling which constitute the everyday. We are looking into what actually happened in those spaces, into what we remember or imagined happening, into what will and what might happen, into what never and could never have happened. These places become settings and opportunities for invention and investment—a breathing into and furnishing of the everyday, a dramatisation and *poietic* production of being. In non linear, pocketed organisations of space, zones overlap, iterate or reflect, shift or fold in relation to reach other. At any moment, a particular space is in palpable relation with several other spaces. The system interweaves and interpenetrates spaces so that the several are present to each other at the same time. Looking into rooms from other rooms creates an impression of a collectivity and constellation of spaces rather than a singularity. If modernity valorised utility, it also valorised the corridor as sole circulational spine and sole provider of connectivity between spaces. A corridor, no matter how "open" it might be, creates relationships of singularity and iterating rhythms of entry-exit. This effectively disjoins spaces from each other since their only mode of communication is the corridor. The corridor does not belong to the order of rooms even though it assures communication between them. The communication is always singular—in the sense of the Latin *singuli*, meaning one after another. It always produces discontinuous sequences that separate as much as connect. The same effect is delivered by the idea of served and servant spaces in Kahn's work. Here, a hierarchical relationship is established through discontinuous compartmentalisation of spaces clustered in zones and defined purely by a kind of utilitarian dependence, based on the subordination of spaces considered servile and of inferior status which generally relegated to a "back" that services a priviledged "front."[103]

This utilitarian system of spaces—lined up along corridors, zoned above or beside servant spaces, or more often a hybrid of both—creates a linear and episodic disposition corresponding to a linear chronological concept of time. Moments exist severally and in severance, succeeding each other so that we can only be in one space at one time from one moment to the next. By contrast, in non-linear folded systems of spaces, at any time we exist in relation to other overlapping spaces and we have an intimation of other overlapping times. These might be arranged regularly and intensively, or irregularly and extensively in the manner of a palimpsest. The architectural trope for the former might be spatial compartmentalisation or *poché*, where the spatial trajectory is always constrained, closed and withheld. For the latter, it might be the *dérive* or architectural promenade, where the spatial trajectory always opens onto new directions, figures of movement and sequences. The latter spaces are experienced and inhabited by deferral—the present moment deferring to past events in other places and projecting possibilities of future events and places yet to be inhabited.

The second dimension of engagement is *contextual* in the broadest sense. This may include obvious aspects such as time in its various phases, climate, ecological, environmental and urban conditions which have the potential to affect the spatiality and temporality of architecture. The most direct way for architecture to register time is to engage with the ambient temporality of its context. Light and sound might be the most evident, although clearly all the senses contribute. The quantitative aspect of time—the chronological time of the clock—is too abstract a register to be useful in this respect. The qualitative aspect of time is in fact its condition of *seasonality*—irrespective of the scale of duration. A season is literally something that flavours time, that gives each moment, each day or month and each climatic phase its own distinctive character. The original sense of the word "season" is agricultural. It relates to the proper time for sowing, the *tempus*. It is also related to the notion and process of tempering, adjusting and moderating. The function of seasoning is to temper flavour so as to bring out or heighten the taste of particular foods and substances. In that sense, seasoning is a fundamental condition of conveyance.[104] The same applies for example to viticulture. A wine essentialises, incorporates or crystalises its *terroir*—the place and spatio-temporal conditions that have produced it and are assimilable in its taste.

In the notion of *kairos*—of opportune or proper time, of the time that makes possible an opening or gate (*porte*) as well as the conveyance of a beneficial influence—the prerequisite for efficacy is that an alignment be achieved between human or existential and cosmic temporalities. It is this alignment that perforates mundane chronological time, opening it up to cosmic influence. The sense of propriety in *kairos* is related to fitfulness— that the moment is fit for planting a particular seed, that the conditions which align at that moment will maximise the potential of the seed to increase. The notion of increase and magnification is fundamental to ideas of proper and opportune time. A season is a circumstance which affords a particular propensity, a kind of time in which certain things become possible, and others not. Seasons are therefore gateways that permit communication between different phases and levels, between different cycles and rhythms. They are times when potentialities might be conjugated and come into productive relationship.

Beyond reference to clocks to tell the time of day and calendars to tell the day of the year, our experience of qualitative time and seasonality comes by way of the senses, severally or in combination. Certain things— things we hear, smell, see, touch and taste—that denote particular events we know to take place at certain times, situate us seasonally in the world. These are embodied not abstract experiences, referring to existential temporalities that are both subjective or individual and common or shared. There are also personalised experiences of seasons, referring concrete times to the recollected times of memory associated with particular events. Buildings are always frameworks which set up certain orientations to the sensory and elemental conditions of the world. They necessarily engage with fire, air, water and earth; with sight, touch, taste, smell and hearing. They can do so accidentally or deliberately. If deliberately, buildings might become instruments for noticing and registering the elemental. Apertures might allow the motion of sun, clouds, wind, rain, smells, stars and planets to be registered within an interior. The orientation and organisation of spaces might amplify the experience of the seasons or of different times of the day. It might selectively foreground certain environmental processes, urban conditions or fine grained circumstantial variabilities. It might become an apparatus for reading the flux of time, the fluctuations of its setting or environment, a part of that setting or the processes that take place in it. To the extent that such fluctuations are permitted to enter into the field of architecture and to interact with the stable elements that constitute it as a fixed framework, they will modify and transform it. Architecture responsive to its context will be less prone to foreground fixity and permanence. It will be open to time and to the processes of change that proliferate around it. It might become a canvas that is sensitive and responsive to such changes. In doing so it might surrender all claim to identity founded on formal expression and distinction. At the limit, such architecture operates as a pure and empty framework for the advent and taking place of the moment.

One of the central functions of the windows in the Christian church—particularly in the early Gothic, Romanesque and Byzantine—was to contribute to the creation of otherworldliness within the interior space. This modification of existential coordinates involved the achievement of an altered temporality. The primary driver of this alteration was tectonic and symbolic. The shift from dark to luminous interiors between Romanesque and Gothic paralleled a theological shift, promoted by St Augustine, from a God identified with darkness to a God identified with light. But the early Christian church is not a dark space. Its gloom immediately transfers into gloaming—into a twilight suspended between darkness and light. Here, the windows do not function to illuminate the interior in a utilitarian sense but in a symbolic sense. Light is modified by the apparatus of the window—its frame and mullions; its dimensions and locations in the wall; its orientation and relation to the space; the physical, optical and chromatic properties of its glass and materiality, and so forth.

These all contribute to a transformation of ambient external light. The window is not an apparatus for framing and viewing the outside; nor a means of exteriorising interiority. From either direction, the window considered in itself has nothing to say. What it does is amplify the dislocation and deterritorialisation of the interior—taking it somewhere else, into an entirely different world. At the same time it establishes a new and altered relationship to the outside. The window not only mediates the ambient light that comes through it. By its occlusion of the outside and its erasure of a visible, differentiated world with which we can engage, the window also fundamentally transforms the inside-outside relationship. It does not function as a means of "dematerialising the wall," since its transparency is not to an outside that lies beyond its boundaries but wholly to an inside that surpasses its limits.

The windows of Chartres Cathedral turn a massive boundary into a pure and diaphanous glassy surface. But the glass does not *let-in* light, or even *filter* light, so much as *resist* it. This resistance defers an optical looking in favour of a materialised luminosity. Looking now becomes a tactile experience of the porosity of the boundary—not to an outside that lies beyond, but to the glimmer of its re-turning surfacing. The building does not function as a representation of Paradise. It does not locate, enclose or embody Paradise. Instead, the architectural fabric is entirely given over to a framing in which Paradise comes to present itself as the aura of a surrounding encompassing.[105] The windows wound and rupture the wall, yet the envelope is far from dematerialised. It skins a surface that seems to have no thickness or depth, no density or mass. It terminates the space but as a returning entrancement in which materiality appears as the pure vibration of an interminable reiterative liminality. In its deferral of distinctions between inside and outside, between the seeing and the seen, the windows slip from being seen *through*, to being looked *at*, to themselves *looking* and throwing glances. To stand at Chartres is to stand inside an outside, to stand in an interior that has been turned inside-out. In this arresting experience the outside is changed and transformed. Not that the outside, as profane, is dissolved for the sake of the sacred; or that an altered state of relationship to the world is brought about. Rather, the inside transfigures an outside by bringing forward a horizon of radiance.[106] Yet that outside—symbolically the sacred, Paradise or the transcendent— does not penetrate or enter the interior space. Rather, it remains in proximate distance, simultaneously present and remote.

The windows perforate the wall and connect two radically different ambiences, two milieux—the everyday and the extraordinary. They relate the rarefied symbolic space of the interior to the circumstantial world and its chronological temporality. But at Chartres, the movements and durations of that temporality are significantly altered. The light admitted into the space does not function to put shape into relief, to disarticulate forms or amplify them by delineating edges and vertices, surfaces and volumes. Rather, it is a light that diffracts, precipitates and condenses into pure atmosphere, materialising the intervallic void and making space itself palpable. The net effect of this, much like the *camera obscura* or the Arab bath, is to slow time down, to lengthen or dilate it. It is maybe less a question of conveying a sense of eternity than of producing interstitial, solsticial or tidal durations in which chronology is suspended. Ambient conditions are thus converted into a kind of twilight where the undecidability of the time it is renders possible and accessible a sense of time itself, of its fluxion and pacing, its rhythm and tempo. Slowing time shifts the diurnal into a different phase and a different setting—altogether larger, more expansive, serene and viscous.

In the typology of the Arab bathhouse (*hammam*),[107] the interior world is radically sequestered from the city. Its spatial organisation is cellular and divided into rooms with water contained in different ways and kept at different temperatures. Interiors are reverberant; the air is saturated with moisture and of viscous grain. The masonry fabric is generally of thick walls, vaults and domes perforated by small unglazed opening in various geometrical shapes. The interior is normally dim, depending on ambient light conditions. Natural light enters the spaces through the roofs either as sky illumination or direct solar rays. As in the *Baños Almirante* (Valencia, 14th C), the *camera obscura* effect is striking.

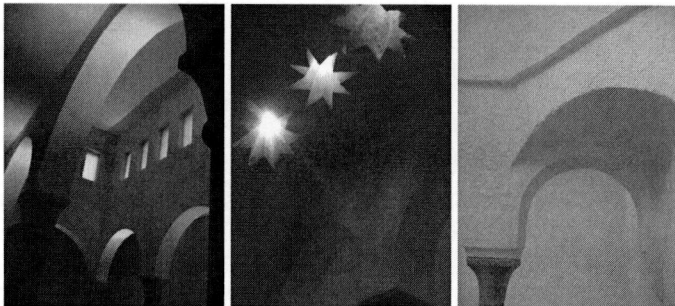

Depending on conditions, the space becomes a camera, transmitting images from the outside world onto wall and floor surfaces—the blue of the sky, passing clouds and muffled sounds. Together these qualities displace the rooms from the city and suspend them spatially and temporally from the ambient milieu. As time passes, light rays produce an inverse trace of the sun's apparent movement in the sky. As the light outside grows bright or dim because of clouds obstructing the sun, the interiors respond by very slowly pulsing so that the space itself appears to expand and contract, to grow and reduce in scale, to oscillate between extremes of brightness and gloom. The changing position of the sun is tracked by bright spots of white light imperceptibly moving across the floors and walls, edges, recesses and columns. These various qualities soon begin to conjugate into complex effects which radically alter the temporality of the space. Its remoteness from the vibrant city streets, the relative evenness of its illumination, the acoustic effect of mass construction and the extremely slow movement of light patterns and changes in light intensity combine to stretch chronological time and bring it to a near standstill.

The aesthetic effects are equally physiological, so that the unhurried and measured ambiance of the space becomes reflected in the rhythm and tempo of those using it. After a long time of remaining with the space and being attentive to changes that interminably manifest within it, the sun's path tracing itself incrementally and imperceptibly across the room becomes discernable as a moving line before giving way to a palpable sense of the earth's mass and inertia in rotational motion. The Arab bath does not simply engage with the ambient world, becoming receptive to changes of time and light. It fundamentally transforms the existential conditions and coordinates of one register of temporality into another. In effectively brings time into perceptibility. Along the way it enables an entirely different regime of attentiveness to become possible—a regime in which visuality is initially present but from which it eventually withdraws in favour of kinaesthetic and psychosomatic modes of reception that are better calibrated to a sense of the languid and the infinitesimal.

Another aspect of the context to which architecture might become receptive is its history and its memory, conserved not only in stories and documents, but in the very materiality of a site. There are multiple climatic, geological, hydrological, environmental and other conditions whose traces are preserved in natural sites and which might be drawn into the terrain of architectural conception and production. Chartres Cathedral achieves this through its remarkable floor. Made of large roughly scaled stone worn smooth by use, the floor slopes up from the entrance to the crossing. Either side of the entrance are long steps up to each aisle. The slope is in two directions—up towards the altar and down on either side as if following a ridge line. The slope appears slight, but underfoot and kinaesthetically it feels steep. The building straddles the ridge through an ingeniously simple and very beautiful cross-section that grounds the space and leads it on. Without geometrically centering, this groundedness stabilises the space which is otherwise extremely elongated vertically and along its axis. The grounding answers something in the windows. It is not a question of an alleged dematerialisation of the building's fabric. Rather, the floor works together with the windows to gather and envelop a space that turns inwards and outwards at the same time. The ancient presence of the hill is retained in a ground that wells up, conferring chthonic energy to the kinaesthetics of pilgrimage that the building enables. The interior is at the same time the most profound underwater space, the lightest forested clearing and the most telluric experience of earth. The still gloaming given to the space by the windows and the arcane presence given to it by the heaving floor both drown and lift—not one after the other in the manner of an alternation, rhythm, or oscillation, but both simultaneously so that one is in the other, the other of the other, and the trace of the other's advancing withdrawal.

There are then social and cultural traces of context, registered in particular landscapes, buildings, remnants, fragments and ruins, or else buried under parks, roads and structures. There are traces of criminal and tragic as well as felicitous events; of individual and collective accounts or experiences of massacres, appropriations, political victories and sporting achievements. Many of these find ways of persisting in publications, exhibitions, art works, recordings and films. Some only remain, fade or disappear with individuals. Others are dissimulated or erased in multiple ways. The majority are probably not the concern of architecture. But if Stiegler is correct in contending that at its origins the city (*polis*) constitutes an apparatus for collective and psychic individuation, for reconstituting an "associated milieu"—a polity, *politeia* or *civitas* that can be policed—then, like all technologies of grammatisation and all techniques of memorisation or *mnemotechniques* such as writing, informatics, cinema and the televisual,[108] architecture must be regarded as a *mnemotechnical object* capable of registering, storing, relaying and mobilising knowledge. Anciently this knowledge was sourced from within mythology and the outward surface of buildings communicated spiritual content and values to the public realm. The shift in priviledged knowledge from mythology to religion, imperialism, politics, commerce and industry before turning lately to informatics and scientific registers, is paralleled by equivalent shifts in the ornamental programme, expression and function of buildings. Now buildings are veiled with active digital surfaces, framed in exoskeletons, skinned in translucent metaphors of molecular networks or suffused with pervasive technologies to become interactive or immersive environments. At the same time they have become apparatuses for data retrieval, surveillance and control. In the midst of such breathless urgency might there remain a capacity for architecture to engage with less evolutionary, possibly more revolutionary or militant and at the same time preservational registers—for example with knowledge and practices that attach to the everyday, with the forgotten memories of individuals and communities, with the marginalisation, trivialisation or erasure of significant events, with spatialities and temporalities or worlds and times that were once common but no longer hold, and with the disappearing traces of global and local environments under threat of oblivion?

More fundamentally, it is in the nature of space as such—its structure and organisation, its materiality and assemblage—to furnish intrinsically multiple dimensions and opportunities for articulation. These multiplicities can be coordinated and resolved or maintained as indefinitely separable and juxtaposable. In the example of an orthogonal spatial system like the cube, the various incommensurable values and patterns integral to its order—irrational roots, axialities, symmetries, iterations, proportional subdivisions, and so forth—can be dislocated in relation to each other to form different overlaid systems of potential conjugation. When these patterns are retained in a virtual state the system conserves its rational coherence and consistency. When they are actualised the system tends to overcoding and chaos. In both cases the result lacks potential and charge since the totalised resolution of the first case leaves no room or impetus for elaboration, while the excessive overlay of systems in the second case depletes and shuts down systemic potential. But it is only where virtual and actual coexist in conjugations of deferred tension—only where they are set off against each other to produce spatial dynamics, inclinations and propensities—that the system can retain potential for transformation as well as the means of mobilising it.

# CHAPTER FOUR

# MATERIALITY

*"Matter,* if we must name in order to couple it with `form,' names the resistance of a form to its deformation. It is not an unformed 'content' that form would come to mold or model, it is the thickness, the texture and the force of form iself."[1]

## Light, sound, architecture

We are accustomed to perceive space visually and privilege light as the primary condition of architectural reception and experience. Le Corbusier's dictum that "architecture is the masterly, correct and magnificent play of masses brought together in light" endures in the formal concerns and visual emphasis of contemporary architecture. Yet in popular culture, the pre-eminence of light and sight (that something needs to be *clear,* that we concoct *vision statements,* that we say "do you *see* what I mean")* is paralleled by a compensatory valorisation of sound and hearing (that something *rings* true, that we say "do you *hear* what I'm saying"). These figures of speech concerning light and sound are traces of more ancient dispositions and attitudes to the world, some of which persist in various ways. They condition the way a work is conceived and made, how it is received, experienced and consumed. For example, in Hinduism the organ of spatial perception is the ear not the eye. Architecture, like the entire world of beings and existents, is considered to be a condensation of sound rather than a crystallisation of light. Numbers and geometric figures have sound bodies that the human body can engage and resonate with. Consequently, light and sound assume cosmogonic and symbolic dimensions and capacities for symbolisation beyond pragmatic, experiential and existential values. Their main function is not communicational, representational or instrumental but *presentational* and *poietic.* That is, their fundamental role is to carry or convey presence, to directly and concretely manifest realities, existences and beings.

Architecture operates as a receptor, modifier and transmitter of light and sound. The materiality of architecture is significant here. Materials absorb, reflect and transmit light, or modify the spectrum of white light in different ways. Tied to time and the seasons, light can make these palpable within architectural space depending on how it is received, modified and transmitted—for example high summer sunlight that bleaches colour or dissolves the edges and boundaries of form; low morning or afternoon light that reinforces contour and profile, that darkens shade and shadow or reveals form and its multiple articulations. Different qualities of light, related to different places and climes might also dislocate spaces from their context and send them onwards to other settings and locales. Natural light, particularly direct sunlight, also confers formative qualities to spaces. Diurnal and seasonal variations, the directionality of light and how it is admitted into the spaces of buildings all have a significant effect on the quality of space. Beyond the pragmatic need to adequately illuminate for use, these effects will contribute to the constitutive character of spaces, to their potential to refer to realities beyond the utilitarian, to their capacity to signify and connect architecture to broader levels of meaning—symbolic, aesthetic, emotional, existential, socio-cultural and so forth.

Likewise, materials absorb, reflect and transmit sound in different ways. The acoustic character of materials conveys reverberative and formative qualities to spaces. Some materials—particularly reconstituted materials—have little or no grain and therefore little or no timbre. Compare for example a solid Ironbark timber floor and one made of chipboard. The first is rich in resonant potential, the second is dull and leaden. There are timber structures in which the resonant potential of materials has been conceptualised and mobilised to create rich and evocative acoustic environments. But there are many more in which the materiality assumes a purely visual rather than sonic character. In the same way there are many buildings where light is used in purely utilitarian ways and far fewer where it contributes to atmospheric, emotional and dramatic affects.

The word *light* comes from the etymological root *LEGH, which means to join. Cognate terms such as *ligature* and *ligament* show its relation to the motif of joining and connecting; as do *league*, *legs*, *legislation* and *law*. Also cognate is the Greek: *logos* = word, speech, lecture. Articulation is from Latin: *ars*, which gives art and artifice—fundamentally processes of joining. As for the word *join*, this comes from the etymon *YEUG, *GEN, cognate with earth (Greek: *ge*), generation and knee (Greek: *goneus*). The knee is a point of articulation of movement, just as the joint functions as a point around which something pivots—a gesture, a force or an idea. The motif of light connects these three notions of speech (the word, *logos*), legislation, (the law) and connection/joining (generative pivot). The word *connect* derives from the etymon *NEK, found in *night, night, negative, not, knot, neck, nape, nap* and *map*. The key theme is of an emptiness clutched by something articulated, functioning as the pivot of a turning—for example, the vacancy of night, the hollow space in a knot, a knee joint, the hub of a wheel, the nap of a cloth or a landscape. In this web of associations, articulate and inarticulate, light and dark, radiation and absorption, advance and retreat, presence and absence, emptiness and fullness, remembrance and forgetfulness interminably double and eclipse each other.

The motif of the knot is aligned with weaving, where a shuttling play between horizontal and vertical threads of warp and weft constructs a fabric—that is, a network of knots whose structure and character depends on how the loom is set up and how the shuttle discriminates and directs the emerging pattern. The warp establishes a predetermined pattern-context within which certain possibilities can be manifest according to how it interacts with the weft. The shuttle discerns amongst latent possibilities open to the weft a selected number present in the predetermined order of the warp.[2] The various possible configurations are held virtually and statically in the warp and it is the visible and dynamic action of the weaver, controlling the weft through the shuttle, which manifests the actual pattern of the fabric.[3] Weaving has long been a symbol for creation. The demiurge is a master weaver, an *arche-tecton* whose *techne* or know-how is tied to techniques of assemblage and articulation. In the dialogues, Plato uses the motif of weaving to develop ideas about philosophical and dialectical practice. The key notion is one of the deconstitution or deconstruction of a given problem *at the joints*—an analytical process which loosens (Latin: *ana-lusis* = to loosen apart) and liquidates the knots that constitute the problem as a contused assemblage of ideas. Plato refers to the dismantling of a chicken carcass—not by hacking away at it indiscriminately, but by identifying the gaps and weaknesses which are located at the joints, then levering these knots open to separate the carcass in the most efficacious way. The shuttle has the same function in weaving. It moves in the gaps and interstices of warp and weft, infiltrates the hollows and fuses or names-together-across (*diakrinomen*) warp and weft into an interconnected relation, which for Plato is the synthetic fabric of discourse—a "weaving together (*sumploxe*) of forms."[4] Of significant interest is the implication that the joint is a site of both strength and weakness—a pivot of assemblage and disassemblage, construction and destruction, creation and catastrophe.

Sound contributes to architectural experience in two major ways. Because of their dimensions, their manner of assembly and their material conditions, spaces and buildings have inherent acoustic characteristics. Reverberant or absorbent, hollow or viscous, perforated or self-contained, the acoustic qualities of a space condition not only its functionality but also broader registers and capacities of sense and experience. A structural system that conveys all its dead and live loads directly to the ground will give a building or space a substantially different resonance to one where loads are indirectly conveyed to the ground by way of transfer beams and cantilevers. The first will feel static, the second reverberant and dynamic. The building itself might operate as a stretched string instrument, sensitive to ambient vibrations and itself emitting sound, or to a sailing boat whose tackle tensions it against the wind. The floor of the building might be sprung underfoot, its stability might be tenuous, its carcass might receive and transmit sound and movement from other spaces, rooms or floors. The walls might deafen, muffle or amplify ambient sound. Components might be detailed and joined to sound hollow and suggest hidden spaces or to sound firm and convey the completeness and self-sufficiency of the assembly.

The second way in which sound affects architectural space relates to the framing of ambient sound. Whether next to a busy road, the ocean or a forest, a building might exclude or include ambient sound to various degrees. Propagated in time, that sound manifests certain life patterns—the volume of traffic at peak hour, birds at dawn, evening wind through a grove of pine trees, a neighbour's yelping dogs, garbage trucks on an early weekday morning, and so forth. Such sounds enter a space and form part of it. They contribute to the character and quality of space, connect it to events, to other beings, to diurnal, nocturnal, solar, lunar, seasonal and other cycles. They might relate to present events but also evoke the past, subjecting space to the operation of memory which invests places with significance. Because it is time-based, sound will also animate or activate space. It will contest space's formal permanence and stability and connect it to a wider world of mutation, change and transformation. Sound brings into space aspects of the circumstantial, the conditional and the contextual. It opens architecture to its milieu, expanding and deterritorialising space, exposing it to what is outside and radically other, to what might threaten its constitutive firmness, order and consistency. It can be a formative and integral part of the set up of a space, of how it is perceived and engaged with, and of the opportunities it affords.

By way of example, consider an unexceptional lecture room in an ordinary university in southeastern Australia. This room happens to have large windows and high sills overlooking a semi enclosed courtyard thick with evergreen foliage. A class is timetabled on late summer afternoons when the university is largely evacuated of students and outside activities, and the campus is extremely quiet. Around that time the outside spaces become filled with Kurrajong—a kind of local crow with a shrill, resonant and iterative call. The sound of these birds echoes around the gardens and hard surfaces of the buildings outside. The effect is to hollow out or deepen the perceived boundaries of space and bring a reflective, twilight quality to the room. This might be amplified by the quality of light, affected by the orientation of the room away from the setting sun, and the large windows which convey high even and fading light from the eastern sky, filtered through limp, fine and thick foliage. In this room, light and sound work together in more than an ambient way. They have the marked effect of changing the conditions and qualities of the space, but also of conditioning or tempering the disposition of the students, the lecturer and the kinds of interactions that might take place in it. If the lecturer is fortunate, her students might be more absorbed and pensive and the lectures more contemplative than they would be elsewhere or at other times.

In a similar vein, consider a beach in the same region after a substantial late afternoon thunderstorm. Out to sea, dark mauve clouds cover the sky through to the eastern horizon. The sea is very sill and transparent to the white sand below. Behind and beyond the rooftops that cap the flat suburban expanse of the beachside valley, a high ridge obscures the western horizon. The dark clouds extending to the west do not quite reach this ridge, so that as the sun drops below them, it sends rays under their cover out to sea. The low rays are deep orange and throw the entire scene into heightened chromatic contrast. The clouds above the beach deflect these rays and send them vertically down through the glassy surface of the sea. Dotted around and standing waist high amid the shore are a dozen or so people, very still and looking about. The descending rays are again deflected off the white sand under the water, then upwards to light up the under-surfaces of people's faces and skin in an orange glow. The scene lasts only a moment but has a pervasive effect on the people who are thrown into radical quiet, matching the radical stillness of the event. The effect of light has transformed the space and materiality of the beach, as well as the temperament and countenance of the bystanders who are now left with an enduring memory that will always colour their recollection of this place. Normal boundaries between sky, sand and water—even the constitutive opacity of the sea and the horizontality of the beach—have been rendered ambiguous. Those standing find themselves suspended in a weightless limbo that converts the usual boisterousness of the site into a calm waiting and watching.

Architectural parallels are evident in the traditional *havelis* of Rajasthan, the long houses of Vietnam and the shearing sheds of remote Australia. Light deflected from a lush garden, a moist green forest floor or dark red and hot dry sand lends its chromatic and thermal qualities to the space it invades, illuminates and transforms.

An exceptional instance is the *Royal Hammam* at the Red Fort, Delhi. Here the interior space of three contiguous apartments around a central marble pool is effectively separated from the ambient glare, heat and dust outside through minimal openings in the external walls. The floor is a network of marble platforms raised above a pattern of pools and waterways that represent Paradise, or an emblematic distillation of the Yamuna River, which flows just below the Fort's boundary. The arched and domed ceilings are inlaid with mirrors in crisscrossed lines that follow the geometric pattern of the faceted surfaces.

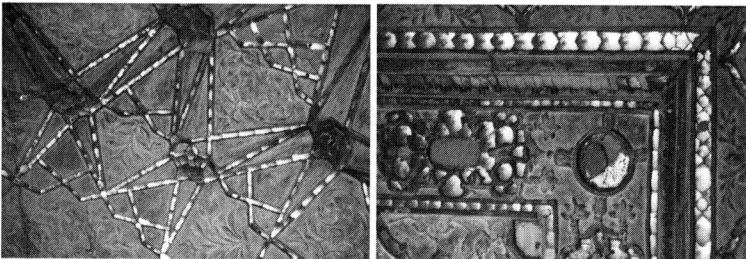

What little light enters the interior from the side walls is reflected off the water surface and up into the web of mirrors within the domes, then back down to create an interminable fluxion and dance of luminous shards. The concrete boundaries of the space are dilated so that it feels indefinite in extent. Its gravity and radical interiority are also transformed into a levitating sense of the in-between. The building's density and mass are dematerialised into fractures of pure light, whose original effect at night, with the space lit only by naked flames, must have been remarkable.

The interior is a conjugation of spaces cooled by the building's mass and shaded water surfaces, darkened by the lack of ambient light, protected from dust by relatively small openings and water and animated by the reflections of fractured light on liquid, marble and the geometric patterns of mirrors. The alignment of form, light, sound and materiality here achieves a substantial modification of thermal comfort, while simultaneously displacing the coordinates of the space from pragmatic to symbolic registers, from earth to Paradise, from ordinary to extraordinary existentiality. This works spatially but also in time, since the space also gains a different, slower, temporality as a result of its transformation.

There is an enduring conjunction of sound and light, particularly in traditional cosmogonies which narrate the creation of the world. In mythology the most charged and commonplace elemental symbol is the conjugation of lightning and thunder.[5] Together these represent a break, tear, or rupture in the everyday and material fabric of the world. This startling injunction is productive. It unclenches alignments, opens up opportunities and precipitates the advent of unmanifest potential. The Judeo-Christian symbolism of sound and light is particularly rich. The world and all its content are created by and identified with the demiurgic pronouncement of the Name (*nomos, nomen*), Word or Verb (*logos, eirein, verbum*). The world is uttered into existence and that utterance shines forth or radiates to open up, fill and measure out space and time. Sound and light are conjoined in the *Numinous*, the luminous aura of the Name—a term coined in the early twentieth century by Rudolf Otto to describe religious experience in terms of the Sublime, which associates mystery, dread and fascination.[6] A parallel cosmogony privileges light as the creative element, articulating beings and existents out of an undifferentiated darkness by mobilising its potential and latent propensity. Here, darkness represents chaos—not as disorder but as inarticulate or as-yet-unarticulated order. Light makes visible the contours, edges, limits and forms of beings concealed in the potentiality of darkness. Sound and silence are conceived in an equivalent cosmogonic way. Sound is the articulated mode of silence which occludes all resonant and enunciative possibilities. Like darkness, silence conceals and holds configurations of sound in the same way that a circle conceals an indefinite sequence of two dimensional polygons and an array of three dimensional volumes. Light, sound and form develop out of the divisions and repartitions of an undifferentiated milieu operating as ground of manifestation—for example, the indefinite chromatic variations of white light, the multiple tonalities and shades of darkness, the inconnumerable names that are modulations of the *Logos*, the interminable numbers and spatial configurations conjugated from the point and the various durational phases and cycles of time modulated from the instant.

An elemental approach to architecture and cinema is useful in this regard. The classical Greek, Hindu and Judeo-Christian views agree on five elements and five corresponding human senses calibrated to the perception of each element: fire, light and vision; air and touch; water and taste; earth and smell; the *quintessence* ether and hearing. Existing things are composed of all five elements in various proportions. The particular combination of elements determines the character of an existent, its constitutive structure, disposition, propensities and behaviour. This applies to animate and inanimate beings, places, peoples and individuals. Each element and each sense associated with it tends to a limit, which is shared with and touches on other elements and senses. This gives rise to the possibility that at their limit, elemental conditions have a propensity to overflow their normal boundaries and milieux, and to trigger affects that properly belong to others. It might be that at a certain limit of luminosity, light will appear to condense and take on the viscous or palpable conditions of earth or water, at another it will appear to mobilise and take on the rhythmic or pulsational character of sound or air. This is mainly due to the presence in all things of all the elements in various constitutive proportions, but more essentially to the inherently vibrational character of elemental existence, ranging from the most decelerated vibrational state in the case of rock to the most rarefied in the case of light or ephemeral realities such as emotional, conceptual or spiritual states of existence. In that sense all things are capable of being smelt, felt, tasted, seen and heard as long as the sensory apparatus has been properly calibrated and prepared.

In Book Ten of Republic, Plato recounts the tale of Er as an allegorical narrative of the last judgement and reintegration of the world with its origin.[7] The story follows the souls of the departed on a four-staged journey to "a mysterious region," where Plato conjugates metaphors of weaving, space, time, sound and music, light and colour. Precipitated by thunder, the souls encounter an extraordinary construction resembling an armillary sphere—an astronomical model or world-machine. Eight interpenetrant whorls are sheathed around a luminous Spindle of Necessity, which stands as a cosmic axis to the whole construction,

"extended from above throughout the heaven and the earth, a straight light like a pillar, most nearly resembling the rainbow, but brighter and purer...

they saw there at the middle of the light the extremities of its fastenings
stretched from heaven, for this light was the girdle of the heavens like the
undergirders of triremes, holding together in like manner the entire
revolving vault. Its staff and its hook were made of adamant, and the whorl
of these and other kinds was commingled"[8]

These eight sheaths correspond to an astronomical and symbolic
structure numbering the outermost sphere of fixed stars and the seven
spheres of Venus, Mars, the Moon, the Sun, Mercury, Jupiter and Saturn:

"The first and outermost whorl had the broadest circular rim, that of the
sixth was second, and third was that of the fourth, and fourth was that of the
eighth, fifth that of the seventh, sixth that of the fifth, seventh that of the
eighth, eighth that of the second... And that of the greatest was spangled,
that of the seventh brightest, that of the eighth took its colour from the
seventh, which shone upon it. The colours of the second and fifth were like
one another and more yellow than the two former. The third had the whitest
colour, and the fourth was of a slightly ruddy hue; the sixth was second in
whiteness."[9]

This organisation is tied to the ancient heptatonic musical scale, the
musical octave of two tetrachords and the structure of the lyre. Plato
conjugates four states of number that later became the scholastic
curriculum of the Medieval *Quadrivium*—static non-dimensional number
(arithmetic), static number in two and three dimensions (geometry),
arithmetic in motion (music) and geometry in motion (astronomy). The
scheme is centred on the Sun, the brightest sphere corresponding to the
musical tonic or *mese*; with the Moon, the swiftest spherical revolution
corresponding to the *nete* and Saturn, the slowest spherical revolution
corresponding to the *hypate*. The whole Spindle revolves in one direction
according to the movement of the Same, while the inner whorls revolve in
the opposite direction according to the movement of the Different. Here
Plato juxtaposes another conjugation between time, light, speed, rotational
direction and music. The three fates *Lachesis* (the past of "things that
were"), *Clotho* (the present of "things that are") and *Atropos* (the future of
"things that are to be") turn the inner and outer, the outer, and the inner
spheres respectively. Each sphere is given the voice of one of eight sirens,
who together chant the eight notes of a cosmic "harmony of the spheres."
Each planet has a distinctive *ethos* within the whole astronomical system,
correlated to the character of tones within the modal musical system that
gives sound-body to proportional conjugations of number.

The entire construction is an apparatus of discrimination and
judgement according to which each soul is allotted its destiny. Once

judged, souls undertake a last journey "to the Plain of Oblivion, through a terrible and stifling heat, for it was bare of trees and all plants, and there they camped at eventide by the River of Forgetfulness, whose waters no vessel can contain." Drinking this water brings forgetfulness and a return of souls "upward to their birth like shooting stars." Only the bold Er, "son of Armenius, by race a Pamphylian," is prevented from drinking the water, and so is able to return to "save" the tale, and through the tale to secure for those remaining a safe passage across the River of Lethe—threshold of lethargy, forgetfulness and death. Plato's fantastical narrative functions on numerous levels—philosophical, scientific, musical, moral, political, spatial and temporal. At every level it is saturated with materiality in every sense and for all the senses—sound, music, light, colour, water, taste, wind, touch. In it, light plays a central role as connective *axis mundi*, pivot of space and time and locus of discrimination. Its motion manifests as the multiple resonances and luminous material emanations of harmonic proportions that underlie the world's ontological and existential rhythmic structure.

Light engages more obvious symbolic registers in sacred architecture—for example at Chartres Cathedral which is dedicated to the Virgin Mary. Here, the deep blue windows plunge the interior into an oceanic gloaming. The visceral and emotive aesthetics of the space doubles the symbolic character of Mary, whose subjectivity is a pre-eminent site of interiorisation, circumspection and individuation. By contrast, Palladios' *Il Redentore* works a cerebral and intellectual aesthetic in which white, undecorated, evenly lit and featureless spaces suggests the undifferentiated and unmanifest unity from which all existence develops and into which it will be reabsorbed. Evidently such lighting strategies have little to do with the pragmatics of health and safety or wayfinding that one might encounter in a hospital or a superstore, or with the ubiquitous prerecorded messages in lifts and trains that immobilise and disable the citizen within an impoverished mundanity. The lighting of Chartres and *Il Redentore* create distinctive places which transport the visitor somewhere else. They modify the ambient environment to such an extent that they bring about ruptures in its fabric, enabling the emergence of other disjunct spaces otherwise dissimulated in the context of the everyday.

There is then the pragmatic lighting of what Marc Augé has called the *non-spaces of supermodernity*, where it takes on a homogenising function or operates as an apparatus for surveillance, control and the mobilisation of consumption. Hence the ubiquity of its radical *glare*—a kind of glaring look emitted by vast commercial buildings, or by external "sensor lights" that convert every citizen into a potential trespasser and every public realm into a no-go zone and site of interrogation. This glare of supermarkets, airports and shopping centres effaces chromatic difference by the exclusion of contrast and atmosphere. It stuns and immobilises the citizen, erases and wastes critical singularities in favour of a crowd wholly subject to consumption and removes any capacity of space to yield to the unexpected, the surprising, the strange and the uncanny. This effacing glare may well appear nefarious. Yet it is clearly implied in the predisposition for white unadorned architectural materiality broadcast equally by Le Corbusier in the 20$^{th}$ C, as by Vasari and Filarete's critiques of the Gothic in the 15$^{th}$ and 16$^{th}$ C. In Le Corbusier it may have been to reanimate a kind of Platonic archetypalism and essentialism; to erase the old city in the utopian guise of valorising hygiene; or to champion the modernist ideals of *carte blanche*, *tabula rasa* and *creatio ex nihilo*. In Vasari and Filarete it may have been to promote professional and financial self-interest among friends and acolytes in the guise of conducting a moralising and political debate; or to valorise a new aesthetic. In any case, such designs on the world are seldom mutually exclusive. In Antonioni's cinematic imagination however, this glare assumes a radically different metaphorical function. There, excess of light conveys the withdrawal, evanescence and dematerialisation of the world, its conversion from utopia to dystopia, together with the dysfunctional world-forming or place-making capacities of the human being.

## Light and sound in cinema

In mainstream cinema, ambient conditions of light and sound create stable settings for narratives to unfurl in real time and space. Materiality is backgrounded and operates as a support or ground for narrative development. Light and sound do not contest but fill-in and round-off the story line. Such might be the case with documentary or straightforward historical genres, where the aim is to depict realistically the environments in which narratives take place; but it does not necessarily exclude artifice. D. A. Pennebaker's *Don't Look Back* (1967) is ostensibly *cinema verité*, yet the control of light, dark, shadows, sound and silence, time, rhythm and duration are all deliberately contrived, cut and assembled through editing and montage to heighten the sense of nocturnal realism, of *being-there* with Dylan, the journalists, acolytes and fans, the taxis, hotel rooms, streets and venues in which the action takes place. It is a recurrent declaration of cinematographers that one has to engage a high level of artifice in order to depict an event realistically. At the other extreme, but also strangely adjacent, is Jarmusch's *Year of the Horse* (1997). Here, the materiality of film is integral to its cinematic and semantic content. Rough grain and shuddering images, largely produced by hand held Super-8 equipment shot in available light, appear as pictorial equivalents to Young and Crazy Horse's rough soundcapes and expansive, rippling sheets of pure vibration. The dematerialisation of light into colour field sequences of streaks, stains and mists of shifting colour convey the music's capacity to dissolve the formal stability of things, as well as the *depaysement*, disorientation and interminable deterritorialisation of a band on the road. As for sound, other than faithfully rendering the music in all of its loose, grainy and weighty presence, Jarmusch interposes two moments by splicing an image sequence from a 1976 concert of Young's over a soundtrack of the same song performed in 1996. The synchronisation is seamless. With it Jarmusch concatenates a twenty year interval into a single coalescence of past and present. In *Year of the Horse*, light and sound are not used to simply communicate the narrative of a musical road movie. They are integral to the construction of the film, to its tectonic organisation, its material grain and its existential presence. Nevertheless, in this and Pennebaker's film, light, sound, materiality, montage and the apparatuses and technologies employed all function to convey a level of realism or hyper-realism which amplifies yet remains faithful to the subject matter.

In Jarmusch's *Dead Man* (1995), Young's persistent and ethereal improvised soundtrack also amplifies key themes of the narrative, but it simultaneously transports the story into broader registers. The protagonist's peregrinations through the wildest and most desolate of Wests, is also an initiation into what Heidegger called being-towards-death—the fundamental disposition and destiny of beings. Dead man walking, cipher of homelessness and clueless eremite subject to a destiny that escapes him, William Blake—"foolish white man"—fades at the last into the oblivion of a landscape suspended in an effaced horizon between earth, sea and sky. The pace, articulation, harmonics and dynamics of the music parallel the protagonist's wandering into the unknown. But Young's multilayered soundtrack combines guitar chords, harmonium, characteristic feedback, rumblings, engines and slamming car doors in an acoustic assemblage whose anachronism displaces the historical time of the film somewhere between the wilderness of a sublime landscape and the catastrophic potential of instrumental technology. Just in case the thematics don't register, the town where Blake is mortally wounded and where his world begins to unravel is called Machine.

With Bergman, light, darkness and colour take on predominantly emotional and psychological dimensions. In *Cries and Whispers* (1972), the light quality of an autumnal landscape and the vibrant red of interiors parallel physical and emotional conditions in the characters. The sequence at the summer house in *Persona* (1966) takes place in light that is atmospheric and wholly ambient. Light condenses almost as if refracted through a fine mist which saturates the space inhabited by two women— one speechless and convalescing, the other her nurse. This space has several registers. It conveys the distance between the two women, whose individual identities are emergent and ambiguous conditions that eventually merge into a single face, a single persona. The diffracted luminosity of the setting also suspends chronological time, sending it into the *temps mort* of an evanescent watching and waiting. This suspended time which is also a dilated duration, non-time or whatever-time, conveys the uncertain rhythm, process and place of the womens' distinctive individuation and subjectivation. The characters enter into and emerge from this mist as if of one substance with it, as if differentiations and modulations of its precipitated materiality.

Bergman explained that for *Winter Light* (1963), a strict formal construction was deployed using a bare architectural setting (a church in Skattungbyn, Dalarna) conjugated by the grey, shadowless light of far north Sweden in November. The way in which light moved through the interior of the church was carefully mapped and a kind of artificial light that casts no shadows was devised. Filming interior scenes in the church, Bergman accentuates the dislocation of the characters from their context by setting up strictly symmetrical and static shots of the central axis, altar and priest which he alternates with asymmetrical shots of people as they tentatively move about. With the first he amplifies the bare, reverberate and empty space's highly structured, hierarchical and religious character. A combination of the hollow sounding bells which toll the film's opening sequence and the priest's sombre disposition and tone reinforce the constraining character of this context. With the second he films people in all their awkwardness, uncertainty, resignation and *humanity*. Central here is Bergman's emphasis on the look and sound of peoples' clothing—stiffly done up and starched but awkwardly folding and rustling as they move, in contrast to the silence of the space and the tacitly enforced silence of the occasion. The even light throws no shadows, produces no contrast and only barely delineates form. The outlook from windows is to an effaced winter landscape also devoid of contrast, in which bare interlaced branches read as an imprisoning briar. The church interior is consequently unresponsive to the changing conditions outside, giving it a static, disassociated quality. There is no architectural ornamentation, and the little decoration there is reinforces the religious and hierarchical tone of the space—a wooden triptych above the altar, implements of the mass, carved balusters of the communion barrier, pointed arches which frame the priest, clustered pilasters buried into the plaster of walls. In this way Bergman creates an impassive setting, distanced from the human condition of the characters that move within it. He amplifies the space's disassociation from the ambient world and the characters' disassociation from the religious world they uncomfortably inhabit. All of this is achieved largely by the way he arranges, frames and films the architectural materiality of the space and the embodied materiality of the characters' faces, clothing, disposition and movement. In a striking sequence, Bergman frames the actress Ingrid Thulin in closeup, straight to camera, speaking the words of a letter she had written to the priest that simultaneously questioned his faith and declared her love. The woman's face is itself a screen, sensitive to the turbulence that wells up and surfaces as the materialisation of her emotional undergoing. In spite of evident inner strength, she is not presented as a distinctive identity or a subject without conflict. Rather, her face registers the emergent subjectivation of the subject that she is and is becoming. In this case, the materiality of the body and the face are not neutral or passive. They do not function as grounds of reception but as contested fields and sites of advent in which any sense of ground, background or substance become indistinguishable from the events that take place *on* them and as variations and modifications *of* their material propensities.

In Tarkovsky, cinematic materiality evidences the affective potential of settings. Light conveys the temporality of places; the articulation and passage of time; what place harbours of memories and perceptions, visions and insights, moments and atmospheres. His cinema foregrounds an elemental imaging of nature through a material tectonics of the image whose register is not metaphorical but existential and direct:

> "Rain, fire, water, snow, dew, the driving ground wind—all are part of the material setting in which we dwell; I would even say of the truth of our lives. I am therefore puzzled when I am told that people cannot simply enjoy watching nature, when it is lovingly reproduced on the screen, but have to look for some hidden meaning they feel it must contain. Of course rain can just be seen as bad weather, whereas I use it to create a particular aesthetic setting in which to steep the action of the film… When the screen brings the real world to the audience, the world as it actually is, so that it can be seen in depth and from all sides, evoking its very `smell,' allowing audiences to feel on their skin its moisture or its dryness…I want to create my own world on the screen, in its ideal and most perfect form, as I myself feel it and see it… I am recreating my world in those details which seem to

me most fully and exactly to express the elusive meaning of our existence."[10]

A different kind of landscape has haunted modernity; the desert which has driven everything from the imperialist colonialist project to the prominence of philosophical, artistic and literary practices such as nomadism and deterritorialisation in the thought of Deleuze; Albert Camus' evocative descriptions of the Mediterranean light of Algiers as a double for the existential condition of the modern subject; and the seminal abstract peregrinations of Paul Klee. Why this should be is a key question for understanding modernity. The cinema of Antonioni and others is helpful in this regard. In *L'Avventura*, but also in several sequences of *The Passenger*, Antonioni uses light as a means of dematerialising landscape, people and place. It is above all *glare*—an excess of light that dissolves the formal solidity of things and disables any sense of discrimination. In both films the desert prevails as a place, a state of mind and a disposition to the world. It is a desolate place evacuated of any sacred dimension in which the disorientated subject wanders without country, identity or trajectory. For Camus, the desert is akin to "the black flame that, from Cimabue to Franscesca, the Italian painters raised amid Tuscan landscapes like the lucid protestation of man thrown upon an earth whose splendour and light relentlessly speak to him of a God who does not exist." [11]

The desert persists as a kind of existential limbo—the ultimate liminal zone for an eschatology of disappearance. In *L'Avventura*, the holidaying bourgeoisie are at first depicted in striking contrast to the rough materiality of the island. The profile of their uncomfortable bodies and movements and the cut of their ludicrous clothes causes them to stand out as aliens in an alienating landscape. They progressively lose definition, dissipating into the materiality of the island in the same way that their tentative and ephemeral identities are progressively exposed and their material presence deteriorated. These subjects now float as so many spectral beings in an oblivious milieu whose light and colour have been drained and effaced.

The effect is multivalent. Two conditions are brought into an unstable assemblage—the political subject, by definition urbanised (*polis, politeia*) and accordingly sharply individuated, is deterritorialised within a site that corrodes the very boundaries which determine that subject's identity. The landscape not only corrodes, but ejects and distantiates. It does this at several levels. Firstly at a *narrative* level through collusion between the island and the sea, dissimulating the exit from the story of a woman that the group will spend the rest of the film searching for. It also does this *politically* and *morally* through the solid persistence of a setting that fundamentally contests the fragile and amoral condition of all characters except the protagonist. It then does it *aesthetically, pictorially* and *spatially* by playing the impermanent forms, patterns and textures of people over and against the enduring material presence of the island. And yet it is the island's gravity, bulk and monumentally static variegated surfaces which unclench the deconstitution to inconsistency of the subjects' emergent disappearance. It appears that the rock surfaces, the sea and wind are in constant unsettling motion, while the characters' tentative and nervous movements are reduced to set pieces and tableaus. The existential and spatial distances between individuals and between people and the landscape of rocks, sea and sky, are compressed to the point where they merge—or rather, to such a point that the subjects find themselves dissipating into oblivion. This oblivion is nature as pure process, as the bare and crude resistance of unyielding, disinclined and indifferent matter.

The character of light in Kurosawa is entirely different. There, light and darkness assume a cosmogonic dimension. Places emerge out of darkness or diffracted mists; spirits assume a chalky whiteness that perforates the frame; light turns water into a luminous viscous substance; the contours of characters and landscapes dematerialise into a surface of pure light or condense into dripping fluids and diaphanous ephemeral veils. There is an enduring concern for showing the materialisation of immaterial realities—of processes, systems, emotions, moral dispositions and designs. These materialised figures are then assembled into dramatic scenarios where they interact with and conjugate each other in order to carry the often tragic registers of the narrative. Where Antonioni develops a landscape materiality of indifference and resistance with corrosive implications for the human subject, Kurosawa sets up sites of exchange where natural and human beings interpenetrate and mutually affect each other. The mist and forest in *Throne of Blood* have a folded, perforate and yielding materiality. At a dramatic level this materiality enables them to function together as a site of entrapment and dissimulation. But the disposition, patterning and timbre of blacks and whites which articulate and produce the image are in a constant state of transformation. Characters and landscapes emerge and retreat into mists or fuse into the tangle of trees and foliage. Here materiality does not resist but interminably yields. Natural and human are not set over against each other, leading to a contestation in line with classical tragedy where only one prevails. Rather, the natural and the human are in an indefinite process of mutual emergence, dissolution and reformulation. The materiality of Antonioni is solid, sedimentary or crystalline, articulated and reactive; that of Kurosawa is fluid, metamorphic or vegetal, interpenetrant and receptive.

Whereas Antonioni's diffracted light heightens formal articulation and Kurosawa's diaphanous light mobilise it, Lynch's highly saturated, thick and viscous colours deepen the materiality and formal solidity of objects while also destabilising and liquefying it. The tendency in Antonioni is a *fading into light*. In Lynch it is a forwarding *retreat into black*. His use of light owes much to Expressionism in the various techniques used and effects generated. But Lynch takes the formalist atmosphere and aesthetics of Expressionism to an entirely different register. In *Eraserhead*, light and dark shadow double the disturbed psychological states of subjects moving about within environments that bear traces of profound disturbance.

Lynch uses indirect lighting washing over surfaces within deep black backgrounds and edges. The sources of light are uncertain, as are the boundaries of the spaces depicted. The setting of the film—*where* it takes place—is an urban and residential *terrain vague*, a wasteland whose exact location is unknown if not unknowable. The same is true of the time of duration—of *when* the events take place. Because the edges of space and time, the boundaries of rooms and corridors, the arrangement of apartments and of interior and exterior spaces in relation to each other are all ambiguous and indeterminate, the setting and the setup are fundamentally unsettling, disorienting and disconcerting. The *mise en scene* is creepy precisely because it is saturated with the dread of an unknown potential about to emerge from the darkness. The creepiness is a measure of the incommensurable latency crawling just below the tired, stained or black surfaces and borders of rooms and settings. The soundtrack amplifies this dread by way of an indeterminate deep vibration that could be the sound of the earth, the rumbling of an industrial apparatus or the vital beat of the city's machinic substance. In any case, the sources of sound are equally dissimulated within the film's materiality so that the ambiguity of source doubles the unlocatability of the condition and consequently the intensity of its threat.[12]

With Lynch, the darkness is ominous since one is never certain what it will give rise to or what passage it will afford. In *Éloge de l'Amour*, Godard works light and shadow with intense saturation and lustre. Shadows equally harbour and occlude a world of beings and objects which retreat from the gaze to the extent that they become reabsorbed into darkness. However in Godard the darkness is silken. It has grain, depth and space, which allows it to convey something of the sensuousness of substance, as opposed to the grotesque and monstrous materiality of Lynch. The film's gloaming darkness, its patient temporality and a montage that produces numerous disjunctions which enable measured reflection allow Godard to say something about love as potentiality for redemption. In that sense, *Éloge de l'Amour* is something of a coda for *Germany 90* and *Histoire(s) du Cinema*.

In the late films, Godard shows himself to be a great colourist. He works with the elemental materiality of the image, with a sort of chemistry if not alchemy of film stock. The materialisation of filmic texture through slow motion, the saturated colouration and rough grain of DV technology, the consequent streaks and smears produced and the deep, aerated blacks enable Godard to achieve a materialisation and de-temporalisation of the image. The first part of *Éloge de l'Amour* is shot in black and white and is set in the present. The second part is in colour and set in the past. The monochrome is not pitch black over against stark white. Rather, it is dusty charcoal gloom and grainy whites that are not set against each other but which appear to give way one to the other, as if one might be a condition of the other's retreat, as if white might be a condition of the distension of black, which in turn might be a condition of the intensification of white. This pulsation of one through the other allows whatever light available to shimmer and gleam in unfocussed points and streaks. Characters, things and images emerge from this darkness and return to it, or are cut to black as if forwarding from and retreating into a primal substance out of which the world is conjured. Shooting the present in monochrome and the past in colour enables Godard to suffuse the present with a darkness into which the past retreats and out of which we live out the interminable experience of an impossible recollection. In our imagined and embodied lives we see ourselves appearing from and disappearing into that same gloom—a gloom that also harbours the impossible narrative and characters of the protagonist's interminable search. This gives the film a profound sense of melancholia which Godard achieves by aligning the material tectonics of the image to the narrative line that is being unravelled.

## Materialised sense

In *A l'Écoute*, Nancy develops a close association between sound, sense and subject through the motif of resonance—more particularly of a resonant ground (*fond*):

> "We should therefore say that at the very least sense and sound share the space of a sending-back (*renvoi*), in which at the same time they send each one to the other, and that in a very general way, that space can be defined as that of a *self*, or of a subject. A *self* is nothing other than a form or a function of relay: a *self* is made of a rapport *to* oneself, or of a presence *to* oneself, which is nothing but the mutual relay between a sensible individuation and an intelligible identity (not only the individual in the accepted sense, but in him the singular occurrences of a state, a tension, or, precisely, of a `sense')—this relay should have been infinite and the point or the occurrence of a *subject* in the substantial sense should have never taken place other than in the relay, therefore within spacing and resonance, and even more so as the point without dimension of the *re-* of this resonance: the repetition whereby sound amplifies and propagates itself as much as it turns back and echoes to make itself heard. A subject *senses itself*: that is its property and its definition. That is to say that it hears itself, sees itself, touches itself, tastes itself, etc., and that it thinks itself or represents itself to itself, nears and distances itself from itself, and thus always senses itself sensing a 'self' which escapes *itself* or subtracts *itself* from itself as much as it resounds elsewhere as within itself, in a world and in otherness."[13]

Nancy explores the motifs of hearing and sight, sound and the image in philosophy, where vision and the look are foregrounded to a greater extent than hearing (*l'ecoute*) and listening or understanding (*l'entendement*)— specifically through the visual referends of key philosophical terms such as idea (from Greek *eidein* = image, the look or aspect of a thing), figure, theatre and theory (from Greek: *theorein* = sighting, scheme), spectacle and speculation:

"Why and how has something of sensed sense privileged a model, a support or a reference of visual presence rather than of acoustical penetration?... Why, on the side of the ear, retreat and pleat, putting into *resonance* but, on the side of the eye, manifestation and ostension, putting into *evidence*? Why though does each of these sides also touch the other and in *touching* put into play the whole regime of sense?... We wish here to lend a philosophical ear: to tug at the ear of the philosopher in order to point it towards that which has always least solicited or represented philosophical knowledge than what is presented to view—form, idea, tableau, representation, aspect, phenomenon, composition—and which rises rather with accent, tone, timbre, resonance and noise... if, since Kant and up to Heidegger, the major stakes of philosophy were found in the apparition or in the manifestation of the being, in a 'phenomenology,' the ultimate truth of the phenomenon... (should not) truth itself as transitivity and incessant transition of a coming-and-going... be heard rather than seen? But isn't it also in this manner that it ceases being itself and identifiable, to become, no longer the bare figure leaving the well, but the resonance of this well—or, were it possible to say it thus, the echo of the bare figure in the open depth?... To 'hear' (*entendre*) also means to 'understand,' as if to 'understand' were before anything else to 'hear said' (rather than to 'hear noise')."[14]

The epistemological register of hearing and resonance parallels an existential dimension that impacts on the experiences of cinema and architecture. More so than light, sound directly affects embodied experience. Hearing and vision necessarily operate within coded intellectual, social, cultural, political, aesthetic, emotional and other frames of reference. However, because of its vibrational character, sound is more likely than images to insinuate itself directly into the physical constitution of a body. The fact of current fascination for materiality and haptic experience in architecture parallels a fascination for the body and embodied experience at a broader sociocultural and artistic level. Both indicate a kind of compensatory function. In an environment where the virtual predominates, where modes of engagement and relation are ephemeral and where multiple kinds of displacement and deterritorialisation pullulate, the call to materiality and physical presence in architecture seem to answer a need for reconnecting body and world.

For the Hindus, the primary sense of spatial perception is hearing. The ear contains the semicircular canals and fluids which are sensitive to gravity, orientation and balance. These are configured in a three dimensional cross which doubles the orthogonal regime of three dimensional space—up and down, left and right, front and back. The apparatus of hearing which operates by way of air and fluid dynamics is therefore ideally calibrated to the perception of spatial position, orientation, measure and relative scale. Compared with vision, for which the perception of space is always mediated by the learned regime of perspective, hearing provides an unmediated sense of space since its apparatus is embodied and produces embodied affects. The acoustic characteristics of a space, which are given by its three dimensional shape and materiality, condition the perception of its size and proportion when experienced through the ear alone. Compare for example the reflective surfaces of a cathedral built of hard granite, the lively and sprung sound of a taught timber room, the indefinitely conjugated echoing of a network of limestone caves or an acoustically dead recording studio. Anechoic chambers artificially produce such variations by manipulating the acoustic reflectivity and absorption of surfaces. But the privilege afforded to sight in the reception and experience of architecture has associated it almost exclusively with regimes of visuality that bring with them an entire economy of the image. This encounter of architecture with the image is radically problematic for a phenomenon whose existential conditions are fundamentally three dimensional and embodied. It also characterises architecture's complicity in the hyperindustrial propensities of the contemporary world order that Stiegler and Ars Industrialis are so forcefully engaged in critiquing. The so called dematerialisation of architecture, the "city of bits," the increasing pervasiveness of ubiquitous computing and other forms of non-physical materiality and dissimulated modes of control simply constitute the replacement of a machinic model of power and economy exercised in the industrial era, a cultural economy model in the post-industrial era and a telematic model in the hyperindustrial era that prevails today.

The key component of sound is vibration, which expresses a relationship of tension between two differing states. A vibrating string in music is the activation, mobilisation, putting into pitch or precipitation of a particular length, distance or interval between two points. The sound produced enunciates or names an interval of separation, a difference of constitution or consistency. Without space and time which permit differentiations in location and duration, there could be no tension, no here or there, no now or then, hence no vibration or sound. Inanimate objects and settings have inherent vibrational potential. Different kinds of stone, metal and wood; a cave, gorge or forest; a tent, pavilion, hearth, hypostyle hall or ceremonial terrace; bells made of different materials—all of these display acoustic properties corresponding to the particular material character, as well as the configurations and assemblages that the materials assume.

There is then the vibrational potential of animate beings. Different human and non human rhythms and behaviors; different human characteristics, states of mind, tremperaments, dispositions, moods and emotions; figures of speech and figures of thought; the pitch, melody, grain, articulation and intonation of a voice; the resonance of ideas and concepts; the rhythm and beat of a gait; different times of the day and different seasons—these also have vibrational capacities which are integral to existential being and presence. In another cultural and intellectual context, the inherent character of a human being might have been called its soul—a particular framing, stringing or tuning of the being which allows the persona to sound-forth and interact with other existential frequencies and tunings within a milieu.

All relationships—cosmic, human, environmental, aesthetic, political, communitarian—are played out in terms of conjugated vibrational potential. To be "in tune" with an epoch, a philosophy, a work of art, a cuisine, a landscape, a microclimate, a musical refrain, a film, a collective, a person—all of these indicate relationships between different vibratory states of a person (their mood, intellectual capacity and interests, emotional proclivity, political and ethical dispositions and so forth) and the environment they find themselves in (the intellectual climate of an epoch, the ambience of a landscape, the tenor of a city, the atmosphere of a room, the mode of a refrain, the colour of a flower). Such relationships can be aligned or misaligned. Alignments and attunements produce resonances and consequent amplification. Something new emerges as an augmentation or increase in the original state and condition—a sense of identity, recognition, elation or delight for example; or a sense that certain things might now be possible, certain avenues opened and certain trajectories initiated. There are then relationships of misalignment in which case discords arise. Misalignments can either drive trajectories of mutual attraction and desire for resonance, or they can cancel out resonant potential by rendering relationships dysfunctional. These analogies are evidently musical and their lineage is Pythagorean, but they do not cease to be useful on that basis. The alignment and attunement of an architectural assemblage with the specificities of the site in which it is situated are prequisite conditions for contextual fit—particularly when the concept of fit is configured not statically or aesthetically, but operationally and strategically in terms of what fitness actually precipitates, delivers and affords over and above the architectural and contextual assemblages on their own.

Two hundred thousand years ago, people living in what is now the French Pyrennes aligned the acoustic conditions of caves with the location and subject matter of wall paintings, thereby indicating a close identity between sound and space. Certain paintings were located in parts of the caves whose spatial configurations and material qualities produced echoes and resonances sensitive to particular notes. In their 1988 study of the caves, Iégor Reznikoff and Michel Dauvois mapped the paintings in relation to the layout and sonorous quality of three caves in the Ariège.[15] They drew three conclusions—the majority of cave paintings and signs are located around points of high resonance; most resonant points are associated with cave paintings and signs; and the significance of paintings and signs is only explainable in relation to the sonority of the location. Such places served ritual functions involving chant, music and procession through networks of passages, tight thresholds and clearings. In this example, acoustic amplification made possible by the spatial and material characteristics of a place are mobilised to ritual, symbolic and cultural ends. The trope of ascribing to certain existential conditions and effects the power to act on and to transform the world, or to align human action with cosmic processes, is commonplace in premodern thought. The interest here is more prosaic. How might similar alignments, coincidences and co-locations between people and place, between the environmental conditions of a place and the tectonic conditions of architecture, between cinematic sound, image and time, enable assemblages that provoke associational thinking and practice with the power to trigger efficacious and productive possibilities?

In addition to vibrational character and frequency, which is more or less arithmetic and abstract, sound also has material, textural and resonant qualities—or *timbre*—which depend on the configuration and materiality of what produces it. Texture can be diaphanous, dense, coagulated, strained, open, closed, expanding, contracting, reverberant, dull, thick, thin, wet, moist, dry and so forth. Because of their physical vibratory character, sound and hearing directly affect the human body and mind. Vibrations can be heard, they can be felt on skin, they can set fluids, organs and their processes into motion. The extraordinary musical columns of the *Vithhala* Temple at *Vijayanagar* are a classic example of alignment between the acoustic dimension of materials and architectural form. Here, a set of 8 massive columns surround the *Mandapa* in which diverse musical and dance performances would take place in front of the temple's main shrine. Each column comprises a cluster of 7 pillars sculpted out of a single piece of granite. When struck, each pillar sounds one of the 7 tones of the octave. More remarkably, each column cluster produces tones which convey the timbre of a different musical instrument—

wind, string, percussion and so forth—to which the cluster is dedicated. The columns are still in production in Mahabalipuram and the exacting know-how needed to sculpt them is scarcely imaginable. What they demonstrate is one of the most direct associations possible between sound, space and materials.

Beyond their curiosity value for Western tourists and local guides, the columns show how architecture can be conceived and realised as a strung instrument with a material sound body that may be struck, played or otherwise activated into palpable resonance. This is precisely what the artist Bill Fontana achieves with works such as *Tyne Soundings* (2009), which transmit assemblages of ambient sound and the sounds of resonant structures producing disembodied and eery presences into contemporary art spaces. Fontana works with extant situations and structures, but the implication of his work is much broader. What would it mean for architecture to take on the resonant potential of its geometric, spatial, technical and material fabric? How might buildings become sensitive and responsive not only to the physical and acoustic conditions of their milieux, but also to their own resonant physicality—if not their luminosity, scent, gust and tactility; and this not by default or accident but by design?

However, the amplificatory potential of resonance can also be destructive. The characteristic tuning of an assemblage can be made to resonate to a limit which constitutes the threshold of its undoing and unraveling. It is the sound of horn and human shouting which destroys the walls of Jericho,[16] and the use of sound and music in physiological warfare is long established. But it is René Guénon who reported the most striking perspective on the deconstitutive potential of vibration in architecture. Buildings are organized according to two and three dimensional geometric systems and patterns, characterised by specific numerical and proportional systems which possess inherent vibratory potential. Consequently, various components of a building and the building as a whole can in theory be sounded, rung or played. Guénon's account is based on the concept of the "vital knot" which holds together living beings, harmonizing them and keeping them from spiritually, mentally and physically unraveling.[17] Certain vibrations or characteristic tonalities of ideas, environments, personalities and voices can so unsettle a person that they become unstrung, inoperative or thoroughly deconstituted. By extension, buildings are also resonant assemblages around a vital knot that can be undone by being set into vibration, thereby disaggregating the structure—much like a certain pitch is capable of breaking a certain kind of glass. The contention may be far-fetched, but it does enable useful reflection.

In music theory, particular vibrations of sound correspond to particular notes situated within musical modes or scales, each of which constitutes a framework with a disctinctive characteristic or *ethos*. This is common to the modal music of ancient Greece and the *ragas* of Indian music. Modes impart particular intellectual, emotional, aesthetic, ethical and experiential characteristics to music set within them. The Appolonian and Dionysiac modes of ancient Greece were thought to produce diametrically opposed musical configurations—the first conveying order and propriety, the second disorder and impropriety. The Doric mode was considered orthogonal and rectilinear, the Lydian melodic and romantic. Each of these modes corresponded to particular peoples, cultural groups and communities, who were in turn associated with particular regions and provenances with specific environmental and climatic conditions. This *ethical* and *ethnical* propensity of modes is paralleled by the dynamic propensities of musical ratios. The octave (equivalent to the ratio 1:2) tends to and conveys resolution and closure. The fifth (2:3) on the other hand leaves resolution hanging. The former will have a stabilising and the latter a mobilising effect on the musical fabric. The same applies modally, so that a note will gain dynamic propensity depending on the mode or scale in which it is set and the sequences of notes within which it is positioned. Musical dynamics are not absolute conditions of tonality but relative conditions emerging with an ambience or milieu.

In ancient Greek and Indian texts on music theory and practice, the key technical problem was the division of the octave. This fact is in the word "music" itself—from the etymon *MU = to speak with the lips closed, to murmur or mutter, hence to utter the inarticulate or un-articulable + *SEC = to cut, section, segment, divide. Music would then be the division and articulation of the unpronounceable, the inexpressible and the incommunicable, which nevertheless cannot-not be uttered in the form of a mumble. This mutism is not an ailment or failure of communication. It is a foundational condition of the speech and convocation of communicant beings who are irremediably caught up in language.

The octave is a natural phenomenon of sound. It is essentially a relation between two tones that conveys a sense of resolution and completeness. The higher tone is an augmented and fulfilled state of the lower. Hence the octave operates as a framework, field or milieu open to subdivision. The problem of dividing the octave aims to produce a set of individual tones which can be grouped into modes and scales, enabling melodic figures and compositions to evolve. The standard division of the octave is into eight tones separated by seven intervals. The Hindus divided the octave into twenty two microtonal intervals. Some Hindu texts refer to

as many as seventy two microtones within the octave, the majority of
which would be inaudible to anything but a highly trained ear. However,
the octave is indivisible into equal intervals without the use of
incommensurable numbers. Like the cycle of polygons which tend to the
circle without ever reaching it, the octave is an interval which cannot be
closed and is always in the process of being over-arched by tonal cycles of
increasing pitch. In that sense it is qualitatively whole, singular and
complete, but quantitatively irresolvable and indeterminate.

In a parallel way, geometric families such as orthogonal, triangular,
pentagonal or circular systems develop out of the subdivision of a primary
spatial interval of difference between two points. Arithmetic sequences (1,
2, 3, 4...) have corresponding geometric sequences (point [1], line [2],
plane/shape [3, triangle; 4, square; 5, pentagon...], volume [4, tetrahedron;
6, cube; 8, octahedron...) that produce configurations with distinctive
characteristics which are not only visual, but by implication conceptual,
ethical and political. Geometric configurations are also rhythmic and
vibrational, as is attested in Hinduism by associations between geometric
ritual diagrams (*yantra*) and their corresponding chanted syllables
(*mantra*). Vibrational configuration in sound and space is essentially a
function of differential measure. The same is true of chromatic variations
and differentiations of white light to produce colours which are open to
association with particular emotions, moods, temperaments, ethical
dispositions, aesthetic experiences, symbolic referends, seasonal phases,
personalities and so forth. Such arithmetic, geometric, acoustic and
rhythmic figures are then susceptible of being put into relation,
combination and conjugation to produce not only complex spatial
configurations, but also qualitative configurations of value. They operate
as frameworks with latent associational potential that design can mobilise,
put to work, unfold and materialise.

Mahler's *Der Abschied* (The Farewell, 1908) from *Das Lied von der
Erde* (The Song of the Earth) exemplifies this associational complex.
Beyond its evident Pastorale, Italianate and Sublime resonances, Mahler
engages an acoustic phenomenon of startling power. A sonic materialisation
of the conditions of the outsider, the homeless and longing are conveyed
essentially by the timbre and vibrational quality of sound rather than by its
melodic or harmonic components or any semantic content. In other words,
the musical sense is conveyed materially rather than formally. It is by the
pure resonance and deep echo of the sound that Mahler achieves
something like the sound of the earth; or silence as the deep noise that
inhabits space—a "muffled growling tied to original disjunction, to the
fundamental heterology of the world."[18] Godard has certainly used Mahler

as part of his strategies of montage to trigger powerful and troubling associations of sense. But his work also achieves a visual double of this telluric resonance purely through the chromatic materiality of images. This is particularly evident in the deep and crisp occluding greens of nature and the manner in which rich shadow works to spatialise the image into profound harbouring depth. This shadow functions as a kind of vanishing point of the image, in the same way that silence is not an absence of sound but its conversion into sound as such. The process is a becoming-non-image of the image, together with its immersive condensation and calorification into pure rhythm and vibration. The image is not consequently abstracted or withdrawn from contingency or concrete existence. Rather, it is rendered hyper-real. Its embodied particularity and excessive, palpable presence are intensified. No longer figurative, sound enters into a phase of pure material emanation and pure vibrational production. It shifts from melodic line to rhythmic beat and pulsation, driven by no other impulse than the material energy of its own production.

In *Nativity of the Mother of God* from *The Protecting Veil* (1987), John Tavener establishes a sound fabric that represent the world as a consistent, homogenous and melodic setting. Into this context he introduces a discordant phrase which tears the harmonic fabric by sharpening and raising the opening melodic line. The effect is equivalent to raising a guttural sound into a nasal then into a cerebral resonance. The resulting phrase develops a diagonal trajectory which rends and striates the smooth fabric, reorienting the generally horizontal character of the piece into an inclined vertical trajectory. The musical and acoustic disjunction carries the sense of a transformative disturbance and eruption within the musical fabric that metaphorically stands for the ambient network of the everyday. The moment of the Virgin's birth—of the birth of an inconceivable and extraordinary woman—is a moment out of time and out of place, or else it is the unsettling moment of an unraveling of existentiality; that is, a collapse of all compossible worlds. Tavener's deformation of the musical sound body, the stress and strain he applies to its materiality, the plasticity to which he subjects it, convey a foundational change undergone within the constitution and entrails of the world. The deforming figure subsists in the midst of a faintly conventional harmonic setting and melodic line, underplayed with minor flurries and delivered wholly within the musical possibilities of that setting. The figure is a shocking and catastrophic moment in which the strange and uncanny breach the limits of the known and the ordinary—a breach all the more troubling because its advent is not from elsewhere but out of the midst of the work's resonant material fabric.

This is perhaps too rapid a summary of very complex, nuanced issues. Yet of particular interest is this close connection between assemblages of sound, formal assemblages which determine architectural order, and environmental or place-based assemblages which gather to them particular ethical dispositions and practices, or particular ways of being-in-the-world and being-with-others. In current architectural practice the dimension of sound and of ambient sound in particular is not consciously foregrounded but has default value. This creates accidental conditions with significant implications for architectural experience. Consider for example the sound of servicing equipment and machinery; air conditioning equipment and ducts; plumbing, drainage and exhaust systems; prerecorded messages in lifts and the multiple buzzing and beeps of various apparatuses that permeate private and public domains. There are then the inaudible frequencies of electronic, communicational and computer systems, power systems, x-rays and so forth. In contemporary buildings the hum of concealed equipment and of the explicitly technological conditions of building performance is ubiquitous. Such effects are generally unmapped, unplanned and unpredictable. They are not taken into account in the conceptualisation and articulation of architectural form and space. The resultant ambient conditions can range from the neutral to the nefarious. But the persistent and ubiquitous pulsating hum that backgrounds contemporary built environments must play a significant formative role in the experiential and existential condition of architecture. In colder parts of the world where sustainability demands thermal efficiency, building techniques which effectively seal architectural space from external conditions through detailing, triple glazing and heat exchange ventilation systems create internal conditions that are effectively disconnected from their milieu. At best, external environments are converted into remote pictorial scenographies which amplify the artificiality of a building's ambience and atmosphere. Because the apparatuses and sources of sound are more often than not concealed, the net effect is to create a strange uncanny sense of permanent, invisible machinic presence suffusing the materiality and interstices of space, or inhabiting and haunting the architectural out-of-frame. The threatening dimensions of this have been well conveyed in films such as Ridley Scott's *Alien* and Lynch's *Eraserhead,* which take place in apparently familiar environments surreptitiouly rendered like the liminal zones, concealed voids and service ducts of excised interstices beyond which nothing exists.

Sound has a formative function in cinema, perdominantly in its conjugation with image sequences. Sound can influence the perception of

time, duration and rhythm, movement and speed. It can temporalise an
image that has no intrinsic time, modify the apparent temporality of an
image sequence or breach it totally by deterritorialising and carrying it into
another register.[19] This depends on relationships established between the
temporality and rhythm of sound and the visual rhythms that form part of
the image or that are implied by it. The temporality of images might
include anything from the rhythm of dramatic action depicted, to the micro
rhythms of movement at the surface of the image (smoke, rain, undulation
of water), as well as the material flickering of the photographic grain itself.
As Michel Chion writes, "these phenomena create rapid and fluid
rhythmic values, establishing in the image itself a shivering vibratory
temporality. Kurosawa uses them systematically in his film *Dreams* (rain
of petals from flowering trees, flakes in a snowstorm, fog, etc.)."[20] Again it
is a matter of assemblage and juxtaposition, convergence and divergence
which are used to generate alignments or misalignments between layers in
the materiality of the film—in this case between sound and image. The
same trope can be used to overlay sounds of different temporalities and
timbres, or images of different graphic and rhythmic quality to create
complex juxtapositions with strategic implications for space, time,
materiality and narrative. The use of ambient sound integral with the
internal logic of images in a film will have indexical value, reinforcing the
specific conditions of where and when the film is set and maintaining a
uniform logic, texture and pace. Through montage, juxtaposition can
introduce disjunctions between sound and image, between soundtrack,
action and place that disturb the filmic texture and render it ambiguous.
Such disturbances might reinforce or amplify the narrative—as in the use
of music to parallel and emphasise the emotional dimensions of a scene; or
they might be deconstitutive—as in the use of music and sound to displace
the narrative into other dimensions and registers. The incommensurability
between constituent parts has the capacity to energise and mobilise
semantic potential, but it requires more complex strategies of engagement,
reception and interpretation since the ordering structure will be more
complex, less obvious to resolve and more susceptible to multiple
interpretations.

Compare for example the soundtracks to Pasolini's *The Gospel
According to St Matthew*, the opening sequences of Lynch's *Lost Highway*
and Roeg's *Bad Timing*. In the first, music as divergent as Bach,
Prokofiev, Mozart, Congolese spirituals, *Missa Luba: An African Mass*
and *Sometimes I feel like a motherless child* repeat or fade in and out
seemingly at random, to underscore figures wandering the deserted
landscapes of the Italian *Meridione* that stands-in for first century

Palestine. Pasolini declared the visual provenance of many of the film's set pieces in the paintings of Masaccio, Giotto and El Greco, which he claimed to have filmed as if scanning a series of paintings. In terms of the soundtrack, Pasolini cites fragments of well known compositions in an entirely syncretic way. There is no logical pattern to their cultural provenance and no evident association with the era or place being depicted. They are roughly edited and matched to the filmic sequences. There is no consistent pattern to the way they increase and decrease in volume. They erupt into scenes, suddenly cease, fade in and out or bridge across several scenarios. The fragments seem to form part of a default and banal canon of "church music" and their use conveys a vague sense of religiosity. At best, the music might function in the traditional dramatic role of a choir, which interrupts worldly events to call attention to divine presence, to indicate the moral implications of human actions or to signal the irruption of a different regime of temporality—the time of destiny or of the gods.

For Tarkovsky, music in film functions as a refrain—a way of returning to and iterating previous emotions, but under an altered regime which deepens the experience. "Music does more than intensify the impression of the visual image by providing a parallel illustration of the same idea; it opens up the possibility of a new, transfigured impression of the same material: something different in kind."[21] Here, the role of music is not to accompany or illustrate the image. It has an essential mobilising role which fundamentally affects the image and its reception. It forms part of a resonant universe and is constitutive of the material of life; of its emotional, aesthetic and chromatic dimensions. It can also cause perceptual distortion of the visual material, making it heavier or lighter, more opaque or transparent, more subtle or coarse. Music triggers and directs the emotional content of images and broadens their semantic implications. Citing Bergman, Tarkovsky considers sound to have a critical function of amplifying the dramatic character of a scene, or of establishing correspondences between particular states of mind and the deep conditions of a landscape—an echo of the earth, its rustling, whispering, trickling, sighing, breathing.[22]

The final sequence of *Blow Up* is set in London's Maryon Park. Antonioni uses the setting to establish visual and acoustic materiality through the site's containment by a thick wood and by foregrounding the rustle of foliage whipped up by a stiff breeze. These shimmering rhythms activate the surface of the screen and develop a contextual presence which counters and supplants the protagonist's search for information. Antonioni sets up sequences of dissimulation as the photographer moves into and out of frame and sight, into and out of fields of foliage that in turn conceal and reveal him; just as they had once revealed and now again occlude or erase the information he seeks. The sound is entirely ambient and amplified, over against the protagonist's frustrated silence. Time and again the impassability of his disposition and face contrast with the shaking and crackling of leaves and canopies around him. The park is almost entirely sequestered from the city, separated by fences and a high wood on all sides except for the odd view through to signs of the urban and industrial fabric beyond. It operates as the inside of an outside; as the evidence of an exposed secret that is as much constructed as construed by the photographer.

The heightened contrast between the visual and acoustic vibration of the park and the silence of the protagonist augments a distantiation of context from content, of the subject from his situation. The park appears to reject the photographer and his quest, sending him on to the last mimetic sequence where he joins in a feigned game of tennis with non existent balls and rackets—the to and fro rhythm and faint sounds of which he eventually follows with his eyes and ears. Just as the photographic image earlier resisted the protagonist's persistence in manufacturing repeated enlargements of frames so that he could discern evidence of a crime he believed had been committed, this time the place itself equally resists his search for concrete evidence. While the indexical nature of the photographic image remains ambiguous and open to interpretation, the place shows no such ambiguity. Nature, metaphorically tousled and contrary, denies the photographer his anticipated find and yields nothing but the total dissimulation and absence of evidence. In both cases, the ground of the image—photographic paper in the first, *hortus conclusus* in the second—remains mute. And it is at the very surface and material resistance of these two grounds—in the chemical body of the photographic image and in the vegetal substance of the park—that the two phases of withholding and yielding evidence their interminable exchange.

Antonioni's final sequence for *L'Eclisse* is an equivalently striking moment of narrative and subjective crisis. In it, the two protagonists conspire to abandon their condition; to definitively depart the story and the setting in which they have been cast. The threshold of departure is again Nature, represented here by a dense canopy of pines framed firstly behind a shop grille, then free of it as the woman Vittoria literally walks out of frame. The scene then shifts to the famous seven minute coda in which cinema, evacuated of its narrative function, returns to pure observation and indexicality.[23] What does this extraordinary sequence point to? What the woman leaves behind, what she leaves to the camera and to cinema is pure observation. The images in this sequence are of largely deserted streets with the long shadows and contrasts of late afternoon sun, followed by the descending gloom of evening. They are collaged in jump cuts with no continuity of location or scale (panning across residential flats that look like an assemblage of industrial buildings; a pile of building materials; a makeshift fence in extreme asymmetrical perspective; buildings under construction shrouded in scaffolding; reflections and shadows on various surfaces; pure visual compositions of horizontals and verticals, of masses, surfaces and lines; smooth sequence shots past a series of cubic forms made ominous by the silent deserted streets; a man reading a newspaper report on the nuclear arms race; a luminous image of translucent foliage dripping in water; vapor trails of distant airplanes framed by a telecommunications tower; abstract forms of modernist buildings against the sky; people looking worriedly behind or across their shoulders; and so on). The framing shifts in scale from distant shots of the urban setting to close ups of people's features and banal circumstances. The sound track juxtaposes ambient noise, unresolved chords and mildly ominous electronic vibrations indicating a denouement-to-come (parkland sprinklers; running water; the rustle of foliage whipped up by wind; ants frantically teeming in the bark of a tree; the sudden roar of trucks and buses, screeching tyres and breaks; individual and collective footsteps; water running out of a breached barrel into a drain, later eroding a trench in the soil; city workers returning to their apartments at dusk; people like lone sentinels waiting in the street, at bus stops, on balconies pointing to the sky, waiting for some ending or the arrival of whatever-being).

In this way Antonioni shifts from cinema's narrative to its material capacity to convey semantic content. Sound and image are separately and severally disjunct. In the soundtrack, ambient noise and suspended chords create a state of irresolution that carries the sense of awaiting a looming encounter. Visually, the discontinuous images juxtapose an assured formal modernity and evacuated urbanism with a collective of troubled subjectivities and an impassive, enduring natural order that threatens the certainty of territorial appropriation. The disjunctions create incommensurable gaps between human beings, objects, contexts and Nature, promoting a sense of their irreconcilability and crisis. Again, it is in the vibratory and pictorial materiality of the film—the concrete and bitumen of the cityscape; the machinic rhythms of vehicles and sprinklers; the flicker of artificial light; the countenance, footfall, flesh and hair of humans; the gleam of leaves; the rustle of trees and the drip and streaming of water—that Antonioni evidences a multivalent crisis and exposes its narrative, political, aesthetic, subjective and environmental face.

With *Lost Highway*, Lynch and Badalamenti construct a soundscape that is both integral to the narrative and infinitely distant. This double character renders it extremely troubling. The sound is a low and deep hum that is vaguely industrial—like the sound of air ducts, faintly heard machinery or a muffled and indiscernible cacophony of shuddering, grinding and sliding squeals. This soundscape underscores a domestic scene set in an internalised and gloomy suburban house where a couple— the male seriously troubled by something he just can't put his finger on— exchanges silences and miscommunications. The sound is clearly not ambient—or at least its ambience, unrelated to the concrete context of the scene, is indicative of the psychological condition of the characters and the latent state of the narrative that is about to unravel. It also contributes to the heightened sense of claustrophobia that permeates the house and the countenance of the characters. Sound drives the narrative on. Its thickness and density dilate and grow; its loudness intensifies and fades; its parts become more or less discernable. It shadows the various actions and characters as they move to the various brinks and thresholds that articulate the story. It is at once otherworldly, radically off-screen and inherent to the premonitory gloom that permeates the sequences.

In *Bad Timing*, Roeg frequently juxtaposes images and soundtracks that are not aligned within the temporality or spatiality of the image. In some cases this is done to create transitions from scene to scene. In others, the function of disjunct juxtapositional montage is to insert a troubling presence within the scene—something which deforms its spatiality and temporality and takes the scene into a different register altogether. Roeg uses sound—in particular sounds that signify inoperative communication and disengaged relationships—to underscore the main narrative line of a dysfunctional affair between the two protagonists. In one late sequence, the detective enters the woman's empty, chaotic apartment. The camera pans across in concert with the detective's gaze to show the same apartment in flashback, this time spotlessly organized and empty. The implication is that the detective is projected as voyeur into the past scene, or at least that at that moment he sees into the past. When the couple meet in the same apartment, Roeg overlays the sound of a ringing telephone. Neither answer because it is not in fact ringing there and then and therefore remains unanswerable. The sound has no function within the internal narrative. What it does is contextualize that narrative in terms of the incommunicability and urgency that permeates the film.

# Monstrous images

The functional and technical relationship between light and the image in cinema is eclipsed by more foundational associations. The word image is from the Latin: *imago, imaginem*, and the etymon \*IM/\*AIM, meaning a copy, an appearance, an imitation. An image has two dimensions and two functions—representational and presentational. According to the first, it stands in for what it represents and as such is destined to be a simulacrum and counterfeit. According to the second, the image is a direct and immediate manifestation or emergence—a monstration and showing-forth. The image advances into and produces the light of its forwarding gesture. Hence its association with the imaginary and the magical, with reflections in mirrors which seem to loom out of a different dimension, and with echoes produced in cavernous spaces. Tied up in this reading of the image is the motif of the *ground*. The image emerges out of, or is fore-grounded over and against a ground. This ground is normally associated with darkness, countering the image's association with light. Darkness is potentiality and latency, the unknown or the not yet; whereas light is the actuality and factuality of the known and produced. The image does not only show itself, it shows itself showing. Hence the trope in much portraiture of the subject's gaze, of mirrors and other reflections and glances that violate the boundary of the frame and the rules of depiction. Monsters loom out from the dark interstices of space, from corners and hollows, from dark rooms and regions. Their nature is to appear and disappear in a double gesture where advent signals impending retreat into oblivion. The image de-monstrates by appearing monstrously on a surface, by being the sur-face or surfeit of a face. Its appearance is a kind of peeling out from a background, an incision into a ground that conceals it, or a disturbance of the ground so that the image is not other-than but simply a particular condition, variation or articulation of the ground. It is simultaneously relief, incision and turbulence. In *The Ground of the Image*, Nancy develops ideas of the ground and monstration in relation to the image[24]:

"The image is separated in two ways simultaneously. It is detached from a ground (*fond*) and it is cut out within a ground. It is pulled away and clipped or cut out. The pulling away raises it and brings it forward: makes it a 'fore,' a separate frontal surface, whereas the ground itself has no face or surface. The cutout or clipping creates edges in which the image is framed: it is the *templum* marked out in the sky by the Roman augurs. It is the space of the sacred or, rather, the sacred as a spacing that distinguishes. Thus, through a process repeated innumerable times in painting, an image is detached from itself while also reframing itself as an image... In this double operation, the ground disappears. It disappears in its essence as ground, which consists in its not-appearing. One can thus say that it appears as what it is by disappearing. Disappearing as ground, it passes entirely into the image. But it does not appear for all that, and the image is not its manifestation, nor its phenomenon. It is the force of the image, its sky and its shadow. This force exerts its pressure 'in the ground' of the image, or, rather, it is the pressure that the ground exerts on the surface—that is, under this force, in this impalpable non-place that is not merely the 'support' but the *back* or the *underside* of the image."

This means that the image detaches itself twice—firstly from a ground and secondly from the thing that it images. It also absents itself twice— firstly by relieving itself of the ground (or relieving the ground of itself) and secondly by relieving itself of what it images. The image is and is not there, is and is not absent:

"The thing as image is thus distinct from its being-there in the sense of the *Vorhanden* [Heidegger's `present at hand', `available,' `apprehendable'], its simple presence in the homogeneity of the world and in the linking together of natural or technological operations. Its distinction is the dissimilarity that inhibits resemblance, that agitates it and troubles it with a pressure of spacing and of passion. What is distinct in being-there is being image: it is not here but over there, in the distance, in a distance that is called 'absence'... The absence of the imaged subject is nothing other than an intense presence, receding into itself, gathering itself together in its intensity. Resemblance gathers together in force and gathers itself as a force of the same—the same differing in itself from itself: hence the enjoyment (*jouissance*) we take in it. We touch on the same and on this power that affirms this: I am indeed what I am, and I am this well beyond or well on this side of what I am for you, for your aims and your manipulations. We touch on the intensity of this withdrawal or this excess. Thus *mimesis* encompasses *methexis*, a participation or a contagion through which the image seizes us."

To the extent that the image is mimetic, imitative and emulative of the thing, it produces itself over above the thing or in its stead. As Nancy observes, this is a fundamentally violent contestation by the stand-in for the presence it seeks to dispute and usurp. It does this by bringing the presence of the thing into a *praes-ensia*, a "being-out-in-front-of-itself, turned towards the outside...posited as subject."[25]

"Thus the image is, essentially, `monstrative' or `monstrant.' Each image is a monstrance (or pattern)—what in French is called *ostensoir*. The image is of the order of the monster; the *monstrum* is a prodigious sign, which warns (*moneo, monstrum*) of a divine threat. The German word for the image, *Bild*—which designates the image in its form or fabrication—comes from a root (*bil-*) that designates a prodigious force or a miraculous sign. It is in this sense that there is a monstrosity of the image. The image is outside the common sphere of presence because it is the display of presence. It is the manifestation of presence, not as appearance, but as exhibiting, as bringing to light and setting froth. What is monstrously shown (*monstré*) is not the aspect of the thing; it is, by way of the aspect or emerging from it (or drawing it up from the depths, opening it out and throwing it forward), its unity and force.... Under this force, forms too deform or transform themselves. The image is always a dynamic or energetic metamorphosis. It begins before forms, and goes beyond them. All painting, even the most naturalistic, is this kind of metamorphic force. Force deforms (and so, therefore does passion); it carries away forms, in a spurt that tends to dissolve or exceed them. The monstrous showing or *monstration* spurts out in *monstruation*."[26]

Monstration signals the immeasurable potential for profusion and excess, monstruousness and outrage. Because monstration is a showing it is also ostentatious, in the sense of tending-out and being out-standing. It is a cipher for Nature as prodigious and unbridled production and presentation. But it also connotes an interminable potential for translation, transformation, and shape-shifting transfiguration—all instances of the transgression and breaching of limits that contain and safeguard from excess. What shows itself in this ostention is thereby properly daimonic and anathema to modernist sensibility, irrespective of the kind of modernity or the era in which it arises. For *our* Modernity, Nature, the ground, grounds, earth, swarms, worms, the muddy, the turbid, gloom, the dark, the wet, the humid, the foreign—are all tropes for monstration, for excess, for chaos. Dampness may well be unhealthy, but only in certain circumstances, only when brought into certain assemblages—for example within particular climates, types of enclosure, materials and domiciliary patterns. It is not unhealthy *per se* and certainly not when forming part of other kinds of assemblages. In Modernity, some of these conditions are demonised and excised, while their opposites are valorised. Modernity's fascination with the desert has already been cited. Consider its abhorrence for of all manner of harboring and concealment, interstice and shadow, recess and fold, secret and crypt. Consider the kinds of urban cleansing promoted by von Hausmann and Le Corbusier; the obsession with hygiene; the banishment of the architectural and human abject—of weeds, garbage, sewerage, insects, masses, crowds, the poor, the sick, the outcast and the dead; the pathological distaste for the makeshift, the unorganised, the unpredictable, the non-orthogonally ordered, the rhizomatic, conflict, disaster, terrorism. What is minimalist architecture but the clearest sign of an inoperative capacity to manage monstration. And what violence this represents.

There always remains something violent about the image, because in emerging it breaches a limit; it tears itself literally from its ground. Breaching the limit is a necessary condition of the appearance of the image. It appears out of a background and manifests itself as separate and looming. The appearance of something engraved, the execution of a graphic mark, is an attack on substance that violates and scars it. In that sense every drawing is a violation; a rupture of the unmarked or a forced release of the latent. For Nancy, the image is a distinctive striking: "always, a picture is also that which subtracts itself from a context and stands out, clear-cut, against a background. Always there is a cut, a framing. The cut prunes the look, trims its borders and its points, lightens its sharpness." The association of light and the evidence of the image is traced by Nancy from the Latin: *evidentia*, a translation of the Greek term *enargeia*, "which speaks of the powerful and instantaneous whiteness of lightning: *argos*—speed in a flash."[27] But the presentation and mobilisation of evidence it is not simply unconcealment, because in its very light, in its provenance and advent, the image always and by nature preserves an essential reserve, a withholding potential.[28] With the image, the real and the enigmatic arrive simultaneously.[29]

Four dimensions of violence accompany the advent of images. Firstly, the image makes its appearance out of a ground. In that appearance as foregrounding it also makes the ground appear. The image breaches and rends the ground in order to deliver, liberate and deploy or unfold its latent potential. The word *appearance* itself indicates it. To appear means to come *through* a limit, through a (withholding) periphery (*PER = through, by means of). The advancing appearance of the image is at the same time a retreating disappearance of the ground. In appearing and discerning one appearance among the multiple latent possibilities of the ground, the image also preserves that potential, sending it disappearing back into the ground. The image always preserves a trace of its simultaneous retreat into the oblivion of ground. Black and silence constitute total absorption and restraint. If anything appears it can only be the surfacing and scintillation of their excessive withholding.

Secondly, every image is metaphorically and practically a capture. It holds something captive in the midst of its captivated emergence. The image is therefore always incarceration and fetishisation of gesture. In capturing, the image also releases and is therefore by nature exclusive.

Thirdly, the image appropriates what it sights, sites or situates—what it cites or quotes, frames, betrays or captures by forcing compliance to another regime and another agency. The image thus becomes part of a different assemblage and its capacity and potential are thereby decontextualised and deterritorialised.

Fourthly, every image excises a moment and arrests the rhythmic transport of its emergence. Destining it to fixity, the moment's passage passes into the past, forgetfulness and death. Such violence might be more explicit in photography than in the moving images of cinema. Yet even while preserving a *sense* of motion through cinematic projection and reception, the actual continuity of movement which the camera seeks to capture will always escape its confines. Because the technology remains founded on the projection of 24 *still* frames/second, something of this discontinuity will persist and haunt the look that cinema casts towards the world. Acknowledging the artifice and abandoning realist pretensions must be foundational to the development of new cinematic, or *kinematic*, practices—if not to the development of what might be called cinema's originary destiny.

What is architecture doing in all of this? The first architectural gesture is the appropriation of territory. It displaces chthonic alliances; ruptures the ground; disturbs microclimate and ecology; consumes resources in production and operation; embodies obsolescence; engages and complies with capitalist, geopolitical and biopolitical regimes; installs apparatuses and mechanisms of prediction and control. In every respect, architecture is fundamentally unnatural. Artificial not only by definition, not only because in terms of nature as *phusis* it does not produce itself, but more significantly because its grounding and enduring gesture is sequestrant, disruptive and consumptive. Disruptive and consuming of its context of installation, but also in the very processes of spatial and formal articulation which are founded on division, disjunction and rupture—the subdivision of measures to space out intervals; the segmentation of circles to produce polygons; the cutting up of space to produce rooms; the incision of doors, windows and voids into surfaces in order to render space usable and so forth. From symbolic origins, the installation of cities and buildings has always been associated with rituals of disestablishment, slaughter and ruination—lifting up valleys, laying waste mountains and making rough places plain[30]; breaking or ploughing soil to release telluric spirits; impaling the daimon of the earth to stabilise a territory; burying a sacrificial infant below a column to consecrate a structure; ornamenting friezes with motifs of garlands and clusters of blood drops to demonstrate its civic and civilising credentials.

Violence is in the word *sacred* itself—from the etymon *SEC = to cut, separate, set aside (from the profane). Paradise, temple, *temenos* and *polis* are all instances of an installed artificial space and world, sectioned-off from a context considered chaotic and threatening, needing to become predictable and controlled. Such violence is embedded in the architectural lexicon and in the tropes and turns of speech common in design practice— inscribing, inserting, engraving, striating, intervening, deconstructing, disassembling, delineating, determining, designating, cutting, splicing, segmenting, sectioning, mutating, transforming. Like cinema, architecture creates a world. It frames the world in reductive ways, cuts it up and zones it for use or view. It separates an ambiance from the territory it installs. It reconfigures new assemblages and relationships which may be constructive and productive or disabling and demeaning. It may set up new assemblages which reestablish for human beings a heightened engagement with the world and with others. But it more commonly conspires to sustain and promote disjunction, disengagement and at worst, contempt. By default at least, this is the persistent danger that haunts every work of architectural conception, design and production. It also happens to be the field that architecture must survey and map out if it is to develop its own originary destiny.

This violence of artifice has its basis in the classical conception of creation—in the *fiat lux* that conditions all cosmogonies in one way or another. The primary demiurgic act is a separation of light from dark, achieved by a speech act which ruptures silence. It constitutes a double violence. Cosmogonic violence is naturally transferred to artistic production when the artist is also, by default or correspondence, a demiurge. The materials worked by the artist correlate to substance and the telluric gravity of the earth. The ideas which inform these materials correlate to essence and the immaterial celestial spheres. Art is what joins and articulates these two irreconcilable entities, bringing heaven and earth into coordinated unity. By implication, the relationship between matter and light demands that the latter redeem the former by illuminating, volatising or rarifying its gravity and structure. Matter is directed downward; it sinks, spreads, weighs, constricts, conceals, prevents, restrains and so forth. Light penetrates matter, leavens it, raises it into the vertical. It loosens and dissolves its constrictive density and grasp. It in- forms, in-structs, organises, orders and destines it. In this regard, the function of art is to save (Latin: *salvus* = safeguard, *salve* = dissolve) matter, to release from it the potential it harbors in concealment and which it is not, in itself, capable of achieving. This unrealised potential is mobilised by the *eidos*, the essence or formative idea which "enters into" matter and frees from incarceration the latent possibilities held in its grasp. In this hierarchical antinomical setup, the notion of *ground* correlates to matter and substance. Its only prospect is deliverance by illumination. As irrelevant or invalidated as this perspective might have become, and as contested it might be in many exemplary works, it nevertheless persists— not only in the expression of architecture and cinema, but in the very technologies that mobilise and regulate their conception and production.

## Ground of artifice

The notion of *ground* is a curious one. There are two main dimensions to the word—the idea of a *principle of reason*, the grounds of a belief or the basis of an architectural rationale for example; and the idea of a *physical foundation* and support. The same ideas cluster around the gendered words *matter* and *substance*, in which notions of metrical, matrical and maternal support persist. Both words convey a dimension of sufficient reason ("on what *grounds*?" that what *matters* is the *substantive* aspect of a thing or concept; what is *essential* to it), as well as of foundation and constitutive material substratum. In that sense, essence and substance, form and matter are not opposing terms but ambivalent phases of one and the same idea. Matter is measure and matrix, configurational force and resistance. The etymon of the word *ground* conveys an additional notion of crushed, worn, ground down or pulverised grit; the grist and grounds that characterise the earth as soil, dirt and sand. Ground can refer to a material that lacks structure and is riddled with voids and hollows—like bulldust or quicksand; inconsistent, unpredictable, susceptible to instability, potential slippage and fluxion. Or it can imply a firm, compact material, a predictable and steady underpinning.

Buildings are obviously grounded, set up upon a ground or foundation. The ground might be the physical topography of a site or it might refer to visual layers against which buildings are read and through which they are experienced. In cinema, image and sound are assembled within framed and layered settings. Layering might be spatial, temporal, acoustic, narrative and so forth. Some might be foregrounded, others backgrounded. In architecture and cinema, constitutive elements might be set over and against a ground which remains static, distinct and simply situates the assemblage. Or the components might interact more fundamentally with that ground so that mutual interchange, exchange and transformation take place between them. In such interaction one might assume an assertive and formative role, the other a supportive and responsive role. Another possibility is for the ground to function both formatively and responsively so that all architectural forms and articulations, all components of a cinematic assemblage would originate in and constitute both the ground of the work as well as its identity and existential texture.[31]

In his 1928 essay *"On the Essence of Ground,"* Heidegger begins with Leibnitz' contention that the problem of ground is fundamentally a problem of the identity and self-sameness of being (*Dasein*), of its true essence (*verum esse*), its "principle of reason" (*principium rationis*) which as "supreme grounding principle" (*Grundsatz*) determines its capacity for individuation and subjectivation. Because of its association with truth, Heidegger then associates the problem of ground with that of transcendence, since "transcendence designates the essence of the subject... it is the fundamental structure of subjectivity. The subject never exists beforehand as a 'subject,' in order then, *if* there are objects at hand, *also* to transcend. Rather, to *be* a subject means to be a being in and as transcendence."[32] The fundamentally transcendent nature of being is therefore vested in the possibility of "surpassing":

"Transcendent Dasein (already a tautological expression), surpasses neither a 'boundary' placed before the subject, forcing it in advance to remain inside (immanence), nor a 'gap' separating it from the object. Yet nor are objects—the beings that are objectified—that *towards which* a surpassing occurs. *What* is surpassed is precisely and solely *beings themselves... In* this surpassing Dasein for the first time comes towards that being that *it* is, and comes toward it *as* it 'itself.' Transcendence constitutes selfhood."[33]

That towards which Dasein tends in its surpassing and transcendence is *world.* "Transcendence is *being-in-the-world,*" a relational condition of being-with (*Mitsein*) others, "belonging among the other beings that we can always multiply to the point where they become unsurveyable"—and not merely human others, but of being in the midst of beings, "beings as a whole." "It is in transcendence alone that beings can come to light as beings." Transcendence is then associated with freedom. Not freedom *from* the world but freedom *for* world, *for the sake of* itself and for the sake of the world. This *for the sake of* is a projective disposition:[34]

"This bringing world before itself is the originary projection of the possibilities of Dasein, in so far as, in the midst of beings, it is to be able to comport itself towards such beings. Yet just as it does not explicitly grasp that which has been projected, this projection of world also always *casts* the projected world *over* beings. This prior casting over (*Überwurf*) first makes it possible for beings as such to manifest themselves. This occurrence of a projective casting-over, in which the being of Dasein is temporalised, is being-in-the-world. 'Dasein transcends' means: in the essence of its being it is *world-forming*, 'forming' (*bildend*) in the multiple sense that it lets world occur, and through the world gives itself an original view (form [*Bild*]) that is not explicitly grasped, yet functions precisely as a paradigmatic form (*Vor-bild*) for all manifest beings, among which each respective Dasein itself belongs."[35]

Transcendence is not a flight into the objective, an escape from the subjective, the existential, matter, substance or ground. Rather, the freedom associated with this transcendence is founded and grounded—that is, *formed*—in an "ontological interpretation of the subjectivity of the subject."[36] It is constitutive and a substantive characteristic of being. In that sense, freedom as transcendence is not a particular kind of ground but "the *origin of ground in general. Freedom is freedom for ground.*"[37]

"We shall name the originary relation of freedom to ground a *grounding* (*Gründen*). In grounding, freedom *gives* and *takes* ground. This grounding that is rooted in transcendence is, however, *strewn* into manifold ways. There are three such ways: (1) grounding as establishing (*Stiften*); (2) grounding as taking up a basis (*Bodennehmen*); (3) grounding as the grounding *of* something (*Begründen*)... This `first' form of grounding is nothing other than *the projection of the 'for the sake of'*... It indeed always pertains to Dasein's projection of world that in and through its surpassing Dasein comes back to beings as such. The 'for the sake of' that is projectively cast before us points back to the entirety of those beings that can be unveiled within the horizon of world.... Dasein in its projecting is, *as projecting*, also already *in the midst* of such beings... *Transcendence means projection of world in such a way that those beings that are surpassed also already pervade and attune that which projects*. With this *absorption* by beings that belongs to transcendence, Dasein has taken up a basis within beings, gained 'ground'... This grounding that establishes, as the projection of *possibilities of itself*, entails, however, that in this process Dasein in each case exceeds itself. In accordance with its essence, the projection of possibilities is in each case richer than the possession of them by the one projecting... Certain other possibilities are thereby already *withdrawn* from Dasein... Yet precisely this *withdrawal* of certain possibilities pertaining to its potentiality for being-in-the-world—a withdrawal entailed in its being absorbed by beings—first brings those possibilities of world projection that can 'actually' be seized upon *toward* Dasein as its world... *Corresponding to these two ways of grounding, transcendence at once exceeds and withdraws*. The fact that the ever-excessive projection of world attains its power and becomes our possession only in such withdrawal is at the same time a transcendental testimony to the *finitude* of Dasein's freedom."[38]

These first two forms of grounding—projecting world and being absorbed in a pervasive attunement—both give way to, or "co-temporalise, a *third* manner of grounding: *grounding as the grounding of something*," "*making possible the why-question in general*," which "illuminates the transcendental origin of the 'why' as such... Why *in this way* and not otherwise? Why this and not that? *Why something at all and not nothing*."[39]

> "Transcendence explicitly unveils itself as the origin of the grounding, however, when such grounding is brought to *spring forth* in its threefold character. In accordance with this, ground means: *possibility, basis, account*. Strewn in this threefold manner, the grounding that is transcendence first brings about in an originarily unifying manner that whole within which a Dasein must be able to exist in each case. Freedom in this threefold manner is freedom for ground. The occurrence of transcendence as grounding is the forming of a leeway into which there can irrupt the factical *self-maintaining* of factical Dasein in each case in the midst of beings as a whole.... *The essence of ground is the transcendental springing forth of grounding, strewn threefold into projection of world, absorption within beings, and ontological grounding of beings*."[40]

This suggests identity and contiguity between ground, grounds and grounding, principle of reason, ontological truth or ontic cause. Ground is not separate from principle, idea, cause. It is not a thing but a gesture, a trajectory, a process, an operation: transcend*ing*, project*ing* and so forth. It is ground*ing* in the same way that world is not world but world*ing:* "World never *is*, but *worlds*."[41] This operation is characterised by a projection or throwing that is free and transcendent, but which is also constituted of a double gesture of concealment/withholding and unconcealment/releasing. This grounding springs forth from "finite freedom." In its throw, being is not directed transcendentally in one direction, *away* from itself and beings, but is folded back *into* beings. The ground that it is and that it establishes is therefore not terminal or solid but abyssal. In this way, Heidegger posits an un-analysable disjunction, gap or *distance* that is constitutive of being, and that can be overcome but never eliminated :

> "The ground that sprigs forth in transcending folds back upon freedom itself, and freedom *as origin* itself becomes 'ground.' *Freedom is the ground of ground*. Yet not simply in the sense of a formal, endless 'iteration'... As this ground, however, freedom is the *abyss of ground (Ab-grund)* in Dasein. Not that our individual, free comportment is groundless; rather, in its essence as transcendence, freedom places Dasein, as potentiality for being, in possibilities that gape open before its finite choice,

i.e., within its destiny. Yet in its world-projective surpassing of beings, Dasein must surpass itself so as to be able to first of all understand itself as an abyss of ground from out of this elevation. And the character of this abyssal ground of Dasein is in turn nothing that lends itself to a dialectic, or to psychological dissection. The irruption of this abyssal ground in transcendence as grounding is rather the primordial movement that freedom accomplishes with us ourselves and thereby 'gives us to understand... The essence of the finitude of Dasein is, however, unveiled in *transcendence as freedom for ground*. And so the human being, existing as a transcendence that exceeds in the direction of possibilities, is a *creature of distance*. Only through originary distances that he forms for himself in his transcendence with respect to all beings does a true nearness to things begin to arise in him. And only being able to listen into the distance awakens Dasein as a self to the response of the other Dasein in whose company (*Mitsein*) it can surrender its I-ness so as to attain itself as an authentic self."[42]

The implication here is that transcendence is not delivered by an eclipsing of matter, by a tectonics of immateriality or dematerialisation, but by working the very core and interstices of matter through a fundamentally existential and material engagement, embeddedness and embodiedness. Central to this operative material existentiality is a double and simultaneous gesture of exceeding and withdrawing, surpassing and grounding which weave an abyssal orginary distance in which the possibility of nearness and of being-with-others is vested. There is a revealing tectonic equivalent of this non-oppositional double gesture in the North Indian Hindu temple. The temple's spire (*śikhara*) is a vertical extension of the central point at the crossing of the ground plan. The latter is the *garbhagṛha*—commonly the "womb-house," or literally "grasped-seed" of the deity, sheathed and invested by the masonry structure. The sexual symbolism is patent; but less evident is the notion that the *śikhara*, as shown here at *Khajuraho*, also represents the emanation and emerging presence of the deity whose breath, irradiating reflux and manifestation are conveyed by the highly worked carved plaster and stone surfaces.

The tectonic theme is the undecidability of solid and void by way of a surface that is literally teeming surfeit and exchange of two apparently opposing conditions. The carved motif is a deeply etched pattern of iterating reflections and inversions, symmetries and asymmetries, folds and scores, which in extremely sharp sunlight amplify the effect of exfoliating figure-ground to a radical degree. This causes solid and void to alternately advance and retreat, waver and become ambiguous so that the surface begins to shimmer, pulsate and reverberate. The tectonic effect conveys the symbolic message—the deity's presence is not wrought upon a separate ground. The god emerges in and as the ground itself by a kind of aeration or leavening of its materiality, which also mobilises and renders the architectonic substance fluid. The god is not transcendent or otherwise remote. Neither is the god immanent in the sense of the imminence of an about-to-be-present. What is presented here is neither the presence nor absence of the deity, but its fundamental manner of being nothing other than the gesture of a pure evanescent materiality.

In a similar register, the carved surfaces of the Buddhist *Bayon* at *Angkor Thom* convey various dispositions, orientations and countenances of the deity *Avalokiteshvara* looking out towards the world. Likewise is the Hindu *Descent of the Ganges* relief at *Mahabalipuram*. This latter is carved into a rock cleft below a natural pool, so that the mythological sculptural program narrating the cosmogonic irrigation of the world into existence by *Visnu* and the serpent *nagas* amplifies and transforms the material conditions found on site to create a conjunction of natural and artificial referends. In each case, the work involves two gestures. The first calibrates and aligns symbolic matter to the materiality and matrix of a context. The second relieves materiality from its burden of potential by releasing it from telluric and ponderous gravity. In a sense, matter is loosened and salved into the open by a thematic and tectonic, technical and tactical play of alternating rhythm between antinomies that never resolves in favor of one or the other, but is sustained in a state of interminable exchange.

Such non-dual conceptualisations of ground in which two such gestures coincide overlays a transcendent going-away—a surpassing or unfolding that projects beyond a limit that would ground it, and returns inwards or withdraws back into its ground. This allows non-oppositional readings of the nature and function of ground and by implication of light and dark, sound and silence. There is, for example, a condition of extreme ambiguity between light and dark which is the twilight. The uncertainty that permeates this period at so many levels conveys a heightened sense of the uncanny. Day and night, the outlines of things, depth and contrast, the layering of space, the pace of duration and the direction and provenance of time are all rendered indeterminate. The overall effect is one of premonition, intrigue and unexpected, impending encounter—that something may or may not be there, may or may not appear, could or could not be present; that something immanent might crystallise or something present vaporise at any moment. This moment is also perilous. Like all thresholds, doorways and gates it harbors uncertain threats and dangers. The twilight is a palpable example of a liminal zone—not a limit *per se* since it is not an interface but an interval, a middle place. It is the milieu par excellence because it harbors an indefinite profusion of possible worlds and beings. Lacking distinct boundaries, firm edges and sharply delineated formal contents, the twilight is not so much subject to the structure of orthogonal and sedentary space but to a space of interactions, transformations, trajectories and gestures.

Twilight manifests what André Leroi-Gourhan has called "itinerant space"—the infiltrating space of nomadism, opposed to the radiating, centralised space of sedentarism.[43] In this space, light cannot serve to render oppositional form, contrasting pattern and shape. Rather, it functions to create atmosphere and ambiance—subsisting as a kind of deconstituted, volatised materiality, or a pervasive gossamer mist that holds indefinite possibilities of combination and recombination, assemblage and alignment. This is to say that here, space is not formal but *ambient*, not hot or cold but *calorific*, not colorful but *chromatic*; and that its qualities are invested less in the objects that populate it than *in the air* that permeates it. Such spaces and the temporalities that belong to them allow us to think of light and dark in non-oppositional ways. The ambiance of twilight is neither light nor dark but gloaming—a condition that is both gloom and glow, one indiscernibly yielding to and inducing the other.

Space consequently grows in mystery rather than clarity, and in becoming
darker, it begins to shimmer and gleam.

## Surfeit

Paradjanov's *Sayat Nova* (1969), which Deleuze considers portentous
("ponderous matter roused by the spirit. *Sayat Nova* is definitely the
masterpiece of a material language of object")[44] and Jameson pretentious
and detestable ("despite the naïf-folk splendour of its images.")[45] is
undoubtedly a weighty film. In large part this is because materiality is so
prominently foregrounded. As Paradjanov says in the opening credits, the
film is not intended to be a historical account of the life of Armenian poet
Sayat Nova, but a reflection on his "inner world… the trepidations of his
soul, his passions and torments, widely utilising the symbolism and
allegories specific to the tradition of Medieval Armenian poet-
troubadours." Clearly the setup owes much to the theatre of medieval
troubadours, but the theatricality of the work operates across several
registers—symbolic, existential and haptic, as well as stylistic; even
political if one accounts for the artistic and religious suppression which the
cinematographer suffered.

The images constructed by Paradjanov have several important tectonic
characteristics. Because of their flatness and non-perspectival setup, they
detach themselves from any kind of existential context, setting or ground.
The gestures of actors are highly stylised and movement is decelerated to
such an extent that the film conveys a distinctive slow and viscous
temporality. This again detaches the images from anything like a
normative spatial and temporal context. The stylised setup allows
Paradjanov to organise the images as highly charged fields in which
people, settings, gestures, objects and sounds interact dynamically. The
subjects and objects featured—faces, hands, eyes, skin, shells, fire, wind,

water, earth, milk, blood, flesh, bread, ash, walls, domes, columns, paving slabs, books, script, garments, carpets, birds, feathers, fish, lamb, chalices, knives, the sound of water flowing, of cloth fluttering, of pages turning, of recited poetry, of wind instruments, of chanting in resonant chambers—are all excised from their normal contexts. They are reconfigured in ways that amplify their individual power as objects. Their elemental character and the starkness of their re-assemblage sets them over and against each other in ways that develop surprising metaphorical alliances and resonances. The procedure is strictly iconic and delivers both heightened existential affects and symbolic reference. Colours are relentlessly saturated and restricted to modulations of one or two—predominantly deep blood red and indigo blue, together with bone, gold, silver, black and white. Chromatic and elemental Christian symbols abounds—white roses, veils of thorns, fish, sheep, and water. Pomegranates bleed on white cloth, the liquid spreading its stain to fill the frame; a bare foot crushes crimson grapes into an inscribed stone slab; stormwaters flow down a stone wall over books stashed in a recess; a child lays out ancient manuscripts to dry on the tilted roofs of a monastic library; carpets are laid on shallow domes for washing with water and the shuffle of womens' feet; a bride weaves in front of a gilded mirror reflecting a spiralling gold statue of cupid.

Compositionally, the images are more often than not frontal and symmetrical. The frame is subdivided by horizontal and vertical lines in dynamic symmetry and layered through shallow screens, cloths and carpets hanging on frames. People and animals are positioned within the frame to activate compositional dynamics. The frontality of images, the abstraction of objects and their assemblage achieve a series of iconographic tableaux or set pieces. Because of this, the sequence of images is disjunctive. Each frame maintains its own boundaries and evokes its own world. In some cases, as with the gilded mirror, Paradjanov separates the mirror's frame from the image and background so that each element has its own motion—a static background, spiralling reflections and a frame that swings from side to side. The assemblage is characterised by a series of individual compositions which unfold the narrative through fracture and flash rather than sequence and continuity. Representational and narrative power are achieved by resonances produced between these fragments, as well as by music and imaged/enunciated texts which overlap the individual frames, sometimes emanating from beyond their boundaries. The film generally features no ambient sound. The soundtrack, like the images, is artificially constructed of natural sounds—Russian Orthodox harmonic plainchant; the singing of children and women accompanying everyday activities; shrieks and wails that appear otherworldly; the reed instruments, cymbals and drums of medieval troubadours; poetic verse and so forth. In cases where sounds bear some relation to the actions depicted, they nevertheless seem to come from elsewhere, off-screen, other regions of the spaces shown or somewhere beyond the world of the narrative.

The disjunctive effects allow Paradjanov to escape the logic of given existential conditions. At the same time, they permit a dramatisation and amplification of those conditions by conjugating them with each other; and with the fact of their disembodied, disengaged status according to which objects and sounds gain power and efficacy beyond what is available to them in their normal milieu. A fish flapping out of water by the seaside is common enough, but consider its position in the following sequence of images: three pomegranates staining a white cloth blood red; pages from a book, presumably the poet's diary; the words "I am the man whose life and soul are torture"; a silver knife on a blood stained white cloth; the diary and text again; a bare foot crushing grapes on an inscribed memorial stone; the diary and text again; the suffocating fish; a silver sword and sphere next to a white rose in a bronze vase; the diary again; the words "I am the man whose life and soul are torture" overlaid on the image of a veil of thorns.

Paradjanov repeats images, texts and verses, often in sequential proximity to iterate, emphasise and articulate themes. Together with the flat intensity and charged character of the image field, these iterations fold the semantic and aesthetic character back into the images, rather than releasing them into a separated space of reception. A deep sense of internalisation, if not claustrophobia, ensues. The images, like icons generally, are entirely self-referential. There is no escaping the ambiance and presence they convey by recourse to anything off-screen, to any referends beyond the structure and semantic content of the image or even spatio-temporally within the setup of the image itself; devoid as it is of any depth, hollows or intervals. All of these tropes convey a radical compaction, densification and materialisation of the image—a kind of throwing-towards/against (ob-jet), an objecti-fication (making-object) or factionalisation of the imaged subject. The contents of images and the various subjects and objects that populate it are always gathered into neighbourhoods and collectives. They are always *with* other subjects and objects, in a milieu that they share and that is mutually formative. The setting might be recognisably architectural, religious and sometimes ruinous; or it might consist of desolate surfaces that could be deserts, grassland or terrains vague. In any case, the settings indicate no horizon; and the normative three dimensionality of space—above, below, left and right—are not explicitly articulated. Shots are generally directed downward so that subjects and objects are read against pure surfaces whose edges are definitively out of frame. In many cases, subjects and objects appear to be modulations of each other and of their setting, rather than being components projected forward as relief against a background. It is in this sense that the images become themselves the ground from which they are conjured up. They are the self-articulations of a matrical ground of potentiality which they surpass by coming forward into visibility; but into which they also reiteratively withdraw as they defer one to the other and fold back into their provenance.

In architecture there is a world of difference between deep materiality and the mere designation and application of diverse materials to a framework for expressive ends. By deep materiality I mean the achievement of material presence and gravity through the close and intricate working and stressing of form and space to produce the kinds of compaction and densification that Paradjanov achieves in film—that is, putting into question or putting to the test the very fabric and ground of architecture. In many architectural projects the conceptualisation of materiality and the application of materials follow the manner of a sampling, which rarely evokes more than a simulacrum of material presence. Assigning a palette of materials to a structural frame for aesthetic ends turns out to have nothing but emblematic value—a gabion retaining wall below a rain screen of sustainably sourced oak boards overlaid by a patinated perforated metal plate screen folded to form an awning or soaring eave above a polished concrete slab floor cast with salvaged rusted or bronze fasteners framed by large walls of beeswaxed set *stucco lustro* plaster, and so forth. These kinds of moves in architecture do produce a level of materiality, at times extraordinary, but always aestheticised, commodified and fetishist. They leave normative tropes of architectural conceptualisation, design and production largely intact and are therefore fundamentally conservative. Deep materiality on the other hand is a fundamentally militant disposition to material and spatial practices. Its field of operation is not applicative but transformative. Its focus is not on the separable components of spatial structuring and organisation but on space itself, on the material presence and corporeality of space. Here, materials are not applied *to* something. Rather, that something—space—is *worked materially*, in a material way, in a way that matters and weighs. The manner of its being worked and what it works out to become constitute the grounds, the articulated form, presence and potential of existential spatiality and temporality.

Recent work by Alvaro Siza exemplifies this kind of testing of space, materiality and the grounds of architecture. The range of materials used at the *Galician Centre of Contemporary Art* (Santiago de Compostella, 1988-1993) and the *Porto School of Architecture* (1995) is extremely restrained—polished granite and timber floors, matt plaster walls and ceilings with set joints. Siza uses granite for the floors and lower parts of the walls to create a containing base for a more articulated and folded composition of planes in the upper walls and ceilings. The latter carry the bulk of formal manipulation and expression. Geometries are also restrained and limited to orthogonal and circular forms, sometimes strained into wedge and oval segments. The predominant sense is of a compact material that has been iteratively hollowed out and aerated, but that at the same time conveys substantial mass and density.

Siza constructs the materiality of these buildings out of cavities and intervals. In several places cavities reveal themselves as elements slide past each other to uncover apparently concealed hollows. These may be other habitable spaces yet to be discovered in the total sequence, they may be neutral or inaccessible. The tectonic trope is one of interminable folding, turning and returning of surfaces into, through and past each other. The spaces and rooms are never fully declared and always maintain something in reserve, something to be later encountered. This quality dramatises the spatial narrative, keeping it in suspense. Even when spaces are reached and understood, they offer surprising perspectives back towards adjoining spaces one may have already passed through as well as to distant unexpected spaces. In all cases, suspense and surprise activate and drive spatial anticipation and movement, but not with any sense of restlessness or urgency. Spaces are poised between stable and directional, regular and distorted, linear and centred, inside and outside, this side and the other. Movement through the buildings takes the form of infiltration into gaps and pockets opened up within an architectonic material fabric that is not separate from but constitutive of space.

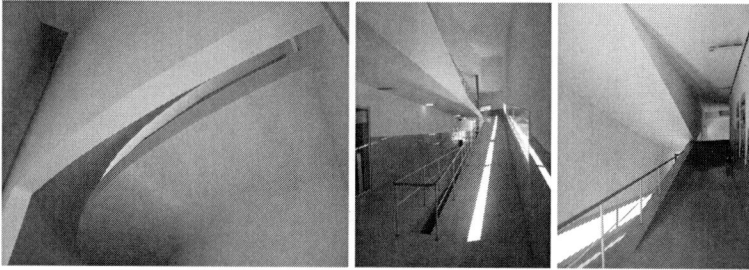

At Porto, the entry and long ramp sequence turns back on itself, becoming more enclosed and shielded as it rises closer to the roof forms, before disappearing into a narrow cleft where roof, wall and floor converge. In this part of the spatial narrative, the materiality of the building first opens to afford entry, then successively closes, conceals and swallows space up, compacting and solidifying itself. Siza's tectonics of folded, layered and hollowed materiality puts into question the relationship and respective status of interior and exterior in a spatial sense; and of interiority and exteriority when such spaces assume subjective dimensions and become places capable of retaining presences.

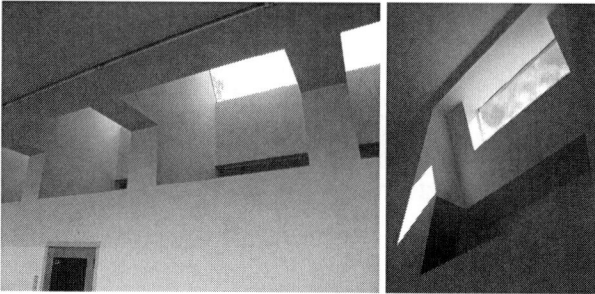

Because the hollows are often inaccessible and their exact location, shape and extent are incommensurable, they are liable to produce inflexions and disturbances within the space. Interiors unexpectedly become exterior to other interiors whose limits cannot be known. Solid boundaries reveal themselves as abyssal, unfathomable and therefore disturbing. The wall, whose accepted function is to produce an unambiguous boundary between interior and exterior worlds, is here folded or perforated to such an extent that it begins to assume interiority.

Contrary to what a pragmatic view might indicate, this quality is in fact integral to the wall, as the etymon itself suggests (from Latin: *valum*, and

*WEL = wind round, turn, roll, spiral; Latin: *voluere* = roll; Greek: *hellisein* = to turn around; Anglosaxon: *wela* = well, spring). The interval, what is *between* the walls, is also what intervenes within the volute and the helix; what is within the spiral or what the spiral turns and pivots about. That is, space, and not simply static space but space as expanding and welling up or springing forth. In that sense, Siza's by turns hollowing and compacting materiality is a foundational architectonic questioning of the nature of enclosure itself—maybe *the* foundational question for architecture. His investigation of the boundary, of its formal and material potential, conveys the impossibility of determining what encloses and what exposes. It foregrounds the undecidable wavering that characterises the limit of inside and outside. Rather than having recourse to an "aesthetics of immateriality" which uses the inter-reflective capacities of glass veils to convey ambiguity and dematerialisation of form, Siza's tectonics pursues its questioning within mass itself, within materiality and within the grounds of architecture in a manner that makes space and materiality integral to and mutually informing of each other.

With Sigurd Lewerentz, an entirely different sensibility to materials is at work but with parallel implications. At the churches of *St Marc* (Björkhagen, 1956-60) and *St Peter* (Klippan, 1962-66), Lewerentz makes predominant use of brick in floor, wall, roof and fixed furnishings. At Björkhagen the brick walls are laid in free running bond, with contrasting light grey mortar for the widely varying beds and perpends. This gives the walls the quality of pure texture and surface rather than the mechanically regular, modular quality normal for brickwork. The surfaces read like a patinated rockface, a tight fabric or gauze that also billows outwards into the birch grove surrounding the building.

While the building stands within the grove as if in a clearing, and while its formal programme is uncompromisingly orthogonal, the material quality of its walls enable it to interact with the bark and foliage of the birches as well as with the dappled quality of light in the grove to such an extent that its mass, surfaces and cubic presence begin to vaccilate. This achieves an unexpected leavening of materiality, a forwarding and receding of surfaces and fields, and a dynamic integration with the diaphanous setting.

The chapel ceiling is of shallow clustered brick vaults, set within steel *I* beams which span across the width of the space. The beams are laid in alternating converging fan shapes in plan, and in an alternating sloping pattern in section. Together, they give the ceiling the quality of a tent fabric billowing upwards. Windows in the main wall have deep internal brick reveals, no frames and are made of single sheets of glass fixed to the external wall. The chapel has few windows and is fairly dark. The combination of these material qualities, or the material assemblage of the building, dramatises the inside-outside relationship in a very specific way. The bright grove outside is projected solidly into the interior through the frameless openings while the relatively darker walls appear to extend outwards into the site. The wall loses its interiorising, enclosing and spatially compressive character. Its limits and the density of its material presence begin to fluctuate and loosen their grip on the interior. The same effects are achieved by the combination of deep brick lintels and vaults in the ceiling.

In terms of both interior and exterior quality, Lewerentz' working of masonry appears to be directed to a dematerialisation of mass and of the sharp edges and outlines that reinforce volumetric gravity and weight. He achieves this by material selection and the way he positions, juxtaposes and overlaps masonry units, forms, surfaces and edges in relation to each other, to the grove and to the birch trunks. Lewerentz both constricts and loosens the rules applying to standard bricklaying processes.[46] He uses only full standard bricks with no cutting or specially shaped units, and he uses bricks for floor, wall, ceiling and furniture. These rules necessitate compensatory moves and enable expressive and tectonic possibilities not available in standard bricklaying practice. For example, the variable proportion of mortar to brick demands a stronger mortar mix that can assume greater structural function. St John Wilson notes that Lewerentz prepared 1:20 scale brick setout drawings and insisted that neither plumb nor level be used in construction: "the effect is of a surface in which bricks appear to be embedded in a matrix of mortar rather than laid up in bonded coursework of conventional joints."[47] Lewerentz turned the regularity and flatness of brick walls into irregular weaves and almost imperceptibly undulating surfaces that achieve a degree of fluidity in material quality, but a more extraordinary pulsation and vibration within the space itself. Lewerentz' deconstitution of the building's materiality was not pursued through a literal fragmentation of forms, a substitution of non-Euclidean geometries or lightweight, transparent and translucent materials. Instead he achieved it in the material itself, using standard components, formal typologies, technologies and processes, but subjecting these to modest shifts and stresses and to modest small scale moves which carry considerable tectonic and experiential implications.

At Klippan, the material and tectonic moves are more risky but also more significant. The three existential and structural dimensions of space—up/down, left/right, front/back—manifest in architecture by the ceiling, wall and floor, are here fused together by a common material. Each becomes a modulation or reverberation of the other, rather than being radically distinguished as three separate and separable components of architectural space. The floor is uneven and slopes to the altar—a visually imperceptible feature because of the low level of light in the space, but obvious experientially. At the baptismal font it bulges up around an incised cut and fountain, implying a connection to an underground water source.

The floor is experienced kinaesthetically as a topographical ground that resists and yields—at once solid and hollow, crystalline and fluid. It appears to be a surface subject and susceptible to telluric forces, heave, fluctuation, rise and fall—all equivalent to an architectural off-screen or out-of-frame that the building's materiality registers. Walls are generally plumb and orthogonal, with variations in thickness, free brick bonding, flush mortar joints and four small windows with deep reveals. Sensed in dim light, the walls appear grave and impermeable but also lively and shimmering because of their variable patterned surfaces. The relatively small scale of the windows and their frameless detailing renders them as bright cubes of light in the space, responsive to outside light conditions. Depending on those conditions and their fluctuation, the walls will appear to expand or contract, advance into or recede from the space, amplify or constrict its volume and boundaries. The frameless fixed glass windows necessitated an alternative ventilation strategy which Lewerentz achieved within the wall cavity and open perpend joints in the wall surface, turning what is normally a pragmatic and technical requirement for thermal isolation and waterproofing into a tectonic quality that aligns with his broader objectives. The perforated character of the walls renders their solidity, mass and gravity ambiguous. There is a circulation of voids and gaps within walls and floors which counters their evident permanence and function as boundaries and limits to the space. To the evident open room of the chapel is added a network of concealed voids for air and water which contribute to the dematerialisation of the walls and the spaces they delimit. The vaulted ceiling is a variation on Björkhagen and produces similar effects. Its form gives it a sense of billowing in uneven waves due to the alternating pattern of ribs which expand and contract in plan, as well as slope slightly towards the centre of the space from each side.

Being made of a single material, all dimensions of the space operate as mutual grounds. However each of the three is also subjected to marginal shifts and discontinuities which have a major impact on the existential quality of the room. The floor reads as a woven surface of homogenous pattern with no predominant direction. The wall functions more like a carved mass, its thickness giving reveals, openings and the interior space itself a cave-like quality. The roof is the most liberated element in its form and its remoteness from light and the ground. The uniformity and palpable difference between the material and tectonic character of these three components allows Lewerentz to conjugate and diversify the ambiguity of the space.

In his reading of Lewerentz' work, St John Wilson cites Heidegger's conception of function of material in a work of art:

> "An eloquent passage in Heidegger's *The Origin of the Work of Art* describes how a Greek temple 'does not cause the material to disappear but rather causes it to come forth for the very first time.' Just so at Klippan: brick was never more brick, steel more steel, glass more glass, wood more wood. In that attention to the essential nature of materials there lies a quality of respect that has its own morality. Ethics and technique become one."[48]

The phrase cited comes from a longer passage, quoted here to give a fuller context:

> "When a work is created, brought forth out of this or that work-material — stone, wood, metal, colour, language, tone—we say also that it is made, set

forth out of it. But just as the work requires a setting up in the sense of a consecrating-praising erection, because the work's work-being consists in the setting up of a world, so a setting forth is needed because the work-being of the work itself has the character of a setting forth. The work as work, in its presencing, is a setting forth, a making... what is the nature of that in the work which is usually called the work material? Because it is determined by usefulness and serviceability, equipment takes into its service that of which it consists: the matter. In fabricating equipment—e.g., an axe—stone is used, and used up. It disappears into usefulness. The material is all the better and more suitable the less it resists perishing in the equipmental being of the equipment. By contrast the temple-work, in setting up a world, does not cause the material to disappear, but rather causes it to come forth for the very first time and to come into the Open of the work's world. The rock comes to bear and rest and so first becomes rock; metals come to glitter and shimmer, colours to glow, tones to sing, the world to speak. All this comes forth as the work sets itself back into the massiveness and heaviness of stone, into the firmness and pliancy of wood, into the hardness and lustre of metal, into the lighting and darkening of colour, into the clang of tone, and into the naming power of the word. That into which the work sets itself back and which it causes to come forth in this setting back of itself we call the earth. Earth is that which comes forth and shelters. Earth, self-dependent, is effortless and untiring. Upon the earth and in it, historical man grounds his dwelling in the world. In setting up a world, the work sets forth the earth. This setting forth must be thought here in the strict sense of the word. The work moves the earth itself into the Open of a world and keeps it there. The work lets the earth be an earth."[49]

For Heidegger, the temple results from a work, an operation on matter. This work does not merely consume matter, using it up without residue in the making of a thing, which is the case in equipmental making. Rather, this work—the work of art and by implication the work of architecture— brings the material to presence in a more originary way. It "draws up out of" the material the "mystery" of its "clumsy yet spontaneous support."[50] As a result of the work, the material *comes into its own* and also *comes into a world*—into the openness of the *world of the work*; in this case of a *templum*, a place in which the deity presents itself to sight.[51] Matter is enabled and ennobled by art to become more *essentially* itself, to come to and to know itself *for the first time*. The purpose of art is thereby to extract, release, reveal and unconceal originary materiality from materials.[52] But this assumes that each material has a paradigmatic form— an *eidos* in the Platonic sense, characterised by certain essential qualities: stone weighs heavy, wood bends firmly, metals shimmer, colours glow and darken, tone clangs, words name, and so forth. This perspective may help to venture plausible interpretations of certain aspects of Lewerentz' work, however, Lewerentz' materiality eclipses any fundamentalist or logocentric reading. St Peter is a masonry building. It rests, stands and supports. It shelters a clearing and illuminates. It weighs heavy and its colouring gloams and darkens. But Lewerentz takes his working of the material to an entirely other level. The masonry is heavy but in the midst of its heaviness, because of how it has been made, that heaviness heaves and becomes animate. For Lewerentz, the transformative character of individual and collective worship is paralleled by a transformation in the material itself, a transformation which takes the material beyond itself and beyond its limits. Through the work, materials are fundamentally altered and for the first time come not into their own but *into their other*. In doing so they defer to other materials and other states of materiality, they suspend their self-sameness, their consistency and individual objective identities in favour of a being-*other*, a being-*with* and a being-*subject to* others.

# CHAPTER FIVE

# AGENCY, CRISIS, DISESTABLISHMENT

"A radical shock can only come from the outside."[1]

## Assemblage

The relative disposition, geometric organisation and motion of camera, frame, actor and setting constitute an *assemblage*—a dynamic field of symmetries, asymmetries, orthogonals and diagonals that can be mobilised, energised and conjugated to create interactions and combinations of compositional and dynamic potential. Assemblages are fundamentally strategic. It is a question of bringing together a framing of components that thereby gain the propensity and capacity to co-function.[2] The field constituted by the framing gathers elements within and outside it so as to play out potentialities and productive conjugations that can develop into patterns, figures and forms—narrative, spatial, temporal, material and in any case dramatic—which were not available to the singularity of elements alone. In that way, the frame *communalises* singularities, but without necessarily resuming or unifying them; without making of them a collective that might be named or labelled. In other words, the frame mobilises singularities in their otherness to each other and to what is other or beyond the frame itself. The containment it offers opens access to what they might become through deferring to each other, their passage past each other, their juxtapositions and conjugations. By containing and including the frame withholds, but only for a moment and only in terms of the proximities and resonances afforded by the potential of the field.

Because the spatial field is both static and dynamic, arrangements within it can mobilise potential relationships, interactions and conjugations between different conditions in the geometric setup. This is done by manipulating frames, registers and regimes to articulate compositional, semantic and narrative objectives. The arrangements are fundamentally strategic and productive and might be usefully articulated Deleuze's notion of *agencement*:

"What is an *agencement*? It is a multiplicity which comports many heterogenous terms, and which establishes liaisons, relationships between them, across ages, sexes, reigns—different natures. Also, the sole unity of *agencement* is that of co-functioning: it is a symbiosis, a `sympathy.' What is important is never filiations but alliances and alignments; these are not heredities, descendences, but contagions, epidemics, the wind.... Not at all a conversation, but a conspiracy, a shock of love or hate. There is no judgement in sympathy, but conveniences between bodies of all kinds... That is what *agencer* is: to be in the middle, on the encountering border between an interior and an exterior world."[3]

The common translation of *agencement* by "assemblage" is problematic. An assemblage implies a static spatial organisation or composition. Deleuze's *agencement* intends a dynamic setup; an arrangement of the mobilisation and putting-to-work of potential that may or may not be spatial. This potential does not rest solely with individual elements that have linear or sequential patterns of association (this *then* that), or that are related by opposition (this *or* that) or negation (neither this *nor* that). Rather, it comes into play out of the relational conjunction, alignment, concatenation or juxtaposition of elements which form non-linear, rhizomatic or folded networks (this *and* that). The elements need not exist in a state of harmony or commensurability. They need not cohere into defined patterns or shapes. The outcome of their interaction is less formal and spatial than temporal or musical. That is, *agencement* a matter of rhythm and resonance, not shape. The more discordant and incommensurable the elements, the more opportunities there will be for productive resonance.

Deleuze's *agencement* has significant implications for an analytics and a poetics of cinematography and architectural design. It is useful for the process of reading films and buildings, but more so for the actual processes, strategies and tactics of practice. Considering films and buildings as combinational assemblages of resonant heterogenous components in relation to place, space, time, materiality and the technologies of production, shifts the focus away from passive reception and mimetics into active and critical engagement in the mobilisation of new trajectories of practice. The process is radically experimental and creative or productive rather than predictive. In both analytical and poetic phases it is a process of drawing rather than designing, of programming "the means of staking out an experimentation that overflows our capacities of prediction."[4]

The building up of a filmic or architectural fabric through montage is a process of the differential assemblage of parts. These parts are akin to fragments with no intrinsic value for cinematographics or architectonics until they are constituted-together to form assemblages. A window is meaningless without the wall it perforates, the zones it links and the prospects it opens up. Likewise, it is in the conjunction—the and-and-and of agency—that the semantic potential of individual images begin to be mobilised. This is Pudovkin's sense of editing as a practice of synthetic assemblage that relays *kinematic* value:

> "I claim that every object, taken from a given viewpoint and shown on the screen to spectators, is a *dead object*, even though it has moved before the camera. The proper movement of an object before the camera is yet no movement on the screen, it is no more than raw material for the future building-up by editing, of the movement that is conveyed by the assemblage of the various strips of film. Only if the object be placed together among a number of separate objects, only if it be presented as part of a synthesis of different separate visual images, is it endowed with filmic life...Every object must, by editing, be brought upon the screen so that it shall have not *photographic*, but *cinematographic* essence."[5]

This assemblage, fabric or network of mobilised agencies is what Deleuze and Guattari term the *plane of immanence*.[6] The frame is precisely such a plane of immanence—a charged zone of neighborhoods and immanent relational opportunities, with no discernable form, shape or dimension, no definable boundaries and no semantic value. It is entirely constituted by the associations that never cease to form and unravel, assemble, disassemble and reassemble, stabilise and mobilise as the relational potential articulates itself. These actualisations may be intended by design and concretely registered, or they may remain virtual until they are variously and differently actualised by the spectator of a film or the user of a space. For Deleuze, the plane of immanence is both a topographical and cinematic condition—that is, a plane surface and a cinematic *plan* or shot. Motifs of traversal, crossing, trajectory—in any case of displacement rather disposition, of dynamics rather than stasis, of energies rather than configurations and of drawing (*dessin*) rather than design (*dessein*)—are paramount in assemblages that characterise *agencement*:

> "It is no longer a matter of forms but of cinematographic relations between unformed elements; there are no longer subjects, but dynamic individuations without subject, which constitute collective *agencements*... It is this very plan(e), uniquely defined by longitude [speed] and latitude [intensity], which opposes the organizational plane. It is truly a plane of immanence, because it has no other dimension to supplement what takes

place on it... it is no longer a teleological plane, a design, but a geometric plane, abstract drawing, which is like the section of all forms whatever, whatever their dimensions... It belongs to this plane of immanence or consistency to include fogs, pests, voids, jumps, immobilisations, suspensions, precipitations. Because failure is part of the plane itself: one must in effect always retake, retake by the middle, to give elements new relations of speed and slowness which cause them to change *agencements*, to jump from one *agencement* to another... Certain contemporary musicians [Pierre Boulez, John Cage] have pushed to the end the practical idea of an immanent plane which no longer has a hidden principle of organization, but where the process must be understood no less than what proceeds from it... where themes, motifs and subjects are maintained only in order to liberate floating affects."[7]

Working(in) the plane is not a matter of taking up a position or of declaring a thesis, but of working transversally—interminably traversing positions in order to liberate the charges latent in the assemblage, working by and through the middle rather than top down (deductively) or bottom up (inductively). It is evidently a concept which privileges movement, variation and transformation over stability and permanence. In this, Deleuze extends Simondon's concept of *transduction* as the process proper to the individuation of a being, in which relation is a constitutive modality of being rather than something that a pre-given being undergoes:

"We understand by transduction an operation—physical, biological, mental, social—by which an activity propagates itself gradually within the interior of a domain, by establishing this propagation on the structuration of the domain worked from place to place: each region of constituted structure serving the following region as principle and model, priming its constitution, so much so that a modification thus extends itself progressively at the same time as this structuring operation. A crystal which, from a very small grain, grows and extends itself in all directions in its supersaturated solution furnishes the simplest image of the transductive operation: each molecular layer already constituted serves as structuring base to the layer in formation; the result is a reticular amplifying structure. The transductive operation is an individuation in progress; in a physical domain it can take place in the simplest manner as a progressive iteration; but in more complex domains, such as domains of vital metastability or psychic problematics, it can advance in constantly variable steps, and extend itself in a domain of heterogeneity; there is transduction when there is structural and functional activity beginning from the centre of a being, and extending itself in diverse directions starting from that centre, as if multiple dimensions of the being were to appear around that centre; transduction is correlative appearance of dimensions and structures within a being of preindividual tension, that is in a being which is more than unity and more than identity, and which has not yet dephased into multiple dimensions in relation to itself[8]... in the domain of knowledge, (transduction) defines the veritable start of invention, which is neither inductive nor deductive but transductive... transduction does not seek elsewhere a principle to resolve the problems of a domain: it draws the resolving structure from the very tensions of that domain... neither is it comparable to induction, as induction does indeed maintain the character of terms of reality comprised in the domain studied, drawing the structures of analysis from those terms themselves, but it only conserves what is positive, that is to say what is common to all the terms, eliminating what they have that is singular."[9]

The two key conditions of the transductive operation are, firstly, that it has no recourse to any external, transcendent organising principle; and secondly, that it is not selective. It preserves and accounts for the differences between terms that it brings into communication and productive neighborhood—Simondon's word is *disparate*, disparateness. The process genuinely accounts for heterogeneity and multiplicity within a metastable field, rather than seeking stable uniformity and unity out of an unstable field. In transduction, disparateness is incorporated within the resolving operation and becomes constitutive of signification—there being no impoverishment of information. Whereas induction always results in a loss of information and a degradation of the original state in order to deliver the requisite resolution of tension. Simondon's concern is to preserve the potential for evolution and fecundity within a system—its "capacity to illuminate new domains" and "engender pregnant forms"—by ensuring its metastability: "In every domain, the most stable state is a state of death; it is a state degraded from which no transformation is any longer possible without the intervention of an energy external to the degraded system."[10] Simondon's aim is also to show the inadequacy of the classical notion of form, of the "Theory of Form" and of the privileging of pure "Good Form" in order to replace it with that of information,[11] which,

"in contrast to form, is never a unique term, but the signification which surges out from a disparation (*qui surgit d'une disparation*)... the Theory of Form ignored metastability. We wanted to take up the Theory of Form and, by way of introducing a quantum condition, show that the problems posed by the Theory of Form cannot be directly resolved by way of a notion of stable equilibrium, but only by one of metastable equilibrium; the Good Form is then no longer the simple form, the geometrically pregnant form, but *the significative form*, that is to say that form which establishes a transductive order within a system of reality comporting potentials. This good form is one that maintains the energetic level of the system, conserves its potentials by making them compatible: it is the structure of compatibility and viability, it is the invented dimensionality according to which there is compatibility without degradation."[12]

The "Theory of Form"—whether archetypal (Platonic), hylemorphic (Aristotelian) or gestaltic[13]—always implies an oppositional duality between what gives form and the matter which receives it; as well as a hierarchy which privileges form as active and informative over matter as passive and uninformed. In the Platonic theory of Ideas, the forms (*ta eide*) are non-degradable, immutable and subject to no progress or change. Only engendered beings are degradable. Forms organise the instability of matter to produce stable entities by uniformalising and totalizing its component parts. It involves a non-reciprocal, irreversible, asymmetrical action. The archetype is anterior and superior to matter. By contrast, the "Theory of Information" privileges reciprocity, equivalence and reversibility between active and passive terms, between emitter and receptor. In a transductive operation, the metastable equilibrium of the field is worked to liberate potential energy by the surging forth of a new structure which functions as a modulator[14]:

"It is the energy of metastability of the field, therefore of matter, which permits the structure, and therefore the form, to advance: potentials reside in matter, and the limit between form and matter is an amplifying relay... the relation form-matter is thereby transposed into a transductive relation, and in accordance with the progress of the structuring-structured couple, across an active limit constituted by the passage of information."[15]

A key motif of this concept is that of the field (*champ*), which establishes a plural reciprocity of ontological and constructive or operative modal status between whole and part, through a productive dynamic coupling exemplified by the electromagnetic field.[16] Characteristic of the field is that the elements contained by it also constitute it and integrally determine it by way of their interactions. The field is an intensive condition with the capacity to produce energetic effects once something is introduced into it. It is laid out like a network or web, a schema that is a plurality of "rich correlations between different and distinct terms." This allows Simondon to propose an energetic rather than morphological theory of form—of the "good form" that operates across Platonic, Aristotelian, gestaltic and scientific registers:

"Instead of conceiving of an archetypal form which dominates the totality, and radiates over it, like the Platonic archetype, could we not propose the possibility of a transductive propagation for form taking, advancing stage by stage, within the field... with an energetic theory of form taking, we would have a non-probabilistic method, according no privilege to stable configurations... it is the form taking accomplished in a metastable field that creates configurations."[17]

Metastability is a dynamic equilibrium that needs to be kept in permanence. It implies a series of successive new structurations without which the metastable equilibrium cannot be maintained. This means that a form is not an abstract totalised entity or configuration over and above the milieu in which it is found. Rather, it is the trace and vestige of a process of individuation.[18] This idea gives rise in Deleuze to the notion of a *mobile section*—the temporary registering of a given state, or the particular phase of a longer, fuller process of becoming, irrespective of the mass, permanence or materiality of the form. Simondon's informational and perceptual concept of spatial form and formation has fundamental implications for an architecture that might seek to eclipse purely formal concerns.[19] He explains the concept firstly by differentiating the structural logic and topological schema of pure and simple geometric forms from the notion of potential which is inherent in a *system* but not in a *structure*:

"A form like the square can be very stable, very pregnant, and contain a minor quantity of information, in the sense that it can very rarely incorporate in itself different elements of a metastable situation; it is difficult to consider the square as a solution to a perceptual problem. The square, the circle, and more generally the simple and pregnant forms, are structural schemes rather than forms... The physical problem of individuality is not only a problem of topology since what is lacking in topology is the consideration of potentials; potentials, precisely because they are potentials and not structures, cannot be represented as graphic elements of a situation. The situation in which the birth of physical individuation takes place is spatio-temporal, since it is a metastable state. Under these conditions, physical individuation, and more generally the study of physical forms, derives from a theory of metastability, envisaging the processed of exchange between spatial and temporal configurations. This theory can therefore be named allagmatic."[20]

Simondon then considers the perception of forms in terms of their relative complexity and the degree of information they convey. He privileges irregularity over regularity as a quality that assures liveliness, intensity and greater scope for meaningful engagement by a subject. The degree of subjective engagement potential in the setup is a critical condition for the process of individuation to take place:

"The theory of Form privileges simplicity and pregnancy of forms; on the contrary, the quantity of information that the theory of information defines is as high as the number of decision to be made; the more a form is predictable... the easier it is to transmit it with a lesser number of signals. It is on the contrary what escapes all monotony and all stereotyping which is difficult to transmit and which requires the greater quantity of information. The simplification of forms, the elimination of details, the augmentation of contrasts correspond to a loss in the quantity of information.... The geometric rigor of a contour often has less intensity and meaning for a subject than a certain irregularity. A perfectly round or oval face, incarnating a good geometric form, would be lifeless... Pregnant geometric forms do not allow us to orient ourselves; they are schemes innate to our perception, but these schemes do not introduce a preferential sense. It is at the level of different gradients, luminous, coloured, sombre, olfactory, thermal, that information takes on a predominant intensive sense. The quantity of signals only gives a terrain without polarity; the structures of good forms only furnish frames. It is not enough to perceive details or ensembles organised within the unity of a good form: these details and ensembles must also make sense in relationship to us, that they could be seized as intermediaries between the subject and the world, as signals which enable a coupling between subject and world... But there also exists an intensive diversity, which renders the system subject-world comparable to a supersaturated solution; perception is the resolution which transforms the tensions which affect this supersaturated system into organised structure; we could say that every veritable perception is the resolution of a problem of compatibility... that the system world-subject is an overdetermined or supersaturated field. Subjectivity is not deforming, since it itself produces the segregation of objects according to the forms it brings to bear; it could however be hallucinatory if it were to detach itself from the signals received from the object."[21]

An *ensemble* whose unity is purely structural and non-energetic should be distinguished from a metastable *system*, constituted of a plurality of ensembles between which there is analogy and energetic potential. The ensemble has no information and its becoming can only be one of degradation and increase in entropy. A system on the other hand maintains its condition of metastability because of the constant exchange of information which characterises its state.[22] To what extent then are cinema and architecture *ensembles* or *systems*, under what conditions and to what individuating ends? The answer is perhaps more straightforward for cinema than for architecture. Cinematic montage is a process of assembling filmic material according to narrative, tectonic, aesthetic and semantic objectives. The assemblages produced are fields of multiple components—visual, acoustic, and so forth—organised so as to work with

and across each other. These correspond to Simondon's metastable fields
and Deleuze's plan(e) of immanence/consistency. As such they are
conceptual and tectonic systems open to transductive operations seeking to
mobilise agency. The same is true in the experience of film. The primary
condition of reception for cinema is predominantly perceptual. The screen
operates as a "perceptual field," which Simondon numbers among his list
of systems. In those fields, images, texts and sounds circulate, enter into
neighborhood, digress, coalesce, overlay, juxtapose or otherwise come into
relationship in order to signify or produce sense. The "information" will be
structured spatially, temporally and materially, but it will also have
potential, tension, suspense and dynamics which allow it to take on
intensive value. The simpler the perceptual field, the less supersaturated,
metastable and charged it will be. The more complex and characterised by
"different gradients, luminous, coloured, somber, olfactory, thermal...,"
the greater will be its capacity to trigger and enable individuation, as well
as the development of relationships between subject and world.

At an obvious level buildings are ensembles and not systems. They do
not "possess information" in the way cybernetic systems do. They are not
networks of potential energy in a process of individuation. They are
totalised entities which can only weather and degrade by an increase in
entropy. At another level, buildings do not exist in isolation and they do
form part of systems of all kinds. They are situated within and form part of
an organic system—a natural, seasonal, climatic and environmental
milieu. They form part of an urban system with historical, cultural,
political, infrastructural, and material dimensions. They are influenced by
local, national and global demographics, migrations and deterritorialisations
of all kinds—circulations of information, data, communicational waves
and frequencies; fluxions of finance, markets, raw material resources,
industrial systems and products; processes of aestheticisation,
commodification and exchange. Buildings also form part of perceptual
fields and are open to diverse regimes of looking—from the disinterested
look of a passer by, the intense looking of a "user" who is probably just as
disinterested in the architecture, to the captivated and captivating look of a
magazine photographer, stylist or architect. However they happen to be
looked at, buildings always frame a way of being seen according to the
way they are sited and related to their context; the way they front onto or
face a public realm; the way they are organised and planned or massed,
composed, assembled and put together. They foreground certain aspects
and dissimulate others. They make certain aesthetic and historical
references and evade others. Buildings also always frame ways of seeing.
They frame their context in particular ways by foregrounding certain

aspects and excluding others. They might accommodate particular sensitivities to light, climate and season, or produce internalised self-referential spaces that amplify disconnections between people and place.

Buildings are not only artifacts. They have been conceived, designed, produced and erected. Each of these stages and processes leave traces in the building's concrete presence. Some might be literal and visible; others virtual, implicit or otherwise dissimulated. Such processes take place within conceptual and thematic assemblages entertained by designers, which themselves form part of larger intellectual, sociocultural and religious environments. There are multiple tacit conditions—for example industrial, technical, legislative, instrumental, social and political—that affect the conceptualisation, production and look of buildings. Most importantly buildings form part of an individuating milieu for human beings. They contribute to a metastable field in which subjects find and define, change and transform themselves. Such fields can be given the status of unstable even turbulent systemic contexts whose metastability must be overcome because of architecture's remit to guarantee stability and permanence. However, the fields can also be considered genuinely constitutive in three ways: constitutive of the processes which deliver architecture—that is, the design process; constitutive of the architectural formal and material ensemble as such—that is, its tectonic and technical assemblage; constitutive finally of the processes that condition its reception and experience within the spatial and temporal field in which it stands. In order to enable subjectivation and individuation buildings cannot simply function as forms and frames, irrespective of how *good* their form is. In Simondon's terms, they would also need to "make sense in relationship to us," they would need to be grasped and to "operate as intermediaries between the subject and the world, as signals which enable a coupling between subject and world."

## Agencies of the frame

Deleuze distinguishes between the *plan* as a formative directing and transcendent idea for design and the *plane* of consistency "which only knows relationships of movement and rest, speed and slowness, between unformed elements, relatively unformed, molecules or particles carried by fluxions."[23] The plane is a thoroughly deregulated topography of becoming and advent on which are produced "continuums of intensity, conjugations of fluxions of variable speed,"[24] with their trajectories of displacement along *lines of flight* which *territorialise* and *deterritorialise* those continuums:

"Lines of flight are a kind of delirium. To be delirious is exactly to exit the furrow (like `messing about' (*déconner*), etc.). There is always something demoniacal, or demonic, in a line of flight. Demons are different from gods, because gods have attributes, properties and fixed functions, territories and codes: they have to do with furrows, borders and cadastres. What is proper to demons is to leap across intervals, from one interval to another."[25]

The topographical and geographical nature of the plane implies the need for cartographical diagramming and mapping of its constitutive intensities, dilations, consistencies and fault lines, circuits and short circuits, trajectories, relays, fluxions, conjunctions, conjugations, mutations and territories. The landscape is not fixed, but made up "at any time of variable lines that are differently combinable."[26] Mapping this landscape is not geared to ascertaining fixed configurations once and for all, but to discern multiple combinational dispositions, possibilities, and affordances by way of an indefinite process of figuration, configuration, defiguration and reconfiguration. Neither is the landscape self contained or determined by an inside: "all is departure, becoming, passage, leap, demon, relation to the outside."[27] Deleuze describes three kinds of line which populate the plane. The first is a cutting, segmenting line that establishes a hard boundary—a line of sedentary demarcation, determination or definition. The second is a supple line of migration that traces faults, thresholds, fluxions, modifications and detours. The third is a line of nomadism, a line of flight whose function is to rupture, detach, mobilise and deterritorialise. The three lines are immanently complicated one inside the other:

"Three lines, of which one would be like the nomadic line, the other migrant, the other sedentary (the migrant, not at all the same thing as the nomad). Or else there would be only two lines, because the molecular line appears only as oscillating between the two extremes, one minute carried away by the conjugation of deterritorialising fluxions, the other returned to the accumulation of reterritorialisations… Or else there is only one line, the first line of flight, of a bordering or frontier, which relativises itself in the second line, which lets itself be stopped or cut in the third."[28]

"What we call by diverse names—schizo-analysis, micro-politics, pragmatics, diagramming, rhizomatics, cartography—has no purpose other than the study of these lines, individually and in groups."[29] The first kind of line effects binary oppositions through an apparatus or dispositif of power. It is the State apparatus, an "abstract machine which organises the dominant enunciations and established order of a society, its dominant languages and knowledge, its conforming actions and sentiments." This abstract machine is what produces the concepts and practices of Greek geometry, installing the organised social spaces of the *agora* and *oikos* according to an *agencement* of the *polis*—the concrete political power of the City.[30] Such hard lines also comprise the idea of the plan, of planning, prediction and predetermination—in other words, of every organisational plan and *design* that ordains forms and their development, subjects and their formation. The other kinds of lines do not determine boundaries and beings but becomings. They mark continuums of intensity and conjugations of flux. They are also produced by abstract machines but what they in turn produce are not designs on the world but "planes of consistency or immanence" on which binary machines have no purchase. They produce destabilising "molecular lines that release, between binary segments, fluxions of deterritorialisation which no longer belong to either one, but which constitute the becoming asymmetrical of them both... (through a third term) which always comes from elsewhere and deranges the duality of both, refusing them both opposition and complementarity."[31]

Deleuze's *agencement* is clearly *not* a configurational arrangement but a radically *strategic* field. The frame that assembles operates as a mobilising agent and not simply a static armature for collection or gathering. In other words, the frame *agences*—it unclenches, puts into play, promotes, affords, enables, produces. It is not simply an establishment or installation, but the condition of a putting-into-world, producing, performing and showing-forth. Following Heidegger's terminology, it is a *worlding*—a releasing into the free and the open. *Agencement* assumes that things exist as relational assemblages, heterogeneous collectives, conjunctions and disjunctions exhibiting patterns of adjacency and distantiation. Each framing represents a snapshot, a momentary section through an indefinitely mutating assemblage of mobile elements that come into and out of frame.[32] Elsewhere, the frame itself is mobile and shifts to differently register the elements and call forth relational possibilities, which in turn mobilise further assemblages. Read through Deleuze's concept of the movement-image, cinematic *agencement* is a putting into variation, or a conjugation of indefinite modulations which are fundamentally *gestural* trajectories rather than formal entities:

> "By producing in this way a mobile section of movements, the shot is not content to express the duration of a whole which changes, but constantly puts bodies, parts, aspects, dimensions, distances and the respective positions of the bodies which make up a set in the image into variation. The one comes about through the other. It is because pure movement varies the

elements of the set by dividing them up into fractions with different denominators—because it decomposes and recomposes the set—that it also relates to a fundamentally open whole, whose essence is constantly to 'become' or to change, to endure; and vice versa."[33]

The frame selects and assembles components (places, spaces, times, materials) into neighbourhoods in order to construct worlds and settings, which in turn become theatres of exchange, action and transformation. In that sense the frame operates as an apparatus, a prosthetic device or *machinic assemblage*.[34] It is a *dispositif* that mobilises the potentialities available in the setup. It disposes in both the sense of *making available* and *effectuating* the dispositional efficacy of the framework.[35] In Alfred Hitchcock's *Rear Window* (1954), the major setup is the window of Jeffries' apartment, looking out onto a courtyard and other apartments around it. Beyond to the left, a gap in the wall of apartments frames a busy street. This is the only portion of external world allowed into the tight frame of the film. Everything takes place in the courtyard or apartments, heightening the division and lack of communication between the inside and outside of worlds constructed to frame the narrative. The window is a narrative frame corresponding to the frame of cinema itself. It frames a world which is itself a frame, constituted of multiple secondary frames to other worlds in which particular actions take place. The patent artificiality of the staging and lighting indicates that the whole setup is in fact a setup. Most of the action is seen through these frames but equally imagined into the out-of-frame by both the viewer and the invalid press photographer Jeffries as he recuperates from a broken leg and begins to observe what is going on, first in the courtyard then in the apartments.

Everything in the film is a prosthetic device, a *dispositif*: J.B. Jeffrie's plaster cast, his wheelchair, binoculars, camera and telephoto lens; his apartment, the window frame, ledge and mullions; the courtyard, a passageway to the street, windows of other apartments; a telephone, flashlight, knife. Even the characters are prosthetic to the narrative, extending the protagonist's physical and scopic reach—the maid, Grace Kelly, the dog. The prosthetic character of the spatial and architectural setup is used to frame multiple narrative possibilities; playing what is seen and what is occluded against what the viewer and characters see, what they don't see and imagine they see, what they know or think they know. Hitchcock's exploration of factuality—of the undecidability between fact and fiction, visibility and occlusion, appearance and disappearance, plausibility and implausibility—is a meditation on the essentially fictional or plastic nature of storytelling, which is fundamentally a *poietic* undertaking.[36] In other words, stories are always made (up).

The prosthetic apparatus of Rear Window works in two ways. It frames a series of events which might be read and related in several ways to construe several plausible stories, and it does this by framing both the seen and the non seen. In other words, it is fundamentally a separating and discriminating apparatus which sets up discontinuities between the events depicted. The non-seen, or the events imagined into the non-seen, build suspense. When Jeffries' neighbour arrives at the door of his apartment, he is seen from the courtyard through a window into the common hallway. His wife, in bed, is seen two windows away. She is not yet aware that he is home. The setup for a confrontation is established. As he enters the apartment and crosses the second window towards the bedroom, his wife realises he is there and becomes restless. Again he crosses an unseen space between two windows obscured by brickwork and reappears in the third window, in the same frame as his wife. What looks like an argument follows. Hitchcock will return to this same setup and sequence later in the film to suggest what Jeffries reads as a possible murder. Jeffries' conclusion is based on him having slept through a crucial moment involving the man leaving the apartment in the rain—a moment that is shown to the viewer but not to Jeffries. What Jeffries doesn't see leads him to see something that may not have happened. His story is made up into the unseen, into the discontinuous and the out-of-frame. It is a *poietic* practice shared by the protagonists and the viewer, albeit asymmetrically as the two are not given equivalent information to work with. Knowing something Jeffries doesn't know allows the viewer to identify and side with him as the suspense builds.

In a short scene from *L'Avventura* (1960) which resumes the entire film, Antonioni orchestrates a tight framing of space to convey dramatic value to the narrative. Antonioni's work is noted for deliberate and nuanced use of spatial organisation for strategic and aesthetic ends. Here he frames a premonitory moment in the narrative by setting up a charged spatial field between three characters and their setting. In an apartment, Sandro is embracing his fiancée Anna, while her friend Claudia waits for them in the town square. Claudia is framed looking up at the apartment through a partially opened window in the corner of the screen. The geometry and spatial dynamics of the scene are critical. Through the window, the horizon is occluded by thick trees so that the room, while clearly a private domestic realm or interiority, also reads as an exterior which extends the civic square. The way Antonioni frames the scene, inside and outside exchange their normal status: the public realm becomes a subset of the private, while the private world of the couple becomes exposed to an outside that is normally occluded.

The framing compresses and telescopes various layers of space towards the couple who are central to the frame. The camera is set up parallel to the back wall of the room, but shoots at a diagonal, downward angle in relation to the frame. The window occupies the upper right corner so that the diagonal is both *across* the two dimensional frame of the screen and *through* the three dimensional frame of the window. The axis of the couple's embrace is also directed diagonally towards Claudia standing outside. Anna has her back to the window and obscures Sandro and Anna's view of each other. The two women create an axis that is countered by the man's orientation and reinforced by the prominence of his back. Anna functions as a doubling and modulation of Claudia, projected into the apartment; while Claudia represents a projection of Anna outside the room—metaphorically out of Sandro's arms since she is considering leaving him. Both women face the man, but with different degrees of proximity and engagement, inversely proportional to their actual relationships with him. The axis that links and separates them has variable intensity and operates as a line of flight and deterritorialisation towards and away from Sandro. Anna stands *between* Sandro and Claudia, who will later develop a relationship with him after Anna mysteriously disappears during a boating trip to the desolate island of Lisca Bianca. Claudia is the *other* of Anna, as well as the *other woman* that Anna will later make way for. Anna is also contained by them. She is both a trigger for their eventual relationship and a premonition of the inoperative space between them. This conjugation of the diagonal, its trajectory across the screen and its penetration through the window destabilises the privacy of the moment and the boundary between private and public realms at an urban and psychological level. But even the furtiveness of the encounter between Sandro and Anna is feigned, since all three know of each others' presence, and there is only a nonchalant attempt to draw a curtain across the window. Most importantly, the diagonal geometry of the scene constructs juxtapositions between the permissive indolence of the couple—projected by Antonioni onto all the idle and jaded *petit bourgeois* who populate the narrative—and Anna's fragile trust and faithfulness which endure to the end. The scene is clearly an assemblage of spatial geometries and tensions, calibrated to the psychological tensions of the narrative and mobilised for dramatic ends. The agency of the assemblage drives the general themes of contempt and recklessness characterising the individuals' relationships with each other and their environment. Spatial order and dynamics are manipulated to convey states of psychological and subjective crisis, together with their moral and ethical implications. They condense the chronological temporality and dynamics of the narrative into a single a-chronic spatial figure which stands-in for the entire film.

Antonioni's use of space has evident implications for tectonic practice in architecture. The disposition of several geometric systems, overlaid by multiple dynamic trajectories, develops potential energies and tensional interactions within a spatial field. These can be used to create specific relationships between spaces of different kinds, to stabilise and amplify their connections or to unsettle and destabilise them. They can stretch and dilate relationships, converting them from tenuous static associations into lines of deterritorialisation and flight. They can reinforce the dominance of a spatial system or produce fractures, modulations and variations within it. They can convey certain relationships between interior spaces, between interior and exterior spaces, between private and public domains, between the various zones of a building or environment or between components and materials of a building's technical assembly. There are also implications for a consideration of architectural space not in terms of distinctive form or aesthetic value, but in terms of the dynamic interactions that are mapped out, registered and promoted in the character of its fabric and the programmatic opportunities it affords.

What is inescapable in cinema is its origin in discontinuous forms of representation—that is, its kinematic character as animated photographic stills. The experience of continuity is an illusion made possible by conditions of speed and the natural limits of visuality. It may be that the human regime of visuality is inherently set up to experience continuity; that it will call for continuities and see them even where they are not there. Cinema is a medium of discontinuity not continuity, while the movements of the human being and the word which it seeks to capture and frame are continuous. Such movement cannot be reduced to a series of stills without the photographic or cinematographic apparatus, which are technologies of discontinuity. In digital programs that approximate continuous motion there is always a discrepancy; there is always something not quite right. This is not because the technology has not yet advanced far enough. It is simply that an apparatus constructed and operated on the basis of discontinuity will always be incapable of capturing continuous phenomena.

The machinic condition of cinema is constitutive. The apparatus, and with it the entire technological enterprise, necessarily functions by making available to view and to common usage—or in Agamben's terms by profaning—the things, places, animals or people that had once been consecrated into a separate, sacred sphere.[37] In *The Question Concerning Technology*, Heidegger reads the technological in terms of revealing (*das Entbergen/aletheia* = unconcealment, truth—"every bringing forth is grounded in revealing"), Enframing (*Gestell*—"the way in which the real reveals itself as standing reserve"), and letting-be (*Gelassenheit*, and taking-place—*Ereignis*: "the disclosing coming-to-pass within Being itself"). The technological is a calculating disposition to the world which regards it as a standing reserve, a resource available for profit and consumption. This disposition occludes the "essence of technology," the essence of art (*techne*) and the essence of the human being. In of all these essences, the critical disposition is one of watching-over, attending-to and safeguarding a coming to presence, a bringing forth and production (*poiesis/phusis*). This coming to presence is poised on a double gesture— an ambiguous state that simultaneously advances and retreats; that reveals the truth (*Aletheia*) even as it preserves for truth a measure of withdrawal and concealment. This is the danger that haunts every advent (*Ereignis*), every production and every bringing into presence—a danger that shows itself in the flash of a shimmering limit, or in the halo that rings every look and every appearance (*Eraügnis, Auge*, eye).[38] The consequent danger is that the apparatuses of technology will profane what they reveal by so exposing them to the absence of sheltering-concealment and care that the truth in them becomes destined to forgetfulness and oblivion. For cinema this might be the danger of exposing the image to bare meaning, to an excess of clarity that erases in it, and in its very material presence as light, all possibility of ambiguity and darkness through which it preserves the right to withhold and dissimulate. This applies to the image's representational and indexical registers as much as to its semantic and symbolic registers. In architecture, the danger might translate into an excess of intentional clarity, tectonic lucidity or operational legibility—all of which erase the potential of built environments to unfold the unpredictable and the surprising, in other words, to endure. Likewise, it might translate into a framing and revealing of place or landscape that leaves nothing in reserve and nothing to the imagination. In *The Gravity of Thought*, Nancy wrote of the problematics of clarity and communicability for language and sense:

> "Certain habits that some claim to be 'Cartesian'… leads one to believe that ideas must be 'clear,' it being understood that 'clarity' is something of the order of pure transparency, perhaps even of the void. But who wants an empty thought? Meaning needs a certain thickness, a density, a mass, and thus an opacity, a darkness by means of which it leaves itself open and lets itself be touched *as meaning* right there where it becomes absent as discourse. Now, this 'there' is a material point, a weighty point: the flesh of a lip, the point of a pen or of a stylus, any writing insofar as it traces out the interior and exterior edges of language. It is the point where all writing *is ex-scribed*, where it comes to rest outside of the meaning it inscribes, in the things whose inscription this meaning is supposed to form. This *ex-scription* is the ultimate truth of inscription. Made absent as discourse, meaning comes into presence within this absence, like a concretion, a thickening, an ossification, an induration of meaning itself; like a becoming heavy or weighty, a sudden destabilising weight of thought. Who would not want a thought that blocks

all passage through it, that does not let itself be breached? Who would not want an impenetrable meaning, a meaning that has consistency and resistance? For it is the communication of this resistance that makes me 'endowed with meaning'—even when this communication represents the noncommunication of a 'meaning' (the nondelivery of a message)."[39]

Whether one considers language instrumentally in terms of communication, representationally in terms of *mimesis* or *poietically* in terms of presentation, it always functions technologically. It not only indicates and represents but also *produces* sense—and it does this to excess, through the kind of *ex-scription* that Nancy alludes to. This foundationally productive capacity of language makes of it an apparatus for the transmission and creation of sense. Language registers, marks and retains the traces and memories of human being in the world. It functions *memotechnically* in the same way as cinema and architecture. All three constitute apparatuses and prosthetic devices whose function is not to transmit but to produce knowledge. Ultimately, the pervasiveness of prosthetic apparatuses is a function of the technological condition to which human existence is subject. It is integral to the circumstances of human being in the same way that for Paul Virilio the accident is integral to the technology whose catastrophic breakdown it predicts.[40] Whether the technological is machinic, linguistic, cinematographical or architectural, it is always on the verge of a collapse that would render *poiesis* inoperable. Yet production does not thereby cease. Rather, it is led-through into an altered or excessive state of production that reveals not some pre-existing idea but production itself, producing.[41] This is the apparatus of language to which we are all destined—an apparatus which flexes to exfoliate sense and the interminable reflux of semantic mobility. If Hermogenes believed in the rectitude or the truth value of names and Cratylus in the theory of the perpetual flux of sense,[42] for Deleuze language is a system, an apparatus in perpetual disequilibrium. Its normative mode is stammering and babbling (*bégayer, balbutier*), according to which language struggles with its own limit even as it enunciates.[43] This struggle is a shuttling rhythm, folding and unfolding to produce sense as weaving and hemming (*ourlant*)—where the hem is a fold that prevents the borders of sense from fraying and the weave from unravelling.[44] With this rhythm, sense ravels and unravels, arrives and departs in the same gesture. Words don't concretise or crystallise meaning. Rather, they are traces of meaning's interminable rhythm of deferral and disappearance. They do not capture sense but captivate it into a withdrawal that is the presentiment of an un-evadable evanescence.

In a parallel register, Martin Arnold's cinematic practice operates through a memory machine or *mnemic* prosthesis. Akira Lippit referred this machine to the Greek figure of Mnemon, who accompanies Achilles for the sole purpose of reminding him of his mortality but which, like all machines, falters and seals Achilles' fate. Arnold's mnemographic machine is an apparatus of repetitive transformation using sampled fragments from classic Hollywood films. These are put through a computer-driven analytic projector that meddles with and reconstructs the space and time of the original by decreasing and accelerating the rhythm of projection, then reconstituting sequences incorporating "rapid shot reversals, supersonic vibrations, masturbatory gestures, paralysed action, aural fragments."[45] In this way, Arnold's machinic cinema plumbs the dysfunctional potential and madness dissimulated in the everyday, and of the normalised institutions and values portrayed in mainstream cinema. He finds this in the breakdowns, short circuits, and gaps that characterise his cinema's violently neurotic machine:

> "Here the projector's systemic dysfunction affects—or rather infects—the diegetic characters with a kind of rhizomatic virus, transmitted from apparatus to subject. An infection because the prosthetic structure of the memory machine makes the border between the natural and unnatural regions of the body, its internal and external organs, virtually indistinguishable. What is outside is always on the inside, while the inside circuits or orbits in the outside. This is the law of technology and that of the unconscious."[46]

In *Alone: Life Wastes Andy Hardy* (1998) Mickey Rooney's filial love turns creepy; while in *Passage à l'Acte* (1993), Gregory Peck's invitation for a boy to join the family meal turns aggressive. These astonishing and troubling moments arrive as a function of Arnold's meddling with apparently inoffensive moments in the original films. But they trouble precisely because they are already there, dissimulated as repressed tensions that contaminate the fabric of the original from inside. This ambiguity is what makes Arnold's work, the films he recycles and the re-presented scenes of love and domesticity uncanny. The technology of cinematic projection unclenches meanings which are not external to the narrative but inherent in the discontinuities of narrative moments—a furtive thought, a withheld feeling, a glance, a gesture or a word. Such discontinuities are overlaid onto and in turn modify the otherwise continuous spatial, temporal and material conditions in which they take place. In Arnold's work, the troubling and disturbing character of the scenes arise within gaps introduced by the subdivision of gestural and

spatio-temporal continuity into distinct frames. What troubles the images
and the narratives is the technological itself, not merely the technical
apparatus that achieves the work. In that sense, everything made is
technological and harbours the potential of its own dysfunction, erasure
and catastrophe. But the troubling character is also in the setup itself as
installation, framing and appropriation. It is the violence within the setup,
the ghost in the machine that corresponds, in Arnold's work, to the other
side of the everyday and the familiar: to the Other of what normally
arrives without critique and without question—for example, love, a kiss, a
glance, family values, community and patriotism.

In *Rear Window*, the prosthetic frame is used to drive a narrative of
suspense; in *Baby Doll*, a narrative of violation and in *Cinemnesis*, a
narrative of catastrophe. In each case, the prosthetic device is indispensable.
It sets-up, makes possible and activates the characters' dramatic
engagement. It animates and drives the narrative. While in a sense
supplementary to the characters, it is also inseparably identified with them.
It enters what Agamben has called a "zone of indiscernibility" where the
distinction between prosthesis and prosthetist, orthoses and limbs, parasite
and host, instrument and operator become ambiguous and begin to waver.
Here the prosthesis does not so much add to or extend the "natural"
conditions or propensities of the characters. Rather, it is itself the natural
condition of characterisation. It is one with the presentation of what
presents itself in and as cinematic frame and filmic texture.

In a similar vein, Ivan Ladislav Galeta's experimental work in the
cinematic structure of time and space challenges the narrative limits of
film and its propensity to record discrepant and dysfunctional potential. In
his *Two Times in One Space* (1976-84),[47] Galeta superimposes two
projections of a scene from Stojanovic's film *In The Kitchen* (1968). The
scene is an ordinary family meal in a small kitchen. Galeta superimposes
image and soundtrack of the two projections with a delay of 216
frames/second. His method is a strictly controlled process of mathematical
and rhythmic manipulation of material, together with a concern for
serialisation, symmetry and circularity in montage. The geometric rigor of
this process is not necessarily carried over into cinematic expression, but
functions more as a preparatory work for a freer contestation of cinema's
capacity to put into question structuralist and formalist spatiality and
temporality. In this case the result is a doubling and ghosting of the
characters and their movements, producing a sense of simultaneous
multiple subjects of solid and translucent presence. The temporal delay
and imaged traces cause time to reiterate and the characters and events to
separate into virtualities. The past is drawn into the present as a mobile

residue that dissolves figures and their movements into fluid auras. This sets up a rhythmic texture to the sequence which puts into question the temporality of the scene and the relation between past, present and future. The virtualities conveyed do not so much represent the compossible existents or subjectivations theorised by Simondon and Deleuze or depicted by Lynch. Rather, they function to deconstitute the spatial and temporal fabric that supports existentiation as such, leading to a dismantling, vaporisation or deterritorialisation to infinity of the subject and the conditions of its being. At the same time, the manipulated materiality and technology of the film complicates its tectonic and semantic texture, producing fragmentary, evanescent and parallel narratives that convey something extra-ordinary and uncanny.

# Crisis

With *Mirror* (1975), Tarkovsky achieves a cinematographic parallel to Deleuze's treatment of virtuality and actuality, twenty years before the philosopher's 1995 text *The Actual and the Virtual*.[48] Deleuze begins with the concept of multiplicity. A multiplicity implies actual and virtual components which surround them like a fog of images along extended, coexistent distributional circuits. These images are "souvenirs of different order" akin to unrealized potentialities maintained "under a principle of unconsciousness,"

"since, as Bergson showed, the souvenir is not an actual image formed after the perceived object, but the virtual image which coexists with the actual perception of the object. The souvenir is the virtual contemporaneous image of the actual object, its double, its `mirror image.' Also there is coalescence and scission, or rather oscillation, perpetual exchange between the actual object and its virtual image: the virtual image never ceases to become actual, like in a mirror which seizes the person, devours them, and leaves nothing in turn than a virtuality... The virtual image absorbs the entire actuality of the person, at the same time as the actual person becomes nothing other than a virtuality. This perpetual exchange of the virtual and the actual defines a crystal. It is on the plane of immanence that crystals appear. The actual and the virtual coexist, and enter into a tight circuit which brings us constantly from one to the other... the distinction of the virtual and the actual corresponds to the most fundamental scission of Time, when it advances by differentiating itself following two major ways: to make the present pass and to conserve the past... It is the present which passes that defines the actual... The two aspects of time, the actual image of the present which passes and the virtual image of the past which conserves itself, distinguish themselves in actualisation, while maintaining an unassignable limit, but exchange themselves in crystallisation to the point of becoming indiscernible, each one assuming the role of the other."

For Deleuze, the virtual acts on actuality. Neither is separable from the other. Actualities and virtualities are in states of mutual transformation through which they crystallise or dissolve. The ambience in which this process is played out is the plane of immanence:

"As Leibnitz has shown, force is a virtual in the process of actualisation, as much as the space in which it displaces itself. The plane (*le plan*) therefore divides itself into a multiplicity of planes, following the cuts of the continuum and the divisions of the impulsion which mark an actualisation of the virtuals. But all the plans constitute a single one, following the way which leads to the virtual. The plane of immanence comprises at the same time the virtual and its actualisation, without there being any assignable limit between them. The actual is the complement or the product, the object of actualisation, but this one only has the virtual for a subject. Actualisation belongs to the virtual. The actualisation of the virtual is singularity, whereas the actual itself is individuality constituted. The actual falls out of the plane like a fruit, whereas actualisation returns it into the plane as one converting the object into a subject."

In an extraordinary sequence of *Mirror*, the author is shown as a child before his mother's dressing table mirror. As he looks into it the scene shifts to the past and to his young mother, washing her hair with elemental poise. The woman is framed within a dark space glistening with reflections from oil-black walls, wet hair and clothing, and mirrors dissimulated into the deep background. Her slow and deliberate gestures decelerate time and convey a premonitory tone to the scene. As she stands dripping in the centre of the space the entire room begins to weep water from all surfaces and collapse. Tarkovsky films this moment in slow motion. The young woman is then shown reflected in her mirror, surrounded by surfaces of extreme elemental materiality—water washing over glass; rough, opaque and wet masonry; walls with gnarled welts like oozing bitumen. The scene then shifts to a dark room, presumably the same room at a later time, in which the author's now elderly mother approaches the glass. The mirror doubles a window set alongside it, suggesting a black night outside. It is unframed and so does not read as an opening in a wall like the window beside it, but as pure surface and pure aperture.

Its position in the room is ambiguous and it appears suspended in space rather than fixed to the wall. It has a transparent immateriality yet reflects multiple overlaid images—a painted twilight landscape of clouds, earth or sea, tree and open fire; reflections of a ceiling cornice and floral wallpaper patterns in the room behind; images of the remaining cornice and wallpaper behind its surface; a floating plane, like a table that reinforces the threshold; reflections of the arched window and the mother slowly nearing the mirror's surface, as if from its other side. She raises her hand and places it on the glass. This gesture not only validates but produces the duality of the two sides and the filmic boundary that separates them. She looks into the mirror as if questioning the materiality of its surface, as if it were on the verge of yielding and giving access to the multiple spatialities and temporalities of memory. The surface of mirrors operates in several ways but always as a cipher of cinema itself. It is a filmic screen onto which images are projected—but from both directions, and exchanged into both of the spaces that front onto its surface. It is a frame which delimits and veils compossible worlds; a translucent doorway connecting places and times; an apparatus of memory, recollection and projection and a surface of monstration.

The collapse of the room marks a crisis in the concrete reality and existential milieu of the scene. The actual time of the sequence is left ambiguous by Tarkovsky since multiple temporalities are simultaneously fielded. There is clearly a looking back to the author's childhood in the early scenes. The old mother might herself be looking back, looking forward, returning from the dead or returning to meet her younger self. The question is less a matter of conveying chronological accuracy than of showing the circulation of real and imagined, actual and virtual, remembered and projected places, times and events within a single setting made possible by this rupture. The implausibility of the event amplifies this condition of crisis, enabling the images to convey more *realistically* what an experience of this rupture might feel like. It is not only the room that collapses but all the spatial, temporal and subjective coordinates of concrete existence. The moment triggers a disorientation in the subject and an avalanche of images which had welled up, to only now break through the resistance of forgetfulness—just as water violates the architectural skin and takes with it all guarantee of stability, shelter and safety. The sequence works metaphorically to convey, through a monstrous architectural catastrophe, the exposure of consciousness to a surfeit of the repressed memory and potentiality of the subject.

Deleuze's plan(e) is such a multiplicity of actual and virtual components in constant exchange. It can be read in relation to both architectural plans and cinematic shots. Both kinds of plans set up circumstances for interaction and conjugation, amplification or elimination. They are assemblages in which propensities circulate, cross-over, interpenetrate, touch, fluctuate and produce. They provide situations in which agencies can be mobilised to exploit potential to productive ends. These components and propensities are not only multiple in number but also in provenance and implication. In both cases they are at least spatial, temporal and material—comporting situational, geometric, dynamic, rhythmic, proportional, calorific, acoustic, chromatic and concrete dimensions. At the geometric level, the coexistence of actual and virtual conditions in an architectural plan is commonplace. In principle this is because the adoption of an *actual* geometric system, say an orthogonal pattern, will naturally produce implicit *virtual* systems—in this case the "hidden" incommensurable values of $\sqrt{2}$, $\sqrt{3}$, $\sqrt{5}$. These virtual systems can be developed into offset orthogonal overlays that complexify, reinforce, embellish or disturb and deterritorialise the original pattern.

The plan of Le Corbusier's *Villa Savoye* is a simple case in point. It consists of several simultaneous overlaid spatial patterns, all following a consistent orthogonal scheme. These are carried by different components of the tectonic system. One is explicitly manifest by the regular column grid. Another by the line of beams in the ceiling, the pattern of which is offset from the grid to create interstitial zones—for example in the living room where a line of columns is spaced away from the external wall to create an intermediate zone along the ribbon window. Another is conveyed by the transparency of the boundary between living room and terrace, which stretches that internal space from a rectangle with one predominant direction into an expanded and more centralised square, comprising the living room and outside terrace as one larger living area. The value of such overlays is to complexify a simple layout by zoning it into several sub-spaces with varying degrees of explicitness or actualised presence. This enriches the spatiality of the house, but also enables it to differentiate and particularise itself in response to different potential uses—the larger rectangular space of the living room has a more formal character; the excised space along the window can function as a less formal zone while still being part of the larger room; the connection of internal room and outside terrace can reorient the axiality of the formal space towards the landscape and less formal activities associated with the terrace, and so forth.

Considering that different activities have different temporalities, their associated spaces will also imbue the house with different rhythms of use; different senses of time, pace and tempo; different existential temperaments and dispositions. In this way a single space can become multiple through the virtualities embedded in its structure, framework and setup. Frank Lloyd Wright's domestic work is likewise exemplary. In the Thomas House (1901),[49] the masonry fireplace stabilises and centralises an intensely dynamic spatial system of radiating rooms, which at the same time are subjected to a pattern of pinwheel rotation. The conjugation of centrality, offset overlays, asymmetry and rotation create a multivalent setup. The actual shape and boundaries of each space; the variable extent of fenestration in each one; their differing orientations; the overlay of patterns created by columns and beams, the position of bay windows that stretch spaces into the surrounding environment; the coffering and stepping of ceilings; the stepping of walls in plan which create diagonal tensions—all of these geometrical moves and zonings form part of a highly complex spatial system in which some components are actualised while others remain virtual.

The virtual systems are either inherent but hidden in the actual patterns used, or else they are systems foreign to the actual pattern on which they have been superimposed. In either case, the overlay of systems establishes a framework or assemblage that enables design to proceed. They also provide infrastructural and existential contexts which can enable or disable use depending on how they are calibrated to need. The virtual components of a spatial, temporal or material infrastructure may not be perceptible or tangible, but they are not neutral. On the contrary, the virtual has substantial purchase and affect on the actual. It can amplify or neutralise it. It can radically alter, contest or transform it. At the limit, it can bring about a state of *crisis* in the system by unsettling the controlling governance of the actual.

Simondon's treatment of crisis draws on the physics of crystallization (the taking form of crystals) to develop a concept of formation with implications for epistemology (the taking form of concepts), perception (the taking form of vision), psycho-sociality (the taking form of individuation), and so forth.[50] In all cases, the process involves a pre-formal, pre-individual metastable and "supersaturated" field that is acted upon by a structuring principle or "seed" to trigger formation and individuation within the milieu. This state of supersaturation, "the moment when potential energy is at its maximum," corresponds in the psycho-social domain to a pre-revolutionary state "where an event is just about ready to produce itself, or where a structure is just about ready to gush out."[51] It is a state of tension which puts at the disposition of the faintest local accident a considerable energy. These liminal moments are critical because they mark a threshold of destabilisation in a being, a collective or a milieu. Consequently, the extant structure can no longer hold. It is no longer adequate for, adjusted to, or adapted to, or compatible with what it structures. In other words, it becomes unsustainable. This state of crisis is not terminal, because it is at this very moment that a system reaches supersaturation of potential and presents a capacity for modulation, leading to the appearance of new structures, systems and forms. The significant implication is that the good form produced by the field thereby approaches a state of paradox or contradiction, without itself becoming paradoxical or contradictory:

> "This good form or form rich in potential would be a complex under tension, a systematised plurality, concentrated; in language, it would become a semantic organism. There would be in it tallying and internal reverberation of a scheme… The pregnancy of forms would not be stability in the sense of the thermodynamics of stable states and convergent series of transformations, but its capacity to traverse, to animate and to structure a variable domain, domains more and more varied and heterogenous… There can only be a taking up of form if two conditions find themselves reunited: an informational tension, brought about by a structural germ, and an energy contained by a milieu which takes form: the milieu—corresponding to the ancient matter—must be in a tensed metastable state, like a supersaturated solution or one in surfusion, which waits for the crystalline germ to be able to pass into a stable state by liberating the energy it contains."[52]

Deleuze's plan(e) of consistency is such a metastable or "surfused" field. The field is worked by transductive operations but with a critical difference in relation to Simondon's scenario. In Deleuze, there is no structuring seed (*germe*) around which the crystallization or individuation takes place. Even in Simondon, the structuring seed has no archetypal, hierarchical or causal value. In the crystallization metaphor, it does need to be of a kind with the field that it structures and it does need to have an "informational tension in relation to that field." But it can be a mere fragment, grain or grit, devoid of any eidetic function. Its agency is not formative. Rather, it works by interrupting the network of flows in the field in order to create a knot or point of densification and aggregation. This then serves to orient "the structuration that survives after de-differentiation,"[53] and the formal accretion which begins to take place and cannot-not continue to take place:

> "There must be a field that externally dedifferentiates itself because internally and essentially it potentialises itself; this field would possibly correspond to matter in Aristotle, which is capable of receiving a form. The field which is capable of receiving a form is that system in which the accumulating potential energies constitute a metastability favorable to transformations. A behavior which deadapts itself [adaptation no longer corresponding to the external world], then dedifferentiates itself [inadequation in relation to the internal milieu] in a domain in which there is incompatibility and tension: it is a domain whose state becomes metastable."[54]

The double condition of externally directed "de-adaption" and internally directed "in-adequation" creates incommensurables and reverberations within the organism, corresponding to "a problem to be resolved" as the being cannot continue to live without a change of state, a reorientation or an altered structural and functional condition. This state of supersaturation applies to knowledge and language as much as to experience and perception. Simondon offers an example that foreshadows his later work on perception.[55] Direct perception and retention of all the information received by the left and right retinal fields would lead to double vision if not for the discernment brought by awareness of perspective and relative depth in three dimensional space. Reading figure on ground for example is a kind of individuation of an object out of an incompatible and supersaturated perceptual and informational field. The moment when a coherent form appears—notwithstanding the perceptual habitus which eventually normalises it—is a moment of crisis that is at the same time discriminating and creative. Of significance for design is the condition of having to pass through such a state of supersaturation and confusion, of informational excess, before the overcoded field begins to accrete and produce perceptible lines, shapes, configurations and forms.

This is particularly relevant in architectural and urban mapping practices which, through design, are geared to understanding and engaging the multivalent complexities of a place—dimensional, ecological, systemic, topographical, geomorphological, hydrological, climatic, socio-cultural, historical, political, infrastructural, and so forth. The mapping process must take survey to a state of layered and folded supersaturation before the cartographic procedure is able to yield insight into opportunities and implications for design.[56] Simondon's work on perception is therefore not only useful in terms of the reception of cinema and architecture. It has much to offer a reconsideration of the conceptualisation, design and production of films and buildings towards non-representational means and ends.

## Disestablishment

Cinema and architecture construct worlds by establishing and installing ways of looking and ways of being. These constructions frame place, space and time by the manner in which the materials of film and architecture are organised and coordinated. Such assemblages constitute spatial, temporal and material fields of potential and agency that can be mobilised to various ends. In cinema such constructions are achieved by *montage*—the particular way of organising, sequencing and editing images and sounds; of establishing particular adjacencies, spatialities, temporalities and rhythms; of conjoining frames, scenes and sequences. Continuous montage conveys homogeneity and constancy in compositional and narrative sequence. It might be achieved through continuous takes or by maintaining consistency in chronology and setting across separate takes. The narrative might be continuous or episodic. There may be shifts in the various settings or flashbacks which introduce more complex time structures. Nevertheless the filmic texture remains stable and self-referential as the narrative unfolds linearly towards a predestined end. The resulting narrative appears to take place in real time and in real space, with no disturbance to duration or setting and no suggestion of other times or worlds apart from the one depicted. This is the case with the classic montage of mainstream cinema. It is also a form of narrative adopted by avant garde cinematographers who, by subjecting the genre to extreme subversive stress, manage to extract extraordinary registers out of a banal, readymade format.

Assemblage implies sameness—bringing parts into semblance, even into resemblance. This classical notion, underpinned by the principle of *mimesis* or mimetic accuracy, is counteracted by assemblages in which the components are incommensurable, disparate, heterogenous and fragmentary—for example in non-continuous sequences, shots or jump-cuts which set up breaks and disrupt the filmic transport. Such breaks can still allow continuity—for example in the staggered sequence shots which proliferate in Hal Hartley's *The Book of Life* (1998). Others are radically discontinuous. The discontinuity can be minimal and still allow the narrative line to continue, or it can involve extreme discontinuities in narrative, image, place, spatiality, temporality and materiality—for example the jump cuts between love and surgical scenes in Roeg's *Bad Timing*. At one level, these cuts produce extreme disjunction through juxtaposition. At another they are extremely potent techniques of foregrounding thematic content, elaborating or transforming narrative, shifting dynamics or otherwise amplifying the central concerns of a film. They can bring different places and times into proximity or alignment, introduce radical and disorienting ruptures and create conditions of undecidability which cause the narrative texture to waver. In that sense, disjunctions can be constructive and creative, they can energise and mobilise the apparently fragmented component parts of an assemblage— much like the *caesura* of versification and poetry which suspends rhythmic transport while still providing the impetus and energy for that rhythm to persist.[57]

The strategic value of rhythm becomes foregrounded as a means of unsettling the continuity, logic and stability of form. In music it is rhythm which, in its tonal and temporal dimensions, has the capacity to unsettle the coordinating function of melodic line and harmonic order by introducing tensions and dynamics which give the musical fabric a propensity for deterritorialisation. Likewise in space it is the rhythmic component of form—the implicit but undeclared structures of articulation and the systems of latent incommensurabilities within geometric forms— which can destabilise apparently permanent and legible configurations. Sauvanet has recognised the strategic value of rhythm in the language, figures of speech and figures thought played out in the work of Heidegger. Here, rhythm is not a motif or theme for investigation, nor an aspect of linguistic style, manner or aesthetics. Rather, it is an integral part of the very materiality and practice of a thinking that is fundamentally and strategically destabilising and deconstructive, but which at the same time and interminably *makes* sense:

"Rhythm in the Heideggerian sense should not be considered simply as a metaphysical conception related to the motif of representation, but rather as a subversive aspect of Heideggerian language, against the rule of logic and signification. In other words, 'rhythm' is not exactly a concept used by

Heidegger, but the proper matter and manner of his thought. Thus the 'language of Heidegger' is itself, in itself, voluntarily, intensely rhythmic—mobilised against representation. Rhythm then becomes thought as ontological rapport, as a relation in itself prior to that which it seeks to relate. The very rapport of Dasein to the being would again be rhythm as an asymmetrical movement, according to which there are interrelationships (*entrelacs*) without any representable union. Within such a perspective, 'rhythm' becomes a site of the erasure of the border between philosophy and poetry. This is how rhythm and its uses can appear today as a recurrent but undeclared image of the discourse of deconstruction. The theoretical interest is to make of rhythm something originary, ontological, which comes to subvert the discourse on the origin, and its rapport with language."[58]

The connection between rhythm and subversive thinking—that is, thinking whose objective is to put concepts into question so as to open up new perspectives and potentialities of sense—suggests that rhythm has this dislocating capacity to shift and reconfigure. Its dislocational value is semantic and disciplinary. It dislocates sense, but it also disclocates the field within which sense is constructed. It shifts the philosophical into the poetic, the cinematic into the architectural and so forth. What applies in language and philosophy must also apply in practices more firmly situated in space and time where rhythm is an integral and foundational condition. Processes of architectural design are fundamentally processes of elaborating and editing contextual, spatial, temporal and material possibilities. They involve putting conceptual patterns, situational patterns, patterns of human use and occupation together with spatial, temporal and material patterns. This putting together creates assemblages with propensities for alignment or misalignment between different elements. How a room is conceived; how it is shaped and scaled; how it is related to external and internal environments; how floor, wall and ceiling are connected; how light is admitted; how views are framed or occluded; what materials are assigned to different roles in the space; how spaces are co-located and sequenced; what geometrical rules are established and where they are applied or contested; and the ends to which these various technologies and tactics are deployed—all of this constitutes a kind of architectural or *architectonic montage*. The purpose of such montage might be geared to achieving the flawless unity of a *good form*—a harmony of parts such that none dominates and all are subject to the rule of the whole; such that nothing could be added or taken away without compromise. In this enduring concept of harmonic assemblage, the objective is *seamless* and *seemly* arrangement—the first a tectonic or technical concern, the second an ethical or moral concern.[59] Here, the coordination of difference is directed to a kind of uniform intensity, smooth homogeneity and legible formal stability that is predictable and settled, if not safe. This is the normative approach to architectural tectonics, montage and assemblage—classicist, modernist, logocentric, complicit, conforming to the rule of established law, promoting clarity, consistency and control.

By contrast, montage might be directed towards conditions of instability and discord, multiplicity and difference. This might be argued as more relevant to contemporary conditions of unconformity, fluctuations and vicissitudes of all kinds, the generalised contempt for hierarchy, radical altereity and heterogeneity predominating in the milieu, and so forth. Such montage might foreground dynamic processes, data flows, gestural dynamics of systems, discordant juxtapositions and irresolvable conjunctions. But in current architectural practice, the dichotomy of stability and instability remain unproblematised and mired in aesthetic, formal and representational concerns. It produces reactive architectures which either conserve the typologies and hegemony of harmonics and stability, or generate new typologies and hegemonies of discord and instability. Beyond this impasse, the theoretical works of Simondon and Deleuze imply another possibility for cinema and architecture, by which stable and unstable would be imperceptibly folded into assemblages of high tension, intensity and potential. The objective might be to see films and buildings as metastable fields prompting indefinite processes of transduction at numerous stages of conceptualisation, design, production, reception and experience. It might be to realise cinematic and architectural settings which are not closed in on themselves but develop as indefinitely emergent self-reconfigurations, as settings in which things are not quite as they seem, in which an apparent order and stability is being imperceptibly but palpably challenged, unsettled and deterritorialised into others. The tectonics of space, time and materiality would then enable possible overlays of multiple systems, calibrated to maintain imperceptible disjunctions, various degrees of actuality and virtuality, manifest and latent materiality and so forth. Such settings would be both resolved and at odds with themselves. Their double condition would create incommensurabilities that charge cinematic works and architectural places, producing intensive conditions open to indefinite interpretation and reading. The approach would mobilise processes that are not formal or aesthetic but strategic and operational. It would install enabling contexts which do not impose but invite emergent possibilities for human engagement and individuation at personal, collective, physical and psychosocial registers.

Writing of montage in Antonioni, Bernardi highlights the contestational and productive character of disturbance and crisis that are central to his work:

> "Fault lines opened up between images, scenes, spatial sequences and places, temporal sequences and moments, aspects of the characters—these `errors of montage' create a disorientation in the cinematic fabric: unexpected, unpredictable, surprising, running against human character and against the anticipated and familiar character of landscapes, places, cities and buildings. Through these, Antonioni contests classical montage by retaining only the conventions of framing—paralleling the destruction of the perspectival line and of the form of objects in the paintings of Cezanne early in the 20th C."[60]

Antonioni allows substantial leeway for a film to emerge under continuous invention, respecting opportunities provided by specific circumstances of setting and take—even if these alter the predetermined substance.[61] But he also contests the linear, chronological and logical continuity of classical montage by using non-linear editing and unorthodox shot-countershot or field-counterfield framing. He eliminates smooth and logical narrative transitions and expected connections between sequences. The texture of his films are characterised by disjunctions which have the strategic function of highlighting and more forcefully conveying the relevant thematic issues:

> "I set out to do a montage that would be absolutely free, poetically free. And I began searching for expressive ways and means, not so much through an orderly arrangement of shots that would give the scene a clear-cut beginning and end, but more through a juxtaposition of separate isolated shots and sequences that had no immediate connection with one another, but which definitely gave more meaning to the idea I had wanted to express."[62]

Godard also contests classical montage, but in a more literal and extreme manner through a process of *demontage* and *remontage*—the deconstitution and reconstitution of cinematic content and components. In contrast with Antonioni, this approach takes Godard outside of classical narrative altogether. Godard's *demontage* strikes at the foundational constituents of cinema—image and sound—by rupturing their logical connection in numerous ways. He severs the image's representational and indexical function by disassociating it from a logical sequence of signification. The image henceforth operates autonomously as pure affect, force and power.[63] The same applies to sound by the displacement of acoustic material from the evident conditions of its source, the superimposition of violent sounds over music or speech, the juxtaposition of music and image in ways that dismantle the music's emotional or harmonic referends, and so on. There are many other ruptures—for example between an event and the place and time in which it takes place; between the demeanor and countenance of an actor and the content of their speech; between the content of a soundtrack and a landscape or event depicted on screen; between the chromatic and emotional conditions of a scene; between a word and its semantic content; between a word and its constituent letters. Godard's method is primarily one of interminable fragmentation and recombination. He severs connections at all levels in order to unsettle logical systems, epistemologies, syntaxes and technologies which for him have become obsolete and have lost their capacity to produce. It is as if nothing can eclipse the highlights of classical cinema, yet its exhausted tropes of montage and narrative no longer have anything of any substance to say.

Consequently, his work develops two parallel threads. There is an element of grief and melancholia around the "end" of classical cinema; which appears in his work either through emulation/*mimesis*, or through sampling/quoting particular scenes from favored directors, sourced historical footage, photographs and so forth. There is then an element of reinvention through an entirely new montage technique based on the multiple recombinational potential of the fragment, which constitutes the work's logic, substance and aesthetic. Here narrative is not conveyed through linear sequencing or continuity but through the resonances made possible by assemblages of fragments.[64] These are sequenced by jump-cut editing, overlaid as multiple simultaneous images or depicted in separate simultaneous sequences on a subdivided screen. In addition to discontinuities between images there are discontinuities between image and sound, varying from unsynchronised lip-voice images to disassociated if not dysfunctional image-soundtracks relationships. There are discontinuities in duration between different narrative periods and historical epochs, as well as in the rhythms and speeds of image projection through acceleration and slow motion. The sheer multiplicity of ruptures and disruptions to classical linear narrative has aesthetic and strategic functions. Godard's conveyance of catastrophe and melancholia reach sublime proportions precisely because of the irreparably disjunct fragments juxtaposed to create associations that are not possible using continuous linear narrative. In this way he is able, for example, to correlate crises in the history of cinema; the demise of nations, nation states and political movements; the identity of the contemporary subject; the ubiquity of capitalist consumption; the trivialisation of culture; the hegemony of technological instrumentalism and the degraded state of the natural world. Narratives emerge out of the juxtaposition of elements which are individually highly loaded and charged, but which have no systematic or organic continuity between them. It is precisely their autonomous power as images, texts and sounds, together with the disassociated proximity which Godard exploits that trigger alignments and conjugations of sense, permitting the narrative to slowly build and elaborate itself over the time of the film.

In his analysis of montage in Godard's *Histoire(s) du Cinema*, Rancière proposes two contradictory principles at work.[65] Firstly there is a counterpoint of the image as autonomous visual presence and singular power of silent form over against the commercial conventions of history and the dead letter of the text. Secondly, images operate like the elements of language which possess value only by dint of the combinations they authorise—combinations that create assemblages of visual and sound fragments mobilising signification by juxtaposition rather than adherence. Rancière suggests that the image in Godard operates as pure form and pathos. It possesses a liberating power which has the capacity to contest classical structures of storytelling, narrative and action. Working the gap between the image's material presence and meaning, between its visibility and signification, Godard assembles heterogenous visual, sound and textual elements whose immediate connections on the screen are difficult to grasp and therefore become enigmatic:[66]

"What is the fit between the power of conjunction assumed by montage and the power of disjunction involved in the radical heterogeneity between an unidentified shot of a nocturnal staircase, testimony about the end of the Warsaw ghetto, and the inaugural lecture of a professor at the College de France who dealt neither with cinema nor with the Nazi extermination?"[67]

Godard uncouples the power of the visible (image), the audible (sound) and the legible (text) through discontinuous montage. Fragments ave no common measure yet possess specific affective materiality—"verbal, plastic, sonorous or whatever," that is mobilised through juxtaposition. They are appropriated from the history of cinema, photography, painting, music, philosophy and literature, and then combined as "pseudo-metamorphoses" which valorise their incommensurability in accordance with what Rancière calls "a distinguishing feature of the art of our time."[68] He equates this with Lyotard's view that the absence of common measure is assimilable to the original and catastrophic undoing of a stable relationship between the idea and its empirical presentation.[69] The "disjunctive conjunction of Godard's image sympathises with the modernist teleology of purity—especially, obviously, in its catastrophic form... (opposing) the redemptive virtue of the image/icon to the original sin that has ruined cinema and its power of witness: submission of the 'image' to the 'text,' of the material to 'history.'"[70] The key condition of this fundamentally discontinuous and rhythmic, rather than continuous and melodic montage is what Rancière calls "the great parataxis,"[71] whose power derives from the lack of measure and apparent chaos of the assemblage. This is a power of contact based on a "fraternity of metaphors," not a power based on translation or explanation. "This power of connecting is not that of the homogenous... It is that of the heterogenous, of the immediate clash between three solitudes: the solitude of the shot, that of the photograph, and that of the words which speak of something else entirely in a quite different context. It is the clash of heterogenous elements that provides a common measure."[72] Godard's work foregrounds the "power of the uncoupled" through a "disruptive power of community" in which radical incompatibility and distantiation of components present "the strangeness of the familiar." Two methods intermingle their logics in Godard's montage. There is a dialectical way which "invests chaotic power in the creation of little machineries of the heterogeneous. By fragmenting continuums and distancing terms that call for each other... by assimilating heterogeneous elements and combining incompatible things, it creates clashes."[73] There is then a symbolist way which "also relates heterogeneous elements and constructs little machines through a montage of unrelated elements... (but in order) to establish a familiarity, an occasional analogy":

"Godard's (symbolist) montage doubtless offers the best example of the extreme proximity of contrasted logics... always to do two things at once: to organise a clash and construct a continuum... the collage of heterogeneous elements... The paradox of Histoire(s) du Cinema thus does not reside where it first of all seemed to be situated: in the conjunction of an anti-textual poetics of the icon and a poetics of montage that makes these icons the endlessly combinable and exchangeable elements of a discourse. The poetics of Histoire(s) simply radicalises the aesthetic power of the sentence-image as a combination of opposites. The paradox lies elsewhere: this monument was in the nature of a farewell, a funeral chant to the glory of an art and a world of art that have vanished, on the verge of the latest catastrophe."[74]

The opening scene of *Caché* (2005) establishes Michael Haneke's contention that reality is not only existentially subjective. On the one hand it is a lived reality and on the other a reality mediated by technologies of the image, televisuality and techniques of surveillance. Reality is therefore never singular, clear cut or unambiguous. The problematics set up by the narrative are never resolvable within it. Rather, the role of the narrative is to call into question the nature of the real, to play out the ambivalence between the fictional reality that we see and the lived reality that we experience.[75] Haneke describes the film as a moral tale about the manner in which one accepts or rejects but in any case endures repressed secrets and hidden guilt. The unexpected surfacing of this culpability exposes the fragility and dysfunction of human subjectivity, interpersonal and familial relationships. The trigger for this revelation is a series of videotapes accompanied by menacing childlike drawings, showing that the film's protagonist is henceforth under persistent surveillance. Throughout the film Haneke conflates the real content of remembered events with imaginary dream passages, and video surveillance footage with real time sequences to create uncertainties in the provenance and veracity of images. This amplifies the incompleteness of available information and foregrounds the impossibility of closing the narrative circle. The source of the menace is never declared but only suggested on the basis of the protagonist's guilt, rather than on narrative evidence. "One never knows," as Haneke himself says—but in fact the responsibility slips between several characters, again opening up the narrative to disjunctions and incommensurabilities which are unsolvable but which also mobilise and drive it.

Patricia Pisters explains how Deleuze's time-image has the potential to falsify narration, in contrast to the movement-image of classic cinema:

"When the virtuality and possibility of time become part of the actual image, when the present becomes at the same time past and future, it is more difficult to say what distinguishes the real from the imaginary or to tell the difference between true and false. Whereas the classic movement-image does everything possible to avoid fooling the spectator, this is not the case with the time image; false cuts, aberrant movements, never explained gaps in the narration, they all make the actual open up to the virtual (and the possible) and at the same time make truth impossible to grasp: we can only guess what happens between, before, and after. In the movement-image, truthful narration is developed organically according to reliable connections in space and chronological connections in time... In the time-image, the duration of time, which implies change and becoming, provokes undecidable alternatives and inexplicable differences between true and false. Real and imaginary become undecidable alternatives, and differences between true and false become unexplainable."[76]

But the truly unsettling character of *Caché* is Haneke's concealment of the time-image's capacity for undecidability, under the guise of classical movement-images deploying an apparently straightforward narrative. His objective in producing highly legible images for the viewer—by using long fixed camera takes and long sequence shots for example—does work to establish a simple and stable narrative base that can then be more effectively put into question. The episodic montage serves a similar function, before it is manipulated to augment tension and suspense. Strangely, what drives the suspense and the expected denouement towards which it moves but which is never declared (who sent the video tapes and drawings?) is in fact irrelevant, since it has no bearing on the protagonist's guilt. What is hidden in *Caché* and yet remains open to interpretation is the truth, conveyed by a dissimulation of images within images. The narrative is never resolved and in the last scene is left hanging. In a passage to rival Antonioni's final sequence for *L'Eclisse*, Haneke sets up a wide fixed shot, tightly framing the crowded steps of a high school. The depth of field is flattened, the boundaries of the frame constraining and the geometry closed. This keeps the eye fully contained within the image surface and the theatricality of the setting. The nature of the shot is such as to prompt the viewer to scan the scene, searching for clues and familiar faces in order to make sense of the story and close the narrative. But the point is to put into question the very fact of looking, of one's attentive capacity to notice, to see and not see, to miss seeing or to mistakenly see. The contradition between the simultaneously constraining spatial and visual setup and the opening up of narrative possibilities amplifies the unsettling quality of the scene. In the animated fluid crowd, the two young sons of the protagonist and antagonist appear momentarily, the latter seeming to be explaining something and reassuring the other. This dissimulated moment puts into question the entire plot sequence since it throws wide the culpability that until then had been plausibly projected onto the protagonist. In any case and whether or not the young men are noticed, what Haneke achieves with this sequence is a sense of the indefinite narrative potentialities available in the setup, of which this film has been only one possible, albeit ambiguous actualization. By returning the subjectivities foregrounded in the film to a state pure latency in the undifferentiated collective, Haneke also returns the narrative to a state of pure virtuality, leaving it radically suspended and open to indefinite reconfiguration.

*Caché* appears to follow a straightforward episodic narrative structure; but from the very start this structure is placed under siege. The status and provenance of the image is always uncertain (real-time, replayed videotape, flashback, future event or dream). The expectation that the narrative will deliver a concrete resolution to the apparent central problem of the film is never satisfied (who is the blackmailer?). The particular details of the characters and the story are interminably deferred towards global registers (the ubiquity of surveillance and its relation to subjective and collective paranoia; the irremediably shared political culpability for neo-colonial practices; contemporaneous societal inequity and racism; dysfunctional familial and intergenerational communication). The unsettling character of the film owes as much to the subject matter and the events depicted as it does to the contested and undermined narrative structure, by which Haneke subjects to radical questioning all the standard hierarchies, roles, tropes, expectations and certainties of mainstream storytelling.

In terms of architectural parallels, it is useful to consider the way in which Haneke first establishes a standard familiar narrative structure, with all of its expectations as to type, rules and codes, plot development, scenario, characters, props, montage and denouement. How he then subtly and imperceptibly interferes with the logic and consistency of this structure by introducing different kinds of discontinuities and gaps, thwarting expectations in the same gesture as their delivery, denying the code its applicability, currency and efficacy, and doing so while maintaining the appearance of structural familiarity and predictability. The resulting disorientation is therefore subliminal and all the more troubling for it. Haneke wants to say that nothing is as it seems, that there is an irrevocable disjunction between what appears to be the case and what the case is in fact. But by never declaring the fact of the matter, the *truth* of the matter, he keeps the disjunction irresolvable. And by dissimulating that irresolvability, he creates a structure that is unknowingly at odds with itself—disturbed and unsettled from within, in turn disturbing and unsettling for the viewer. This is a precise expression of the uncanny—an apparently familiar condition haunted and rendered strange by an otherness which is not external but dissimulated within.

The manipulation of structure, type, predictability and expectation which form part of Haneke's method is transferable into architectural settings. Architecture adopts registers, formal types, spatial grammar and syntax, patterns of design, geometric layout, three dimensional composition and materiality. It works with and works *into* those types, appropriating them holistically or contesting them by putting them under stress through modification, translation, overlay, discontinuity and so forth. With adopted types come anticipations and expectations that the architecture will appear, function and be experienced in certain ways. For example, a series of spaces might be organised to give the impression of normative layering in depth by the clear articulation of foreground, mid-ground and background. An orthogonal geometry adopted might imply a centre and an axially symmetrical disposition. However by offsetting and overlaying the same geometry, and expressing this second system virtually through peripheral patterns and secondary components of the architecture, the original geometry will be contested and the spatial order rendered ambiguous. What appears stable and permanent might then be subjected to slight discrepancies and incommensurabilities that charge or otherwise animate the space. Space now carries several systems in simultaneity, becoming a field of tensions, energies and potentials—a metastable field. Such tensions could be resolved and aligned or remain misaligned so that the question of resolution is deferred and kept open.

In Lewerentz' *Björkhaagen* (1956-64) project for example, and in Jörn Utzon's house *Can Lis* (1971), there exist ways of detailing a window which eliminate any trace of the frame from the inside.[77] This creates the sense that there is no "window" since the expectation that accompanies it is always of a frame surrounding the opening that perforates a wall. The impression is then of an inside that gives immediate access to the outside, of an interior that is a subset of external space. Yet in both cases the openings are glazed. This creates effects against expectations since external ambient sound is attenuated and internal ambient sound is modified by the continuity of reverberation in the space. The unexpected and ambiguous result renders the boundary indeterminate. One is inside and outside yet strangely neither one nor the other, since each condition (closure and openness) presents a contradiction or at least a reservation, resistance and deferral to the other. One is at once directly accessing the outside while at the same time being excluded from it by the glass.

This is a minor example, but the principle is applicable at numerous scales—from the layout geometries of master plans to the detailing of a door threshold in architecture; from the sequencing of shots to the precise overlay at a single instant of an image and sound in cinema. This principle involves establishing a framing strategy that forms part of normative practices of montage and composition. The expected stability of that framing is then undermined to produce unsettling effects which destabilise the established order. The narrative or semantic anticipation that comes with the established order is contested, often subliminally but also radically. The simultaneous experience of anticipated stability and its disestablishment creates an uncanny dimension in the work, a sense of mismatch or misalignment—hence a gap or absence in the fabric, an irreconcilability, ambiguity or indeterminacy that remains unexplained and prevents the system or narrative from closing; even the possibility that the entire spatial, temporal and narrative structure might at any moment vaporise at the same time as it persists. For both cinema and architecture, the trajectory of purpose then shifts from the communication of specific meaning to the pure articulation of means and production of sense.

Framing gathers together an assemblage in which is maintained a high intensity of potential through the differentiated component that populate it. The intensity is achieved by a supersaturation or overcoding of the layers which constitute the fabric of the assemblage. The critical matter is not the nature of the components held and released by the frame but what circulates *between* them, how they circulate amongst each other in a milieu that is both context and content. The layers maintain discrepancy, tension and irresolution between them but they also maintain agency—that is, a capacity to do, to prompt, trigger, work, direct and produce. Agency mobilises components of the assemblage towards states of interminable resolution and infinite finishing that are complete at any moment, yet energised to remobilise and transform. Their mobilisation functions through the conjunction *and*—not by consuming or subsuming difference, nor by harmonising, aligning or assimilating difference towards any kind of whole. When framing assembles elements between which there is irreconcilable discrepancy, the boundaries and delimitations of the frame become uncertain, unstable and begin to waver. The established regime is systematically unsettled so that it no longer has any purchase or currency. Expectations are thwarted in the same gesture as their delivery, denying the code its applicability, currency and efficacy. This creates a disorientation and loss of footing which abandons the frame and the narrative to the unfamiliar, to an impasse through which there is neither passage nor return.

Such conditions may be fascinating and interesting in themselves, but they are more significant to the extent that they contest established structures of meaning around foundational issues such as visuality, dwelling, place, space, time, community, materiality and so forth. The implications are radically trans-disciplinary and have substantial ethical and political, as well as aesthetic and formal registers well beyond cinema or architecture. They open and inflect meaning into new regimes of sense by mobilising a questioning and testing of predetermined boundaries, and by making possible opportunities to project thinking and practice into new territories. The function of this is to provide a charged field that can enable ongoing development, evolution, becoming, individuation and subjectivation. This operation takes place at every level—conceptualisation, design, montage, technical production, materiality, reception and experience. The operation is transductive and functions to gather into neighborhood and compatibility, to conjugate and articulate, to enable the production of new assemblages to emerge and take place.

Assemblages work to produce by cooperative engagement. Or they trigger inoperativeness at the core of the work which then suffers synaptic disjunction or seizure, dysfunction or catastrophe. The latter is always potential in every machinic assemblage, in every apparatus and prosthesis, in every technology and technique of production. For Agamben, the gestural character of language represents "the communication of an incommunicatability. It has precisely nothing to say because what it shows is the being-in-language of human beings as pure mediality." This pure mediality, which is "a process of making a means visible as such" manifests as a silence or gag: "a gesture of not being able to figure something out in language." This is "the unsayable which exhibits language itself, being-in-language itself as a gigantic loss of memory, as an incurable speech defect."⁷⁸ Deleuze's *balubutiement* and Agamben's gag are moments potential in every frame. They correspond to the frame's double phase of tightening and releasing its hold on the assemblages it has made possible, only to return them to the interminable fluxion of *agencement*. This conveys the double sense of every framing—constraining and gathering as well as expanding and affording in order to *make* sense. Framing attends to and cares for possibilities arising through the agency that it fields. In the same gesture, framing *frames*—that is, it traps, constricts, and incarcerates what it gathers—betraying it by exposing and delivering it over to an outside that exceeds its bounds.

In architecture as in any kind of spatial practice, there is always an engagement with framing—that is, with containing and showing, excluding and dissimulating. Things and events can be framed in terms of occlusion, for anticipation, for suspense, or they can be framed so that everything is seen and available. The plan of the *Palace Museum* in Beijing (15ᵗʰ C) conforms to a strict orthogonal, symmetrical and hierarchical organisation. Axes divide the site into grids proportioned in response to varying symbolic, political and social values. The system applying to the whole is inflected in each part, so that major avenues and shrines along the axes which have royal or civic scale are iterated in miniature within institutional, executive and domiciliary zones. These grids-within-grids function at the level of the plan, but also volumetrically and experientially to establish a perforated spatial texture and various narratives of exclusion, inclusion, infiltration and transgression. The individual courtyard houses, with their gate, laneway and boundary walls are folded into multiple reparations and function as individual microcosms of the city.

The geometry is pervasive and totalising. Every part is controlled by an overarching order and yet this geometric apparatus is far from panoptic. It may represent the spatial correlate of a political system but it also allows for surprising variations and contestations of the system's surveying power. Across the entire city, in whole and part, symmetries are never static. There are radical differences in the grid's occupation by the network of streets, gardens, courtyards, pavilions, squares and walls. This works both orthogonally and diagonally and is especially marked the further one is away from the royal and civic zones. This "further" is not necessarily in distance, since the fabric of the city is effectively woven and folded into itself so that what is hierarchically distant may be spatially proximate. In that sense the urban fabric reads more like a heterogeneous web of variable spatial intensities and densities than a regular latticework of even pattern. In the residential quarters, individual houses are so removed by the incessant turns and returns of linking pathways that they become radically safeguarded from the totalising schema. In these spaces it is the privacy and individuality of the household that dominates. Each dwelling becomes not only *another* centre, equivalent to its neighbors, but *the* centre of the entire city. In this way, the imbricate texture of the city begins to vacillate. The geometric control evident at the large scale becomes uncertain and elusive, if not entirely erased by a system that occludes itself in its most secret part.

Peter Markli's *La Conjiunta* (1992) is a gallery for the work of sculptor Hans Josephsohn. The pieces exhibited are barely figural, yet they touch on the tragic—a kind of *terribilità* which conjoins despair and ecstasy. Markli's narrative response is a deceptively simple building—an enfilade of three rooms, of the same width but different heights, separated by doorways and lit by a skylight. The rooms have no external prospect. The materials are in-situ concrete and metal. The physical and experiential qualities of the spaces manage to heighten the dramatic value and presence of Josephsohn's work without making any explicit gesture towards them, but simply by letting them be against a highly controlled, apposite background. Clearly the quality of the spaces owe much to Markli's handling of material and light, mobilising a sensibility to the sublime evident in both the physical context of the building and in Josephsohn's work. But there is a less evident aspect of the building that contributes a great deal to its unsettling and uncanny qualities.

Markli's *parti* appears to be a simple axial and symmetrical enfilade in plan, section and elevation. However there is a series of shifts that effectively contest and unsettle the framework established. The attenuated axiality and linear constriction of the spaces are countered by the opposed alignment and disposition of the reliefs and sculptures, located along one of the side walls. The effect is to create an asymmetry between the two sides of the space—a more constricted space on one side where the reliefs and sculptures are positioned, and a more open space opposite. This in turn exaggerates the disjunction between the scales of the viewer, the spaces and the works, amplifying their monumental and tragic dimension.

The entire building is constructed around this series of displaced frames within frames that create a geometric system of discrepancies and gaps. This self-contested spatial system conveys a palpable yet virtual ambiguity defined not by the imposition of external forces but by the breakdown of an intrinsic order. At its limit, space is displaced. At odds with itself, it begins to lose self-consistency. Unsettled by the discrepancies that constitute it, the constricted and reductive formal character of the spaces begins to fluctuate. Various explicit ordering systems become discontinuous and separated, which causes the space to assume a palpable indecisiveness while simultaneously conveying the image of a highly ordered simple arrangement. The play between explicit minimal order and its own implicit maximal dismantling charges and enlivens the space. But it also prompts a questioning of space as (dis)order and (dis)installation. In a surprising turn, the totally interiorised space that is also formally totally alien to its context begins to expand its boundaries and engage the very qualities of the desolate axiality, containment and infinite variability of the landscape in which it is set.

By 1972, Carlo Scarpa had completed his cemetery for the Brionvega family at San Vito d'Altivole. In Scarpa's own words, "I wanted to show some ways in which you could approach death in a social and civic way; and further what meaning there was in death, in the ephemerality of life."[79] There is a curious quality to Brionvega. A slow, persistent becoming-aware of something uncanny in the disposition of the spaces, the organisation and layering of floor and wall surfaces and the way the boundary wall engages the immediate and distant landscape.

In the floor plan, there is a distinct sense of repeatedly moving around something which remains unseen and yet palpable. Scarpa had worked the geometries of spatial sequence around a series of pivot-points, about which there were shifts in direction, orientation and prospect. The explicit pivot of the composition is in the corner of the L shape plan which Scarpa used to fringe and frame an existing cemetery. He did this, as with Castelvecchio and elsewhere, by using a new intervention to complete and foreground the old. There are several other geometric pivots around which the spaces turn and shift—shortly after entry; the "artesian well"; the cloister; a reorientation towards the water garden; the aedicule floating on water; the Brionvega tomb itself and, aligned with it in the crook of the L and *outside* the walls in a place both central and excluded, Scarpa's own tomb.

Both floor and wall surfaces are deeply perforated, yet the spaces they open into are concealed from full view. In the case of walls, the openings are to fragments of dense foliage in the original cemetery, around which Brionvega forms an L in plan, or to secondary or distant other spaces in the complex. In the case of the floor, there is an enduring sense of the whole surface being suspended over a dark and still water body—a well, underground pool or spring: here and there, the sound of water dripping, draining or flowing underfoot.

The ground plane of concrete decking produces hollowness underfoot, reinforcing the sense of walking over a deep and cavernous space. The overall sense is of being surrounded by inaccessible spaces of arcane power—forest, grove, spring, well, cavern; of moving between these spaces, being aware of their presence but unable to verify that awareness. This sense of an absent presence builds as the spaces, gardens and rooms are infiltrated and traversed.

The metaphorical sense of absence is achieved through a set of concrete spatial tropes, using simultaneous antinomical qualities to create ambiguity and undecidability. A vista opens in one direction, turning on a pivot associated with dense enclosure and occlusion. The floor plane is a heavily grounded platform which at the same time hovers over a hollow sub-space, and is effectively separated from the boundary walls by a continuous recessed trench that allows it to float in relation to the walls and surrounding landscape. The boundary walls clearly delimit a defined precinct or *templum*, establishing a horizontal screen against which the distant town and hills are read, while at the same time expanding beyond those limits to frame and gather them into the interior spaces of the garden.

In this way, the project simultaneously includes *and* excludes, reveals *and* conceals, opens *and* closes, grounds *and* hovers, delimits *and* expands, frames *and* gathers, interiorises *and* exteriorises. Tectonic elements—floor, wall, screen, volume; and spatial forces—enclosure, openness, expansion, contraction, rotation, torsion, centrality, periphery, are mobilised in simultaneity to develop an intricate and overlaid spatial texture in which no antinomy predominates. Here the *and* does not have an additive function but a mobilising and iterative one, which conjugates antinomies both within and without the frame into a network or agency. Conjugated, the antinomies begin to co-operate, and in the interstices, to produce and weave the spatial narrative's ambiguous, and uncanny dimension.

The entire architectural setup is calibrated to a palpable sense of absence—to conveying the absence and withdrawal of the deceased among those who remain. The project's multiple dissimulated spaces remain invisible yet are manifestly sensed. They are occluded spaces one moves alongside; implicit pivots around which one rotates; edges that resist and deflect away from spaces that may or may not be there; pocketed spaces behind walls and under the floor that are patently there but unoccupiable; fluids that drip or drain in resonant cavities below; a telluric understorey that wells up around the caskets and in fountains and pools. The place is constructed of tensions and suspensions between containment and release—between inside and outside, the everyday and the unexpected that interminably threatens its borders. This force field converts the distant and monumental into the proximate and intimate. It gathers the milieu into an artifice of tectonic delimitation. Architecture and landscape conspire within a locational, spatial, temporal and material framework in which the existential presence of the absent one is made haptic and conspicuous. At the same time the individual—whose death hypostasises their radical incommutability and placelessness—is returned to a region of familial and communitarian exchange and to an enduring being-there-with-others.[80]

Lewerentz' reworking and challenging of classical design typologies is a recurrent feature of his architecture. Interpreting his *Chapel of the Resurrection* at the Woodland Cemetery, Stockholm, St John Wilson notes the disengagement of the building's portico and its slight angular shift from the main volume, as well as the chapel roof and eaves that hover above the wall cornice. He reads such modifications to or "abandonment" of classical architectural syntax as having both programmatic and symbolic functions. They create an enigmatic, ramifying and insistent strangeness: "There is something haunting about this insistence, its juxtaposition and transformation that hints at some metaphor we cannot grasp—a quality to which de Chirico ascribed the status of the 'metaphysical.'"[81]

"So to what end did Lewerentz, the most poetic master of the classical language of architecture in this century, abandon that language? As a student of Schinkel, Lewerentz would have been aware of that master's own conviction that the means of architecture would have to be 'created anew. It would be a wretched business for architecture... if all necessary elements... had been established once and for all in antiquity' but Lewerentz' concern lay at a much deeper level than the pursuit of novelty.... In the Church of St Peter... an unprecedented austerity of means prevails. But this austerity is not an end in itself—it is the means by which the tragic aura of the Mass envelops us with a breathtaking primitiveness. Once again there is the element of strangeness... The building's mystery lies in the discrepancy between its apparent straightforwardness and its actual obliqueness. The harder you look, the more enigmatic it becomes."[82]

To venture an explanation of how this enigmatic quality is achieved, St John Wilson cites Lewerentz' own motto for his work: "*Mellanspel*"— meaning a playing (*spel*) between (*mellan*). The contention is that Lewerentz sets up various antinomical oppositional themes, which he then plays or shuttles-between to create discrepancy, ambiguity, indeterminacy and obliquity. From that result a sense of enigma and unexplainable mystery that St John Wilson implies might be proper to a sacred building. The discrepancies which Lewerentz plays out in the geometry and materiality of St Peter do confirm this. The plan is square rather than basilican, therefore centralised rather than linear. This foregrounds a communitarian rather than hierarchical liturgy—the celebrant is *among* the community of worshipers who surround the performance of the sacrament *in their midst*, rather than *before* them. But the altar is not literally centralised in the space. It is located just to one side of the central axis and diagonally opposite the entrance door.

While the space is a square, which in an ideal or abstract version no single direction would predominate, Lewerentz carefully but forcefully differentiates between several of the axes which traverse and bisect the space. There are four entrances into the chapel. These are differently proportioned and unaligned to each other, to the room's cross axes or to anything in the four quadrants. One entrance is into the north-west corner from the wedding chapel; another is into the south-west quadrant from outside; a third is into the south-east quadrant from the external L shaped courtyard and the last into the north-east quadrant from the sacristy. The position of these doors does relate to the conditions that surround each type of entrance. The western door, which is the chapel's formal civic address, is aligned to the west-east axis of the altar in common with the layout of traditional churches. The more informal wedding chapel entry in the north-west adjoins the baptismal font. It establishes a diagonal relationship with the space and the altar, prompting a turning or spiralling trajectory of entry—a sequence that is the most extended but also the most gradual and anticipatory of the four. The south-east entry is smaller and more proximate to the altar, being an entry most likely to be used regularly by the private church community. Finally, the north-east entry between organ and choir is reserved for the clergy and located not quite opposite the community's entry door. The two axes linking these three doors and the altar form a cross that is unaligned to the cross axis of the geometric centre of the room, or the cross axis through the central column.

Lewerentz clearly adopts and departs from the key formal and co-locational rules of church layout at the same time. He works the space and he works *into* the space so as to overlay multiple overlapping geometrical alignments, directions and dynamics which contest the apparent simplicity of the square and distort its rational order. The offset position and different orientation of elements—floor paving patterns, vaulted ceiling, entry doors, windows, baptismal font, congregation, choir, altar, organ and so forth—create a web of geometric and spatial tensions which begin to charge the space. The vaulted ceiling billows in uneven waves due to the alternating pattern of ribs which expand and contract in plan as well as slope slightly towards the centre of the space from each side. The undulating and folded brick ceiling is read against a pair of deep steel beams which give midspan support to the vaults and span the full width of the space. These beams are supported on a secondary beam, almost imperceptibly asymmetrical to the single column that supports it. The column is marginally off centre within a space that is exactly square. The column and beams are themselves assembled from two unequal sections with gaps between them sufficient to allow light through their mass. The asymmetry of the column is reinforced by the offset assembly of beams— the two major cross beams also having the effect of countering the orientation of the vaults. This steel assembly effectively subdivides the square chapel into four smaller regions. The altar is marginally offset to the south of the central axis of the room and placed in the quadrant opposite the entry door. The baptismal font is in the quadrant closest to the entry. In both cases this is in accordance with normal liturgical practice. The lectern and organ occupy the third quadrant and the major portion of the congregation occupies the fourth. None of the windows or doors is symmetrical to or aligned with the geometric axes of the whole space, or with the quadrants in which they are located. The combined effect of this highly complex but barely perceptible setup, made of very slight nuanced geometrical shifts and overlays, is considerable.

In terms of directionality and dynamics, the ceiling vaults run west-east towards the altar to emphasize a processional direction. This conforms to a traditional liturgical orientation. At the same time, the vaults rise from each side to a north-south pitching ridge above the column assembly. The combined effect is to stretch the west-east dimension and at the same time to gather, centralise and raise the space upward. This tension between two tendencies holds the space in suspense, in an indiscernible state somewhere between stability and dissolution. In the brick floor the bed joints run north-south, but at an angle to the square plan. Within this linear pattern Lewerentz inserts several areas of paving at other angles—like rugs or patches set within a larger web. Only the paving in the zone of the altar conforms to the orientation of the walls. Despite reading more like a woven multidirectional surface than a linear array, the heterogenous patterning of the floor counters the orthogonal alignment of the overall space and the altar, as well as the walls. The directionality of the paving resists and decelerates that of the vaults. These contrasting shifts in pattern and geometry create disjunctions and incommensurabilities in the spatial order of the room.

The intricate juxtaposition of geometries, spatial directions, tensions and proportions tends to overburden, materialise and condense the space; turning it from an empty container into a solid woven network. At the same time, Lewerentz mobilises the materiality of the space, causing it to fluctuate, alternate and oscillate—but in minor, almost imperceptible ways. This imperceptibility, made more acute by the dimness of the interior, conveys Lewerentz belief that "the nature of the space has to be reached for, emerging only in response to exploration."[83] St John Wilson has read this as a desire of Lewerentz' to convey and represent the numinous. But the tectonic implications exceed any semantic, metaphorical or symbolic readings that could be ventured for the building. What Lewerentz achieves spatially, tectonically and materially has important value in terms of transferable strategic agency. The central armature that supports the roof may well evoke the cross on Calvary, but it also has a significant role in zoning the space to foreground the differentiated collectivity that characterises a congregation. It works to gather and amplify a distinctive weightiness in the space—a gravity which corresponds to the internalised disposition of grief and joy which surround reflection, prayer and celebration in the Christian mass. It acts as a pivot which keeps the various sectors and trajectories of movement in asymmetrical balance; as if to convey a sense of anticipation and suspense, or to frame the conditions of advent and of the uncanny. As such, the armature enables and mobilises before it represents. It turns an abstract spatial structure into a world or a place, calibrated to specific modes of being, of being-with-others, and of being-with-otherness. Lewerentz does not achieve this through formal complexity, large scale compositional moves, distinctive articulations and separations between parts or unusual geometries. The scale of his tectonic endeavor is extremely modest, but every move carries considerable weight and enduring affect. He does not abandon architecture's foundational tectonic dimensions or remit but works *at* the tectonic by subjecting it to significant strain and working it until it *yields*.

# NOTES

## Introduction

1. See Adrian Snodgrass, *Architecture, Time and Eternity. Studies in Stellar and Temporal Symbolism* (New Delhi: Aditya Prakashan, 1990).
2. Gilles Deleuze and Claire Parnet, *L'Abécédaire de Gilles Deleuze*, DVD (Paris, Éditions Montparnasse, 2004), "Culture," "Désir."
3. Deleuze and Parnet, *Abécédaire*, "Désir."
4. Andrey Tarkovski, *Sculpting in Time*, translated by Kitty Hunter-Blair (Austin: University of Texas Press, 2006), 72.
5. This sense of furniture as what is essential in architecture will be taken up in my forthcoming book *Theorising the Project. A Thematic Approach to Architectural Design*. See my "Furnishing Place: What is Architecture Fit For," in *Content(s)*, edited by Barbara McConchie (Canberra: Craft and Design Centre, 2005), 10-16.
6. This kind of semantic assemblage is elaborated in my *Design Lexicon*, available in pilot form at http://ensemble.va.com.au/ti/designlexicon/index.html.
7. Plato, *Republic*, 534a.
8. I use the term "singular" in Jean-Luc Nancy's sense, where it is derived from Latin *singuli*, which does not refer to isolated units but to a plurality or community of co-appearance—or to use Nancy's term, *compearance*—describing the interminable deferral of singularities out of which communities emerge. For Nancy, "This is the singular plural in such a way that the singularity of each is indissociable from its being-with-many and *because*, in general, a singularity is indissociable from a plurality... In Latin, the term *singuli* already says the plural, because it designates the `one' as belonging to the `one by one.' The singular is primarily each one and, therefore, also *with* and *among* all the others. The singular is plural." See *Being Singular Plural*, translated by Robert D. Richardson and Anne E. O'Byrne (Stanford: Stanford University Press, 2000), 32. This emergence is also an emergence of sense—not as distinct and separable meaning or content, but as the singular relationships that constitute our being with-one-another (*étant l'un-avec-l'autre*). Nancy is evidently working with Heidegger's *Mitsein*—the condition of being-*with* which characterises Dasein's existential being-there: "it needs to be made absolutely clear that Dasein, far from being either 'man' or 'subject,' is not even an isolated and unique 'one,' but is instead always the one, each one, with one another (*l'un avec l'autre*)," ibid., 26. In both cases, singularities are not merely following, alongside or juxtaposed over each other. They are *with* each other in the ethical sense of attending to each other, yet without forming any surpassing or transcendent unity. This sense of the singular can be read in relation to Agamben's treatment of the example: "the example is characterised by the fact that it holds for all cases of the same type, and, at the

same time, it is included among these. It is one singularity among others, which, however, stands for each of them and serves for all. On one hand, every example is treated in effect as a particular case; but on the other, it remains understood that it cannot serve in its particularity. Neither particular nor universal, the example is a singular object that presents itself as such, that *shows* its singularity. Hence the pregnancy of the Greek term, for example: *para-deigma*, that which is shown alongside (like the German *Bei-spiel*, that which plays alongside). Hence the proper place of the example is always beside itself, in the empty space in which its undefinable and unforgettable life unfolds... These pure singularities communicate only in the empty space of the example, without being tied by any common property, by any identity. They are expropriated of all identity so as to appropriate belonging itself, the sign ε. Tricksters or fakes, assistants or 'toons,' they are the exemplars of the coming community." See *The Coming Community*, translated by Michael Hardt (Minneapolis: University of Minnesota Press, 1993), 9-11.

9. Gilles Deleuze and Claire Parnet, *Dialogues* (Paris: Flammarion, 1996), 68-9.

10. Ibid., 71-2.

11. Ibid., 73.

12. Ibid., 81.

13. Ibid., 11.

14. Ibid., 13 and 16.

15. Deleuze and Parnet, *Abécédaire*, "Style." Nancy has developed this theme in relation to art in *The Muses*, translated by Peggy Kamuf (Stanford: Stanford University Press, 1996).

16. Deleuze and Parnet, *Dialogues*, 42.

17. The relevant etymological roots for the word *sit* are *SED/T = sit (seat, saddle, sedentary, settle); go (away), settle-apart (sedge, sediment) and *SEQ = cut, cleave (sedge, segment, segregate, sector, section, secant, seclude, secret, sect, secular, second). My use of etymology throughout this book is not intended to suggest any transcendent meanings of words. In spite of the arguably problematic sources used—in particular Fabre D'Olivet—it is not a contribution to the recovery of an original universal language. Nor does it engage philological norms or processes, although it patently displays a love of words and of the "tectonic" potential of sense that they imply and unclench. It is simply word-play—where the word *play* takes on a Derridean sense of production and deferral and a Barthean sense of delinquency. The objective is to enable the liberal and excessive conjugation of metaphor and allusion, so that sense begins to pullulate and meanings no longer cohere in the words themselves but in the potential resonances *between* them. Etymologies are drawn from William W. Skeat, *Etymological Dictionary of the English Language* (Oxford, Oxford University Press, 1978), J. Strong, *The Exhaustive Concordance of the Bible* (Riverside, Iowa Falls, undated), and Fabre D'Olivet, *La Langue Hébraïque Restituée* (Vevay: Delphica, L'Age D'Homme, 1985). In the text, etymological roots are indicated by the sign *.

18. The question of the use of theory in design will be treated in a forthcoming book, *Theorising the Project. A Thematic Approach to Architectural Design*.

19. Greek: *hetoimos* = ready; from *heteos* = adjusted, fitness (for), readiness; *hetes* = friend; *heteros* = other, different, altered. The same conjunction of familiar and

alien is evident in the German *Fremde* = alien, other and *Freunde* = friend, kin. See Greek: *kataskeuazo* = to be prepared, to equip, construct, create, ordain—from *kata* = distributed *down* (by, after the manner of) + *skeuos* = vessel, implement, equipment. Compare Hebrew: *kuwn* = set-up, appoint, fashion, fasten; *KHN = to render apt for, designate by naming, produce; *hasah* = to do, make, accomplish, furnish; *hesheb* = glisten.

20. Greek: *mello* = expectation, intention, to be about to do, to purpose, to be at the point of; *melo* = to be of interest, to concern, care.

21. Greek: *paraskeuazo* = to equip for—from *para-* = near, beside, aside, in the sight of, for the sake of + *skeuos* = vessel, implement, equipment, gear, apparatus.

22. Anglosaxon: *raedan* = to discern; *raed* = to counsel, advise, persuade; to be prepared, ready (for); *ridan* = to ride; Teutonic/Sanscrit: *radh* = to make favourable, propitiate; to be favourable to; to achieve, accomplish, prepare [ratio, ration, reason, arraign, riddle, region]; Icelandic: *reidi* = harness, gear, implements, dressed; prepared for a raid or ride. Reading is therefore not for information or communication. It is essentially a provisional and preparatory practice. Relevant etymons are *RE = to think upon; *REDH/*RED =to provide, accomplish; *REIDH = to ride, be conveyed. Compare Latin: *rota* = wheel; Sanscrit: *ratha* = charior, cart; Middle English: *retoryke*; Latin: *rhetorica*; Greek: *rhetorike techne* = art of rhetoric—from *eirein* = to speak, say, utter + *-tor* = agent; in turn from *WER = speak (word, verb); Sanskrit: *svar* = sound as "resounding," speech; compare *WERT = to turn, become; Sanskrit: *vrt* = turn, exist, be; Latin: *uertere* = turn; Anglosaxon: *weordan* = become. The notion of whirling and swerving are inherent in the idea of rhetorical speech, where *turns* of phrase and answers in return characterise a fundamental rhythm of deferral not geared towards the determination of singular meanings but of the swarming of indefinitely varying sense.

23. Hebrew: *qara* = to call out, address by name, call for, pronounce; encounter, happen, meet; *qarah* = to light upon, bring about, happen; establish, erect timbers for floors or roofs; *qiryah* = flooring, pavement, platform, city; *qereth* = building, city; *qeren* = projection, horn, cornet, peak of a mountain, ray of light. Compare *qiyr, qiyrah* = wall of a trench, side, town, fortress—all in the sense of *curving* to enclose. Enclosure is therefore not determined by the orthogonal segmentation or sectioning of an abstract spatial extent applied from without (by a demiurge or architect) but by a (re)turning and environing gesture in the milieu itself. The etymon is *KR/KIYR = what is incisive, penetrant; that which engraves, digs; that which serves as sign to conserve the memory of things. The sense is of that which produces characters, script, writing—hence technology itself as the means of enabling retentions of all kinds.

24. Image and imitation are cognate words. The mysterious dimension of the image that Huillet refers to is implied in the etymology of the word, which can be deconstructed either from Latin: *im-itari* = to imitate, produce a likeness—from *im-* = in + *iterare* = to repeat, that is, an iteration-in; or else from *im-* = in + *magi*; Greek: *magos* = enchanter, wizard, magician, allied to Latin: *magn*, Greek: *megas* = great, Anglosaxon: *maegen*, and the etymon *MAG/MAK = strong, great, might, much; *MAGH = to have power. Compare. Greek: *mechane*; Latin: *machine* =

machine, contrivance, instrument; Greek: *machos* = means, contrivance. The overall sense is of a magnification of power and scale by iteration.
25. Jacques Rancière, *The Future of the Image* (London: Verso, 2007), 1-31.
26. Jean-Luc Nancy, *The Evidence of Film* (Bruxelles, Yves Gevaert, 2001), 18.
27. Ibid., 46.
28. Ibid., 24-6.
29. Ibid., 29-30.
30. Ibid., 40-1.
31. Ibid., 14-16.
32. Ibid., 38.
33. Ibid., 38.
34. Ibid., 56.
35. I will pursue this line of enquiry in *Theorising the Project. A Thematic Approach to Architectural Design.* See my "Makeshift Stalls," *Broadsheet* 28, no.4 (2000): 6-7.

# Chapter One: Place and Setting

1. Martin Heidegger, *The Fundamental Concepts of Metaphysics*, translated by William McNeil and Nicholas Walker (Bloomington: Indiana University Press, 1995), 365.
2. See my "Limit and leimma. What remains for architecture," in *Limits* (Melbourne: SAHANZ/RMIT, 2005), 455-460.
3. See the discussion of Carlo Scarpa's Brion Vega cemetery in the last chapter.
4. J. E. Malpas' survey of this idea is notable. See his *Place and Experience. A Philosophical Topography* (Cambridge: Cambridge University Press, 1999). See also Edward S. Casey, *The Fate of Place. A Philosophical Enquiry* (Berkeley: University of California Press, 1998) and *Getting Back into Place. Towards a Renewed Understanding of the Place-World* (Bloomington: Indiana University Press, 1993).
5. Malpas, *Place and Experience*, 32. This theme is central to the work of Augustin Berque on the relationships of societies to space and nature. See for example *Mediance de Milieux en Paysages* (Paris: Belin, 2000), *Écoumène. Introduction a l'Étude des Milieux Humains* (Paris: Belin, 2000) and *La Pensée Paysagère* (Paris: Archibooks, 2008).
6. This concept is based on Cartesian and Newtonian notions of space as "a single homogenous and isotropic 'container' in which things are located." Ibid., 26.
7. Ibid., 18.
8. Ibid., 25.
9. Gilbert Simondon, *L'Individuation Psychique et Collective* (Paris: Aubier/Flammarion, 2007), 12.
10. Ibid., 12, 66 n 1.
11. Ibid., 13.
12. Ibid., 16.
13. Ibid., 17.
14. Ibid., 23-25.

15. Ibid., 28.
16. Malpas, *Place and Experience*, 176, 178.
17. Ibid., 180, 186.
18. Referring to Proust's *Remembrance of Things* past, Malpas notes that "one recalls, not just the person, but person and place, and both as part of the same image, part of a single remembrance." Ibid., 176. See also Edward S. Casey, *Remembering: A Phenomenological Study* (Bloomington: Indiana University Press, 1987) and Drouwe Draaisma, *Metaphors of Memory. A History of Ideas About the Mind* (Cambridge: Cambridge University Press, 2000).
19. Jean-Yves Trépos, "La Sociologie Postmoderne," in *Le Portique* 1, no.1 (1998): 60.
20. Benoît Goetz, *La Dislocation. Architecture et Philosophie* (Paris: Les Editions de la Passion, 2002).
21. The fundamental spacing of here from there (and of now from then in time) leads to a typology of multiple antinomies which regulate the architectural production of modernity—albeit according to different registers (cosmological, existential, tectonic, mythical, and so forth). For example, order/chaos; same/other; interior and exterior; private/public; served/servant; known/unknown; familiar/unfamiliar; safe/dangerous; memory/oblivion; orientation/disorientation; clearing/forest; domicile/wilderness, sedentary/nomadic and so forth.
22. *Place* is from Anglosaxon: *place;* Middle English: *plekke* = open space, plot of ground, patch, piece. Compare Middle English: *plakken* = to patch, fasten; strike; plaster or besmear with lime or chalk; *pate, plate* = (shaven) crown of the head; Latin: *platta* = clerical tonsure—from *PET = to spread out; Latin: *patere* = to lie open, spread out, extend. The Hebrew word for place is *makom* = standing, spot, locality, condition. Compare *makor* = something dug, source of water, fountain, issue, well, spring—from *kuwm* = to rise, abide, accomplish, perform, set-up; and the etymon *QUWM = to substantialise, to be extended, consolidated, constituted; to exist, subsist, consist of, persist, resist. The two common Greek words for place are *topos* = occupied spot, tract, position, home; condition, opportunity; and *khora* = room, space as undetermined or undifferentiated expanse, uninhabited region— the latter related to the etymon *KHA = chasm, chaos. Compare Sanskrit *kha* = emptiness, zero—not as (de)void but as indefinite potential. For the latter, see Ananda K Coomaraswamy, "Kha and other words denoting 'zero,'" in *Selected Papers Volume 2* (Princeton: Princeton University Press, 1977), 220-230. This text is available on-line: http://aryan-buddhism.blogspot.com/2007/07/kha-and-other-words-denoting-zero-in.html (accessed November 1, 2009).
23. The word *site* means locality, situation, place where a thing is set down or fixed—from Latin: *situs* and *sinere* = to allow, put, place; *situare* = locate, place; *situs* = site; *sedere* = sit. Compare Anglosaxon: *settan* = settle down, fix, sink to rest, subside; Sanscrit: *sad*; Greek: *sedyomai* and *ktisis* = foundation; Sanscrit: *kshiti* = abode—from *kshi* = to dwell; Latin: *sedere* = I sit. All are from the etymon *SED = sit—but, as with the idea of *flattening out* in the word *place*, the sense is of a spreading-out-apart, therefore a sedition. See Latin: *sed-* = scatter, sow-apart (seed) and lead-apart (seduce). The word *seize* is related in the sense of a laying hold of or grasping; but also appropriating, confiscating and withdrawing.

Related words are saddle, set, seat, settle, preside, reside, residue, sedate, sedentary, sediment; siege, size. *Steady* is related to *stand* through the etymon \*STHA = to stand and \*STHEU = to fix firmly, stand fast. Compare Sanscrit: *stha*; Greek: *hesten*, *histemi*; Latin: *stare*; German: *stehen* = stand, set, place; Anglosaxon: *stede* = place, stead, steady; *stow* = a place; Sanskrit: *sthavira* = fixed, firm; Greek: *sthulos* = pillar; *stoa* = porch; *stavros* = upright pole, stake; Latin: *instaurare* = construct, build; Anglosaxon: *steor* = paddle, rudder. Related words are stage, station, statute, stool, stall, static, apostasy, stammer (literally *disposed to come to a stand still*), stem, stamen, stamina, steer, store, restore.

24. Martin Heidegger, *Fundamental Concepts of Metaphysics*, translated by William McNeil and Nicholas Walker (Bloomington and Indianapolis: Indiana University Press, 1995), 80.

25. Giorgio Agamben's *whatever being* and Gilles Deleuze's *any place whatever* are discussed in terms of space in Chapter 3.

26. "God is in every thing as the place in which every thing is, or rather as the determination and the 'topia' of every entity. The transcendent, therefore, is not a supreme entity above all things; rather, *the pure transcendent is the taking place of every thing.*" See Giorgio Agamben, *The Coming Community*, translated by Michael Hardt (Minneapolis: University of Minnesota Press, 1993), 13-14.

27. Jean-Luc Nancy, "Uncanny landscape," in *The Ground of the Image*, translated by Jeff Fort (New York: Fordham University Press, 2005), 54.

28. See my "Place, country, chorography: towards a kinaesthetic and narrative practice of place," in *Architectural Theory Review* 7, no.2 (November 2002): 45-58; and "Liru and Kuniya: Greg Burgess' Aboriginal centre at Ayers Rock," in *Architecture Australia* 85, no.2 (1996): 48-55.

29. See my "Grounding the Question. Implications of Indigenous Narrative Practice for Architectural History," in *On What Ground(s)* (Adelaide: Society of Architectural Historians of Australia and New Zealand, 1997), 221-227.

30. See my "Mapping: Design," *Architectural Theory Review* 3, no.1 (1998): 35-45.

31. Stephen Muecke, borrowing the term from Gilles Deleuze and Felix Guattari, refers these practices to "nomadology." See Krim Benterrak, Stephen Muecke and Paddy Roe, *Reading the Country* (Fremantle: Fremantle Arts Centre Press, 1984), 15; and Deleuze and Guattari, *A Thousand Plateaus. Capitalism and Schizophrenia*, translated by Brian Massumi (Minneapolis: University of Minnesota Press, 1993).

32. Between 2000 and 2004 I collaborated with staff and students of the University of NSW, the University of South Australia and the Nganajarra community around Patjarr and Warburton in the Gibson Desert of Western Australia. A community arts centre was designed, prefabricated in Sydney and Adelaide, transported and constructed in situ built by students with assistance from the community. During the project we met the same people and families that had featured in Dunlop's film, and spent some time in several of the places depicted.

33. "In those days there was no such thing as handheld sync sound shooting, where your sound was automatically linked to the film. If you wanted to use sound, this was a whole big deal because the camera made a lot of noise. So the camera had to

be put in what we called a blimp, which meant it couldn't be handheld. The sound equipment was a huge amount—another vehicle full of equipment, another couple of people, sound engineers. So, it was logistically ridiculous to think of shooting synchronised sound. I decided to shoot it silent. What we used to do often in those days with documentary films was put artificial sound on. We'd make sound in the studio and lay it in. But the kind of style of filming I wanted was to be as truthful as possible. If I didn't have sound, I didn't want to make artificial sound, so I decided to have it silent except for a very simple commentary, which I gave myself. Again, because I didn't want it to be a professional commentator, I wanted it to be the voice of someone who was there and had seen what was going on.... I shot in black-and-white. Why? Because I thought this was probably the last chance ever perhaps to film this remarkable and, I thought, really beautiful way of life. These people living in this incredible environment, a harsh but beautiful environment with seemingly so few resources, but having a rich and meaningful life. I wanted it to be as beautiful as possible and I thought that Black-and-white was actually more beautiful than colour. And as it turned out, black-and-white lasts much longer than colour—it doesn't fade. So these films will probably be around long after all my colour films have faded. And I think black-and-white must have suited Richard Tucker because he was able to get really beautiful tones on people's skin with the 35 mm." Ian Dunlop, Film Australia interview available at http://www.filmaust.com.au (accessed February 22, 2009).
34. Martin Heidegger, "On the essence and concept of *phusis* in Aristotle's Physics B, 1," in *Pathmarks*, edited by William McNeil, translated by Thomas Sheehan (Cambridge: Cambridge University Press, 1998), 199.
35. Latin: *natura*—from *nasci* = to be born, to originate; cognate with Greek: *gen-*.
36. Heidegger, "On the essence and concept of *phusis*," 183.
37. Jean-Christophe Bailly, *Le Champ Mimétique* (Paris: Editions du Seuil, 2005), 228.
38. Ibid., 211-212.
39. The first city builder is the metalworker *Tubalcain* (Latin: *Vulcan*), whose father, the sedentary Cain, kills his nomadic brother Abel. This myth is read by René Guénon as a metaphor for the destruction of time (nomadism) by space (sedentarism); and by implication of the uncivilised by the civilised, of the earth by the city, of the organic by the crystalline and of nature by culture. See the chapter "Time changed into space," in *The Reign of Quantity and the Signs of the Times*, translated by Lord Northbourne (New York: Sophia Perennis, 2001), 159-164.
40. Latin: *domus* = house is from the etymon *DEM/*TIM = to build. Compare Greek: *domos* = building; Gothic: *timrjan* = to build—from which the word *timber* is derived; Greek: *demos* = country district, as well as the local people who live or build their houses there; *demokratia* = the (creative, discriminating) power, strength and rule of those people—trivialised in the facile definition of "popular government." See *DHE = to put, place, set, do; Sanskrit: *dha*; Greek: *tithemo*, *thema, thesis* = place, put, propose; and *DO = to give; Sanskrit: *da* = to give; Greek: *dosis*; Latin: *donum* = gift, dose. The notion of the house as a "gift" from architect to client is a standard enough cliché. Less foregrounded is the implied idea of the house as a constructed setting, milieu—or more properly infrastructure,

frame or system which "gives," "donates," or enables multiple opportunities for being-with-others and for being-with-place.

41. Heidegger, "On the essence and concept of *phusis*," 189.
42. Ibid., 190-1. "Making, *poiesis*, is one kind of production, whereas 'growing' the going back into itself and emerging out of itself), *phusis* is another. Here 'to produce' cannot mean 'to make' but rather: to place something into the unhiddenness of its appearance; to let something become present; presencing," ibid., 221.
43. Ibid., 198.
44. Ibid., 195.
45. Ibid., 216.
46. Ibid., 217.
47. Ibid., 227-8.
48. Ibid., 229-30.
49. Ibid., 212-13.
50. Ibid., 206.
51. Ibid., 205-6. See also "Building Dwelling Thinking," in *Poetry, Language, Thought*, translated by Albert Hofstadter (New York: Harper & Row, 1975), 145-161; and my "Limit and leimma. What remains for architecture," in *Limits* (Melbourne: SAHANZ/RMIT, 2005): 455-460.
52. Greek: *Logos*—from *LEG = to join*—variously means relation, proportion, analogy, correspondence. Heidegger reads it as a gesture of collecting and gathering—"to bring various dispersed things together into a unity, and at the same time to bring this unity forth and hand it over…into the unhidden of presencing (*parousia*)… to reveal what was formely hidden, to let it be manifest in its presencing, to let it be seen." See "On the essence and concept of *phusis*," 205-6.
53. Maurice Blanchot, *L'attente l'oubli* (Paris: Gallimard, 1962), 39.
54. Alain Mons, "Le bruit silence ou la plongée paysagère," in *Les Paysages du Cinema*, edited by Jean Mottet (Champ Vallon: Seyssel, 1999), 242-3.
55. Inid., 244
56. Nancy, "Uncanny landscape," 51-2.
57. Cadastral is commonly derived from Latin: *capitastrum* through the Greek: *katastikon*—from *kata* = down, by + *stikon* = line; that is, *line by line*. It is a list or register of land tenure based on lines between markers or corners as a basis for taxation. But the word can also be decomposed in relation to the Latin: *quadrum* = square, *quadrus* = four-cornered + *aster* = star. In this case, the register would be symbolic and the cadastre would refer to a means of stabilising or *cornering* (that is framing and double crossing) stellar motion by way of a diagram which in turn becomes an apparatus for mobilising cosmic energies associated with those stars. In that sense, to be without cadastre would constitute a *disaster*—literally a being-without(*dis-*)-stars(*aster*); hence a state of disorientation and placelessness. In the *Cardo* and *Decumanus,* which *crossed* the Roman settlement, the *cardo,* a correlate of *cardinal*—from the Latin: *cardo* = hinge, pin, prick, functions to pin-down the geometrical/spatial arrangement and by implication the territory. The proximity of *cardo* to card, chart, charter and cart foregrounds the politicising, institutionalising and mobilising power of the map. In this regard, see the

exceptional multivolume *The History of Cartography*, editors J. B. Harley and David Woodward (Chicago: The University of Chicago Press, 1987).

58. Nancy, "Uncanny landscape," 57, 59.

59. Ibid., 52.

60. Ibid., 59.

61. Ibid., 59-60.

62. Martin Heidegger, *Parmenides*, translated by André Shuwer and Richard Rojcewicz Bloomington: Indiana University Press, 1992), 117.

63. Nancy, "Uncanny landscape," 61-2.

64. Ibid., 58.

65. Latin: *desertus* = waste, desert—from *de-* = to undo + *serrere* = join, link, bind together, tighten; *desertare* = abandon. The main sense is the idea of unthreading and disassembling a weave, hence of deconstituting an order—be it psychosomatic, conceptual, political or aesthetic.

66. Sandro Bernardi. *Antonioni. Personnage Paysage* (Paris: Presses Universitaires de Vincennes: 2006), 35.

67. Ibid., 56.

68. Michelangelo Antonioni, *The Architecture of Vision. Writings and Interviews on Cinema* (Chicago: The University of Chicago Press, 1996), 8-9 and 20.

69. Roland Barthes, "Dear Antonioni," quoted in Geoffrey Nowell-Smith, *L'Avventura* (London: BFI, 1977), 63-68.

70. Antonioni, *The Architecture of Vision*, 98.

71. Ibid., and Bernardi, *Antonioni*, 38.

72. Antonioni, *The Architecture of Vision*, 23.

73. Bernardi, *Antonioni*, 39.

74. Ibid., 36.

75. Ibid., 72.

76. Antonioni, *The Architecture of Vision*, 27, 29.

77. Bernardi, *Antonioni*, 64.

78. Ibid., 55.

79. Ibid., 75.

80. Ibid., 97.

81. Ibid., 63.

82. Ibid., 74.

83. Ibid., 94.

84. Ibid., 128-9.

85. "Depopulated, the landscape estranges, it renders uncanny (*le paysage dépayse*): there is no more community, no more civic life, but it is not simply 'nature.' It is the land of those who have no land, who are uncanny and estranged (*le pays des dépayses*), who are not a people, who are at once those who have lost their way and those who contemplate the infinite—perhaps their infinite estrangement." Nancy, "Uncanny landscape," 61.

# Chapter Two: Spatiality

1. Rancière, *The Future of the Image,* 91.

2. Pierre Sauvanet, *Le Rythme Grec d'Héraclyte à Aristote* (Paris: Presses Universitaires de France, 1999).

3. Emile Benveniste's scrupulous analysis of the word rhythm can be found in *Problèmes de Linguistique Générale* (Paris: Gallimard, 1966), 327-335.

4. Sauvanet, *Le Rythme Grec,* 124.

5. Benveniste, *Problèmes de Linguistique Générale*, 331-333.

6. Plato, *Laws*, 665a, 728e; Aristotle, *Physics*, Book 4, 219, 221.

7. Plato, *Banquet*, 187a and Sauvanet, *Le Rythme Grec*, 85-93.

8. Sauvanet, *Le Rythme Grec*, 23-4.

9. For Aristotle, what is not yet formed or organised is *arruthmistos*, arrhythmic. See *Metaphysics*, 1014b.

10. Book 1, Chapter 2.

11. *Skhema* corresponds to the German *Gestalt* and *rhuthmos* to *Gestaltung*. See Sauvanet, *Le Rythme Grec*, 40-50.

12. Rancière, *The Future of the Image,* 91.

13. Gilles Deleuze, *Cinema 1: The Movement Image*, translated by Hugh Tomlinson and Barbara Habberjam (Minneapolis: University of Minnesota Press, 1986), 26, n.25: "The cinema presents... two very different aspects of depth of field which were analysed by Bazin. Despite all his reservations about Bazin's thesis, Mitry concedes the essential point: in a primary form, depth is cut up into superimposable isolable slices each of which is valid on its own (as in *Feuillade* in Griffith); but in Renoir and in Welles, another form replaces slices with a perpetual interaction, and shortcircuits the foreground and the background."

14. All from the etymon *PER = to go through, experience, fare, travel; Sanscrit: *paraya* = to conduct across; *paras* = beyond, further; Greek: *peras* = I pass through; *poros* = a way; *peran* = beyond; *para* = beside; *peri* = around; Latin: *porta* = gate; *portus* = harbour; Anglosaxon: *faran* = to go, fare (experience, peril, far, for, from, part, parent, periphery, portal, opportunity). Forbearance is patient endurance; a form of resistance or abstinence suggesting that bearing and carriage, while moving forward, simultaneously retreat in order to conserve for themselves a measure of unactualised potentiality, hence of impending power.

15. Jacques Derrida, "Parergon," in *La Vérité en Peinture* (Paris: Flammarion, 1978).

16. Ibid., 63, 85.

17. See my "Limit and leimma," 455-460.

18. Paul Virilio, *The Lost Dimension*, translated by Daniel Moshenberg (New York: Semiotext(e), 1991).

19. *The Pleasure of the Text,* translated by R. Howard (New York: Hill and Wang, 1973), and "Rhetoric of the image," in *Image-Music-Text*, translated by Stephen Heath (London: Collins Sons and Co.), 32-51.

20. Roland Barthes, *Le Plaisir du Texte* (Paris: Editions du Seuil, 1973), 19 (my translation). For Barthes, "The *brio* of the text (without which, after all, there is no text) is its will to bliss: just where it exceeds demand, transcends prattle, and

whereby it attempts to overflow, to break through the constraint of adjectives – which are the doors of language through which the ideological and the imaginary come flooding in." See *The Pleasure of the Text*, translated by Richard Miller (Oxford: Blackwell, 1990), 13-14. Such excess of what Michael Moriarty calls "simultaneously inapprehensible meanings" (*Roland Barthes* (Stanford: Stanford University Press, 1991), 145) cause the "signifiying mass of the text to fall (*basculer*)," triggering disorientation (*déboussollement*) and vertigo in the reader, for whom the illegibility of the text opens to an erotics and bliss of reading. See *Prétexte: Roland Barthes*, edited by Antoine Compagnon (Cerisy-La-Salle: Centre Culturel International de Cerisy-La-Salle, 1978), 300.

21. Deleuze, *Cinema 1,* 16-18.

22. Ibid., 15-18: "In one case, the out-of-field designates that which exists elsewhere, to one side or around; in the other case, the out-of-field testifies to a more disturbing presence, one which cannot even be said to exist, but rather to 'insist' or 'subsist', a more radical Elsewhere, outside homogenous space and time."

23. Ibid., 17 & 18.

24. Ibid..

25. Ibid., 27.

26. See Rancière, *The Future of the Image.*

27. Martin Heidegger, *Parmenides*, 104. Numerous kinds of looking feature in Greek terminology: *blepo* = voluntary observation; *horao* = stare at, discern, experience; *optomai* = gaze in wonder, with wide open eyes; *eido* = to see, know, behold; *eidos* = form, appearance; *eidolon* = image; *theoreo* = look closely at, inspect; *theatron* = spectacle, apparition, show; *theo* = to place, ordain, purpose; *theoria* (*theo + horao*) = spectatorship, spectacle; *thereuo* = hunt, catch; *skopeo* = passively observe.

28. *Speculation* is from the etymon*SPEK = to spy. Greek: *spektomai* = I see; Latin: *specere* = see; *species* = appearance. See Ivan Illich, who relates species to "the characteristic or nature of something,... the visible sign of the substance or essence." See "Guarding the Eye in the Age of Show," in *Conference at the International Meeeting of Inter-Face in Hamburg* (1993), 9—12. Illich gives valuable references for a historical study of the gaze in antiquity. The word "face" (German: *Gesicht*, Greek: *emphasis*) meant countenance and appearance until the 15th. C. Compare Latin: *superficies* = upper face; Greek: *huper* = above, upper; Sanskrit: *upari* = near, close, under, over, sub. William Skeat reads *sub-* as an upward movement, as in Latin: *subregere* = surge, rise (super, superb, supernal). See his *Etymological Dictionary*, 419. Compare Anglosaxon: *up*; Old High German: *uf* = under, *ufar* = over; Greek: *hupo* = under; Anglosaxon: *open* = that which is lifted up; Middle English: *surfet*; Old French: *sorfait, surfaire* = excess; Latin: *factus, facere* = to make, hold, do (fact, faculty); *facies* = face, front, countenance; French: *facile* = easy, yielding.

29. Heidegger, *Parmenides*, 107-8. See also Jacques Derrida, *The Gift of Death* (Chicago: The University of Chicago Press, 1995), 98-102.

30. See my "In(side)out: the face that turns towards and looks: Chartres Cathedral, 1989," *Interzones*, 1997, http://www.altx.com/au2/tawa.html.

31. Bernard Stiegler, *Économie de l'Hypermatériel et Psychopouvoir* (Mille et une Nuits, 2008), 122-3. "Attention is something that is formed slowly, across a complex system of care (*soins*), going from the first gestures that a mother devotes to her child up to the most elaborate forms of sublimation… attention is not simply a psychological concentration: it is also a social comportment towards the other who precisely appears as *other*, including across his objects, which, inasmuch as they are his objects, are invested with the other's spirit." (My translation).

32. Stiegler, *Prendre Soin. De la Jeunesse et des Generations* (Paris: Flammarion, 2008), 136-7.

33. As Stiegler notes, for deep attention to operate the object of attention must constitute a deferred identity (*identité différante*) which is overdetermined by a context that can be interminably recontextualised—much like a literary text that is recontextualised each time it is read, thereby engendering different readings. Stiegler, *Prendre Soin*, 152-3.

34. Stiegler, *Économie de l'Hypermatériel*, 105-131. Stiegler calls this desire a "spirit of libidinal economy." It is constitutive of human being as such and is targeted for ruination by the control of individual and collective comportment through technologies of attention capture.

35. Martin Heidegger, *Being and Time*, translated by John Macquarrie and Edward Robinson (London: Blackwell, 1995), 156, 225-273.

36. Malpas, *Heidegger's Topology*, 83-104.

37. Stiegler, *Prendre Soin*, 283.

38. Heidegger, *Being and Time*, 158-9.

39. Heidegger, "The Question Concerning Technology" and "The Turning," in *The Question Concerning Technology and Other Essays*, translated by William Lovitt (New York: Harper & Row, 1977), 3-49.

40. *Solicit* is from the Latin: *sollus-* = whole, entire + *citus*, *ciere* = shake, excite, cite. Greek: *kinemai* = I hasten—from *kinein* = to move—is cognate.

41. The allusion here is to Nancy's term *compearance* which refers to the co-appearance of singular (beings) in the commonality of their difference. See his "La Comparution/The Compearance: From the Existence of 'Communism' to the Community of 'Existence,'" translated by Tracey B Strong, *Political Theory* 20, no.3 (August, 1992): 371-398.

42. Nancy, *The Evidence of Film*, 42. This is evident in Kiarostami's photographic work *The Roads of Kiarostami*, Centre Georges Pompidou, January 2007.

43. *Pasolini L'Enragé*, DVD, directed by Jean-André Fieschi (Paris: La Sept, AMIP, INA, in association with Channel Four, 1966).

44. Agamben, *The Coming Community*, 1.

45. Deleuze, *Cinema 1*, 120.

46. Marc Augé, *Non-Places. Introduction to an Anthropology of Supermodernity*, translated by J. Howe (London & New York: Verso, 1995).

47. Yukata Saito, *Louis I. Kahn Houses 1940-1974* (Tokyo: Toto Shuppan, 1994), 40-83.

48. Consider this sequence from Burgess' unpublished notes (1999), for an ABC Television program (capitalisation in the original): "re-enchantment, opportunities… gentle, exploring, sensitive; lyrical, poetic, inclusive; the dark,

unknown, trust to question; myth, healing, rhythm, slower, quiet; tolerance, friendship; the earth, nurturing, children, mother; feeling, courage, quiet; time to observe, to feel; relationship, generosity, prayer, RECEIVE, GIVE, OPEN; move towards, wait, patience, SERVE..." Burgess notes the role of the architect as being to "SERVE people and their activities... (to) set up connections between people and nature, past and present... to make a life enhancing difference, then challenge, delight, surprise, inspire."

49. Rancière has noted the privileging of gestural rather than formal motives in recent architecture: "a new state of the spatial phenomenon where a coalescence between the physicality and materiality of space and the materiality of the designer's gesture is imposed in place of the representative privilege of form that organised and cancelled matter." The issue is not as simple since what is at play is a shift from a representation of stable form to the representation of emergent formation. The representational regime operates in both cases. See *The Future of the Image*, 56-7.

50. Burgess, unpublished notes.

51. Nancy, *Hegel. The Restlessness of the Negative*, translated by Jason Smith and Steven Miller (Minneapolis: University of Minnesota Press, 2002), 14, 20.

52. William Blake, "The Marriage Of Heaven And Hell, Proverbs Of Hell, 10 and 7," in William Blake, *The Complete Illuminated Books* (London: Thames and Hudson with the William Blake Trust, 2000), 116.

53. *Ecstasis* is used here in the Heideggerian sense of a "rapture of resolute openness in which Dasein is carried away toward whatever possibilities and circumstances are encountered in the situation, but a rapture that is *held* in this absolute openness." See *Being and Time*, 338 and William McNeill's treatment of Heidegger's *Augenblick* in *The Glance of the Eye. Heidegger, Aristotle and the Ends of Theory* (New York: State University of New York Press, 1999).

54. Job, 39: 29. For *shekinah*, see René Guénon, *Le Roi du Monde* (Paris: Gallimard, 1927), 22-30.

55. E. Baldwyn Smith, *The Dome. A Study in the History of Ideas* (Princeton: Princeton University Press, 1971), 88.

56. John James, "The Canopy of Heaven," in *In Search of the Unknown in Medieval Architecture* (London: Pindar Press, 2007).

57. See Jean-Pierre Vernant, *Myth and Thought Amongst the Greeks* (London: Routledge & Kegan Paul, 1983), 135-140.

# Chapter Three: Temporality

1. St Augustine, *Confessions*, translated by R. S. Pine-Coffin (Harmondsworth: Penguin, 1979), Book 11: 15.

2. Plato, *Parmenides*, 137d-e.

3. Ibid., 138b.

4. Ibid., 139a.

5. Ibid., 139b.

6. Ibid., 141e.

7. See A. E. Taylor, *The Parmenides of Plato* (Oxford: Clarendon Press, 1934), 37.

8. Plato, *Parmenides*, 165b.
9. Ibid., 164d, 165a-e.
10. Plato, *Timaeus*, 37d-38c, 29a-b. See Ananda K. Coomaraswamy, *Time and Eternity* (Bangalore: Indira Ghandi National Centre for the Arts, 1990), 64, 67.
11. Plato, *Parmenides*, 152d.
12. Ibid., 156d-e.
13. See Coomaraswamy, *The Rg Veda as Land-Náma Bók* (New Delhi: Bharatiya Publishing House, 1980), 10-12.
14. Plato, *Cratylus*, 437a. See the etymon *STHA = to be born/to subsist; Sanskrit: *astam* = home. History can be decomposed into *STA = standing (Greek: *stasis*; Sanscrit: *sthiti*) + *REO = to flow (Latin: *riuus* = a stream)—hence the *standing of flow* (of time, causality, and so forth). Compare Greek: *ereo* = to speak, utter, command; *rhema* = an utterance. The suffix *t*, conveying the sense of arrest or termination, produces words such as *right, rite* (Sanscrit: *rta* = order, law; *rota* = wheel of the law; *ratha* = chariot), *road, root, current, street, articulate, orator*. According to Plato, the letters *D* and *T* have a compressive *dynamin*—that is, they imitate the idea of bondage (*desmou*) and restraint (*staseos*). See *Cratylus*, 427b. For *rhema* = locution/manner of speaking, see Plato, *Republic*, 601a; *Theatetus*, 168b; Cratylus, 399b; Laws, 840c. For *rhoe* = flux, see *Cratylus*, 424a, 440c; *Theatetus*, 152c. For *rhein* = to flow, see *Cratylus*, 439c, 411c; *Theatetus*, 182c-d. For *ruthmos*, see *Banquet*, 187d; *Republic* 397b, 398d, 399e, 400d, 401d; *Laws*, 655a, 661c, 669e, 672c.
15. Greek: *histo* = weft; *histao* = to be standing. Of the various senses of *stasis* in the Platonic dialogues, three predominate: a state or condition (*Phaedrus*, 253c), stability/rest (*Cratylus*, 437a, 438c; *Sophist*, 250a; *Timaeus*, 57e), and discord (*Republic*, 351d, 440e, 444a, 470b-70d; *Laws*, 628b).
16. The rotation of the earth's own rotational axis causes it to wobble as it completes a full cycle in around 25920 years. This curious number belongs to sexagesimal arithmetic: $25920 = 4320 \times 6$, where $4320 = 2160 \times 2$; $216 = 2^3 \times 3^3$; $432 = 72 \times 6$; $72 = 8 \times 9$ or $2^3 \times 3^2$; $36 = 2^2 \times 3^2$; $18 = 2 \times 3^2$. It appears in the Old Testament, the Vedas and Upanishads, the Platonic dialogues and what remains of Pythagorean doctrine. It is there in the Perfect or Great Year of Greek and Persian astronomy (432,000 years). See Plato, *Republic*, 427b-c; *Timaeus*, 39c-d and Van der Waerden, "The Great Year in Greek, Persian and Hindu astronomy," in *Archive for the History of the Exact Sciences* 18, no.4 (1978): 359-384. The motif of the 4 Ages surfaces in the Bible and Plato (gold, silver, bronze and iron) and the Vedic *caturyuga* (four ages) consisting of *krita* (1728 years), *treta* (1296), *dwapara* (864) and *kali* (432). In *Republic*, 543, Plato assigns four temporalities to these ages, with distinctive ethos, political systems, and corresponding spatialisations in the form of 4 paradigmatic cities: Athens (royalty, aristocracy), Callipolis (aristocracy, oligarchy), Magnesia (oligarchy, democracy) and Atlantis (democracy, tyranny). The sequence of 4 ages indicates a fall from the most pure (gold/*krita*) to the most admixed and impure (bronze/*kali*). The end of time is equated with discord and the complete overturning of natural hierarchy between spiritual authority and temporal power. The last age is one of dregs and psychic residues of all past ages. The descent from first to last also expresses a decrease in

duration and a compression of time for each succeeding *yuga*, leading to an eventual suppression of time as it falls into an "ocean of unlikeliness." See Plato, *Sophist*, 268d. The compression of time implies a sense of accelerated temporality, with a consequent restlessness or urgency that characterises the ambient world. This is inversely proportional to a simultaneous expansion and dilation of space, with a consequent distantiation and dislocation that characterises the existential milieu.

17. The solstices are generally identified with gates that enable an escape from temporality. In pre-Christian and Christian conceptions, the summer solstice is the gate of hell, *Januae Inferni*; and the winter solstice the gate of heaven, *Januae Coeli*. The two-faced god Janus, the janitor who gives his name to January, is a symbol of the door and threshold. See Guénon, *Le Roi du Monde*, 62, and *L'Esoterisme de Dante* (Paris: Galilee, 1981), 149.

18. See Coomaraswamy, *Selected Papers* (Princeton: Princeton University Press, 1977), Volume 1, 528-31, 542-4; and *Time and Eternity*, 45.

19. *Door*—Sanscrit: *dvara, torana, torii*; Greek: *thuran, thura* = door, portal, gate; *thuris* = aperture, window; *thera* = trap, destruction; French *tuer* = to kill; Greek: *thusiasterion* = altar; *dvandra* = delusion of the pairs. The words *two, duality, divide* and *devil* are cognate.

20. Elías Torres Tur, *Zenithal Light* (Barcelona: Col-legi d'Arquitectes de Catalunya, 2005).

21. Heidegger, "Building Dwelling Thinking," 154. See also Casey, *The Fate of Place*, 63.

22. For a political reading of potentiality and actuality in Aristotle's *de Anima* in terms of power, see Agamben, "On potentiality," in *Potentialities*, translated by Daniel Heller-Roazen (Stanford: Stanford University Press, 1999), 177-184; "The Idea of Study," and "The Idea of Power," in *Idea of Prose*, translated by Michael Sullivan and Sam Whitsitt (New York: State of New York University Press, 1995), 63-65, 71-72.

23. *Le Littré* gives for *étale* "that which has ceased to rise and is not yet falling." *Étale* is cognate with German *stillstehend*—still-stand, or standstill. The Shorter Oxford defines still-stand as a "geographical term for a condition or period in which there is a pause in a process such as crustal uplift, sea level change, or glacial advance or retreat." Still water is also referred to as *slack* water.

24. *Labile* = subject to slide, fall, lack—from Latin: *labare* = to totter, sink; in the sense of being subject to a heavy weight. *Labour* is cognate. At this intertidal moment of slack water the sea labours under the weight of its own mass.

25. Nancy, "*Lumière étale*," in Anne Immelé and Jean-Luc Nancy, *Wir* (Trézélan: Filigranes Éditions, 2003), 57. (My translation).

26. *Limit*—Middle English: *limiten* = to limit, assign a boundary; Latin: *limitem, limes* = boundary; *limen* = threshold; *limus* = transverse, oblique; *limbus* = border, edging, edge; *lamina* = thin plate, layer; Greek: *limen* = harbour, haven; Latin: *limne* = lake, pond (as restricted by a close shore). Greek: *leimma* = remainder, remnant; from *leipo* = to leave, fail, be absent or destitute, wanting, lack—from the etymon *LEP = to peel, a scale. Compare *LEIP = smear, cleave, remain; Sanscrit: *lip* = smear, anoint; Gothic: *bi-leib-an* = to remain behind; *laiba* = remnant;

Anglosaxon: *liban* = live, leave; Greek: *lupe, lipeo* = sadness, distress, grief, heavy sorrow; *loipon* = something remaining; remaining time; Middle French: *limbe* = mouth, brink. In astronomy, a limb is the outermost border of the solar or lunar disc in an eclipse. *Limbo, limbus* are the borders of hell or the place bordering on hell.

27. Hebrew: *gebul* = (twisted) chord, boundary, enclosed territory—from *gabal* = to twist, bound, be a border, set bounds about; *GB = convexity, concavity—as a *turning* of space. The word can be decomposed as*GA = increase, augmentation, enlargement + *BL = dilation, distension, abundance, inundation.

28. *Horizon*—Greek: *horizo* = mark out, bound, appoint, decree, determine, ordain, limit; *horos* = boundary line, frontier, region, border, coast; *horkos* = fence, restraint. Compare *oros* = to rise, lift up; and *orthos* = right, erect, perpendicular, straight, upright, arisen.

29. *Ferry*—Middle English: *ferien* = to carry, convey, bear; Anglosaxon: *faran* = to go; Gothic: *farjan* = to travel by ship; Greek: *poreomai* = I travel, go; *pherein* = to carry, bear; to make; *poros* = a way through, experience; Latin: *ferre* = to bear; to make—in the sense of ferrying across from potentiality to actuality. All these words are from the etymon *PER = go through, experience, travel, fare, bear, carry.

30. *Periphery*—Greek: *peri* = around + *pherein* = to carry, bear; to make. Compare *peril* = an experience, a trial one passes through; Middle English: *peril*; Latin: *periculum* = danger, trial, proof; *periri* = to try; Greek: *peirao* = I try, prove; *peras* = I press through, pass through—allied to Gothic: *faran* = travel, fare. Compare Latin: *fermentum* = leaven; *feruere* = to boil, be agitated; *fertilis* = fertile, fruitful.

31. Heidegger, "On the essence and concept of *phusis*," 217.

32. Agamben, *Le Temps qui Reste. Un Commentaire de l'Épître aux Romains*, translated by Judith Revel (Paris: Bibliotheque Rivages, 2004), 99-139. (My translation). See *The Time that Remains. A Commentary on the Letter to the Romans*, translated by Patricia Dailey (Stanford: Stanford University Press, 2005).

33. See my *"Limit and leimma,"* 455-460.

34. Agamben, *Le Temps qui Reste*, 96-7.

35. Ibid., 112.

36. Ibid., 113.

37. Ibid., 124.

38. Heidegger, *Contributions to Philosophy (From Enowning)*, translated by Parvids Emad and Kenneth Maly (Bloomington: Indiana University Press, 1999), 289.

39. Agamben, *Le Temps qui Reste*, 133-4.

40. Marcel Martin, *Le Langage Cinematographique* (Paris: Les Editions du Cerf, 2001), 245-275.

41. Walter Benjamin relates the fundamental alliance between the image and time: "The true image of the past *escapes*. It is only in the image, which appears as lightning once and for all in the very moment of its knowability, that the past allows itself to be fixed... Since it is an irrevocable image of the past which risks fainting for every present unable to recognise itself in its sights." Walter Benjamin,

"Theses on the Concept of History," in *Illuminations*, edited by Hannah Arendt, translated by Harry Zohn, (New York: Schocken Books, 1969), 253-265.
42. Bernardi, *Antonioni*, 94-5.
43. "Cinema masters time, and in this way, is susceptible of representing movement. On the other hand, it is the radical suspension of all movement which gives to the best photographs their surest impact." Paul Adams Sitney, "Le paysage au cinema, les rythmes du monde et la camera," in Mottet, *Les Paysages du Cinema*, 109.
44. *Fabulation*—Latin: *fabula* = story; *faber* = an artisan, maker; a liar. The equivalent term in Greek is *poiesis* = to produce; *poiein* = to make.
45. Agamben, *Image et Mémoire. Écrits sur l'Image, la Dance et le Cinéma*, translated by Marco Dell'Omodarme, Suzanne Doppelt, Daniel Loayza and Gilles A. Tiberghien (Paris: Desclée de Brouwer, 2004), 91.
46. Ibid., 94.
47. Agamben, *Means Without End. Notes on Politics, translated by* Vincenzo Binetti and Cesan Casal'ina (Minneapoli: University of Minnesota Press, 2000).
48. Tarkovsky, *Sculpting in Time*, translated by Kitty Hunter-Blair (Austin: University of Texas Press, 2006), 193-4.
49. Ibid., 114-116.
50. Ibid., 116-117.
51. Heidegger, *Langue de Tradition et Langue Technique* (Brussels: Leeber-Hossmann, 1990), 19. (My translation).
52. Tarkovsky, *Sculpting in Time*, 117.
53. Ibid., 94.
54. Malpas, *Heidegger's Topology*, 92-96.
55. Tarkovsky, *Sculpting in Time*, 108-9.
56. Agamben, *The Coming Community*, Chapter 3.
57. Tarkovsky, *Sculpting in Time*, 112.
58. Ibid., 104-113. Tarkovsky distances his method from structuralist theory: "Cinema is an art which operates with *reality*. This is why I resist structuralist attempts to look at a frame as a sign of something else, the meaning of which is summed up in the shot," ibid., 177. Likewise, he criticises Eisenstein's abstract framing and montage which "contradicts the very basis of the unique process whereby a film affects an audience. It deprives the person watching of that prerogative of film, which has to do with what distinguishes its impact on his consciousness from that of literature or philosophy: namely the opportunity to live through what is happening on the screen as if it were his own life, to take over, as deeply personal and his own, the experience imprinted in time upon the screen, relating his own life to what is being shown," ibid., 183.
59. Ibid..
60. See Agamben, "The Passion of Facticity," 185-204: "Heidegger distinguishes Dasein's *Factizität* from *Tatsächlichkeit*, the simple factuality of intraworldly beings. At the start of his *Ideas*, Husserl defines the *Tatsächlichkeit* of the objects of experience. These objects, Husserl writes, appear as things found at determinate points in space and time that possess a certain content of reality but that, considered in their essence, could be elsewhere and otherwise. Husserl thus insists

on contingency (*Züfalligkeit*) as an essential characteristic of facticity. For Heidegger, by contrast, the proper trait of facticity is not *Züfalligkeit* but *Verfallenheit* [fallenness—absorption in the world]. Everything is complicated, in Heidegger, by the fact that Dasein is not simply, as in Sartre, thrown into the 'there' of a given contingency; instead, Dasein must rather be its 'there,' be the 'there' (*Da*) of Being... The origin of the Heideggerian use of the term 'facticity' is most likely to be found not in Husserl but in Augustine, who writes that *facticia est anima*, 'the human soul is *facticia*,' in the sense that it was made by God. In Latin, *factitius* is opposed to *nativus*; it means *qui non sponte fit*, what is not natural, what did not come into Being by itself... What is important here for Heidegger, this experience of facticity, of a constitutive non-originarity, is precisely the original experience of philosophy, the only legitimate point of departure for thinking.... Facticity is the condition of what remains concealed in its opening, of what is exposed by its very retreat."

61. Tarkovsky, *Sculpting in Time*, 68-9, 75.

62. Robert Bresson, *Notes sur le Cinématographe* (Paris: Gallimard, 1988), 100. (My translation).

63. André Bazin, *Qu'est-ce que le Cinéma?* (Paris: Édition du Cerf, 1958-1962), volume 1, 132, 148 ; volume 4, 96. (My translation).

64. Werner Herzog, *Manuel de Survie* (Nantes: Capricci, 2008), 79. (My translation).

65. Deleuze, *Cinema 1,* 11.

66. Giles Deleuze, *Cinema 2. The Time-Image*, translated by Hugh Tomlinson and Robert Galeta (London: Continuum, 2005), 41.

67. Godard's montage contests the urgency that characterises totalitarian, technological and commoditised time, whose headlong rushing tends to obscure or abolish the moment. He does this either literally by inserting slow motion sequences and images, or by montages of narrative, spatial and temporal dislocations which undermine the logic, authority and easy acceptance of time's continuity and eventuality. As a consequence he allows extended experiences of the present as slow time, as the time of waiting and watching over what comes, rather that of time focussed on interminable and inexorable passage. See Jean-Luc Godard and Youssef Ishaghpour, *Cinema. The Archaeology of Film and the Memory of a Century*, translated by John Howe (Oxford: Berg, 2005), 19-21.

68. Éric Dufour, *David Lynch: Matière, Temps et Image* (Paris: Vrin, 2008), 86, 89. (My translation)

69. *Accident*—Latin: *accidens* = what arrives—in the sense of something happening or be-falling (*ad-cadere*); Greek: *katastrophe*, from *kata-* = down + *strophe* = turn. See Paul Virilio. *L'Accident Originel* (Paris: Galilee, 2008), 27. Virilio notes that the accident is a coeval and teleological condition of every discovery, every invention, every act of creation and every apparatus.

70. Dufour, *David Lynch*, 84-5.

71. Ibid., 100-1.

72. Antonioni, *The Architecture of Vision*, 24-5.

73. Herzog, *Manuel de Survie*, 26: "The time of the image can, in the manner of a stasis, be situated outside relationships of causality and chronology."

74. *Ecstasy*—Greek: *ekstasis* = to stand (*stasis*) outside (*ex-*)—that is, outside oneself, one's familiar place or time; to have a sense of altereity or otherness.
75. Herzog, *Manuel de Survie*, 35.
76. Ibid., 21.
77. Heidegger, *The Fundamental Concepts of Metaphysics*, 157-8.
78. Ibid., 106-7
79. Ibid., 115-9.
80. Ibid., 122.
81. Ibid., 123-5.
82. Ibid., 127.
83. Ibid., 135-6.
84. Ibid., 136.
85. Ibid., 138.
86. Ibid., 140-1.
87. Ibid., 143.
88. Ibid., 144.
89. "What is entrancing in this attunement is not the determinate time-point at which the specific boredom arises; for this determinate `now' sinks at a stroke; the sign of this is that we do not worry at all about the clock and suchlike. Nor is that which entrances, however, a more stretched `now,' such as the span of time during which boredom persists. This boredom does not need such things at all, it can take hold of us in an instant like a flash of lightning, and yet precisely in this instant the whole expanse of the entire time of Dasein is there and not at all specifically articulated or delimited according to past and future. Neither merely the present nor merely the past nor merely the future, nor indeed all these reckoned together—but rather their unarticulated unity in the simplicity of this unity of their horizon all at once," ibid., 147-8.
90. Ibid., 149.
91. Ibid., 150.
92. Ibid., 295.
93. Ibid., 151-2.
94. Ibid., 284.
95. Ibid., 180.
96. Agamben, "Potentiality," 177-184.
97. Agamben, "The Passion of Facticity," 189-195. *Aletheia*, unconcealment, is *a-* = without + *lethe* = forgetfulness.
98. Le Corbusier, *Towards an Architecture*, translated by John Goodman (Los Angeles: Getty Research Institute, 2007), 102.
99. Consider for example the disjunction between carrier and carried which characterises Simondon's second stage of architectural development. The separation between space defining and loadbearing functions of architectural assemblies in ancient buildings—for example the trabeated temples of Greece; and more recent architecture—for example the frame and skin structures of early high rise buildings or the separation of services, structure and enclosure at the Pompidou Centre, are distinctive examples that delineate an aesthetics of disarticulation and independence of parts within an assemblage. See Gilbert

Simondon, *L'Invention dans les Techniques. Cours et Conférences* (Paris: Seuil, 2005), 129.
100. François Jullien, *Éloge de la Fadeur. A Partir de la Pensée et de l'Esthétique de la Chine* (Paris: Philippe Piquier, 1991). See also *In Praise of Blandness. Proceeding from Chinese Thought and Aesthetics*, translated by Paula M Varsano (New York: Zone Books, 2004).
101. See G. R. Kaye, *The Astronomical Observatories of Jai Singh* (Delhi: Archaeological Survey of India, New Imperial Series, Vol. XL, 1973). An interactive site for the observatories is available at http://www.jantarmantar.org/ (accessed March 18, 2009).
102. François Jullien, *"Du Temps." Eléments d'une Philosophie du Vivre* (Paris: Grasset/Le Collège de Philosophie, 2001).
103. Inferior, hence infernal and below; superior, hence supernal and above. Or again, left—Italian: *a sinistra*; French: *gauche*; right—Italian: *a destra* = dexterous, adroit; French: *droite* = upright. The words *tree* (Greek: *drus* = oak) and *true* are cognate through the etymon *DREU = firm, reliable.
104. Stiegler notes the important alignment between the word savour (*saveur*) and knowledge/wisdom/sapience (*savoir*): "If it is true that knowledge (*les savoirs*) is what, as *sapere*, renders the world sapid, and that the inverse is true: a world, to the extent that a world only constitutes a world (*fait monde*) on condition of being sapid, is what assumes this sense of knowing-how-to-be-in-the-world (*savoir-être-au-monde*), that precisely we call *savoir-vivre*." See Stiegler & Ars Industrialis, *Réenchanter le Monde. La Valeur Esprit Contre le Populisme Industriel* (Flammarion: 2006), 45. (My translation)
105. *Environment*—Old French: *environner* = to surround, make place for, contextualise; *environ* = round about—from *en-* = in + *virer* = turn around, change direction, wind. The etymon is *WEI = twist about (ferrule), bind, plait. Compare Sanskrit: *vaya* = weave; Latin: *uitis* = vine, *uiere* = bind; Anglosaxon: *wir* = wire (wind, winding); Latin: *gyrare* = gyrate, whirl about. The relevant etymons are *WER = surround, protect and *WERT = turn, become.
106. See my "In(side)out: the face that turns towards and looks: Chartres Cathedral, 1989," http://www.altx.com/au2/tawa. html.
107. I limit myself to examples from Spain—specifically Cordoba and Valencia.
108. Stiegler, *Réenchanter le Monde*, 28-9.

# Chapter Four : Materiality

1. Nancy, *Le Plaisir au Dessin* (Paris: Galilée, 2009), 17.
2. Coomaraswamy, "The Iconography of Durer's Knots and Leonardo's Concatanations," *Art Quarterly* 7 (1944): 109-128. On the symbolism of weaving, see René Guénon, *Symbolism of the Cross*, translated by Angus Macnab (London: Luzac, 1975), 65-70; Coomaraswamy, *Selected Papers*, *edited by* Roger Lipsey (Princeton: Princeton University Press, 1977), Volume 1, 465 and Volume 2, 189, 351n; and Snodgrass, *Stellar and Temporal Symbolism in Sacred Architecture* (PhD, University of Sydney, 1985), 58-60, 111, published as *Architecture, Time*

*and Eternity: Studies in the Stellar and Temporal Symbolism of Traditional Buildings* (New Delhi: Aditya Prakashan, 1990).

3. In Persian weaving, the ground of the pattern (*zemin*) corresponds to a spatial aspect, and the pattern itself (*zeman*) to a temporal aspect. Time is what puts to work the spatial potential of the frame—in this case, the warp.

4. Plato, *Theatetus*, 259e; *Cratylus*, 388a. In Greek mythology, *Circe* (from *kirkos* = circle) is situated at the navel of the world and sings as she works the cosmic loom using a golden shuttle identified with the sun. See Eric Alan Schofield Butterworth, *The Tree at the Navel of the World* (Berlin: Walter de Gruyter, 1970), 8, 180. In the Hindu *Vedas*, unworthy speech is speech weaved "on a weft of rags, without understanding," *Rig Veda*, 10: 71, 10.

5. On thunder and lightning in the Pythagorean tradition, see Armand Delatte, *Études sur la Littérature Pythagoricienne* (Paris: É. Champion, 1915), 298.

6. Rudolf Otto, *The Idea of the Holy*, translated by John W. Harvey (Oxford: Oxford University Press, 1950).

7. *Republic*, 614b-621d.

8. Ibid., 661b-d.

9. Ibid., 616d-e. See Robert Allendy, *Le Symbolisme des Nombres* (Paris: Chacornac, 1921), 190.

10. Tarkovsky, *Sculpting in Time*, 212-13.

11. Albert Camus, "Le Desert," in *Œuvres Complètes 1931/1948* (Paris : Gallimard, 2006), Volume 1, 129.

12. Michel Chion discusses the cinematic role of sounds whose sources are not seen *(acousmatic)*. These have formative, dramatic and narrative value when conjugated with techniques of the out of frame (where the sound conforms to the on-screen action but remains unseen), the on screen and the off screen (where the sound source is not only unseen but logically other, of another time and/or space, than what is taking place on-screen). See his *L'Audio-Vision. Son et Image au Cinema* (Paris: Nathan, 2002), 63-70.

13. Nancy, *À l'Écoute* (Paris: Galilée, 2002), 24-5.

14. Ibid., 14.

15. Iégor Reznikoff and Michel Dauvois, "La dimension sonore des grottes ornées," *Bulletin de la Société Préhistorique Française* 85 (1988): 238-246.

16. Joshua, 6: 20.

17. Gaston Bachelard, *La Dialectique de la Durée* (Paris: Presses Universitaires de France, 1950), 131: "the most stable figures owe their stability to a rhythmic discord... our houses are constructed with anarchy of vibrations... An enchanter, conductor of the orchestra of matter, would volatise all these stones... due to a synchronising action upon the superimposed times relative to different elements." (My translation). In Masonry, the *vital knot* is a point within every existent—including beings, things and architectural structures. It functions like a *Gordian knot* whose undoing deconstructs the existent. This process is tied to the "power of keys" (*potestas ligandi et solvendi*) in Hermeticism, and the *coagula-salva* in Alchemy. See René Guénon, *Études sur la Franc-Maçonnerie et le Compagnonnage*, (Paris: Chacognac, 1983), Volume 1, 10-11: "The cathedral

constructed according to the rules constitutes a veritable organic ensemble, and that is why it too has a `vital knot.'"
18. Alain Mons. "Le bruit silence ou la plongée paysagère," in Mottet, *Les Paysages au Cinéma*, 235.
19. Chion, *L'Audio-Vision*, 12-19.
20. Ibid., 18.
21. Tarkovsky, *Sculpting in Time*, 158.
22. Ibid., 162-3.
23. I use the word in its etymological sense of both "disclosing" and "showing." It derives from the Latin: *index, indices, indicare*—where *in-* = towards + *dicare* = to proclaim, make known, say. The etymon is *DEIK = to show, point out, teach, function as a token or index. Compare *DEUK = to pull, draw, lead; and *DEK = fitting. Cognate words include *conduct, duct, educate, ductile, deduct, tow, tug, touch, tie, tuck* and *decent, decorum, disciple*. But the sense is also, through the word *deck*, to "cover up" or "hide." To *deck out* would then mean to disguise, to clothe or equip in such a way that the one clothed is both shown/indicated/made operative and concealed/covered up/made inoperative. This is the double sense of every vestment, every ornament and by implication every investment—be it an investment in representation and the image, in the tectonic strategies of cinema and architecture, in politics or finance. An indexical image is therefore not limited to showing the factical nature of a thing—its *reality-value*—but must also account for its propensity to fictionalise, to occlude if not occult reality. The index must always be poised between indicating and concealing. These resonances of sense should also account for the alliance between *DEIK/*DEK and *TEK/TEKTH = fit, prepare, weave, make. *Techne* (art), technology, texts, textures, textiles, tectonics and architecture are all implicated in the deferring play between showing and hiding. In Platonic terms, anything made by art—that is by *techne* as "know-how"—both points to and occludes the *eidos* that governs it and of which it is an indication.
24. Nancy, *Ground of the Image*, 9.
25. Ibid., 21. Nancy notes the etymology of the word image from Latin: *imago* which refers to *imitor* and *aemulus,* so that *mimesis* and the image are tied by the double gesture of emulation and rivalry. The theme of ground or foundation (*fond*) is recurrent in Nancy. See his *The Muses*, and *The Gravity of Thought,* translated by François Raffoul and Gregory Recco (New Jersey: Humanities Press, 1997). *Fond* is an etymological correlate of words with a general sense of deep sinking and spreading—such as fund, fundamental, font, found, fount, founding, founder and bottom.
26. Nancy, *Ground of the Image*, 21-2.
27. Nancy, *The Evidence of Film*, 42.
28. Ibid..
29. Ibid., 44.
30. Isaiah, 40: 4.
31. Rancière's reading of gestural tendencies in contemporary architecture, where they are not constrained by formalist motives or registers, implies the production of new cinematic and architectural spaces that are not sites for representation and

presence, but of an alliance and conjugation of materiality and gesture within a
framework and rhythm of emergent rather than imposed form. See *The Future of
the Image*, 81-2. By implication, the same strategies have brought about
32. Heidegger, *Pathmarks*, 108.
33. Ibid., 108.
34. Ibid., 121-2.
35. Ibid., 123.
36. Ibid., 125.
37. Ibid., 127.
38. Ibid., 128-9.
39. Ibid., 129-30.
40. Ibid., 131-2.
41. Ibid., 126.
42. Ibid., 134-5.
43. André Leroi-Gourhan, *Le Geste et la Parole*, Volume II (Paris: Albin Michel,
1964), 128-205.
44. Deleuze, *Cinema 2*, 28.
45. Federic Jameson, *The Geopolitical Aesthetic: Cinema and Space in the World
System* (Bloomington and Indianapolis, 1995), 111.
46. Here I follow Colin St John Wilson's attentive reading of the building. See
"Sigurd Lewerentz. The Sacred Buildings and the Sacred Sites," in *Sigurd
Lewerentz 1885-1975*, edited by Nicola Flora, Paola Giardiello and Gennaro
Postiglione (Milan: Electa, 2001), 17-23.
47. Ibid., 18-19.
48. Ibid., 22.
49. Heidegger, "The Origin of the Work of Art," in *Poetry, Language, Thought*,
45-6.
50. Ibid., 42.
51. "A building, a Greek temple, portrays nothing. It simply stands there in the
middle of the rock-cleft valley. The building encloses the figure of the god, and in
this concealment lets it stand out into the holy precinct through the open portico.
By means of the temple, the god is present in the temple. This presence of the god
is in itself the extension and delimitation of the precinct as a holy precinct."
Heidegger clearly considers architecture as an apparatus which enables the
unconcealment of presence—the presence of a god who is an irradiation of the
location and the place. Hence the temple does not "represent," "image," or "stand
in" for the god. It *is* the god, and it is the god as place, world and orientation to that
world: "The temple, in its standing there, first gives to things their look and to men
their outlook on themselves. This view remains open as long as the work is work,
as long as the god has not fled from it. It is the same with the sculpture of the god,
votive offering of the victor in the athletic games. It is not a portrait whose purpose
is to make it easier to realise how the god looks; rather, it is a work that lets the
god himself be present and thus is the god himself," ibid., 41-3.
52. In Aristotle, matter (*hyle*) and form (*morphe*), or content and form, are not in
opposition. *Hyle* refers to a forest or woods, to wood, to the basic material of
building and production. *Morphe* is "shape," "the form into which the `material' is

brought by imprinting and moulding." *Morphe* has to be read in terms of *eidos*, which is the appearance and sight of a thing; its look. This look is an act of standing in and "placing itself into appearance." It is a mode of presencing and a way of being. See Heidegger, *"On the essence and concept of phusis,"* 210-11.

# Chapter Five: Agency, Crisis, Disestablishment

1. Jacques Derrida, *Marges de la Philosophie* (Paris: Éditions de Minuit, 1972), 1.
2. Deleuze and Parnet, *Dialogues*, 65: "The truly minimal unit is not the word, nor the idea or the concept, nor the signified, but the agencement. It is always an *agencement* that produces enunciations... The writer invents *agencements* beginning with *agencements* that have invented him, he makes one multiplicity pass into another. The difficulty is to have all the elements of a non-homogenous ensemble conspire together, to make them function together."
3. Ibid., 66.
4. Ibid., 60.
5. V.I Pudovkin, *Film Technique and Film Acting. The Cinema Writings of V.I Pudovkin*, translated by Ivor Montagu (New York: Bonanza Books, 1960), xiv- xv.
6. Gilles Deleuze and Felix Guattari, *What is Philosophy*, translated by Janice Tomlinson and Graham Burchell (New York: Columbia University Press, 1994).
7. Deleuze and Parnet, *Dialogues,* 112-113.
8. According to Simondon, a "being does not possess a unity of identity, which is that of the stable state in which no transformation is possible; the being possesses a transductive unity, which is to say that it can dephase itself (*se déphaser*) in relation to itself, to overflow itself on both sides of its centre," See *L'Individuation Psychique et Collective*, 24-5.
9. Ibid., 25-7, 66n, 95n. *Metastability* is a condition or state presupposing two orders of scale, together with an absence of communication between them. Likewise, a *milieu* is a *system*—a synthetic grouping of two or more echelons of realty, with no intercommunication prior to individuation. Metastability is a heterogeneous state, but with potential to provoke becoming. Simondon gives the counter example of granite, which is heterogeneous but not metastable.
10. Ibid., 49.
11. Ibid., 29. Simondon differentiates his use of the term from the common instrumental notion of information as transmission of messages promoted by the technological theory of information. For him, the primary sense is "information as signification."
12. Ibid., 29.
13. Ibid., 31-2.
14. Ibid., 37. This term designates an operation "accomplished in an amplifying relay with an indefinite number of states, like, for example... a transistor."
15. Ibid., 33.
16. Ibid., 57.
17. Ibid., 61, 63.
18. Ibid., 80.
19. Ibid., 78-82.

20. Ibid., 82. Allagmatic is from the Greek: *allagma* = change, vicissitude, from *allos* = other, different; *alla* = otherwise, differently, contrariwise. Simondon intends more a sense of ex-change—but the exchange is founded on a radically differentiated field.

21. Ibid., 82, 88, 91.

22. Ibid., 94n.

23. Deleuze and Parnet, *Dialogues*, 110-111. Haecceity is *quidditas*, this-ness, in contrast to what-ness. Deleuze's use of this Medieval term preserves the sense of the non-qualitative, non-symbolic, non-transcendent property responsible for individuation, although clearly it rejects any reference to ontological or transcendent referends for the idea. See http://plato.stanford.edu/entries/medieval-haecceity/ (accessed July 31, 2009).

24. Deleuze and Parnet, *Dialogues*, 117.

25. In that sense, lines of flight describe a properly hermeneutic practice, doubling the peregrinations of Hermes—the messenger and peripatetic boundary rider who complements Hestia's guardianship of the hearth in the ancient Greek *oikos*. The tension between these two figures and trajectories is between concentration, fixation, and permanence, and expansion, impermanence and mutability—between centripetal involution or enclosure of space, and centrifugal development or distraction to the outside; or again between sedentary and nomadic modes of existence. In the *oikos*, Hestia, goddess of the hearth, is seated in the *omphalos*, while Hermes, the angel-messenger (*aggelos*) and deity of the threshold, is stationed at the door. Hestia is the centralizing principle of spatial, temporal, and domestic identity while Hermes is the principle of spatial, temporal and domestic difference and deterritorialisation. He is the obtuse "wall piercer" who glides "edgeways through the keyhole." See Jean-Pierre Vernant, *Myth and Thought*, 128, 133, 141; and "Hestia-Hermès. Sur l'Éxpression Religieuse de l'Éspace et du Mouvement Chez les Grecs," *Revue Française d'Anthropologie* 3 (1963): 12-50.

26. Deleuze and Parnet, *Dialogues*, 122, 47-63.

27. Ibid., 48.

28. Ibid., 165.

29. Ibid., 152-3, 164-176.

30. Ibid., 156-7.

31. Ibid., 157-8.

32. Deleuze, *Cinema 1*, 23.

33. Agamben reads the Greek notion of the *eidos* not as immobile archetype, "but rather a constellation in which phenomena arrange themselves in a gesture. Cinema leads images back to homeland of gesture. According to the beautiful definition implicit in Beckett's Traum und Nacht, it is the dream of a gesture. The duty of the director is to introduce into this dream the element of awakening." See *Means Without Ends*, 55.

34. The operation of agencement within an assemblage is by implication machinic: "*il n'y a de désir qu'agencé ou machine.*" See Deleuze and Parnet, *Dialogues*, 115.

35. "I call *dispositif* everything that has, in one way or another, the capacity to capture, to orient, to determine, to intercept, to model, to control and to assure the gestures, conducts, opinions and speech of living beings." Agamben, *Qu'est-ce*

*qu'un Dispositif, translated by* Martin Rueff (Paris: Rivages, 2007), 31. (My translation). Following Foucault's classification of prisons, asylums, the *panopticon*, schools, confessionals, factories, disciplines, juridical measures and architecture, Agamben counts language (together with writing, literature, philosophy, agriculture, cigarettes, navigation, computers and mobile phones) as perhaps the most ancient of *dispositifs*. For *dispositional efficacy* see François Jullien, *The Propensity of Things. Towards a History of Efficacy in China*, translated by Janet Lloyd (New York: Zone Books, 1995).
36. From the Greek: *poiein* = to make, produce.
37. Agamben, *Profanations*, translated by Jeff Fort (New York: Zone, 2007).
38. Maurice Blanchot. *L'Ecriture du Désastre*, 152.
39. Jean-Luc Nancy, *The Gravity of Thought*, translated by Francois Raffoul and Gregory Recco (New Jersey: Humanities Press, 1997), 79-80.
40. See Paul Virilio and Sylvère Lotringer, *The Accident of Art*, translated by Michael Taormina (New York: Semiotext(e), 2005), 91-111.
41. Technology is from the Greek: *techne* = to make, to produce, as well as the manner in which a thing is made or produced. In Heidegger's terminology *techne* is "know-how," the knowledge of how to lead-through (Latin: *pro-* = through + *ductere* = to lead) and bring forth out from concealement into unconcealement. See Heidegger, "On the essence and concept of *physis*," 192, and "Letter on Humanism," in *Pathmarks*, 259: "For technology does not go back to the *techne* of the Greeks in name only but derives historically and essentially from *techne* as a mode of *aletheuin* (unconcealement), a mode, that is, of rendering beings manifest."
42. Bailly, *Champ Mimétique*, 260.
43. Deleuze and Parnet, *Abécédaire,* "S pour Style"
44. Giles Deleuze. *Le Plis* (Paris: Les Editions de Minuit, 1988), 248.
45. Akira Lippit, "Cinemnesis. Martin Arnold's Memory Machine," in *Cinemnesis,* DVD, directed by Martin Arnold (Paris: Re:Voir Video CNC EDV 519, 1999), 12.
46. Ibid., 7.
47. *Obsession: Structuring Time and Space*, DVD, directed by Ivan Ladislav Galeta (Vienna: Arge Index, DVD 028: Film 02).
48. Deleuze and Parnet, *Dialogues*, 179-185.
49. William Marlin, *Frank Lloyd Wright. Houses in Oak Park and River Forest, Illinois. 1889-1913* (Tokyo: A.D.A Edita, GA24, 1973), 25-6, 44.
50. Simondon, *L'Individuation Psychique et Collective*, 65.
51. Ibid., 53.
52. Ibid., 54.
53. Ibid., 58.
54. Ibid., 59.
55. Ibid., 73-95. See his *Cours sur la Perception (1964-1965)* (Chatou: Les Editions de la Transparence, 2006), 175-350, for a treatment of the perception of movement, form, space and duration.
56. See my "Mapping: Design," in *Architectural Theory Review* 3, no.1 (1998): 35-45

57. On the caesura of verse, see Agamben, *Idea of Prose*, 43-4, and the preceding discussion on rhythm in Chapter Three.

58. Sauvanet, *Le Rhythme Grèque*, 60.

59. The etymological sense of assemblage is to *bring-together-into-semblance*, to make self-similar, to produce sameness. In the classical notion of assemblage implied in the Platonic theory of forms that Simondon glosses, the objective is resolutely mimetic. It is to cause the artifact to resemble, as closely as possible, its archetypal form. The aesthetic character of mimetic resemblance hinges on the seemliness that results from the extent to which a work seems alike to its archetypal *eidos*. Every existent is a composite and as such must be necessarily seamed or jointed, but the assumption in classical aesthetics is that perfect semblance, like Christ's cloak, must be a seamless unity. The word *semblance* is not without fascinating dissemblance. Compare *assimilation*, from the Latin: *assimilare* = to collect; *simulation*, from *assimulare* = to pretend, feign; and *similar*, from *simul* = together. The Sanskrit: *sam* and English: *same, similar*, are cognate. Philippe Lacoue-Labarthe deals with the way in which notions of forgery, fiction and inadequation haunt Platonic *mimesis*, and the way in which for Heidegger, *mimesis* is disinstallation, "fall, decline, diminution, obfuscation, and so on." See Philippe Lacoue-Labarthe, *Typography. Mimesis, Philosophy, Politics,* translated by Cristopher Fynsk (Stanford: Stanford University Press, 1998), 120, 132.

60. Bernardi. *Antonioni*, 52, 58n.

61. Antonioni, *The Architecture of Vision*, 19.

62. Ibid., 24.

63. *Notre Musique*, DVD, directed by Jean-Luc Godard, (Optimum Releasing, OPTD0176, 2005).

64. For Simondon, the proper mode of transduction is *internal resonance*—a primitive form of communication between realities of different order. It comprehends a double process of amplification and condensation. See *L'Individuation Psychique et Collective*, 67n.

65. Rancière, *The Future of the Image*, Chapter 2.

66. Ibid., 35.

67. Ibid., 38.

68. Ibid., 34.

69. Ibid., 41.

70. Ibid., 41.

71. Ibid., 42.

72. Ibid., 55.

73. Ibid., 56-7.

74. Ibid., 60, 67.

75. *Caché*, DVD, directed by Michael Haneke (Artificial Eye, VFC88342, 2005).

76. Patricia Pisters, *The Matrix of Visual Culture. Working with Deleuze in Film Theory* (Stanford: Stanford University Press, 2003), 84.

77. See St John Wilson, "Sigurd Lewerentz. The Sacred Buildings," 19, and for Utzon's "tamed yawning apertures," see Richard Weston, *Utzon* (Hellerup: Bløndal, 2002), 373.

78. Agamben, *Means Without Ends,* 51.

79. Peter Nover, *The Other City. Carlo Scarpa: the Architect's Working Method as Shown by the Brion Cemetery in San Vito D'Altivole* (Berlin: Ernst & Son, 1989), 17-18.

80. This was confirmed to me as a plausible reading by the architectural theorist and historian Marco Frascari, who had worked in Scarpa's office. Frascari noted that Brionvega was initially built following the death of the patriarch, while his spouse was still alive. The absent presence that Scarpa appears to have realised tectonically might then parallel the palpable presence of the deceased to those remaining behind.

81. See St John Wilson, "Sigurd Lewerentz. The Sacred Buildings," 13-14.

82. Ibid., 21, 16.

83. Ibid., 20.

# BIBLIOGRAPHY

Agamben, Giorgio. *Qu'est-ce qu'un Dispositif,* translated by Martin Rueff. Paris: Rivages, 2007.
—. *Profanations,* translated by Jeff Fort. New York: Zone Books, 2007.
—. *La Puissance de la Pensée,* translated by Joël Gayraud and Martin Rueff. Paris: Rivages, 2006.
—. *Image et Mémoire. Écrits sur l'Image, la Dance et le Cinéma,* translated by Marco Dell'Omodarme, Suzanne Doppelt, Daniel Loayza and Gilles A. Tiberghien. Paris: Desclée de Brouwer, 2004.
—. *Le Temps qui Reste. Un Commentaire de l'Épître aux Romains,* translated by Judith Revel. Paris: Bibliotheque Rivages, 2004.
—. *Means Without End. Notes on Politics,* translated by Vincenzo Binetti and Cesan Casal'ina. Minneapoli: University of Minnesota Press, 2000.
—. *Potentialities,* translated by Daniel Heller-Roazen. Stanford: Stanford University Press, 1999.
—. *Idea of Prose,* translated by Michael Sullivan and Sam Whitsitt. New York: State of New York University Press, 1995.
—. *Infancy and History. Essays on the Destruction of Experience,* translated by Liz Heron. London: Verso, 1993.
—. *The Coming Community,* translated by Michael Hardt. Minneapolis: University of Minnesota Press, 1993.
Allendy, Robert. *Le Symbolisme des Nombres.* Paris: Chacornac, 1921.
Antonioli, Manola. *Abécédaire de Jacques Derrida.* Mons: Sils Maria, 2006.
Antonioni, Michelangelo. *The Architecture of Vision. Writings and Interviews on Cinema.* Chicago: The University of Chicago Press, 1996.
Augé, Marc. *Non-Places. Introduction to an Anthropology of Supermodernity,* translated by J. Howe. London: Verso, 1995.
Augustine, St *Confessions,* translated by R. S. Pine-Coffin. Harmondsworth: Penguin, 1979.
Bachelard, Gaston. *La Dialectique de la Durée.* Paris: Presses Universitaires de France, 1950.
Bailly, Jean-Christophe. *Le Champ Mimétique.* Paris: Editions du Seuil, 2005.

Barthes, Roland. *Comment Vivre Ensemble. Cours et Séminaires au Collège de France (1976-1977)*, edited by Claude Coste. Paris: Seuil, 2002.

—. *Le Neutre. Cours au Collège de France (1977-1978)*, edited by Thomas Clerc. Paris: Seuil, 2002.

—. *La Préparation du Roman I et II. Cours et Séminaires au Collège de France (1978-1979 et 1979-1980)*, edited by Claude Coste. Paris: Seuil, 2002.

—. *The Pleasure of the Text,* translated by Richard Miller. Oxford: Blackwell, 1990.

—. *Camera Lucida*, translated by Richard Howard. London: Fontana, 1984.

—. *Empire of Signs*, translated by Richard Howard. New York: Hill and Wang, 1982.

—. *Image-Music-Text*, translated by Stephen Heath. New York: Hill and Wang, 1977.

—. *Le Plaisir du Texte*. Paris: Editions du Seuil, 1973.

Basili, Giancarlo. *Spazio e Architettura Nel Cinema Italiano*. Alexa, 2000

Bawden, Liz-Anne. *The Oxford Companion to Film*. London: Oxford University Press, 1976.

Bazin, André. *Qu'est-ce que le Cinéma?* Paris: Édition du Cerf, 1958-1962.

Benjamin, Walter. *Illuminations*, edited by Hannah Arendt, translated by Harry Zohn. New York: Schocken Books, 1969.

Bennett, Tony, Lawrence Grossberg and Maeghan Morris editors. *New Keywords. A Revised Vocabulary of Culture and Society*. Oxford: Blackwell, 2005.

Benterrak, Krim, Stephen Muecke and Paddy Roe. *Reading the Country*. Fremantle: Fremantle Arts Centre Press, 1984.

Benveniste, Emile. *Problèmes de Linguistique Générale*. Paris: Gallimard, 1966.

Bergson, Henry. *Matter and Memory*. New York: Zone Books, 1990.

Bernardi, Sandro. *Antonioni. Personnage Paysage*. Paris: Presses Universitaires de Vincennes: 2006.

Berque, Augustin. *La Pensée Paysagère*. Paris: Archibooks, 2008.

—. *Médiance. De Milieux en Paysages*. Paris: Belin, 2000.

—. *Écoumène. Introduction a l'Étude des Milieux Humains*. Paris: Belin, 2000.

—. *Du Geste à la Cité. Formes Urbaines et Lien Social au Japon*. Paris: Gallimard, 1993.

Berque, Augustin, Alessia de Biase and Philippe Bonin, *L'Habiter dans sa Poetique Premiere. Actes du Colloque de Cerisy-la-Salle*. Paris: Editions Donner Lieu, 2008.

Blake, William. *The Complete Illuminated Books*. London: Thames and Hudson with the William Blake Trust, 2000.

Blanchot, Maurice. *L'Écriture du Désastre*. Paris: Gallimard, 1980.

—. *L'attente l'oubli*. Paris: Gallimard, 1962.

Bogue, Ronald. *Deleuze on Cinema*. New York and London: Routledge, 2003.

Bonfand, Alain. *Le Cinema de Michelangelo Antonioni*. Paris: Editions Images Modernes, 2003.

—. *Ecrits. Michelangelo Antonioni*. Paris: Editions Images Modernes, 2003.

Bresson, Robert. *Notes sur le Cinématographe*. Paris: Gallimard, 1988.

Bruno, Giuliana. *Atlas of Emotion. Journeys in Art, Architecture and Film*. London: Verso, 2002.

Butterworth, Eric Alan Schofield. *The Tree at the Navel of the World*. Berlin:Walter de Gruyter, 1970.

Camus, Albert. *Œuvres Complètes 1931/1948*. Paris : Gallimard, 2006.

Casey, Edward S. *The Fate of Place. A Philosophical Enquiry*. Berkeley: University of California Press, 1998.

—. *Getting Back into Place. Towards a Renewed Understanding of the Place-World*. Bloomington: Indiana University Press, 1993.

—. *Remembering: A Phenomenological Study*. Bloomington: Indiana University Press, 1987.

Chatman, Seymour and Paul Duncan, editors *Michelangelo Antonioni. The Complete Films*. Köln: Taschen, 2004.

Chion, Michel. *L'Audio-Vision. Son et Image au Cinema*. Paris: Nathan, 2002.

Compagnon, Antoine, edited by *Prétexte: Roland Barthes*. Cerisy-La-Salle: Centre Culturel International de Cerisy-La-Salle, 1978.

Coomaraswamy, Ananda K. *Time and Eternity*. Bangalore: Indira Ghandi National Centre for the Arts, 1990.

—. *The Rg Veda as Land-Náma Bók*. New Delhi: Bharatiya Publishing House, 1980.

—. *Selected Papers*, edited by Roger Lipsey. Princeton: Princeton University Press, 1977.

—. "The Iconography of Durer's Knots and Leonardo's Concatanations." *Art Quarterly* 7 (1944): 109-128.

Corbusier, Le *Towards an Architecture*, translated by John Goodman. Los Angeles: Getty Research Institute, 2007.

Cosgrove, Denis, editor. *Mappings*. London: Reaction, 1999.
Crary, Jonathan and Kwinter, Stephen, editors. *Incorporations*. New York: Zone Books, 1992.
Cronin, Paul, editor. *Herzog on Herzog*. London: Faber and Faber, 2002.
Deleuze, Giles. *Cinema 2. The Time-Image*, translated by Hugh Tomlinson and Robert Galeta. London: Continuum, 2005.
—. *Francis Bacon: the Logic of Sensation*, translated by Daniel W. Smith. Minneapolis: University of Minnesota Press, 2003.
—. *Le Plis*. Paris: Les Editions de Minuit, 1988.
—. *Cinema 1: The Movement Image*, translated by Hugh Tomlinson and Barbara Habberjam. Minneapolis: University of Minnesota Press, 1986.
Deleuze, Gilles and Claire Parnet. *L'Abécédaire de Gilles Deleuze*. Paris, Éditions Montparnasse, 2004. DVD.
—. *Dialogues* (Paris: Flammarion, 1996).
Deleuze, Gilles and Felix Guattari. *What is Philosophy*, translated by Janice Tomlinson and Graham Burchell. New York: Columbia University Press, 1994.
—. *A Thousand Plateaus. Capitalism and Schizophrenia*, translated by Brian Massumi. Minneapolis: University of Minnesota Press, 1993.
Delatte, Armand. *Études sur la Littérature Pythagoricienne*. Paris: É. Champion, 1915.
Derrida, Jacques. *Le Toucher, Jean-Luc Nancy*. Paris: Galilee, 2000.
—. *The Gift of Death*, translated by David Wills. Chicago: The University of Chicago Press, 1995.
—. *Demeure. Maurice Blanchot*. Paris: Galilee, 1998.
—. *Khôra*. Paris: Galilée, 1993.
—. *Positions*, translated by Alan Bass. Chicago: University of Chicago Press, 1981.
—. *La Carte Postale, de Socrate à Freud et au-delà*. Paris: Flammarion, 1980.
—. *La Vérité en Peinture*. Paris: Flammarion, 1978.
—. *Marges de la Philosophie*. Paris: Éditions de Minuit, 1972.
Draaisma, Drouwe. *Metaphors of Memory. A History of Ideas About the Mind*. Cambridge: Cambridge University Press, 2000.
Dufour, Éric. *David Lynch: Matière, Temps et Image*. Paris: Vrin, 2008.
Dunne, Nathan, editor. *Tarkovsky*. London: Black Dog Publishing, 2008.
Eisenstein, Sergei. *Film Form. Essays in Film Theory*, translated by Jay Leyda. San Diego, New York, London: Harcourt, 1977.
Evans, Robin. *Translations from Drawing to Building and Other Essays*. London: Architectural Association, 1997.

—. *The Projective Cast. Architecture and its Three Geometries*. Cambridge: MIT Press, 2000.

Fitzmaurice, Tony, and Mark Shiel. *Screening the City*. New York: Verso, 2003.

Fleischer, Alain. *Les Laboratoires du Temps. Écrits sur le Cinéma et la Photographie*. Paris: Galaade, 2008.

Forty, Adrian. *Words and Buildings. A Vocabulary of Modern Architecture*. New York: Thames and Hudson, 2000.

Godard, Jean-Luc and Youssef Ishaghpour, *Cinema. The Archaeology of Film and the Memory of a Century*, translated by John Howe. Oxford: Berg, 2005.

—. *The Future(s) of Film. Three Interviews 2000/1*. Berlin: Verlag Gachnang & Springer AG, 2002.

—. *Histoire(s) du Cinema*. Paris : Gallimard-Gaumont, 1998.

Goetz, Benoît. *La Dislocation. Architecture et Philosophie*. Paris: Les Editions de la Passion, 2002.

—. "Imagiques. Conversation avec Danièle Huillet et Jean-Marie Straub." *Le Portique* 1, no.1 (1998): 164.

Griffith, R. *The Hymns of the Rig Veda*. Motilal Banarasidas, Delhi, 1976.

Guénon, René. *The Reign of Quantity and the Signs of the Times*, translated by Lord Northbourne. New York: Sophia Perennis, 2001.

—. *Le Roi du Monde*. Paris: Galilee, 1983.

—. *Études sur la Franc-Maçonnerie et le Compagnonnage*. Paris: Chacognac, 1983.

—. *L'Esoterisme de Dante*. Paris: Galilee, 1981.

—. *Symbolism of the Cross*, translated by Angus Macnab. London: Luzac, 1975.

Harley J. B. and David Woodward, editors. *The History of Cartography*. Chicago: The University of Chicago Press, 1987.

Heath, Stephen. *Questions of Cinema*. Bloomington: Indiana University Press, 1981.

Heidegger, Martin. *Contributions to Philosophy (From Enowning)*, translated by Parvids Emad and Kenneth Maly. Bloomington: Indiana University Press, 1999.

—. *Pathmarks*, translated by Thomas Sheehan. Cambridge: Cambridge University Press, 1998.

—. *Plato's Sophist*, translated by Richard Rojcewicz and André Schuwer. Bloomington: Indiana University Press, 1997.

—. *Being and Time*, translated by John Macquarrie and Edward Robinson. London: Blackwell, 1995.

—. *Basic Questions of Philosophy. Selected "Problems" of "Logic,"* translated by Richard Rojcewicz and André Schuwer. Bloomington: Indiana University Press, 1994.

—. *The Fundamental Concepts of Metaphysics,* translated by William McNeil and Nicholas Walker. Bloomington: Indiana University Press, 1995.

—. *Parmenides,* translated by André Schuwer and Richard Rojcewicz. Bloomington: Indiana University Press, 1992.

—. *Langue de Tradition et Langue Technique.* Brussels: Leeber-Hossmann, 1990.

—. *The Basic Problems of Phenomenology,* translated by Albert Hofstadter. Bloomington: Indiana University Press, 1988.

—. *The Question Concerning Technology and Other Essays,* translated by William Lovitt. New York: Harper & Row, 1977.

—. *Poetry, Language, Thought,* translated by Albert Hofstadter. New York: Harper & Row, 1975.

—. *Questions I et II,* translated by Kosstas Axelos and others. Paris Gallimard, 1968.

Hertzberger, Ludvig, editor. *Jim Jarmusch Interviews.* Lackson: University Press of Mississippi, 2001.

Herzog, Werner. *Manuel de Survie.* Nantes: Capricci, 2008.

Huntington, Edith and Hamilton Cairns, editors. *Plato. The Collected Dialogues.* Princeton: Princeton University Press, 1999.

James, John. *In Search of the Unknown in Medieval Architecture.* London: Pindar Press, 2007.

Jameson, Federic. *The Geopolitical Aesthetic: Cinema and Space in the World System.* Bloomington and Indianapolis, 1995.

Jullien, François. *Du "Temps." Eléments d'une Philosophie du Vivre.* Paris: Grasset/Le Collège de Philosophie, 2001.

—. *Detour and Access. Strategies of Meaning in China and Greece,* translated by Sophie Hawkes. New York: Zone Books, 2000.

—. *The Propensity of Things. Towards a History of Efficacy in China,* translated by Janet Lloyd. New York: Zone Books, 1995.

—. *Éloge de la Fadeur. A Partir de la Pensée et de l'Esthétique de la Chine.* Paris: Philippe Piquier, 1991.

Kaye, G. R. *The Astronomical Observatories of Jai Singh.* Delhi: Archaeological Survey of India, New Imperial Series, Vol. XL, 1973.

Kracauer, Siegfried. *Theory of Film. The Redemption of Physical Reality.* Princeton: Princeton University Press, 1997.

Kramrish, Stella. *The Hindu Temple.* Delhi: Motilal Banarsidass, 1976.

—. *The Presence of Shiva.* Princeton: Princeton University Press, 1994.

Lacoue-Labarthe, Philippe. *Typography. Mimesis, Philosophy, Politics,* translated by Cristopher Fynsk. Stanford: Stanford University Press, 1998.

Lamster, Mark. *Architecture and Film.* New York: Princeton Architectural Press, 2000.

Leatherbarrow, David. *Uncommon Ground. Architecture, Technology, and Topography.* Cambridge: MIT Press, 2002.

Leroi-Gourhan, André. *Milieu et Technique.* Paris : Albin Michel, 1973.

—. *L'Homme et la Matière.* Paris : Albin Michel, 1971.

—. *Le Geste et la Parole. I Technique et Langage.* Paris: Albin Michel, 1964.

—. *Le Geste et la Parole. II La Memoire et les Rytmes.* Paris: Albin Michel, 1964.

Lippit, Akira. "Cinemnesis. Martin Arnold's Memory Machine." In *Cinemnesis.* Directed by Martin Arnold. Paris: Re:Voir, 1999. DVD.

Lyotard, Jean Francois. *The Inhuman: Reflections on Time.* Oxford: Polity Press, 1991.

—. *The Postmodern Condition: A Report on Knowledge,* translated by Bennington, Geoffrey and Massumi, Brian. Minneapolis: University of Minnesota Press, 1984.

Malpas, Jeff. *Heidegger's Topology. Being, Place, World.* London: MIT Press, 2008.

—. *Place and Experience. A Philosophical Topography.* Cambridge: Cambridge University Press, 1999.

Marlin, William. *Frank Lloyd Wright. Houses in Oak Park and River Forest, Illinois. 1889-1913.* Tokyo: A.D.A Edita, GA24, 1973.

Martin, Marcel. *Le Langage Cinematographique.* Paris: Les Editions du Cerf, 2001.

McNeill, William. *The Glance of the Eye. Heidegger, Aristotle and the Ends of Theory.* New York: State University of New York Press, 1999.

Metz, Christian. *The Imaginary Signifier. Psychoanalysis and the Cinema,* translated by Celia Britton, Annwyl Williams and Ben Brewster. Bloomington: Indiana University Press, 1982.

Mons, Alain. "Le Bruit Silence ou la Plongée Paysagère." In *Les Paysages Du Cinema,* edited by Jean Mottet, 235-249. Champ Vallon: Seyssel, 1999.

Moriarty, Michael. *Roland Barthes.* Stanford: Stanford University Press, 1991.

Mottet, Jean. *Les Paysages au Cinéma.* Seyssel: Champ Vallon, 1999.

Mulvey, Laura. *Death 24x a Second. Stillness and the Moving Image.* London: Reaction, 2006.

Nancy, Jean-Luc. *Le Plaisir au Dessin*. Paris, Galilée, 2009.
—. *The Ground of the Image*, translated by Jeff Fort. New York: Fordham University Press, 2005.
—. *À l'Écoute*. Paris: Galilée, 2002.
—. *Hegel. The Restlessness of the Negative*, translated by Jason Smith and Steven Miller. Minneapolis: University of Minnesota Press, 2002.
—. *The Evidence of Film*. Bruxelles, Yves Gevaert, 2001.
—. *Being Singular Plural*, translated by Robert D. Richardson and Anne E. O'Byrne. Stanford: Stanford University Press, 2000.
—. *The Muses*, translated by Peggy Kamuf. Stanford: Stanford University Press, 1996.
—. "La Comparution/The Compearance: From the Existence of 'Communism' to the Community of 'Existence,'" translated by Tracey B Strong. *Political Theory* 20, no.3 (1992): 371-398.
—. *The Gravity of Thought*, translated by François Raffoul and Gregory Recco. New Jersey: Humanities Press, 1997.
—. *The Birth to Presence*, translated by Brian Holmes and others. Stanford: Stanford University Press, 1993.
Nancy Jean-Luc and Anne Immelé. *Wir*. Trézélan: Filigranes Éditions, 2003.
Nover, Peter. *The Other City. Carlo Scarpa: the Architect's Working Method as Shown by the Brion Cemetery in San Vito D'Altivole*. Berlin: Ernst & Son, 1989.
Nowell-Smith, Geoffrey. *L'Avventura*. London: BFI, 1977.
Oakman, Joan, edited by *Architecture Culture 1943-1968: A Documentary Anthology*. New York: Rizzoli and The Trustees of Columbia University, 1993.
D'Olivet, Fabre. *La Langue Hébraïque Restituée*. Vevay: Delphica, L'Age D'Homme, 1985.
Otto, Rudolf. *The Idea of the Holy*, translated by John W. Harvey. Oxford: Oxford University Press, 1950.
Pallasmaa, Juhani. *The Architecture of Image. Existential Space in Cinema*. Helsinki: Rakennustieto Oy, 2001.
—. *The Eyes of the Skin. Architecture and the Senses*. Chichester: Wiley-Academy, 2005.
—. *Pasolini L'Enragé*. Directed by Jean-André Fieschi. Paris : La Sept, AMIP, INA, in association with Channel Four, 1966. DVD.
Penz, Francois and Maureen Thomas, editors *Cinema & Architecture: Melies, Mallet-Stevens, Multimedia*. Cambridge: Cambridge University Press, 1995.

Pisters, Patricia. *The Matrix of Visual Culture. Working with Deleuze in Film Theory.* Stanford: Stanford University Press, 2003.

Pudovkin, V. I. *Film Technique and Film Acting. The Cinema Writings of V.I Pudovkin,* translated by Ivor Montagu. New York: Bonanza Books, 1960.

Rajchman, John. *Constructions.* Massachusetts: MIT Press, 1998.

Rancière, Jacques. *The Future of the Image,* translated by Gregory Elliott. London: Verso, 2007.

—. *La Fable Cinématographique* (Paris: Seuil, 2001).

Reznikoff, Iégor and Michel Dauvois. "La Dimension Sonore des Grottes Ornées." *Bulletin de la Société Préhistorique Française* 85 (1988): 238-246.

Rodley, Chris, edited by *Lynch on Lynch.* London, 1997.

Rodowick, David. *Gilles Deleuze's Time Machine.* Durham and London: Duke University Press, 1977.

Saito, Yukata. *Louis I. Kahn Houses 1940-1974.* Tokyo: Toto Shuppan, 1994.

Sauvanet, Pierre. *Le Rythme Grec d'Héraclyte à Aristote.* Paris: Presses Universitaires de France, 1999.

Shaviro, Steven. *The Cinematic Body.* Minneapolis: University of Minnesota Press, 1993.

Shonfield, Katherine. *Walls Have Feelings: Architecture, Film and the City.* Oxford: Routledge, 2001.

Simondon, Gilbert. *L'Individuation Psychique et Collective.* Paris: Aubier/Flammarion, 2007.

—. *L'Invention dans les Techniques. Cours et Conférences.* Paris: Seuil, 2005.

—. *Cours sur la Perception (1964-1965).* Chatou: Les Editions de la Transparence, 2006.

Skeat, William W. *Etymological Dictionary of the English Language.* Oxford: Oxford University Press, 1978.

Smith, E. Baldwyn. *The Dome. A Study in the History of Ideas.* Princeton: Princeton University Press, 1971.

Snodgrass, Adrian. *Architecture, Time and Eternity. Studies in Stellar and Temporal Symbolism.* New Delhi: Aditya Prakashan, 1990.

Stiegler, Bernard. *Pour une Nouvelle Critique de l'Économie Politique.* Paris: Galilée, 2009.

—. *Le Design de nos Existences a l'Époque de l'Innovation Ascendante.* Mille et une Nuits, 2008.

—. *Économie de l'Hypermatériel et Psychopouvoir.* Mille et une Nuits, 2008.

—. *Prendre Soin. De la Jeunesse et des Generations.* Paris: Flammarion, 2008.

—. *Réenchanter le Monde. La Valeur Esprit Contre le Populisme Industriel.* Paris: Flammarion: 2006.

—. *La Technique et le Temps 3. Le Temps du Cinéma et la Question du Mal-Être.* Paris: Galilée, 2001.

—. *La Technique et le Temps 1. La Faute d'Épiméthée.* Paris: Galilée, 1994.

Stiegler, Bernard, Alain Giffard and Christian Fauré. *Pour en Finir avec la Mécroissance. Quelques Réflections d'Ars Industrialis.* Paris: Flammarion, 2009.

St John Wilson, Colin. "Sigurd Lewerentz. The Sacred Buildings and the Sacred Sites." In *Sigurd Lewerentz 1885-1975*, edited by Nicola Flora, Paola Giardiello and Gennaro Postiglione. Milan: Electa, 2001, 17-23.

Strong, J. *The Exhaustive Concordance of the Bible.* Riverside: Iowa Falls, undated.

Szendy, Peter, editor. *L'Ecoute.* Paris: L'Harmattan, IRCAM—Centre Pompidou, 2000.

Tarkovsky, Andrey. *Sculpting in Time*, translated by Kitty Hunter-Blair. Austin: University of Texas Press, 2006.

Tawa, Michael. "*Furnishing Place: What is Architecture Fit For.*" In *Content(s)*, edited by Barbara McConchie,10-16. Canberra: Craft and Design Centre, 2005.

—. "Design Lexicon." http://ensemble.va.com.au/ti/designlexicon/index.html.

—. "Limit and Leimma. What Remains for Architecture," in *Limits*, edited by Harriet Edquist and Hélène Frichot, 455-460. Melbourne: SAHANZ/RMIT, 2005.

—. "Place, Country, Chorography: Towards a Kinaesthetic and Narrative Practice of Place." *Architectural Theory Review* 7, no.2 (2002): 45-58.

—. "Making-for." In *Warm Filters*, edited by Linda Marie Walker, 4-9. Adelaide: Contemporary Art Centre of South Australia, 2000.

—. "Makeshift Stalls." Broadsheet 28, no.4 (1999/2000): 6-7.

—. "Mapping: Design." *Architectural Theory Review* 3, no.1 (1998): 35-45.

—. "Grounding the Question. Implications of Indigenous Narrative Practice for Architectural History." In *On What Ground(s)*, edited by Sean Pickersgill, 221-227. Adelaide: Society of Architectural Historians of Australia and New Zealand, 1997.

—. "Liru and Kuniya: Greg Burgess' Aboriginal centre at Ayers Rock." *Architecture Australia* 85, no.2 (1996): 48-55.

—. "In(side)out: the Face that Turns Towards and Looks: Chartres Cathedral, 1989." *Interzones* (1997). http://www.altx.com/au2/tawa.html.

Taylor, A. E. *The Parmenides of Plato*. Oxford: Clarendon Press, 1934.

Torres Tur, Elías. *Zenithal Light*. Barcelona: Col-legi d'Arquitectes de Catalunya, 2005.

Toy, Maggie, editor. *Architecture + Film*. London: Academy Editions, 1994.

Trépos, Jean-Yves. "La Sociologie Postmoderne." *Le Portique* 1, no.1 (1998) : 57-8.

Tschumi, Bernard and Berman, Matthew, editors. *Index Architecture*. Cambridge: MIT Press, 2003.

Vernant, Jean-Pierre. *Myth and Thought Amongst the Greeks*. London: Routledge & Kegan Paul, 1983.

—. "Hestia-Hermès. Sur l'Éxpression Religieuse de l'Espace et du Mouvement Chez les Grecs." *Revue Française d'Anthropologie* 3 (1963): 12-50.

Vidler, Anthony. *The Architectural Uncanny*. Cambridge: MIT Press, 1992.

—. "The Explosion of Space: Architecture and the Filmic Imaginary." *Assemblage* 9 (1993): 46-53.

Virilio, Paul. *L'Accident Originel*. Paris: Galilee, 2008.

—. *The Art of the Motor*, translated by Julie Rose. Minneapolis: University of Minnesota Press, 1995.

—. *The Vision Machine*, translated by Julie Rose. Bloomington and Indianapolis: Indiana University Press, 1994.

—. *The Lost Dimension*, translated by Daniel Moschenberg. New York: Semiotext(e), 1991.

—. *Speed and Politics*, translated by Mark Polizzotti. New York: Semiotext(e), 1986.

Virilio, Paul and Lotringer, Sylvère, *The Accident of Art*, translated by Michael Taormina. New York: Semiotext(e), 2005.

Weston, Richard. *Utzon*. Hellerup: Bløndal, 2002.

Williams, Raymond. *Keywords. A Vocabulary of Culture and Society*. London: Fontana Press, 1988.

Wingårdh, Gert and Rasmus Wærn, editors. *Crucial Words. Conditions for Contemporary Architecture*. Basel: Birkhauser, 2008.

# INDEX

abject; in modernity, 78-9, 84,
140, 235
adaptability, 25; design for
adaptational capacity, 190-
1, 285
Agamben, Giorgio; *dispositifs*,
73, 335n35; messianic time,
144-7; power, potentiality and
impotentiality, 181-2; time,
repetition and arrest in cinema,
155
*agencement*, 39, 258-69, 299,
333n2, 334n34
agency, 174, 237, 258, 260, 273,
285-6, 298-9, 304, 308
*akhronos*, 144
ambient sound, 203, 223, 227-8,
247, 297
*Angkor Thom*, 244
Antonioni, Michelangelo;
alienation and dislocation, 53-4,
84-5, 153; *Blow Up*, 88, 152,
229; crisis of representation, 84-
5, 87, 90, 290; desert, 83, 150;
*l'Avventura*, 83, 86-7, 214, 272;
landscapes of estrangement, 83;
*l'Eclisse*, 53, 83, 151, 230, 295;
narrative, 86; *The Passenger*,
83, 113, 150, 214
any-space-whatever, *See*
whatever being
Arab bathhouse; light, time and
duration, 196-7
architecture; and cinema, 2, 17,
19; deterritorialisation, 5;
dislocation, 187, 195; enabling
infrastructure, 33;
mnemotechnical object, 198;
music, 10-11; other disciplines,

3; representation, 32-5, 43; light
and sound, 15, 18, 38-9, 200-1
Arnold, Martin; *Cinemnesis*,
277-8
assemblage, 4-5, 10, 13-19, 22-
36, 48, 258; and agency, 39-40;
and destabilisation in Antonioni,
215; and disassemblage, 202,
223-4; and framing, 298-9; and
milieu, 44, 115; and the
makeshift, 115; and weaving,
202; architectural and
contextual, 221; etymology,
270, 336n59; in architecture and
cinema, 94-6; in Bergman's
Cries and Whispers, 137; in
Godard, 136; in Paradjanov,
247; in space, 199; spatial and
material in Lewerentz, 252-7;
mobilisation of, 286; semblance
and mimesis, 286
Augé, Mark; non-spaces of
supermodernity, 114, 218

Bailly, Jean-Christophe; and
*mimesis*, 72
*Baños Almirante*, 196
Barthes, Roland, 11; *jouissance*,
13, 99; *studium* and *punctum*,
28; vacillation of sense, 84
*Bayon*, 244
*begaiement* (stammering,
stuttering), 13, 276, 299
Beijing *Palace Museum*, 299-
300
being-with (*Mitsein*); in
Heidegger, 227, 240, 243, 257,
308, 310
Bergman, Ingmar; *Cries and*

*Whispers*, 137, 211; *Persona*,
    212; *Winter Light*, 212-3
boredom; in Heidegger, 23, 107,
    147, 174, 176-181; profound
    boredom and the moment of
    vision, 181. *See* time
Bosch, Hieronymus; *Triptico de
    Los Improperios*, 142-4
Burgess, Gregory; *Hackford
    House*, 121-2; *Uluṟu-Kata
    Tjuṯa Cultural Centre*, 59

care, 31, 33, 37, 45, 57, 106; in
    Burgess' work, 123-5; in
    Dreyer's *Joan of Arc*, 109-110;
    in Heidegger, 108; in Stiegler,
    108-9
*Chartres Cathedral. See*
    window
floor, 197
close-up, 112-3; in Godard's
    *Éloge de l'Amour*, 165; political
    function in Pasolini's *Gospel
    According to St Matthew*, 112
colour; in Bergman's *Cries and
    Whispers*, 212-3; Godard's
    *Éloge de l'Amour,* 167, 217-8;
    in Jarmusch's *Year of the Horse*,
    211; in Paradjanov's *Sayat
    Nova*, 246-7; in Lynch, 171
compossibility, 168-9, 279-81;
    in Lynch, 168-170
concealment; and evidence in
    Nancy, 236; and potentiality,
    182; and privation (*steresis*), 75-
    6, 93, 181-182; and self-hiding
    in Nature (*phusis*), 75-6; and
    truth (*Aletheia*) in Heidegger,
    275, 328n97; 332n51; and
    unconcealment, 141, 242; in
    Antonioni's *Blow Up*, 89-90; in
    Haneke's *Caché*, 295; matter
    and light, 238-9
conjugation, 11, 40, 44; in
    Deleuze's Plane of Immanence,
    268-9; in geometry, 282; in

time, 134; of cosmic and human
    registers in sacred architecture,
    94; of narrative layers in
    Zumthor's *Sumvigt Chapel*; of
    rhythm, 134; of sound and
    image in cinema, 227; of sound
    and image in Tarkovsky, 78; of
    sound and light in cosmogony,
    206; of spatial systems, 96-7,
    199, 258, 283; of subject and
    object, 57; programmatic, 139
Cordoba, Mosque, 47
country, 57
crisis, 3, 7, 11, 14, 25, 48, 68,84-
    90, 92, 105, 258; in cinema,
    279-290; in the image, 164-6; in
    time, 148; narrative and
    subjective, 230-232, 273; in
    Simondon, 284

darkness, and light, 106, 127,
    141, 194, 206; and materiality in
    Lewerentz, 275; and materiality
    in Tarkovski's *Mirror*, 280-2;
    and modernity, 235; and
    potentiality, 233; in Antonioni's
    *Blow Up*, 89; in Godard,
    Jarmusch and Lynch, 165-172;
    in Kurosawa's *Dreams* and
    *Throne of Blood*, 68; twilight
    and the gloaming, 245
Deleuze, Gilles, cinematic
    frame, 101-2; compossibility,
    168; instantaneous-images,
    movement-images and time-
    images, 164, 294; lines of flight
    and deterritorialisation, 4, 278;
    out-of-field, 101; *plan*(e), 267-
    8; plane of immanence, 49, 114-
    5, 260-1, 284-5; The Actual and
    the Virtual, 279-282;
    transduction, 261; whatever-
    space, 114. *See* assemblage,
    *agencement,* deterritorialisation*,*
    Simondon, space, time,
    transduction, whatever-being

*dépaysement*, 211
Descent of the Ganges, 244
desert, *Ngannyatjarra* Lands
  (Gibson Desert), 57-8, 136; in
  Antonioni, 83-87; in modernity,
  214; in Antonioni's *Passenger*,
  150; in Dunlop's *People of the*
  *Western Desert*, 65; in Herzog's
  *Fata Morgana*, 175; etymology,
  318n65
deterritorialisation, 5, 7, 13, 15-
  17, 40, 56, 63-4, 88, 96, 107,
  116, 170, 220, 266-9, 273-4,
  279, 287; and Hermes, 334n25;
  in Deleuze, Camus and
  Antonioni, 214; in Jarmusch's
  *Year of the Horse*, 211; of the
  interior space, 195
disestablishment, and
  dislocation, 53; and
  displacement, 79; and landscape
  in Nancy, 79; and lines of flight,
  267; and motion in Nature, 73-
  4; in Antonioni, 53, 85-90; in
  contemporary spatiality, 319; in
  Deleuze's Plane of Immanence,
  260-1; in Herzog's *Where the*
  *Green Ants Dream*, 64; in
  Lynch, 170; of sound from
  sense, 290; of spatiality in
  modernity, 114; of time and
  narrative in Herzog, 163-4. *See*
  crisis
*dispositif*, 73, 335-336n35; and
  agencement, 268-70; and spatial
  framing in Hitchcock's *Rear*
  *Window*, 270
drawing; drawing for, 19;
  drawing from cinema, 18, 20;
  drawing parallels, 1-4;
  interpretative, presentational
  and representational, 17-18
Dreyer, Carl, *The Passion of*
  *Joan of Arc*, 104, 109
Dunlop, Ian, representation of

place and landscape in *People of*
  *the Western Desert*, 65-6
duration, 1, 5; alteration in
  architecture, 196; and boredom,
  179; and event, 191; and
  seasonality, 193; and time, 131-
  8, 144-5, 191, 323n16; and
  twilight, 245; in Bergman's
  *Winter Light*, 212-3; in Lynch's
  *Eraserhead*, 216-7; in
  Pennebaker's *Don't Look Back*,
  219-11; in time and cinema, 38,
  40, 147-165. *See* time, *khronos*,
  boredom, light

*eidos*, and configuration
  (*skhema*, form) 92; and matter,
  239, 256, 332n52; and *mimesis*,
  10, 334n33, 336n59; and the
  look, 106, 176; etymology,
  320n27; in Plato, 43-4
enframing, in Heidegger, 63, 77,
  80, 109, 121, 274
*ethos*, and place (*topos*), 52, 58-
  9, 85; and modes in music, 224

field, and care in Heidegger,
  108; and crisis in Simondon,
  284-9; and landscape in Nancy,
  82; and metastability, 40, 49-52,
  262-3;and tension in Kurosawa's
  *Dreams*, 69; as frame and
  assemblage. 10, 14, 16, 20, 23-
  4, 37, 40, 91, 94-8, 104, 115-6,
  258-67; charged fields in
  Paradjanov's *Sayat Nova*, 246-8
  and Antonioni's *l'Avventura*,
  272-4; of estrangement in
  Antonioni, 83-87; out-of-field
  (*hors champ*), 97-8, 100-2,
  320n22; spatial, 108, 273-4;
  temporal, 168; visual fields in
  cinema, 87, 151
Fontana, Bill, *Tyne Soundings*,
  223
framing, 5, 10, 33-4, 37; and

appropriation, 80; and betrayal,
109, 117; and dislocation in
Simondon, 50; and enframing in
Heidegger, 80; and Derrida's
*parergon / hors-d'œuvre*, 97-8;
and ethics, 106-8; and
dislocation, 107; and limit, 98;
and narrative, 116; and out-of-
frame, 87-88, 97-101; and place,
35-6, 42; and surface, 110; and
world formation, 37; as pure
observation 113-4; cadre and
care, 106; geometric, 91; spatial,
94-7; in cinema, 6, 18; in
cinema and architecture, 106; in
Antonioni's *Passenger*, 113 and
*l'Eclisse*, 53-5; in Burgess'
*Uluru-Kata Tjuta Cultural
Centre*, 59-62; in Deleuze, 101-
2; in Dreyer's *Joan of Arc*, 34,
104-5; in Herzog's *Where the
Green Ants Dream*, 63-5; in
Hitchcock's *Rear Window*, 270-
2; in Kazan's *Baby Doll*, 103; in
Kurosawa's *Dreams*, 67-8; in
Paradjanov's *Sayat Nova*, 101-2;
in Roeg's *Bad Timing*, 70. *See*
assemblage, *agencement*, care,
*milieu*, space, time, Simondon
Galeta, Ivan Ladislav; Two
Times in One Space and In the
Kitchen, 278-9
gaze. *See* look
glare, 210, 214
Godard, Jean-Luc; *Éloge de
l'Amour*, 165, 167, 172, 217;
*Germany 90*, 76, 136;
*Histoire(s) du Cinéma*, 16, 76,
217, 292-3
Goetz, Benoît, dislocation, 53
ground, 242; and non-duality,
263; and matter, 93, 155; 172,
176, 178, 218, 230; and the
image in Nancy, 233-6; and
transcendence, 241-2; in

Heidegger's *On the Essence and
Concept of Ground*, 240-243

Haneke, Michael; *Caché*, 293-5
Hartley, Hal; *The Book of Life*,
287
Hayles, Katherine, attention
deficit, 107
Heidegger, Martin; and
homelessness, 56; and nature
(*phusis*), 71, 76, 83, 237-275;
*On the Essence and Concept of
Ground*, 240-243; *The Origin of
the Work of Art*, 255-6
Herzog, Werner; and dislocation
in *Where the Green Ants
Dream*, 63-4; and temporality,
172; fact and otherness of the
image, 163; *Fata Morgana*,
172-5; *Lessons of Darkness*,
174; *Where the Green Ants
Dream*, 63-5
Hitchcock, Alfred; *Rear Window*,
270
homelessness. See Heidegger
*hortus conclusus*, 73, 89, 230

image, and artifice in
Tarkovsky, 170; and
dematerialisation in
architecture, 220; and
monstration, 233; and reality in
Tarkovsky, 78, 157-165; and
representation in architecture,
32; and sound in cinema, 227-
232; and the cinematic gaze in
Nancy, 29-32, 111, 233-5; and
time, 147-8; and violence, 236;
crisis of the image in Godard,
166-7, 217-18; *eidos* and the
look, 106, 218; etymology, 233;
in Agamben, 155-7; regimes of
the image in Rancière, 27-9;
sight, sound and image in
Nancy, 218; verisimilitude and

unframing in Antonioni's *Blow Up*, 88-90, 152-3
Inarritu, Alejandro Gonzales, *21 Grams*, 149
instant, 131; and time, 133; *caesura* and standstill, 142; etymology, 134
intentionality, in cinema and architecture, 21-6, 130

*Jantar Mantar*, 185
Jarmusch, Jim; *Dead Man*, 211; *Stranger Than Paradise*, 167; *Year of the Horse*, 210
Jullien, François, blandness, 184

*kairos*, 135, 144-5, 193; and *khronos*, 144-7
Kazan, Elia, *Baby Doll*, 103-4
Keith Jarrett, 12
Khajuraho, 243
*khronos, See kairos*
Kiarostami, Abbas, *And Life Goes On*, 111
kinaesthetic, experience of place, 36, 57-62
kinematic, 16, 74, 237
*kinesis*, and cinema, 31
Kurosawa, Akira, *Dreams: Sunshine Through the Rain*, 67; *Throne of Blood*, 68, 215

landscape, and absence, 80-1; and framing in Scarpa's *Brionvega*, 304; and place, 42-90; and representation, 79; and the uncanny in Nancy, 79
Le Corbusier, five points, 119; *Villa Savoye*, 127, 282
*leimma*, 43, 98, 144; etymology, 324n26. *See* limit
Lewerentz, Sigurd, *Chapel of the Resurrection*, 305; *St Peter and St Mark*, 252-7, 305-9; *Woodland Crematorium*, 45
light, 201; and dark, 127; and

place, 201; and shadow in Godard and Lynch, 216; and sound, 204; and sound in cinema, 210; etymology, 201-2; in Antonioni's *l'Avventura* and *Passenger*, 214; in Kurosawa, 215; in Le Corbusier, 182; in Lynch's *Eraserhead*, 216; in Plato's myth of Er, 207; in sacred architecture, 206; knot, night, connection, 127, 202; sky and shadow (*skotos/skia*), 127, 130
limit, 14, 43; *aporia* and *caesura*, 139; and *leimma*, 43, 98; and rhythm, 92; etymology, 145
lines of flight, 267, 334n25
look, and evidence in Nancy, 29-37; and framing, 27, 96, 117; and glaring, 106; and Platonic *eidos*, 106; ethical dimensions, 106; etymology, 106; in Antonioni, 85-87, 113, 151-2; in Bosch's *Triptico de Los Improperios*, 142-4; in Dreyer's *Joan of Arc*, 109-110; in Godard's *Éloge de l'Amour*, 165-7; in Herzog, 172; in Lynch, 168; in Paradjanov's *Sayat Nova*, 168; in Tarkovsky, 162-4; in Roeg's *Bad Timing*, 153; in Plato and Heidegger, 106; of the architectural plan, 116; of the landscape, 88
loose fit, 25
Lynch, David, *Eraserhead*, 216; *Inland Empire*, 169-170; *Lost Highway*, 167-172; *Mulholland Drive*, 168-171

Mahler, Gustav, *Der Abschied*, 225
makeshift, 21-2, 33, 37, 115, 235-6
mapping, 14, 17, 40, 186, 268,

286
Markli, Peter, *La Conjiunta*,
300-302
materiality, 32-3, 38-9, 61, 118,
200-257; and potential in
architecture, 190, 200; in
Antonioni's *l'Eclisse*, 231; in
architecture, 244-5, 249; in
Bergman's *Cries and Whispers,
Persona* and *Winter Light*, 212;
in Dreyer's *Joan of Arc*, 109-
110; in Jarmusch's *Year of the
Horse* and *Dead Man*, 211-12;
in Kurosawa's *Dreams* and
*Throne of Blood*, 68-70; in
Lewerentz, 252-7; in Lynch,
216; in Mirales and Tagliabue's
*Torre de Gas Natural*, 100; in
Paradjanov's *Sayat Nova*, 102-3,
246; in Plato's Myth of Er, 209;
in Siza, 250-2; in Tarkovsky,
213-16l; of light and colour in
Godard, 217-8; of time, 148; of
the image in Tarkovski and
Herzog, 157-8, 161-76. *See*
ground, matter
matter, 43-50, 78, 110, 117, 200,
215, 263, 284-5; and light, 238-
239; in Aristotle, 93, 332n52;in
Heidegger's *The Origin of the
Work of Art*, 256. *See* ground,
materiality
metastability, 50, 261-7, 285,
333n9, 274
*milieu*, 12-19, 42; and
architecture, 39, 41, 203; and
assemblage, 44; and
environment, 189; and place,
56-7; and spatial framing, 107-
9, 298, 316n39; and time, 197;
in Deleuze, 114-5; in Simondon,
49-52, 264-267, 284-289, 333n9
*mimesis*, 10-11, 110-111; and
forgery, 23; and representation,
10, 117
Miralles Tagliabue, *Torre de*

*Gas Natural*, 100

Nancy, Jean Luc, *À l'Écoute*,
218; and landscape, 79-83; and
the image, 30, 331n25; on
singularity and community,
310n8; *The Evidence of Film*,
29, 111; *The Gravity of
Thought*, 275-6; *The Ground of
the Image*, 233-6; *Uncanny
Landscape*, 79-81
narrative, 2; and
disestablishment in space, 297-
9; and framing, 116; and
juxtapositional montage, 228;
and kinaesthetics, 136; and
materiality, 210; and place, 52-
7; and space-time, 148-9;
architectural, 35-44;
architectural and cinematic, 96-
7, 184, 286-7; narrative crisis in
Antonioni, 83-8, 91, 150-2, 215,
230, 272-8; in Bosch's *Triptico
de los Improperios*, 142; in
Burgess' *Uluru-Kata Tjuta
Cultural Centre*, 60-63; in
Godard, 291-3; in Haneke's
*Caché*, 293-7; in Herzog, 163,
174-5; in Hitchcock's *Rear
Window*, 270-2; in Inarritu's *21
Grams*, 149-50; in Jarmusch's
*Stranger than Paradise*, 167 and
*Dead Man*, 211; in Le
Corbusier's *Villa Savoye*, 118-
20; in Lewerentz and Asplund's
*Woodland Crematorium*, 45; in
Lynch, 167-172, 232;
Paradjanov's *Sayat Nova*, 101-2;
in Roeg's *Bad Timing*, 70-1,
153-5, 232; in Tarkovski, 154;
in Wilder's *Double Indemnity*,
149; in Zumthor's *Sumvigt
Chapel*, 126-130; spatial, 247-
50
nature, and late modernity, 76,

235-7; and time, 131-2, 138, 191-4; as *phusis* in Aristotle and Heidegger, 71-6, 93, 125; in Antonioni, 55, 83-9, 230-5; in cinema, 36; in Godard, 76-8, 136; in Herzog, 175; in Kahn's *Korman House*, 121; in Kurosawa, 67-8; in Le Corbusier's *Villa Savoye*, 119-20; in Nouvel's *Quai Branly*, 99; in Tarkovsky, 78-9, 213-5
Nouvel, Jean, *Fondation Cartier* and *Quai Branly*, 99

Palladio, *Il Redentore*, 209
Paradise, and *Chartre Cathedral*, 195;etymology, 47
Paradjanov, Sergei, *Sayat Nova* (The Colour of Pomegranates), 101, 168, 246
Pärt, Arvo, *Festina Lente*, 160
Pasolini, Pier Paolo, *The Gospel According to St Matthew*, 112, 228
Pennebaker, D. A., *Don't Look Back*, 210
place, 348-55; and architecture, 33, 40; and cinema, 5; and displacement, 43, 53-54, 79-90; and *ethos*, 52, 91, 108; and framing, 71-79; and homelessness in Heidegger, 56; and memory, 52, 203; and setting, 36, 42; and space-time, 52; and *topos*, 37, 145; etymology, 55, 314-15n22 and 23; 316-17n40, 329n105; in Heidegger, 180, 275, 332n51; taking place, 27, 31, 55-71, 111, 114, 116
Plato, and *dynamis*, 181; *eidos* (idea/look), 43, 106; and *ethos/topos*, 8; and history, 134, 323n14; and *mimesis*, 10-11, 23, 110-111; and music, 208; and time, 133, 323n16; and

weaving, 51, 202; myth of Er, 202; parable of the cave, 30; Theory of Form, 263, 336n59
programme, and the unprogrammable, 12, 37, 117, 189-90; in architecture, 109, 115. *See* makeshift

Rancière, Jacques, and geometric regimes, 94; and the image, 27-9; on image and montage in Godard, 292-3
reading, and being ready, 26-7; and illegibility in cinema and architecture, 91, 320n20; for potential, 23; for communication, 25; etymology, 27, 312; for the proliferation of sense, 26
representation, 10; and drawing, 17; and the image, 27, 29-32; and *mimesis*, 117; in architecture, 32-35; of landscape in Dunlop's People of the Western Desert, 66. *See* drawing, image, *mimesis*, nature
rhythm, 73-78; and *caesura*, 155-8; and place, 136-8; and time, 132, 145, 147; vibration in sound and space, 225-228; arrest and flow in Aristotle, 92-4, 134; etymology, 92; form, proportion and *skhema*, 92-94; potential for disestablishment, 288
Roeg, Nicholas, 20, 16; *Bad Timing*, 70-1, 153-5, 165, 228, 232, 287

Scarpa, Carlo, Brionvega, 302-5
Scott, Ridley, Alien, 227
setup. *See* framing
*shakti*, 142
Simondon, Gilbert, crisis, 284; distinction between carrier and carried in architecture, 328n99;

field, milieu, 40; metastability,
50, 266-7, 333n9; perception,
285-6; Plato's *eidos* and Theory
of Form, 263-4; *Psychic and
Collective Individuation*, 49;
transduction, 261, 336n64. *See*
crisis, field, milieu,
metastability
Siza, Alvaro, *Galician Centre of
Contemporary Art* and *Porto
School of Architecture*, 250
sound, ambient sound of
equipment in architecture,
227;and absence in Dunlop's
*People of the Western Desert*,
66, 316n33; and acoustic
materiality in Antonioni, 229-
31; and architecture, 34, 38-40,
184, 200-206, 219, 297, 303;
and dislocation in Herzog, 63,
65, 175; and duration in Arvo
Pärt's *Festina Lente*, 160; and
*ethos* in music, 224-6; and
hearing in Hinduism, 219; and
image in cinema, 210, 227-8,
239, 290-1; and image in
Tarkovsky, 78, 229; and layered
sound in The Necks' *Aether*,
159-60; and light in cosmogony,
206; and materiality in
Paradjanov, 246-280; and
musical columns in the *Vitthala*
Temple, 222-3; and off-screen,
101, 330n12; and place, 193,
196; and space in prehistoric
cave painting, 221-2; and
vibration, 220; etymology,
312n22; hearing and resonance
in cinema, 219; in Godard, 290-
92; in Jarmusch, 210-11; in
Lynch, 34, 232; in Pasolini's
*Gospel According to St
Matthew*, 228-9; in Roeg's *Bad
Timing*, 71, 153-4, 232;
resonance and destruction, 223;

sense and ground in Nancy, 218;
timbre and materials, 220-22
space, 37; abstract, 37, 114, 131;
ambiguous in Lewerentz, 254-
55; and atmosphere in Bergman,
211-3; and disestablishment in
Lewerentz, 305-9; and framing
in Antonioni's *l'Avventura*, 272-
3; and framing in Dreyer's *Joan
of Arc*, 34, 104-5; and framing
in Kazan's *Baby Doll*, 103-4;
and interval, 132-6; and *khora*,
10, 37, 145; and *logos*, 206; and
materiality in Siza, 249-52; and
multiple systems in the *Palace
Museum*, Markli's *La Conjiunta*
and Scarpa's *Brionvega*, 299-
305; and multiple systems in Le
Corbusier's *Villa Savoye*, and
Wright's *Thomas House*, 282-4;
and place, 48, 138; and the look
in Nancy, 30-1; and sound, 39,
203-4, 221-2, 225; and
tabernacle/tent, 115-6; and the
uncanny in Nancy and
Heidegger, 81-3; and time, 38-9,
53, 132, 194, 196-201, 205-6,
220; and time in cinema and
architecture, 2, 131; and
violence, 237; any-space-
whatever in Deleuze, 56, 114-5;
architectural and cinematic, 40-
3, 86, 91, 96, 106, 118, 131,
173-4; as field and milieu, 108-
9; cinematic in Corbusier's *Villa
Savoye*, 1118-21;
decontextualised and disjunct in
Lynch, 34, 167-72, 216-7;
framing and setup, 48, 93-4,
101; makeshift, 115-6; memory
and subjectivity, 39, 52, 191-2;
modernist in Antonioni, 53-5,
83-90, 150-2; multivalent, 189-
91, 296-7; in Burgess' *Hackford
House*, 121-5; in Kurosawa's
*Dreams*, 67-70; Paradjanov's

*Sayat Nova*, 101; in Roeg's *Bad Timing*, 70-1, 154; in Tarkovsky, 78-9, 157, 159, 161, 279-82; spacing, displacement and dislocation, 53, 79; suspended in Zumthor's *Sumvigt Chapel*, 126-130. *See* framing, place, time, field, milieu

St Augustine, *Confessions*, 135

St John Wilson, Colin, on Lewerentz, 253, 255, 305-8; on Lewerentz's *Mellanspel* (playing between), 305

Stiegler, Bernard, attentiveness and care, 106-110

*Strasbourg* Cathedral, and dematerialisation of the facade, 128

Tarkovsky, Andrey, 16; and affective image, 157, 162-3; and crisis of the milieu, 281-2; and landscape, 80; and materiality, 157-8, 165, 213; and space, 78-9; and time, 156, 162, 164-5, 177; artifice and realism, 7, 164; defiguration of the representative image, 78; *Mirror*, 157-161, 279-82; *Sculpting in Time*, 157; *Stalker*, 78, 157;

Tavener, John, *Nativity of the Mother of God*, 226

technology, and Heidegger's enframing, 63, 77, 109, 121, 274

terroir, 137

The Necks, *Aether*, 159

theory, uses of, 21

timbre, 10, 38, 40, 111, 160, 167, 201, 215, 219, 222, 225, 228

time, 1-8, 37-8, 131-9; and boredom in Heidegger, 176-81; and duration in cinema; and landscape in Nancy, 82; and memory in Tarkovsky, 280-2;

and narrative in Inarritu's *21 Grams*, 149; and place, 52, 56, 138; and potentiality in Agamben, 131; and sound, 227-8; and space, 52-3, 131-2, 145; and the instant, 133, 142; and the interval, 132-4; and the windows of *Chartres Cathedral*, 194-6, 209; caesura of time in Bosch's *Triptico de los Properios*, 142-4; dead time in Bergman's *Persona* and *Winter Light*, 212-3; image and materiality in Tarkovsky, 16, 78-9, 156-8, 160-3, 165; immobility and immanence, 17; in Antonioni's *The Passenger*, 150-1; in Bergman's *Cries and Whispers*, 137-8; in cinema and architecture, 1-8, 131-9, 183-5, 193-4, 201, 203-4, 206, 286-8; in Galeta's *Two Times in one Space*, 278-9; in Godard's *Histoire(s) du Cinéma*, *Éloge de l'Amour* and *Germany 90*, 16, 136, 165-7; in Herzog's *Fata Morgana* and *Lessons of Darkness*, 172-5; in Kurosawa's *Dreams*, 67-70; in Lynch's *Lost Highway* and *Mulholland Drive*, 168-72; in Paradjanov's *Sayat Nova*, 168; in Pärt's *Festina Lente*, 160; in Plato, 133, 208-9; in Roeg's *Bad Timing*, 16, 20, 70-1, 153-5; in St Augustine, 131, 135; in the Arab bathhouse, 196-7; in The Neck's *Aether*, 159; in Wilder's *Double Indemnity*, 149; *kairos*, *khronos*, 133, 135, 143-4, 193; messianic time in Agamben, 143-7, 155-6; multivalent time in cinema and architecture, 288-9; of waiting and ethics, 77; sound and light, 38-40; suspension and narrative in Antonioni's *Blow Up* and

*l'Eclisse*, 151-3; time-image in
Deleuze, 164, 294. *See
boredom, duration, place,
rhythm, space*
*Tjukurpa*, 57-63
toponymy, 48, 73
Torres, Elias, *Zenithal Light*,
138
*transduction*. See Simondon
translation, between cinema and
architecture, 7, 35, 188. *See
mimesis*

uncanny, 3, 7, 13, 15, 17, 34, 56;
landscape/district in Heidegger
and Nancy, 74-83

validity, of interpretations, 22
van der Rohe, Mies, Barcelona
Pavilion, 98
violence, in the image and
architecture, 236-8
*Vithhala* Temple, musical

columns, 188, 222

wall, etymology, 251-2
weaving, 51-2, 134, 202, 276.
whatever being, 32, 56, 113-4;
and any-space-whatever in
Agamben and Deleuze, 56, 114,
117
Wilder, Billy, *Double
Indemnity*, 149
window, 118, 121; *Chartres
Cathedral*, 195-6, 209; in
Lewerentz and Utzon, 297; in
the Christian Church, 194-5;
inside and outside, 194-5
withdrawal, of the gods in
Nancy, 82

Wright, Frank Lloyd, *Thomas
House*, 283

Zumthor, Peter, *Sumvigt Chapel*,
126-130